GCC 7.0 GNAT User's Guide for Native Platforms

A catalogue record for this book is available from the Hong Kong Public Libraries.

Published in Hong Kong by Samurai Media Limited.

Email: info@samuraimedia.org

ISBN 978-988-8406-95-1

Table of Contents

4   Building Executable Programs with GNAT

GNAT, The GNU Ada Development Environment

GCC version 7.0.0

AdaCore

Permission is granted to copy, distribute and/or modify this document under the terms of the GNU Free Documentation License, Version 1.3 or any later version published by the Free Software Foundation; with no Invariant Sections, with the Front-Cover Texts being "GNAT User's Guide for Native Platforms", and with no Back-Cover Texts. A copy of the license is included in the section entitled [GNU Free Documentation License], page 317.

1 About This Guide

This guide describes the use of GNAT, a compiler and software development toolset for the full Ada programming language. It documents the features of the compiler and tools, and explains how to use them to build Ada applications.

GNAT implements Ada 95, Ada 2005 and Ada 2012, and it may also be invoked in Ada 83 compatibility mode. By default, GNAT assumes Ada 2012, but you can override with a compiler switch ([Compiling Different Versions of Ada], page 140) to explicitly specify the language version. Throughout this manual, references to 'Ada' without a year suffix apply to all Ada 95/2005/2012 versions of the language.

1.1 What This Guide Contains

This guide contains the following chapters:

* [Getting Started with GNAT], page 4 describes how to get started compiling and running Ada programs with the GNAT Ada programming environment.

* [The GNAT Compilation Model], page 8 describes the compilation model used by GNAT.

* [Building Executable Programs with GNAT], page 76 describes how to use the main GNAT tools to build executable programs, and it also gives examples of using the GNU make utility with GNAT.

* [GNAT Utility Programs], page 169 explains the various utility programs that are included in the GNAT environment

* [GNAT and Program Execution], page 187 covers a number of topics related to running, debugging, and tuning the performace of programs developed with GNAT

Appendices cover several additional topics:

* [Platform-Specific Information], page 235 describes the different run-time library implementations and also presents information on how to use GNAT on several specific platforms

* [Example of Binder Output File], page 263 shows the source code for the binder output file for a sample program.

* [Elaboration Order Handling in GNAT], page 279 describes how GNAT helps you deal with elaboration order issues.

* [Inline Assembler], page 307 shows how to use the inline assembly facility in an Ada program.

1.2 What You Should Know before Reading This Guide

This guide assumes a basic familiarity with the Ada 95 language, as described in the International Standard ANSI/ISO/IEC-8652:1995, January 1995. It does not require knowledge of the features introduced by Ada 2005 or Ada 2012. Reference manuals for Ada 95, Ada 2005, and Ada 2012 are included in the GNAT documentation package.

1.3 Related Information

For further information about Ada and related tools, please refer to the following documents:

* *Ada 95 Reference Manual*, *Ada 2005 Reference Manual*, and *Ada 2012 Reference Manual*, which contain reference material for the several revisions of the Ada language standard.

* *GNAT Reference_Manual*, which contains all reference material for the GNAT implementation of Ada.

* *Using the GNAT Programming Studio*, which describes the GPS Integrated Development Environment.

* *GNAT Programming Studio Tutorial*, which introduces the main GPS features through examples.

* *Debugging with GDB*, for all details on the use of the GNU source-level debugger.

* *GNU Emacs Manual*, for full information on the extensible editor and programming environment Emacs.

1.4 A Note to Readers of Previous Versions of the Manual

In early 2015 the GNAT manuals were transitioned to the reStructuredText (rst) / Sphinx documentation generator technology. During that process the *GNAT User's Guide* was reorganized so that related topics would be described together in the same chapter or appendix. Here's a summary of the major changes realized in the new document structure.

* [The GNAT Compilation Model], page 8 has been extended so that it now covers the following material:
    - The *gnatname*, *gnatkr*, and *gnatchop* tools
    - [Configuration Pragmas], page 26
    - [GNAT and Libraries], page 32
    - [Conditional Compilation], page 40 **including** [Preprocessing with gnatprep], page 46 **and** [Integrated Preprocessing], page 50
    - [Generating Ada Bindings for C and C++ headers], page 69
    - [Using GNAT Files with External Tools], page 75

* [Building Executable Programs with GNAT], page 76 is a new chapter consolidating the following content:
    - [Building with gnatmake], page 77
    - [Compiling with gcc], page 87
    - [Binding with gnatbind], page 150
    - [Linking with gnatlink], page 162
    - [Using the GNU make Utility], page 164

* [GNAT Utility Programs], page 169 is a new chapter consolidating the information about several GNAT tools:
    - [The File Cleanup Utility gnatclean], page 170
    - [The GNAT Library Browser gnatls], page 172
    - [The Cross-Referencing Tools gnatxref and gnatfind], page 175

* The *Compatibility and Porting Guide* appendix has been moved to the *GNAT Reference Manual*. It now includes a section *Writing Portable Fixed-Point Declarations* which was previously a separate chapter in the *GNAT User's Guide*.

1.5 Conventions

Following are examples of the typographical and graphic conventions used in this guide:

* *Functions, utility program names, standard names,* and *classes.*
* *Option flags*
* `File names`
* *Variables*
* *Emphasis*
* [optional information or parameters]
* Examples are described by text

    `and then shown this way.`
* Commands that are entered by the user are shown as preceded by a prompt string comprising the `$` character followed by a space.
* Full file names are shown with the '/' character as the directory separator; e.g., `parent-dir/subdir/myfile.adb`. If you are using GNAT on a Windows platform, please note that the '\' character should be used instead.

2 Getting Started with GNAT

This chapter describes how to use GNAT's command line interface to build executable Ada programs. On most platforms a visually oriented Integrated Development Environment is also available, the GNAT Programming Studio (GPS). GPS offers a graphical "look and feel", support for development in other programming languages, comprehensive browsing features, and many other capabilities. For information on GPS please refer to *Using the GNAT Programming Studio*.

2.1 Running GNAT

Three steps are needed to create an executable file from an Ada source file:
  * The source file(s) must be compiled.
  * The file(s) must be bound using the GNAT binder.
  * All appropriate object files must be linked to produce an executable.

All three steps are most commonly handled by using the *gnatmake* utility program that, given the name of the main program, automatically performs the necessary compilation, binding and linking steps.

2.2 Running a Simple Ada Program

Any text editor may be used to prepare an Ada program. (If Emacs is used, the optional Ada mode may be helpful in laying out the program.) The program text is a normal text file. We will assume in our initial example that you have used your editor to prepare the following standard format text file:

```
with Ada.Text_IO; use Ada.Text_IO;
procedure Hello is
begin
   Put_Line ("Hello WORLD!");
end Hello;
```

This file should be named `hello.adb`. With the normal default file naming conventions, GNAT requires that each file contain a single compilation unit whose file name is the unit name, with periods replaced by hyphens; the extension is `ads` for a spec and `adb` for a body. You can override this default file naming convention by use of the special pragma *Source_File_Name* (for further information please see [Using Other File Names], page 14). Alternatively, if you want to rename your files according to this default convention, which is probably more convenient if you will be using GNAT for all your compilations, then the *gnatchop* utility can be used to generate correctly-named source files (see [Renaming Files with gnatchop], page 22).

You can compile the program using the following command (*$* is used as the command prompt in the examples in this document):

```
$ gcc -c hello.adb
```

gcc is the command used to run the compiler. This compiler is capable of compiling programs in several languages, including Ada and C. It assumes that you have given it an Ada program if the file extension is either `.ads` or `.adb`, and it will then call the GNAT compiler to compile the specified file.

The -c switch is required. It tells *gcc* to only do a compilation. (For C programs, *gcc* can also do linking, but this capability is not used directly for Ada programs, so the -c switch must always be present.)

This compile command generates a file `hello.o`, which is the object file corresponding to your Ada program. It also generates an 'Ada Library Information' file `hello.ali`, which contains additional information used to check that an Ada program is consistent. To build an executable file, use *gnatbind* to bind the program and *gnatlink* to link it. The argument to both *gnatbind* and *gnatlink* is the name of the ALI file, but the default extension of `.ali` can be omitted. This means that in the most common case, the argument is simply the name of the main program:

```
$ gnatbind hello
$ gnatlink hello
```

A simpler method of carrying out these steps is to use *gnatmake*, a master program that invokes all the required compilation, binding and linking tools in the correct order. In particular, *gnatmake* automatically recompiles any sources that have been modified since they were last compiled, or sources that depend on such modified sources, so that 'version skew' is avoided.

```
$ gnatmake hello.adb
```

The result is an executable program called `hello`, which can be run by entering:

```
$ hello
```

assuming that the current directory is on the search path for executable programs.

and, if all has gone well, you will see:

```
Hello WORLD!
```

appear in response to this command.

2.3 Running a Program with Multiple Units

Consider a slightly more complicated example that has three files: a main program, and the spec and body of a package:

```
package Greetings is
   procedure Hello;
   procedure Goodbye;
end Greetings;

with Ada.Text_IO; use Ada.Text_IO;
package body Greetings is
   procedure Hello is
   begin
      Put_Line ("Hello WORLD!");
   end Hello;

   procedure Goodbye is
   begin
      Put_Line ("Goodbye WORLD!");
   end Goodbye;
```

```
      end Greetings;

      with Greetings;
      procedure Gmain is
      begin
         Greetings.Hello;
         Greetings.Goodbye;
      end Gmain;
```

Following the one-unit-per-file rule, place this program in the following three separate files:

greetings.ads

      spec of package *Greetings*

greetings.adb

      body of package *Greetings*

gmain.adb

      body of main program

To build an executable version of this program, we could use four separate steps to compile, bind, and link the program, as follows:

```
      $ gcc -c gmain.adb
      $ gcc -c greetings.adb
      $ gnatbind gmain
      $ gnatlink gmain
```

Note that there is no required order of compilation when using GNAT. In particular it is perfectly fine to compile the main program first. Also, it is not necessary to compile package specs in the case where there is an accompanying body; you only need to compile the body. If you want to submit these files to the compiler for semantic checking and not code generation, then use the **-gnatc** switch:

```
      $ gcc -c greetings.ads -gnatc
```

Although the compilation can be done in separate steps as in the above example, in practice it is almost always more convenient to use the *gnatmake* tool. All you need to know in this case is the name of the main program's source file. The effect of the above four commands can be achieved with a single one:

```
      $ gnatmake gmain.adb
```

In the next section we discuss the advantages of using *gnatmake* in more detail.

2.4 Using the *gnatmake* Utility

If you work on a program by compiling single components at a time using *gcc*, you typically keep track of the units you modify. In order to build a consistent system, you compile not only these units, but also any units that depend on the units you have modified. For example, in the preceding case, if you edit `gmain.adb`, you only need to recompile that file. But if you edit `greetings.ads`, you must recompile both `greetings.adb` and `gmain.adb`, because both files contain units that depend on `greetings.ads`.

gnatbind will warn you if you forget one of these compilation steps, so that it is impossible to generate an inconsistent program as a result of forgetting to do a compilation. Nevertheless

it is tedious and error-prone to keep track of dependencies among units. One approach
to handle the dependency-bookkeeping is to use a makefile. However, makefiles present
maintenance problems of their own: if the dependencies change as you change the program,
you must make sure that the makefile is kept up-to-date manually, which is also an error-
prone process.

The *gnatmake* utility takes care of these details automatically. Invoke it using either one of
the following forms:

```
$ gnatmake gmain.adb
$ gnatmake gmain
```

The argument is the name of the file containing the main program; you may omit the extension. *gnatmake* examines the environment, automatically recompiles any files that need
recompiling, and binds and links the resulting set of object files, generating the executable
file, **gmain**. In a large program, it can be extremely helpful to use *gnatmake*, because
working out by hand what needs to be recompiled can be difficult.

Note that *gnatmake* takes into account all the Ada rules that establish dependencies among
units. These include dependencies that result from inlining subprogram bodies, and from
generic instantiation. Unlike some other Ada make tools, *gnatmake* does not rely on the
dependencies that were found by the compiler on a previous compilation, which may possibly
be wrong when sources change. *gnatmake* determines the exact set of dependencies from
scratch each time it is run.

3 The GNAT Compilation Model

This chapter describes the compilation model used by GNAT. Although similar to that used by other languages such as C and C++, this model is substantially different from the traditional Ada compilation models, which are based on a centralized program library. The chapter covers the following material:

*   Topics related to source file makeup and naming
    *   [Source Representation], page 9
    *   [Foreign Language Representation], page 10
    *   [File Naming Topics and Utilities], page 13
*   [Configuration Pragmas], page 26
*   [Generating Object Files], page 29
*   [Source Dependencies], page 30
*   [The Ada Library Information Files], page 31
*   [Binding an Ada Program], page 32
*   [GNAT and Libraries], page 32
*   [Conditional Compilation], page 40
*   [Mixed Language Programming], page 52
*   [GNAT and Other Compilation Models], page 74
*   [Using GNAT Files with External Tools], page 75

3.1 Source Representation

Ada source programs are represented in standard text files, using Latin-1 coding. Latin-1 is an 8-bit code that includes the familiar 7-bit ASCII set, plus additional characters used for representing foreign languages (see [Foreign Language Representation], page 10 for support of non-USA character sets). The format effector characters are represented using their standard ASCII encodings, as follows:

Character	Effect	Code
VT	Vertical tab	16#0B#
HT	Horizontal tab	16#09#
CR	Carriage return	16#0D#
LF	Line feed	16#0A#
FF	Form feed	16#0C#

Source files are in standard text file format. In addition, GNAT will recognize a wide variety of stream formats, in which the end of physical lines is marked by any of the following sequences: *LF*, *CR*, *CR-LF*, or *LF-CR*. This is useful in accommodating files that are imported from other operating systems.

The end of a source file is normally represented by the physical end of file. However, the control character *16#1A#* (SUB) is also recognized as signalling the end of the source file. Again, this is provided for compatibility with other operating systems where this code is used to represent the end of file.

Each file contains a single Ada compilation unit, including any pragmas associated with the unit. For example, this means you must place a package declaration (a package *spec*) and the corresponding body in separate files. An Ada *compilation* (which is a sequence of compilation units) is represented using a sequence of files. Similarly, you will place each subunit or child unit in a separate file.

3.2 Foreign Language Representation

GNAT supports the standard character sets defined in Ada as well as several other non-standard character sets for use in localized versions of the compiler ([Character Set Control], page 141).

3.2.1 Latin-1

The basic character set is Latin-1. This character set is defined by ISO standard 8859, part 1. The lower half (character codes *16#00#* ... *16#7F#*) is identical to standard ASCII coding, but the upper half is used to represent additional characters. These include extended letters used by European languages, such as French accents, the vowels with umlauts used in German, and the extra letter A-ring used in Swedish.

For a complete list of Latin-1 codes and their encodings, see the source file of library unit *Ada.Characters.Latin_1* in file `a-chlat1.ads`. You may use any of these extended characters freely in character or string literals. In addition, the extended characters that represent letters can be used in identifiers.

3.2.2 Other 8-Bit Codes

GNAT also supports several other 8-bit coding schemes:

ISO 8859-2 (Latin-2)
> Latin-2 letters allowed in identifiers, with uppercase and lowercase equivalence.

ISO 8859-3 (Latin-3)
> Latin-3 letters allowed in identifiers, with uppercase and lowercase equivalence.

ISO 8859-4 (Latin-4)
> Latin-4 letters allowed in identifiers, with uppercase and lowercase equivalence.

ISO 8859-5 (Cyrillic)
> ISO 8859-5 letters (Cyrillic) allowed in identifiers, with uppercase and lowercase equivalence.

ISO 8859-15 (Latin-9)
> ISO 8859-15 (Latin-9) letters allowed in identifiers, with uppercase and lowercase equivalence

IBM PC (code page 437)
> This code page is the normal default for PCs in the U.S. It corresponds to the original IBM PC character set. This set has some, but not all, of the extended

Latin-1 letters, but these letters do not have the same encoding as Latin-1. In this mode, these letters are allowed in identifiers with uppercase and lowercase equivalence.

IBM PC (code page 850)

This code page is a modification of 437 extended to include all the Latin-1 letters, but still not with the usual Latin-1 encoding. In this mode, all these letters are allowed in identifiers with uppercase and lowercase equivalence.

Full Upper 8-bit

Any character in the range 80-FF allowed in identifiers, and all are considered distinct. In other words, there are no uppercase and lowercase equivalences in this range. This is useful in conjunction with certain encoding schemes used for some foreign character sets (e.g., the typical method of representing Chinese characters on the PC).

No Upper-Half

No upper-half characters in the range 80-FF are allowed in identifiers. This gives Ada 83 compatibility for identifier names.

For precise data on the encodings permitted, and the uppercase and lowercase equivalences that are recognized, see the file `csets.adb` in the GNAT compiler sources. You will need to obtain a full source release of GNAT to obtain this file.

3.2.3 Wide_Character Encodings

GNAT allows wide character codes to appear in character and string literals, and also optionally in identifiers, by means of the following possible encoding schemes:

Hex Coding

In this encoding, a wide character is represented by the following five character sequence:

```
ESC a b c d
```

where a, b, c, d are the four hexadecimal characters (using uppercase letters) of the wide character code. For example, ESC A345 is used to represent the wide character with code $16\#A345\#$. This scheme is compatible with use of the full Wide_Character set.

Upper-Half Coding

The wide character with encoding $16\#abcd\#$ where the upper bit is on (in other words, 'a' is in the range 8-F) is represented as two bytes, $16\#ab\#$ and $16\#cd\#$. The second byte cannot be a format control character, but is not required to be in the upper half. This method can be also used for shift-JIS or EUC, where the internal coding matches the external coding.

Shift JIS Coding

A wide character is represented by a two-character sequence, $16\#ab\#$ and $16\#cd\#$, with the restrictions described for upper-half encoding as described above. The internal character code is the corresponding JIS character according to the standard algorithm for Shift-JIS conversion. Only characters defined in the JIS code set table can be used with this encoding method.

EUC Coding

A wide character is represented by a two-character sequence *16#ab#* and *16#cd#*, with both characters being in the upper half. The internal character code is the corresponding JIS character according to the EUC encoding algorithm. Only characters defined in the JIS code set table can be used with this encoding method.

UTF-8 Coding

A wide character is represented using UCS Transformation Format 8 (UTF-8) as defined in Annex R of ISO 10646-1/Am.2. Depending on the character value, the representation is a one, two, or three byte sequence:

```
16#0000#-16#007f#: 2#0'xxxxxxx'#
16#0080#-16#07ff#: 2#110'xxxxx'# 2#10'xxxxxx'#
16#0800#-16#ffff#: 2#1110'xxxx'# 2#10'xxxxxx'# 2#10'xxxxxx'#
```

where the *xxx* bits correspond to the left-padded bits of the 16-bit character value. Note that all lower half ASCII characters are represented as ASCII bytes and all upper half characters and other wide characters are represented as sequences of upper-half (The full UTF-8 scheme allows for encoding 31-bit characters as 6-byte sequences, and in the following section on wide wide characters, the use of these sequences is documented).

Brackets Coding

In this encoding, a wide character is represented by the following eight character sequence:

```
[ " a b c d " ]
```

where *a*, *b*, *c*, *d* are the four hexadecimal characters (using uppercase letters) of the wide character code. For example, ['A345'] is used to represent the wide character with code *16#A345#*. It is also possible (though not required) to use the Brackets coding for upper half characters. For example, the code *16#A3#* can be represented as *['A3']*.

This scheme is compatible with use of the full Wide_Character set, and is also the method used for wide character encoding in some standard ACATS (Ada Conformity Assessment Test Suite) test suite distributions.

Note: Some of these coding schemes do not permit the full use of the Ada character set. For example, neither Shift JIS nor EUC allow the use of the upper half of the Latin-1 set.

3.2.4 Wide_Wide_Character Encodings

GNAT allows wide wide character codes to appear in character and string literals, and also optionally in identifiers, by means of the following possible encoding schemes:

UTF-8 Coding

A wide character is represented using UCS Transformation Format 8 (UTF-8) as defined in Annex R of ISO 10646-1/Am.2. Depending on the character value, the representation of character codes with values greater than 16#FFFF# is a is a four, five, or six byte sequence:

```
16#01_0000#-16#10_FFFF#:        11110xxx 10xxxxxx 10xxxxxx
                                10xxxxxx
16#0020_0000#-16#03FF_FFFF#: 111110xx 10xxxxxx 10xxxxxx
                                10xxxxxx 10xxxxxx
16#0400_0000#-16#7FFF_FFFF#: 1111110x 10xxxxxx 10xxxxxx
                                10xxxxxx 10xxxxxx 10xxxxxx
```

where the *xxx* bits correspond to the left-padded bits of the 32-bit character value.

Brackets Coding

In this encoding, a wide wide character is represented by the following ten or twelve byte character sequence:

```
[ " a b c d e f " ]
[ " a b c d e f g h " ]
```

where *a-h* are the six or eight hexadecimal characters (using uppercase letters) of the wide wide character code. For example, ["1F4567"] is used to represent the wide wide character with code *16#001F_4567#*.

This scheme is compatible with use of the full Wide_Wide_Character set, and is also the method used for wide wide character encoding in some standard ACATS (Ada Conformity Assessment Test Suite) test suite distributions.

3.3 File Naming Topics and Utilities

GNAT has a default file naming scheme and also provides the user with a high degree of control over how the names and extensions of the source files correspond to the Ada compilation units that they contain.

3.3.1 File Naming Rules

The default file name is determined by the name of the unit that the file contains. The name is formed by taking the full expanded name of the unit and replacing the separating dots with hyphens and using lowercase for all letters.

An exception arises if the file name generated by the above rules starts with one of the characters *a*, *g*, *i*, or *s*, and the second character is a minus. In this case, the character tilde is used in place of the minus. The reason for this special rule is to avoid clashes with the standard names for child units of the packages System, Ada, Interfaces, and GNAT, which use the prefixes *s-*, *a-*, *i-*, and *g-*, respectively.

The file extension is `.ads` for a spec and `.adb` for a body. The following table shows some examples of these rules.

Source File	Ada Compilation Unit
`main.ads`	Main (spec)
`main.adb`	Main (body)
`arith_functions.ads`	Arith_Functions (package spec)

`arith_functions.adb`	Arith_Functions (package body)
`func-spec.ads`	Func.Spec (child package spec)
`func-spec.adb`	Func.Spec (child package body)
`main-sub.adb`	Sub (subunit of Main)
`a~bad.adb`	A.Bad (child package body)

Following these rules can result in excessively long file names if corresponding unit names are long (for example, if child units or subunits are heavily nested). An option is available to shorten such long file names (called file name 'krunching'). This may be particularly useful when programs being developed with GNAT are to be used on operating systems with limited file name lengths. [Using gnatkr], page 20.

Of course, no file shortening algorithm can guarantee uniqueness over all possible unit names; if file name krunching is used, it is your responsibility to ensure no name clashes occur. Alternatively you can specify the exact file names that you want used, as described in the next section. Finally, if your Ada programs are migrating from a compiler with a different naming convention, you can use the gnatchop utility to produce source files that follow the GNAT naming conventions. (For details see [Renaming Files with gnatchop], page 22.)

Note: in the case of Windows or Mac OS operating systems, case is not significant. So for example on *Windows* if the canonical name is *main-sub.adb*, you can use the file name `Main-Sub.adb` instead. However, case is significant for other operating systems, so for example, if you want to use other than canonically cased file names on a Unix system, you need to follow the procedures described in the next section.

3.3.2 Using Other File Names

In the previous section, we have described the default rules used by GNAT to determine the file name in which a given unit resides. It is often convenient to follow these default rules, and if you follow them, the compiler knows without being explicitly told where to find all the files it needs.

However, in some cases, particularly when a program is imported from another Ada compiler environment, it may be more convenient for the programmer to specify which file names contain which units. GNAT allows arbitrary file names to be used by means of the Source_File_Name pragma. The form of this pragma is as shown in the following examples:

```
pragma Source_File_Name (My_Utilities.Stacks,
  Spec_File_Name => "myutilst_a.ada");
pragma Source_File_name (My_Utilities.Stacks,
  Body_File_Name => "myutilst.ada");
```

As shown in this example, the first argument for the pragma is the unit name (in this example a child unit). The second argument has the form of a named association. The identifier indicates whether the file name is for a spec or a body; the file name itself is given by a string literal.

The source file name pragma is a configuration pragma, which means that normally it will be placed in the `gnat.adc` file used to hold configuration pragmas that apply to a complete compilation environment. For more details on how the `gnat.adc` file is created and used see [Handling of Configuration Pragmas], page 28.

GNAT allows completely arbitrary file names to be specified using the source file name pragma. However, if the file name specified has an extension other than `.ads` or `.adb` it is necessary to use a special syntax when compiling the file. The name in this case must be preceded by the special sequence -*x* followed by a space and the name of the language, here *ada*, as in:

```
$ gcc -c -x ada peculiar_file_name.sim
```

gnatmake handles non-standard file names in the usual manner (the non-standard file name for the main program is simply used as the argument to gnatmake). Note that if the extension is also non-standard, then it must be included in the *gnatmake* command, it may not be omitted.

3.3.3 Alternative File Naming Schemes

The previous section described the use of the *Source_File_Name* pragma to allow arbitrary names to be assigned to individual source files. However, this approach requires one pragma for each file, and especially in large systems can result in very long `gnat.adc` files, and also create a maintenance problem.

GNAT also provides a facility for specifying systematic file naming schemes other than the standard default naming scheme previously described. An alternative scheme for naming is specified by the use of *Source_File_Name* pragmas having the following format:

```
pragma Source_File_Name (
   Spec_File_Name  => FILE_NAME_PATTERN
 [ , Casing         => CASING_SPEC]
 [ , Dot_Replacement => STRING_LITERAL ] );

pragma Source_File_Name (
   Body_File_Name  => FILE_NAME_PATTERN
 [ , Casing         => CASING_SPEC ]
 [ , Dot_Replacement => STRING_LITERAL ] ) ;

pragma Source_File_Name (
   Subunit_File_Name  => FILE_NAME_PATTERN
 [ , Casing           => CASING_SPEC ]
 [ , Dot_Replacement => STRING_LITERAL ] ) ;

FILE_NAME_PATTERN ::= STRING_LITERAL
CASING_SPEC ::= Lowercase | Uppercase | Mixedcase
```

The *FILE_NAME_PATTERN* string shows how the file name is constructed. It contains a single asterisk character, and the unit name is substituted systematically for this asterisk. The optional parameter *Casing* indicates whether the unit name is to be all upper-case letters, all lower-case letters, or mixed-case. If no *Casing* parameter is used, then the default is all lower-case.

The optional *Dot_Replacement* string is used to replace any periods that occur in subunit or child unit names. If no *Dot_Replacement* argument is used then separating dots appear unchanged in the resulting file name. Although the above syntax indicates that the *Casing* argument must appear before the *Dot_Replacement* argument, but it is also permissible to write these arguments in the opposite order.

As indicated, it is possible to specify different naming schemes for bodies, specs, and subunits. Quite often the rule for subunits is the same as the rule for bodies, in which case, there is no need to give a separate *Subunit_File_Name* rule, and in this case the *Body_File_name* rule is used for subunits as well.

The separate rule for subunits can also be used to implement the rather unusual case of a compilation environment (e.g., a single directory) which contains a subunit and a child unit with the same unit name. Although both units cannot appear in the same partition, the Ada Reference Manual allows (but does not require) the possibility of the two units coexisting in the same environment.

The file name translation works in the following steps:

* If there is a specific *Source_File_Name* pragma for the given unit, then this is always used, and any general pattern rules are ignored.

* If there is a pattern type *Source_File_Name* pragma that applies to the unit, then the resulting file name will be used if the file exists. If more than one pattern matches, the latest one will be tried first, and the first attempt resulting in a reference to a file that exists will be used.

* If no pattern type *Source_File_Name* pragma that applies to the unit for which the corresponding file exists, then the standard GNAT default naming rules are used.

As an example of the use of this mechanism, consider a commonly used scheme in which file names are all lower case, with separating periods copied unchanged to the resulting file name, and specs end with `.1.ada`, and bodies end with `.2.ada`. GNAT will follow this scheme if the following two pragmas appear:

```
pragma Source_File_Name
  (Spec_File_Name => ".1.ada");
pragma Source_File_Name
  (Body_File_Name => ".2.ada");
```

The default GNAT scheme is actually implemented by providing the following default pragmas internally:

```
pragma Source_File_Name
  (Spec_File_Name => ".ads", Dot_Replacement => "-");
pragma Source_File_Name
  (Body_File_Name => ".adb", Dot_Replacement => "-");
```

Our final example implements a scheme typically used with one of the Ada 83 compilers, where the separator character for subunits was '__' (two underscores), specs were identified by adding `__.ADA`, bodies by adding `.ADA`, and subunits by adding `.SEP`. All file names were upper case. Child units were not present of course since this was an Ada 83 compiler, but it seems reasonable to extend this scheme to use the same double underscore separator for child units.

```
pragma Source_File_Name
```

```
        (Spec_File_Name => "_.ADA",
         Dot_Replacement => "__",
         Casing = Uppercase);
     pragma Source_File_Name
        (Body_File_Name => ".ADA",
         Dot_Replacement => "__",
         Casing = Uppercase);
     pragma Source_File_Name
        (Subunit_File_Name => ".SEP",
         Dot_Replacement => "__",
         Casing = Uppercase);
```

3.3.4 Handling Arbitrary File Naming Conventions with *gnatname*

3.3.4.1 Arbitrary File Naming Conventions

The GNAT compiler must be able to know the source file name of a compilation unit. When using the standard GNAT default file naming conventions (*.ads* for specs, *.adb* for bodies), the GNAT compiler does not need additional information.

When the source file names do not follow the standard GNAT default file naming conventions, the GNAT compiler must be given additional information through a configuration pragmas file ([Configuration Pragmas], page 26) or a project file. When the non-standard file naming conventions are well-defined, a small number of pragmas *Source_File_Name* specifying a naming pattern ([Alternative File Naming Schemes], page 15) may be sufficient. However, if the file naming conventions are irregular or arbitrary, a number of pragma *Source_File_Name* for individual compilation units must be defined. To help maintain the correspondence between compilation unit names and source file names within the compiler, GNAT provides a tool *gnatname* to generate the required pragmas for a set of files.

3.3.4.2 Running *gnatname*

The usual form of the *gnatname* command is:

```
$ gnatname ['switches'] 'naming_pattern' ['naming_patterns']
    [--and ['switches'] 'naming_pattern' ['naming_patterns']]
```

All of the arguments are optional. If invoked without any argument, *gnatname* will display its usage.

When used with at least one naming pattern, *gnatname* will attempt to find all the compilation units in files that follow at least one of the naming patterns. To find these compilation units, *gnatname* will use the GNAT compiler in syntax-check-only mode on all regular files.

One or several Naming Patterns may be given as arguments to *gnatname*. Each Naming Pattern is enclosed between double quotes (or single quotes on Windows). A Naming Pattern is a regular expression similar to the wildcard patterns used in file names by the Unix shells or the DOS prompt.

gnatname may be called with several sections of directories/patterns. Sections are separated by switch *–and*. In each section, there must be at least one pattern. If no directory is specified in a section, the current directory (or the project directory is *-P* is used) is implied. The options other that the directory switches and the patterns apply globally even if they are in different sections.

Examples of Naming Patterns are:

```
"*.[12].ada"
"*.ad[sb]*"
"body_*"    "spec_*"
```

For a more complete description of the syntax of Naming Patterns, see the second kind of regular expressions described in `g-regexp.ads` (the 'Glob' regular expressions).

When invoked with no switch -P, *gnatname* will create a configuration pragmas file `gnat.adc` in the current working directory, with pragmas *Source_File_Name* for each file that contains a valid Ada unit.

3.3.4.3 Switches for *gnatname*

Switches for *gnatname* must precede any specified Naming Pattern.

You may specify any of the following switches to *gnatname*:

--version

> Display Copyright and version, then exit disregarding all other options.

--help

> If *–version* was not used, display usage, then exit disregarding all other options.

--subdirs=dir

> Real object, library or exec directories are subdirectories <dir> of the specified ones.

--no-backup

> Do not create a backup copy of an existing project file.

--and

> Start another section of directories/patterns.

-cfilename

> Create a configuration pragmas file `filename` (instead of the default `gnat.adc`). There may be zero, one or more space between -c and `filename`. `filename` may include directory information. `filename` must be writable. There may be only one switch -c. When a switch -c is specified, no switch -P may be specified (see below).

-ddir

> Look for source files in directory `dir`. There may be zero, one or more spaces between -d and `dir`. `dir` may end with /**, that is it may be of the form *root_dir*/**. In this case, the directory *root_dir* and all of its subdirectories, recursively, have to be searched for sources. When a switch -d is specified, the current working directory will not be searched for source files, unless it is explicitly specified with a -d or -D switch. Several switches -d may be specified. If `dir` is a relative path, it is relative to the directory of the configuration pragmas file specified with switch -c, or to the directory of the project file specified with switch -P or, if neither switch -c nor switch -P are specified, it

is relative to the current working directory. The directory specified with switch
-*d* must exist and be readable.

-D*filename*

Look for source files in all directories listed in text file `filename`. There may
be zero, one or more spaces between -*D* and `filename`. `filename` must be
an existing, readable text file. Each nonempty line in `filename` must be a
directory. Specifying switch -*D* is equivalent to specifying as many switches -*d*
as there are nonempty lines in `file`.

-eL

Follow symbolic links when processing project files.

-f*pattern*

Foreign patterns. Using this switch, it is possible to add sources of languages
other than Ada to the list of sources of a project file. It is only useful if a -P
switch is used. For example,

    gnatname -Pprj -f"*.c" "*.ada"

will look for Ada units in all files with the `.ada` extension, and will add to the
list of file for project `prj.gpr` the C files with extension `.c`.

-h

Output usage (help) information. The output is written to `stdout`.

-P*proj*

Create or update project file `proj`. There may be zero, one or more space
between -*P* and `proj`. `proj` may include directory information. `proj` must be
writable. There may be only one switch -*P*. When a switch -*P* is specified, no
switch -*c* may be specified. On all platforms, except on VMS, when *gnatname*
is invoked for an existing project file <proj>.gpr, a backup copy of the project
file is created in the project directory with file name <proj>.gpr.saved_x. 'x' is
the first non negative number that makes this backup copy a new file.

-v

Verbose mode. Output detailed explanation of behavior to `stdout`. This includes name of the file written, the name of the directories to search and, for
each file in those directories whose name matches at least one of the Naming
Patterns, an indication of whether the file contains a unit, and if so the name
of the unit.

-v -v

Very Verbose mode. In addition to the output produced in verbose mode, for
each file in the searched directories whose name matches none of the Naming
Patterns, an indication is given that there is no match.

-x*pattern*

Excluded patterns. Using this switch, it is possible to exclude some files that
would match the name patterns. For example,

    gnatname -x "*_nt.ada" "*.ada"

will look for Ada units in all files with the `.ada` extension, except those whose
names end with `_nt.ada`.

3.3.4.4 Examples of *gnatname* Usage

```
$ gnatname -c /home/me/names.adc -d sources "[a-z]*.ada*"
```

In this example, the directory **/home/me** must already exist and be writable. In addition, the directory **/home/me/sources** (specified by *-d sources*) must exist and be readable.

Note the optional spaces after *-c* and *-d*.

```
$ gnatname -P/home/me/proj -x "*_nt_body.ada"
-dsources -dsources/plus -Dcommon_dirs.txt "body_*" "spec_*"
```

Note that several switches *-d* may be used, even in conjunction with one or several switches *-D*. Several Naming Patterns and one excluded pattern are used in this example.

3.3.5 File Name Krunching with *gnatkr*

This section discusses the method used by the compiler to shorten the default file names chosen for Ada units so that they do not exceed the maximum length permitted. It also describes the *gnatkr* utility that can be used to determine the result of applying this shortening.

3.3.5.1 About *gnatkr*

The default file naming rule in GNAT is that the file name must be derived from the unit name. The exact default rule is as follows:

* Take the unit name and replace all dots by hyphens.

* If such a replacement occurs in the second character position of a name, and the first character is **a**, **g**, **s**, or **i**, then replace the dot by the character ~ (tilde) instead of a minus.

  The reason for this exception is to avoid clashes with the standard names for children of System, Ada, Interfaces, and GNAT, which use the prefixes **s-**, **a-**, **i-**, and **g-**, respectively.

The **-gnatk**nn switch of the compiler activates a 'krunching' circuit that limits file names to nn characters (where nn is a decimal integer).

The *gnatkr* utility can be used to determine the krunched name for a given file, when krunched to a specified maximum length.

3.3.5.2 Using *gnatkr*

The *gnatkr* command has the form:

```
$ gnatkr 'name' ['length']
```

name is the uncrunched file name, derived from the name of the unit in the standard manner described in the previous section (i.e., in particular all dots are replaced by hyphens). The file name may or may not have an extension (defined as a suffix of the form period followed by arbitrary characters other than period). If an extension is present then it will be preserved in the output. For example, when krunching **hellofile.ads** to eight characters, the result will be hellofil.ads.

Note: for compatibility with previous versions of *gnatkr* dots may appear in the name instead of hyphens, but the last dot will always be taken as the start of an extension. So if *gnatkr* is given an argument such as **Hello.World.adb** it will be treated exactly as if the first period had been a hyphen, and for example krunching to eight characters gives the result `hellworl.adb`.

Note that the result is always all lower case. Characters of the other case are folded as required.

length represents the length of the krunched name. The default when no argument is given is 8 characters. A length of zero stands for unlimited, in other words do not chop except for system files where the implied crunching length is always eight characters.

The output is the krunched name. The output has an extension only if the original argument was a file name with an extension.

3.3.5.3 Krunching Method

The initial file name is determined by the name of the unit that the file contains. The name is formed by taking the full expanded name of the unit and replacing the separating dots with hyphens and using lowercase for all letters, except that a hyphen in the second character position is replaced by a tilde if the first character is `a`, `i`, `g`, or `s`. The extension is *.ads* for a spec and *.adb* for a body. Krunching does not affect the extension, but the file name is shortened to the specified length by following these rules:

* The name is divided into segments separated by hyphens, tildes or underscores and all hyphens, tildes, and underscores are eliminated. If this leaves the name short enough, we are done.

* If the name is too long, the longest segment is located (left-most if there are two of equal length), and shortened by dropping its last character. This is repeated until the name is short enough.

As an example, consider the krunching of `our-strings-wide_fixed.adb` to fit the name into 8 characters as required by some operating systems:

```
our-strings-wide_fixed 22
our strings wide fixed 19
our string  wide fixed 18
our strin   wide fixed 17
our stri    wide fixed 16
our stri    wide fixe  15
our str     wide fixe  14
our str     wid  fixe  13
our str     wid  fix   12
ou  str     wid  fix   11
ou  st      wid  fix   10
ou  st      wi   fix   9
ou  st      wi   fi    8
Final file name: oustwifi.adb
```

* The file names for all predefined units are always krunched to eight characters. The krunching of these predefined units uses the following special prefix replacements:

Prefix	Replacement
ada-	a-

```
gnat-                      g-

interfac es-               i-

system-                    s-
```

These system files have a hyphen in the second character position. That is why normal user files replace such a character with a tilde, to avoid confusion with system file names.

As an example of this special rule, consider `ada-strings-wide_fixed.adb`, which gets krunched as follows:

```
ada-strings-wide_fixed 22
a-  strings wide fixed 18
a-  string  wide fixed 17
a-  strin   wide fixed 16
a-  stri    wide fixed 15
a-  stri    wide fixe  14
a-  str     wide fixe  13
a-  str     wid  fixe  12
a-  str     wid  fix   11
a-  st      wid  fix   10
a-  st      wi   fix   9
a-  st      wi   fi    8
Final file name: a-stwifi.adb
```

Of course no file shortening algorithm can guarantee uniqueness over all possible unit names, and if file name krunching is used then it is your responsibility to ensure that no name clashes occur. The utility program *gnatkr* is supplied for conveniently determining the krunched name of a file.

3.3.5.4 Examples of *gnatkr* Usage

```
$ gnatkr very_long_unit_name.ads        --> velounna.ads
$ gnatkr grandparent-parent-child.ads --> grparchi.ads
$ gnatkr Grandparent.Parent.Child.ads --> grparchi.ads
$ gnatkr grandparent-parent-child      --> grparchi
$ gnatkr very_long_unit_name.ads/count=6 --> vlunna.ads
$ gnatkr very_long_unit_name.ads/count=0 --> very_long_unit_name.ads
```

3.3.6 Renaming Files with *gnatchop*

This section discusses how to handle files with multiple units by using the *gnatchop* utility. This utility is also useful in renaming files to meet the standard GNAT default file naming conventions.

3.3.6.1 Handling Files with Multiple Units

The basic compilation model of GNAT requires that a file submitted to the compiler have only one unit and there be a strict correspondence between the file name and the unit name.

The *gnatchop* utility allows both of these rules to be relaxed, allowing GNAT to process files which contain multiple compilation units and files with arbitrary file names. *gnatchop* reads the specified file and generates one or more output files, containing one unit per file. The unit and the file name correspond, as required by GNAT.

If you want to permanently restructure a set of 'foreign' files so that they match the GNAT rules, and do the remaining development using the GNAT structure, you can simply use *gnatchop* once, generate the new set of files and work with them from that point on.

Alternatively, if you want to keep your files in the 'foreign' format, perhaps to maintain compatibility with some other Ada compilation system, you can set up a procedure where you use *gnatchop* each time you compile, regarding the source files that it writes as temporary files that you throw away.

Note that if your file containing multiple units starts with a byte order mark (BOM) specifying UTF-8 encoding, then the files generated by gnatchop will each start with a copy of this BOM, meaning that they can be compiled automatically in UTF-8 mode without needing to specify an explicit encoding.

3.3.6.2 Operating gnatchop in Compilation Mode

The basic function of *gnatchop* is to take a file with multiple units and split it into separate files. The boundary between files is reasonably clear, except for the issue of comments and pragmas. In default mode, the rule is that any pragmas between units belong to the previous unit, except that configuration pragmas always belong to the following unit. Any comments belong to the following unit. These rules almost always result in the right choice of the split point without needing to mark it explicitly and most users will find this default to be what they want. In this default mode it is incorrect to submit a file containing only configuration pragmas, or one that ends in configuration pragmas, to *gnatchop*.

However, using a special option to activate 'compilation mode', *gnatchop* can perform another function, which is to provide exactly the semantics required by the RM for handling of configuration pragmas in a compilation. In the absence of configuration pragmas (at the main file level), this option has no effect, but it causes such configuration pragmas to be handled in a quite different manner.

First, in compilation mode, if *gnatchop* is given a file that consists of only configuration pragmas, then this file is appended to the `gnat.adc` file in the current directory. This behavior provides the required behavior described in the RM for the actions to be taken on submitting such a file to the compiler, namely that these pragmas should apply to all subsequent compilations in the same compilation environment. Using GNAT, the current directory, possibly containing a `gnat.adc` file is the representation of a compilation environment. For more information on the `gnat.adc` file, see [Handling of Configuration Pragmas], page 28.

Second, in compilation mode, if *gnatchop* is given a file that starts with configuration pragmas, and contains one or more units, then these configuration pragmas are prepended to each of the chopped files. This behavior provides the required behavior described in the RM for the actions to be taken on compiling such a file, namely that the pragmas apply to all units in the compilation, but not to subsequently compiled units.

Finally, if configuration pragmas appear between units, they are appended to the previous unit. This results in the previous unit being illegal, since the compiler does not accept configuration pragmas that follow a unit. This provides the required RM behavior that forbids configuration pragmas other than those preceding the first compilation unit of a compilation.

For most purposes, *gnatchop* will be used in default mode. The compilation mode described above is used only if you need exactly accurate behavior with respect to compilations, and you have files that contain multiple units and configuration pragmas. In this circumstance the use of *gnatchop* with the compilation mode switch provides the required behavior, and is for example the mode in which GNAT processes the ACVC tests.

3.3.6.3 Command Line for *gnatchop*

The *gnatchop* command has the form:

```
$ gnatchop switches file_name [file_name ...]
        [directory]
```

The only required argument is the file name of the file to be chopped. There are no restrictions on the form of this file name. The file itself contains one or more Ada units, in normal GNAT format, concatenated together. As shown, more than one file may be presented to be chopped.

When run in default mode, *gnatchop* generates one output file in the current directory for each unit in each of the files.

directory, if specified, gives the name of the directory to which the output files will be written. If it is not specified, all files are written to the current directory.

For example, given a file called `hellofiles` containing

```
procedure Hello;

with Ada.Text_IO; use Ada.Text_IO;
procedure Hello is
begin
   Put_Line ("Hello");
end Hello;
```

the command

```
$ gnatchop hellofiles
```

generates two files in the current directory, one called `hello.ads` containing the single line that is the procedure spec, and the other called `hello.adb` containing the remaining text. The original file is not affected. The generated files can be compiled in the normal manner.

When gnatchop is invoked on a file that is empty or that contains only empty lines and/or comments, gnatchop will not fail, but will not produce any new sources.

For example, given a file called `toto.txt` containing

```
-- Just a comment
```

the command

```
$ gnatchop toto.txt
```

will not produce any new file and will result in the following warnings:

```
toto.txt:1:01: warning: empty file, contains no compilation units
no compilation units found
no source files written
```

3.3.6.4 Switches for *gnatchop*

gnatchop recognizes the following switches:

`--version`

>   Display Copyright and version, then exit disregarding all other options.

`--help`

>   If *–version* was not used, display usage, then exit disregarding all other options.

`-c`

>   Causes *gnatchop* to operate in compilation mode, in which configuration prag-
>   mas are handled according to strict RM rules. See previous section for a full
>   description of this mode.

`-gnatxxx`

>   This passes the given *-gnat'xxx*' switch to 'gnat' which is used to parse the
>   given file. Not all 'xxx' options make sense, but for example, the use of *-
>   gnati2* allows gnatchop to process a source file that uses Latin-2 coding for
>   identifiers.

`-h`

>   Causes *gnatchop* to generate a brief help summary to the standard output file
>   showing usage information.

`-kmm`

>   Limit generated file names to the specified number *mm* of characters. This is
>   useful if the resulting set of files is required to be interoperable with systems
>   which limit the length of file names. No space is allowed between the *-k* and
>   the numeric value. The numeric value may be omitted in which case a default
>   of *-k8*, suitable for use with DOS-like file systems, is used. If no *-k* switch is
>   present then there is no limit on the length of file names.

`-p`

>   Causes the file modification time stamp of the input file to be preserved and
>   used for the time stamp of the output file(s). This may be useful for preserving
>   coherency of time stamps in an environment where *gnatchop* is used as part of
>   a standard build process.

`-q`

>   Causes output of informational messages indicating the set of generated files to
>   be suppressed. Warnings and error messages are unaffected.

`-r`

>   Generate *Source_Reference* pragmas. Use this switch if the output files are
>   regarded as temporary and development is to be done in terms of the original
>   unchopped file. This switch causes *Source_Reference* pragmas to be inserted
>   into each of the generated files to refers back to the original file name and
>   line number. The result is that all error messages refer back to the original
>   unchopped file. In addition, the debugging information placed into the object
>   file (when the *-g* switch of *gcc* or *gnatmake* is specified) also refers back to this

original file so that tools like profilers and debuggers will give information in
terms of the original unchopped file.

If the original file to be chopped itself contains a *Source_Reference* pragma
referencing a third file, then gnatchop respects this pragma, and the generated *Source_Reference* pragmas in the chopped file refer to the original file,
with appropriate line numbers. This is particularly useful when *gnatchop* is
used in conjunction with *gnatprep* to compile files that contain preprocessing
statements and multiple units.

`-v`

Causes *gnatchop* to operate in verbose mode. The version number and copyright
notice are output, as well as exact copies of the gnat1 commands spawned to
obtain the chop control information.

`-w`

Overwrite existing file names. Normally *gnatchop* regards it as a fatal error if
there is already a file with the same name as a file it would otherwise output,
in other words if the files to be chopped contain duplicated units. This switch
bypasses this check, and causes all but the last instance of such duplicated units
to be skipped.

`--GCC=xxxx`

Specify the path of the GNAT parser to be used. When this switch is used, no
attempt is made to add the prefix to the GNAT parser executable.

3.3.6.5 Examples of *gnatchop* Usage

```
$ gnatchop -w hello_s.ada prerelease/files
```

Chops the source file `hello_s.ada`. The output files will be placed in the directory
`prerelease/files`, overwriting any files with matching names in that directory (no files in
the current directory are modified).

```
$ gnatchop archive
```

Chops the source file `archive` into the current directory. One useful application of *gnatchop*
is in sending sets of sources around, for example in email messages. The required sources
are simply concatenated (for example, using a Unix *cat* command), and then *gnatchop* is
used at the other end to reconstitute the original file names.

```
$ gnatchop file1 file2 file3 direc
```

Chops all units in files `file1`, `file2`, `file3`, placing the resulting files in the directory
`direc`. Note that if any units occur more than once anywhere within this set of files, an
error message is generated, and no files are written. To override this check, use the *-w*
switch, in which case the last occurrence in the last file will be the one that is output, and
earlier duplicate occurrences for a given unit will be skipped.

3.4 Configuration Pragmas

Configuration pragmas include those pragmas described as such in the Ada Reference
Manual, as well as implementation-dependent pragmas that are configuration pragmas.

See the *Implementation_Defined_Pragmas* chapter in the *GNAT_Reference_Manual* for details on these additional GNAT-specific configuration pragmas. Most notably, the pragma *Source_File_Name*, which allows specifying non-default names for source files, is a configuration pragma. The following is a complete list of configuration pragmas recognized by GNAT:

```
Ada_83
Ada_95
Ada_05
Ada_2005
Ada_12
Ada_2012
Allow_Integer_Address
Annotate
Assertion_Policy
Assume_No_Invalid_Values
C_Pass_By_Copy
Check_Name
Check_Policy
Compile_Time_Error
Compile_Time_Warning
Compiler_Unit
Component_Alignment
Convention_Identifier
Debug_Policy
Detect_Blocking
Default_Storage_Pool
Discard_Names
Elaboration_Checks
Eliminate
Extend_System
Extensions_Allowed
External_Name_Casing
Fast_Math
Favor_Top_Level
Float_Representation
Implicit_Packing
Initialize_Scalars
Interrupt_State
License
Locking_Policy
Long_Float
No_Run_Time
No_Strict_Aliasing
Normalize_Scalars
Optimize_Alignment
Persistent_BSS
```

```
Polling
Priority_Specific_Dispatching
Profile
Profile_Warnings
Propagate_Exceptions
Queuing_Policy
Ravenscar
Restricted_Run_Time
Restrictions
Restrictions_Warnings
Reviewable
Short_Circuit_And_Or
Source_File_Name
Source_File_Name_Project
SPARK_Mode
Style_Checks
Suppress
Suppress_Exception_Locations
Task_Dispatching_Policy
Universal_Data
Unsuppress
Use_VADS_Size
Validity_Checks
Warnings
Wide_Character_Encoding
```

3.4.1 Handling of Configuration Pragmas

Configuration pragmas may either appear at the start of a compilation unit, or they can appear in a configuration pragma file to apply to all compilations performed in a given compilation environment.

GNAT also provides the *gnatchop* utility to provide an automatic way to handle configuration pragmas following the semantics for compilations (that is, files with multiple units), described in the RM. See [Operating gnatchop in Compilation Mode], page 23 for details. However, for most purposes, it will be more convenient to edit the `gnat.adc` file that contains configuration pragmas directly, as described in the following section.

In the case of *Restrictions* pragmas appearing as configuration pragmas in individual compilation units, the exact handling depends on the type of restriction.

Restrictions that require partition-wide consistency (like *No_Tasking*) are recognized wherever they appear and can be freely inherited, e.g. from a *with*ed unit to the *with*ing unit. This makes sense since the binder will in any case insist on seeing consistent use, so any unit not conforming to any restrictions that are anywhere in the partition will be rejected, and you might as well find that out at compile time rather than at bind time.

For restrictions that do not require partition-wide consistency, e.g. SPARK or No_Implementation_Attributes, in general the restriction applies only to the unit in which the pragma appears, and not to any other units.

The exception is No_Elaboration_Code which always applies to the entire object file from a compilation, i.e. to the body, spec, and all subunits. This restriction can be specified in a configuration pragma file, or it can be on the body and/or the spec (in eithe case it applies to all the relevant units). It can appear on a subunit only if it has previously appeared in the body of spec.

3.4.2 The Configuration Pragmas Files

In GNAT a compilation environment is defined by the current directory at the time that a compile command is given. This current directory is searched for a file whose name is `gnat.adc`. If this file is present, it is expected to contain one or more configuration pragmas that will be applied to the current compilation. However, if the switch *-gnatA* is used, `gnat.adc` is not considered. When taken into account, `gnat.adc` is added to the dependencies, so that if `gnat.adc` is modified later, an invocation of *gnatmake* will recompile the source.

Configuration pragmas may be entered into the `gnat.adc` file either by running *gnatchop* on a source file that consists only of configuration pragmas, or more conveniently by direct editing of the `gnat.adc` file, which is a standard format source file.

Besides `gnat.adc`, additional files containing configuration pragmas may be applied to the current compilation using the switch `-gnatec=path` where *path* must designate an existing file that contains only configuration pragmas. These configuration pragmas are in addition to those found in `gnat.adc` (provided `gnat.adc` is present and switch *-gnatA* is not used).

It is allowable to specify several switches *-gnatec=*, all of which will be taken into account.

Files containing configuration pragmas specified with switches *-gnatec=* are added to the dependencies, unless they are temporary files. A file is considered temporary if its name ends in `.tmp` or `.TMP`. Certain tools follow this naming convention because they pass information to *gcc* via temporary files that are immediately deleted; it doesn't make sense to depend on a file that no longer exists. Such tools include *gprbuild*, *gnatmake*, and *gnatcheck*.

If you are using project file, a separate mechanism is provided using project attributes.

3.5 Generating Object Files

An Ada program consists of a set of source files, and the first step in compiling the program is to generate the corresponding object files. These are generated by compiling a subset of these source files. The files you need to compile are the following:

* If a package spec has no body, compile the package spec to produce the object file for the package.

* If a package has both a spec and a body, compile the body to produce the object file for the package. The source file for the package spec need not be compiled in this case because there is only one object file, which contains the code for both the spec and body of the package.

* For a subprogram, compile the subprogram body to produce the object file for the subprogram. The spec, if one is present, is as usual in a separate file, and need not be compiled.

* In the case of subunits, only compile the parent unit. A single object file is generated for the entire subunit tree, which includes all the subunits.

* Compile child units independently of their parent units (though, of course, the spec of all the ancestor unit must be present in order to compile a child unit).

* Compile generic units in the same manner as any other units. The object files in this case are small dummy files that contain at most the flag used for elaboration checking. This is because GNAT always handles generic instantiation by means of macro expansion. However, it is still necessary to compile generic units, for dependency checking and elaboration purposes.

The preceding rules describe the set of files that must be compiled to generate the object files for a program. Each object file has the same name as the corresponding source file, except that the extension is .o as usual.

You may wish to compile other files for the purpose of checking their syntactic and semantic correctness. For example, in the case where a package has a separate spec and body, you would not normally compile the spec. However, it is convenient in practice to compile the spec to make sure it is error-free before compiling clients of this spec, because such compilations will fail if there is an error in the spec.

GNAT provides an option for compiling such files purely for the purposes of checking correctness; such compilations are not required as part of the process of building a program. To compile a file in this checking mode, use the *-gnatc* switch.

3.6 Source Dependencies

A given object file clearly depends on the source file which is compiled to produce it. Here we are using "depends" in the sense of a typical *make* utility; in other words, an object file depends on a source file if changes to the source file require the object file to be recompiled. In addition to this basic dependency, a given object may depend on additional source files as follows:

* If a file being compiled *with*s a unit X, the object file depends on the file containing the spec of unit X. This includes files that are *with*ed implicitly either because they are parents of *with*ed child units or they are run-time units required by the language constructs used in a particular unit.

* If a file being compiled instantiates a library level generic unit, the object file depends on both the spec and body files for this generic unit.

* If a file being compiled instantiates a generic unit defined within a package, the object file depends on the body file for the package as well as the spec file.

* If a file being compiled contains a call to a subprogram for which pragma *Inline* applies and inlining is activated with the *-gnatn* switch, the object file depends on the file containing the body of this subprogram as well as on the file containing the spec. Note that for inlining to actually occur as a result of the use of this switch, it is necessary to compile in optimizing mode.

  The use of *-gnatN* activates inlining optimization that is performed by the front end of the compiler. This inlining does not require that the code generation be optimized. Like *-gnatn*, the use of this switch generates additional dependencies.

  When using a gcc-based back end (in practice this means using any version of GNAT other than for the JVM, .NET or GNAAMP platforms), then the use of *-gnatN* is deprecated, and the use of *-gnatn* is preferred. Historically front end inlining was more extensive than the gcc back end inlining, but that is no longer the case.

* If an object file O depends on the proper body of a subunit through inlining or instantiation, it depends on the parent unit of the subunit. This means that any modification of the parent unit or one of its subunits affects the compilation of O.

* The object file for a parent unit depends on all its subunit body files.

* The previous two rules meant that for purposes of computing dependencies and recompilation, a body and all its subunits are treated as an indivisible whole.

These rules are applied transitively: if unit *A* *with*s unit *B*, whose elaboration calls an inlined procedure in package *C*, the object file for unit *A* will depend on the body of *C*, in file c.adb.

The set of dependent files described by these rules includes all the files on which the unit is semantically dependent, as dictated by the Ada language standard. However, it is a superset of what the standard describes, because it includes generic, inline, and subunit dependencies.

An object file must be recreated by recompiling the corresponding source file if any of the source files on which it depends are modified. For example, if the *make* utility is used to control compilation, the rule for an Ada object file must mention all the source files on which the object file depends, according to the above definition. The determination of the necessary recompilations is done automatically when one uses *gnatmake*.

3.7 The Ada Library Information Files

Each compilation actually generates two output files. The first of these is the normal object file that has a .o extension. The second is a text file containing full dependency information. It has the same name as the source file, but an .ali extension. This file is known as the Ada Library Information (ALI) file. The following information is contained in the ALI file.

* Version information (indicates which version of GNAT was used to compile the unit(s) in question)

* Main program information (including priority and time slice settings, as well as the wide character encoding used during compilation).

* List of arguments used in the *gcc* command for the compilation

* Attributes of the unit, including configuration pragmas used, an indication of whether the compilation was successful, exception model used etc.

* A list of relevant restrictions applying to the unit (used for consistency) checking.

* Categorization information (e.g., use of pragma *Pure*).

* Information on all *with*ed units, including presence of Elaborate' or *Elaborate_All* pragmas.

* Information from any *Linker_Options* pragmas used in the unit

* Information on the use of *Body_Version* or *Version* attributes in the unit.

* Dependency information. This is a list of files, together with time stamp and checksum information. These are files on which the unit depends in the sense that recompilation is required if any of these units are modified.

* Cross-reference data. Contains information on all entities referenced in the unit. Used by tools like *gnatxref* and *gnatfind* to provide cross-reference information.

For a full detailed description of the format of the ALI file, see the source of the body of unit *Lib.Writ*, contained in file `lib-writ.adb` in the GNAT compiler sources.

3.8 Binding an Ada Program

When using languages such as C and C++, once the source files have been compiled the only remaining step in building an executable program is linking the object modules together. This means that it is possible to link an inconsistent version of a program, in which two units have included different versions of the same header.

The rules of Ada do not permit such an inconsistent program to be built. For example, if two clients have different versions of the same package, it is illegal to build a program containing these two clients. These rules are enforced by the GNAT binder, which also determines an elaboration order consistent with the Ada rules.

The GNAT binder is run after all the object files for a program have been created. It is given the name of the main program unit, and from this it determines the set of units required by the program, by reading the corresponding ALI files. It generates error messages if the program is inconsistent or if no valid order of elaboration exists.

If no errors are detected, the binder produces a main program, in Ada by default, that contains calls to the elaboration procedures of those compilation unit that require them, followed by a call to the main program. This Ada program is compiled to generate the object file for the main program. The name of the Ada file is `b~xxx.adb`' (with the corresponding spec `b~xxx.ads`') where *xxx* is the name of the main program unit.

Finally, the linker is used to build the resulting executable program, using the object from the main program from the bind step as well as the object files for the Ada units of the program.

3.9 GNAT and Libraries

This section describes how to build and use libraries with GNAT, and also shows how to recompile the GNAT run-time library. You should be familiar with the Project Manager facility (see the *GNAT_Project_Manager* chapter of the *GPRbuild User's Guide*) before reading this chapter.

3.9.1 Introduction to Libraries in GNAT

A library is, conceptually, a collection of objects which does not have its own main thread of execution, but rather provides certain services to the applications that use it. A library can be either statically linked with the application, in which case its code is directly included in the application, or, on platforms that support it, be dynamically linked, in which case its code is shared by all applications making use of this library.

GNAT supports both types of libraries. In the static case, the compiled code can be provided in different ways. The simplest approach is to provide directly the set of objects resulting from compilation of the library source files. Alternatively, you can group the objects into an archive using whatever commands are provided by the operating system. For the latter case, the objects are grouped into a shared library.

In the GNAT environment, a library has three types of components:

* Source files,
* `ALI` files (see [The Ada Library Information Files], page 31), and
* Object files, an archive or a shared library.

A GNAT library may expose all its source files, which is useful for documentation purposes. Alternatively, it may expose only the units needed by an external user to make use of the library. That is to say, the specs reflecting the library services along with all the units needed to compile those specs, which can include generic bodies or any body implementing an inlined routine. In the case of *stand-alone libraries* those exposed units are called *interface units* ([Stand-alone Ada Libraries], page 36).

All compilation units comprising an application, including those in a library, need to be elaborated in an order partially defined by Ada's semantics. GNAT computes the elaboration order from the `ALI` files and this is why they constitute a mandatory part of GNAT libraries. *Stand-alone libraries* are the exception to this rule because a specific library elaboration routine is produced independently of the application(s) using the library.

3.9.2 General Ada Libraries

3.9.2.1 Building a library

The easiest way to build a library is to use the Project Manager, which supports a special type of project called a *Library Project* (see the *Library Projects* section in the *GNAT Project Manager* chapter of the *GPRbuild User's Guide*).

A project is considered a library project, when two project-level attributes are defined in it: *Library_Name* and *Library_Dir*. In order to control different aspects of library configuration, additional optional project-level attributes can be specified:

*

    Library_Kind

        This attribute controls whether the library is to be static or dynamic

*

    Library_Version

        This attribute specifies the library version; this value is used during dynamic linking of shared libraries to determine if the currently installed versions of the binaries are compatible.

* *Library_Options*
*

    Library_GCC

        These attributes specify additional low-level options to be used during library generation, and redefine the actual application used to generate library.

The GNAT Project Manager takes full care of the library maintenance task, including recompilation of the source files for which objects do not exist or are not up to date, assembly of the library archive, and installation of the library (i.e., copying associated source, object and `ALI` files to the specified location).

Here is a simple library project file:

```
project My_Lib is
   for Source_Dirs use ("src1", "src2");
   for Object_Dir use "obj";
   for Library_Name use "mylib";
   for Library_Dir use "lib";
   for Library_Kind use "dynamic";
end My_lib;
```

and the compilation command to build and install the library:

```
$ gnatmake -Pmy_lib
```

It is not entirely trivial to perform manually all the steps required to produce a library. We recommend that you use the GNAT Project Manager for this task. In special cases where this is not desired, the necessary steps are discussed below.

There are various possibilities for compiling the units that make up the library: for example with a Makefile ([Using the GNU make Utility], page 164) or with a conventional script. For simple libraries, it is also possible to create a dummy main program which depends upon all the packages that comprise the interface of the library. This dummy main program can then be given to *gnatmake*, which will ensure that all necessary objects are built.

After this task is accomplished, you should follow the standard procedure of the underlying operating system to produce the static or shared library.

Here is an example of such a dummy program:

```
with My_Lib.Service1;
with My_Lib.Service2;
with My_Lib.Service3;
procedure My_Lib_Dummy is
begin
   null;
end;
```

Here are the generic commands that will build an archive or a shared library.

```
# compiling the library
$ gnatmake -c my_lib_dummy.adb

# we don't need the dummy object itself
$ rm my_lib_dummy.o my_lib_dummy.ali

# create an archive with the remaining objects
$ ar rc libmy_lib.a *.o
# some systems may require "ranlib" to be run as well

# or create a shared library
$ gcc -shared -o libmy_lib.so *.o
# some systems may require the code to have been compiled with -fPIC

# remove the object files that are now in the library
$ rm *.o
```

```
# Make the ALI files read-only so that gnatmake will not try to
# regenerate the objects that are in the library
$ chmod -w *.ali
```

Please note that the library must have a name of the form `libxxx.a` or `libxxx.so` (or `libxxx.dll` on Windows) in order to be accessed by the directive `-lxxx` at link time.

3.9.2.2 Installing a library

If you use project files, library installation is part of the library build process (see the *Installing a Library with Project Files* section of the *GNAT Project Manager* chapter of the *GPRbuild User's Guide*).

When project files are not an option, it is also possible, but not recommended, to install the library so that the sources needed to use the library are on the Ada source path and the ALI files & libraries be on the Ada Object path (see [Search Paths and the Run-Time Library (RTL)], page 89. Alternatively, the system administrator can place general-purpose libraries in the default compiler paths, by specifying the libraries' location in the configuration files `ada_source_path` and `ada_object_path`. These configuration files must be located in the GNAT installation tree at the same place as the gcc spec file. The location of the gcc spec file can be determined as follows:

```
$ gcc -v
```

The configuration files mentioned above have a simple format: each line must contain one unique directory name. Those names are added to the corresponding path in their order of appearance in the file. The names can be either absolute or relative; in the latter case, they are relative to where theses files are located.

The files `ada_source_path` and `ada_object_path` might not be present in a GNAT installation, in which case, GNAT will look for its run-time library in the directories `adainclude` (for the sources) and `adalib` (for the objects and `ALI` files). When the files exist, the compiler does not look in `adainclude` and `adalib`, and thus the `ada_source_path` file must contain the location for the GNAT run-time sources (which can simply be `adainclude`). In the same way, the `ada_object_path` file must contain the location for the GNAT run-time objects (which can simply be `adalib`).

You can also specify a new default path to the run-time library at compilation time with the switch *–RTS=rts-path*. You can thus choose / change the run-time library you want your program to be compiled with. This switch is recognized by *gcc*, *gnatmake*, *gnatbind*, *gnatls*, *gnatfind* and *gnatxref*.

It is possible to install a library before or after the standard GNAT library, by reordering the lines in the configuration files. In general, a library must be installed before the GNAT library if it redefines any part of it.

3.9.2.3 Using a library

Once again, the project facility greatly simplifies the use of libraries. In this context, using a library is just a matter of adding a *with* clause in the user project. For instance, to make use of the library *My_Lib* shown in examples in earlier sections, you can write:

```
with "my_lib";
project My_Proj is
```

```
      ...
   end My_Proj;
```

Even if you have a third-party, non-Ada library, you can still use GNAT's Project Manager facility to provide a wrapper for it. For example, the following project, when *with*ed by your main project, will link with the third-party library `liba.a`:

```
   project Liba is
      for Externally_Built use "true";
      for Source_Files use ();
      for Library_Dir use "lib";
      for Library_Name use "a";
      for Library_Kind use "static";
   end Liba;
```

This is an alternative to the use of *pragma Linker_Options*. It is especially interesting in the context of systems with several interdependent static libraries where finding a proper linker order is not easy and best be left to the tools having visibility over project dependence information.

In order to use an Ada library manually, you need to make sure that this library is on both your source and object path (see [Search Paths and the Run-Time Library (RTL)], page 89 and [Search Paths for gnatbind], page 161). Furthermore, when the objects are grouped in an archive or a shared library, you need to specify the desired library at link time.

For example, you can use the library `mylib` installed in `/dir/my_lib_src` and `/dir/my_lib_obj` with the following commands:

```
   $ gnatmake -aI/dir/my_lib_src -aO/dir/my_lib_obj my_appl \\
      -largs -lmy_lib
```

This can be expressed more simply:

```
   $ gnatmake my_appl
```

when the following conditions are met:

* `/dir/my_lib_src` has been added by the user to the environment variable `ADA_INCLUDE_PATH`, or by the administrator to the file `ada_source_path`

* `/dir/my_lib_obj` has been added by the user to the environment variable `ADA_OBJECTS_PATH`, or by the administrator to the file `ada_object_path`

* a pragma *Linker_Options* has been added to one of the sources. For example:

```
      pragma Linker_Options ("-lmy_lib");
```

Note that you may also load a library dynamically at run time given its filename, as illustrated in the GNAT `plugins` example in the directory `share/examples/gnat/plugins` within the GNAT install area.

3.9.3 Stand-alone Ada Libraries

3.9.3.1 Introduction to Stand-alone Libraries

A Stand-alone Library (abbreviated 'SAL') is a library that contains the necessary code to elaborate the Ada units that are included in the library. In contrast with an ordinary library, which consists of all sources, objects and `ALI` files of the library, a SAL may specify a restricted subset of compilation units to serve as a library interface. In this case, the fully self-sufficient set of files will normally consist of an objects archive, the sources of interface units' specs, and the `ALI` files of interface units. If an interface spec contains a generic unit or an inlined subprogram, the body's source must also be provided; if the units that must be provided in the source form depend on other units, the source and `ALI` files of those must also be provided.

The main purpose of a SAL is to minimize the recompilation overhead of client applications when a new version of the library is installed. Specifically, if the interface sources have not changed, client applications do not need to be recompiled. If, furthermore, a SAL is provided in the shared form and its version, controlled by *Library_Version* attribute, is not changed, then the clients do not need to be relinked.

SALs also allow the library providers to minimize the amount of library source text exposed to the clients. Such 'information hiding' might be useful or necessary for various reasons.

Stand-alone libraries are also well suited to be used in an executable whose main routine is not written in Ada.

3.9.3.2 Building a Stand-alone Library

GNAT's Project facility provides a simple way of building and installing stand-alone libraries; see the *Stand-alone Library Projects* section in the *GNAT Project Manager* chapter of the *GPRbuild User's Guide*. To be a Stand-alone Library Project, in addition to the two attributes that make a project a Library Project (*Library_Name* and *Library_Dir*; see the *Library Projects* section in the *GNAT Project Manager* chapter of the *GPRbuild User's Guide*), the attribute *Library_Interface* must be defined. For example:

```
for Library_Dir use "lib_dir";
for Library_Name use "dummy";
for Library_Interface use ("int1", "int1.child");
```

Attribute *Library_Interface* has a non-empty string list value, each string in the list designating a unit contained in an immediate source of the project file.

When a Stand-alone Library is built, first the binder is invoked to build a package whose name depends on the library name (`b~dummy.ads/b` in the example above). This binder-generated package includes initialization and finalization procedures whose names depend on the library name (*dummyinit* and *dummyfinal* in the example above). The object corresponding to this package is included in the library.

You must ensure timely (e.g., prior to any use of interfaces in the SAL) calling of these procedures if a static SAL is built, or if a shared SAL is built with the project-level attribute *Library_Auto_Init* set to `"false"`.

For a Stand-Alone Library, only the `ALI` files of the Interface Units (those that are listed in attribute *Library_Interface*) are copied to the Library Directory. As a consequence, only the Interface Units may be imported from Ada units outside of the library. If other units are imported, the binding phase will fail.

It is also possible to build an encapsulated library where not only the code to elaborate and finalize the library is embedded but also ensuring that the library is linked only against static libraries. So an encapsulated library only depends on system libraries, all other code, including the GNAT runtime, is embedded. To build an encapsulated library the attribute *Library_Standalone* must be set to *encapsulated*:

```
for Library_Dir use "lib_dir";
for Library_Name use "dummy";
for Library_Kind use "dynamic";
for Library_Interface use ("int1", "int1.child");
for Library_Standalone use "encapsulated";
```

The default value for this attribute is *standard* in which case a stand-alone library is built.

The attribute *Library_Src_Dir* may be specified for a Stand-Alone Library. *Library_Src_Dir* is a simple attribute that has a single string value. Its value must be the path (absolute or relative to the project directory) of an existing directory. This directory cannot be the object directory or one of the source directories, but it can be the same as the library directory. The sources of the Interface Units of the library that are needed by an Ada client of the library will be copied to the designated directory, called the Interface Copy directory. These sources include the specs of the Interface Units, but they may also include bodies and subunits, when pragmas *Inline* or *Inline_Always* are used, or when there is a generic unit in the spec. Before the sources are copied to the Interface Copy directory, an attempt is made to delete all files in the Interface Copy directory.

Building stand-alone libraries by hand is somewhat tedious, but for those occasions when it is necessary here are the steps that you need to perform:

* Compile all library sources.

* Invoke the binder with the switch *-n* (No Ada main program), with all the ALI files of the interfaces, and with the switch *-L* to give specific names to the *init* and *final* procedures. For example:

      $ gnatbind -n int1.ali int2.ali -Lsal1

* Compile the binder generated file:

      $ gcc -c b~int2.adb

* Link the dynamic library with all the necessary object files, indicating to the linker the names of the *init* (and possibly *final*) procedures for automatic initialization (and finalization). The built library should be placed in a directory different from the object directory.

* Copy the *ALI* files of the interface to the library directory, add in this copy an indication that it is an interface to a SAL (i.e., add a word *SL* on the line in the ALI file that starts with letter 'P') and make the modified copy of the ALI file read-only.

Using SALs is not different from using other libraries (see [Using a library], page 35).

3.9.3.3 Creating a Stand-alone Library to be used in a non-Ada context

It is easy to adapt the SAL build procedure discussed above for use of a SAL in a non-Ada context.

The only extra step required is to ensure that library interface subprograms are compatible with the main program, by means of *pragma Export* or *pragma Convention*.

Here is an example of simple library interface for use with C main program:

```
package My_Package is
```

```
procedure Do_Something;
pragma Export (C, Do_Something, "do_something");

procedure Do_Something_Else;
pragma Export (C, Do_Something_Else, "do_something_else");

end My_Package;
```

On the foreign language side, you must provide a 'foreign' view of the library interface; remember that it should contain elaboration routines in addition to interface subprograms.

The example below shows the content of *mylib_interface.h* (note that there is no rule for the naming of this file, any name can be used)

```
/* the library elaboration procedure */
extern void mylibinit (void);

/* the library finalization procedure */
extern void mylibfinal (void);

/* the interface exported by the library */
extern void do_something (void);
extern void do_something_else (void);
```

Libraries built as explained above can be used from any program, provided that the elaboration procedures (named *mylibinit* in the previous example) are called before the library services are used. Any number of libraries can be used simultaneously, as long as the elaboration procedure of each library is called.

Below is an example of a C program that uses the *mylib* library.

```
#include "mylib_interface.h"

int
main (void)
{
   /* First, elaborate the library before using it */
   mylibinit ();

   /* Main program, using the library exported entities */
   do_something ();
   do_something_else ();

   /* Library finalization at the end of the program */
   mylibfinal ();
   return 0;
}
```

Note that invoking any library finalization procedure generated by *gnatbind* shuts down the Ada run-time environment. Consequently, the finalization of all Ada libraries must be performed at the end of the program. No call to these libraries or to the Ada run-time library should be made after the finalization phase.

Note also that special care must be taken with multi-tasks applications. The initialization and finalization routines are not protected against concurrent access. If such requirement is needed it must be ensured at the application level using a specific operating system services like a mutex or a critical-section.

3.9.3.4 Restrictions in Stand-alone Libraries

The pragmas listed below should be used with caution inside libraries, as they can create incompatibilities with other Ada libraries:

* pragma *Locking_Policy*
* pragma *Partition_Elaboration_Policy*
* pragma *Queuing_Policy*
* pragma *Task_Dispatching_Policy*
* pragma *Unreserve_All_Interrupts*

When using a library that contains such pragmas, the user must make sure that all libraries use the same pragmas with the same values. Otherwise, *Program_Error* will be raised during the elaboration of the conflicting libraries. The usage of these pragmas and its consequences for the user should therefore be well documented.

Similarly, the traceback in the exception occurrence mechanism should be enabled or disabled in a consistent manner across all libraries. Otherwise, Program_Error will be raised during the elaboration of the conflicting libraries.

If the *Version* or *Body_Version* attributes are used inside a library, then you need to perform a *gnatbind* step that specifies all ALI files in all libraries, so that version identifiers can be properly computed. In practice these attributes are rarely used, so this is unlikely to be a consideration.

3.9.4 Rebuilding the GNAT Run-Time Library

It may be useful to recompile the GNAT library in various contexts, the most important one being the use of partition-wide configuration pragmas such as *Normalize_Scalars*. A special Makefile called *Makefile.adalib* is provided to that effect and can be found in the directory containing the GNAT library. The location of this directory depends on the way the GNAT environment has been installed and can be determined by means of the command:

```
$ gnatls -v
```

The last entry in the object search path usually contains the gnat library. This Makefile contains its own documentation and in particular the set of instructions needed to rebuild a new library and to use it.

3.10 Conditional Compilation

This section presents some guidelines for modeling conditional compilation in Ada and describes the gnatprep preprocessor utility.

3.10.1 Modeling Conditional Compilation in Ada

It is often necessary to arrange for a single source program to serve multiple purposes, where it is compiled in different ways to achieve these different goals. Some examples of the need for this feature are

* Adapting a program to a different hardware environment
* Adapting a program to a different target architecture
* Turning debugging features on and off
* Arranging for a program to compile with different compilers

In C, or C++, the typical approach would be to use the preprocessor that is defined as part of the language. The Ada language does not contain such a feature. This is not an oversight, but rather a very deliberate design decision, based on the experience that overuse of the preprocessing features in C and C++ can result in programs that are extremely difficult to maintain. For example, if we have ten switches that can be on or off, this means that there are a thousand separate programs, any one of which might not even be syntactically correct, and even if syntactically correct, the resulting program might not work correctly. Testing all combinations can quickly become impossible.

Nevertheless, the need to tailor programs certainly exists, and in this section we will discuss how this can be achieved using Ada in general, and GNAT in particular.

3.10.1.1 Use of Boolean Constants

In the case where the difference is simply which code sequence is executed, the cleanest solution is to use Boolean constants to control which code is executed.

```
FP_Initialize_Required : constant Boolean := True;
...
if FP_Initialize_Required then
...
end if;
```

Not only will the code inside the *if* statement not be executed if the constant Boolean is *False*, but it will also be completely deleted from the program. However, the code is only deleted after the *if* statement has been checked for syntactic and semantic correctness. (In contrast, with preprocessors the code is deleted before the compiler ever gets to see it, so it is not checked until the switch is turned on.)

Typically the Boolean constants will be in a separate package, something like:

```
package Config is
    FP_Initialize_Required : constant Boolean := True;
    Reset_Available        : constant Boolean := False;
    ...
end Config;
```

The *Config* package exists in multiple forms for the various targets, with an appropriate script selecting the version of *Config* needed. Then any other unit requiring conditional compilation can do a *with* of *Config* to make the constants visible.

3.10.1.2 Debugging - A Special Case

A common use of conditional code is to execute statements (for example dynamic checks, or output of intermediate results) under control of a debug switch, so that the debugging behavior can be turned on and off. This can be done using a Boolean constant to control whether the code is active:

```
      if Debugging then
         Put_Line ("got to the first stage!");
      end if;
```

or

```
      if Debugging and then Temperature > 999.0 then
         raise Temperature_Crazy;
      end if;
```

Since this is a common case, there are special features to deal with this in a convenient manner. For the case of tests, Ada 2005 has added a pragma *Assert* that can be used for such tests. This pragma is modeled on the *Assert* pragma that has always been available in GNAT, so this feature may be used with GNAT even if you are not using Ada 2005 features. The use of pragma *Assert* is described in the *GNAT_Reference_Manual*, but as an example, the last test could be written:

```
      pragma Assert (Temperature <= 999.0, "Temperature Crazy");
```

or simply

```
      pragma Assert (Temperature <= 999.0);
```

In both cases, if assertions are active and the temperature is excessive, the exception *Assert_Failure* will be raised, with the given string in the first case or a string indicating the location of the pragma in the second case used as the exception message.

You can turn assertions on and off by using the *Assertion_Policy* pragma.

This is an Ada 2005 pragma which is implemented in all modes by GNAT. Alternatively, you can use the *-gnata* switch to enable assertions from the command line, which applies to all versions of Ada.

For the example above with the *Put_Line*, the GNAT-specific pragma *Debug* can be used:

```
      pragma Debug (Put_Line ("got to the first stage!"));
```

If debug pragmas are enabled, the argument, which must be of the form of a procedure call, is executed (in this case, *Put_Line* will be called). Only one call can be present, but of course a special debugging procedure containing any code you like can be included in the program and then called in a pragma *Debug* argument as needed.

One advantage of pragma *Debug* over the *if Debugging then* construct is that pragma *Debug* can appear in declarative contexts, such as at the very beginning of a procedure, before local declarations have been elaborated.

Debug pragmas are enabled using either the *-gnata* switch that also controls assertions, or with a separate Debug_Policy pragma.

The latter pragma is new in the Ada 2005 versions of GNAT (but it can be used in Ada 95 and Ada 83 programs as well), and is analogous to pragma *Assertion_Policy* to control assertions.

Assertion_Policy and *Debug_Policy* are configuration pragmas, and thus they can appear in `gnat.adc` if you are not using a project file, or in the file designated to contain configuration pragmas in a project file. They then apply to all subsequent compilations. In practice the use of the *-gnata* switch is often the most convenient method of controlling the status of these pragmas.

Note that a pragma is not a statement, so in contexts where a statement sequence is required, you can't just write a pragma on its own. You have to add a *null* statement.

```
if ... then
   ... -- some statements
else
   pragma Assert (Num_Cases < 10);
   null;
end if;
```

3.10.1.3 Conditionalizing Declarations

In some cases it may be necessary to conditionalize declarations to meet different requirements. For example we might want a bit string whose length is set to meet some hardware message requirement.

This may be possible using declare blocks controlled by conditional constants:

```
if Small_Machine then
   declare
      X : Bit_String (1 .. 10);
   begin
      ...
   end;
else
   declare
      X : Large_Bit_String (1 .. 1000);
   begin
      ...
   end;
end if;
```

Note that in this approach, both declarations are analyzed by the compiler so this can only be used where both declarations are legal, even though one of them will not be used.

Another approach is to define integer constants, e.g., *Bits_Per_Word*, or Boolean constants, e.g., *Little_Endian*, and then write declarations that are parameterized by these constants. For example

```
for Rec use
   Field1 at 0 range Boolean'Pos (Little_Endian) * 10 .. Bits_Per_Word;
end record;
```

If *Bits_Per_Word* is set to 32, this generates either

```
for Rec use
   Field1 at 0 range 0 .. 32;
end record;
```

for the big endian case, or

```
for Rec use record
   Field1 at 0 range 10 .. 32;
end record;
```

for the little endian case. Since a powerful subset of Ada expression notation is usable for creating static constants, clever use of this feature can often solve quite difficult problems in conditionalizing compilation (note incidentally that in Ada 95, the little endian constant was introduced as *System.Default_Bit_Order*, so you do not need to define this one yourself).

3.10.1.4 Use of Alternative Implementations

In some cases, none of the approaches described above are adequate. This can occur for example if the set of declarations required is radically different for two different configurations.

In this situation, the official Ada way of dealing with conditionalizing such code is to write separate units for the different cases. As long as this does not result in excessive duplication of code, this can be done without creating maintenance problems. The approach is to share common code as far as possible, and then isolate the code and declarations that are different. Subunits are often a convenient method for breaking out a piece of a unit that is to be conditionalized, with separate files for different versions of the subunit for different targets, where the build script selects the right one to give to the compiler.

As an example, consider a situation where a new feature in Ada 2005 allows something to be done in a really nice way. But your code must be able to compile with an Ada 95 compiler. Conceptually you want to say:

```
if Ada_2005 then
    ... neat Ada 2005 code
else
    ... not quite as neat Ada 95 code
end if;
```

where *Ada_2005* is a Boolean constant.

But this won't work when *Ada_2005* is set to *False*, since the *then* clause will be illegal for an Ada 95 compiler. (Recall that although such unreachable code would eventually be deleted by the compiler, it still needs to be legal. If it uses features introduced in Ada 2005, it will be illegal in Ada 95.)

So instead we write

```
procedure Insert is separate;
```

Then we have two files for the subunit *Insert*, with the two sets of code. If the package containing this is called *File_Queries*, then we might have two files

* `file_queries-insert-2005.adb`

* `file_queries-insert-95.adb`

and the build script renames the appropriate file to `file_queries-insert.adb` and then carries out the compilation.

This can also be done with project files' naming schemes. For example:

```
for body ("File_Queries.Insert") use "file_queries-insert-2005.ada";
```

Note also that with project files it is desirable to use a different extension than **ads** / **adb** for alternative versions. Otherwise a naming conflict may arise through another commonly used feature: to declare as part of the project a set of directories containing all the sources obeying the default naming scheme.

The use of alternative units is certainly feasible in all situations, and for example the Ada part of the GNAT run-time is conditionalized based on the target architecture using this approach. As a specific example, consider the implementation of the AST feature in VMS. There is one spec: **s-asthan.ads** which is the same for all architectures, and three bodies:

*

```
s-asthan.adb
        used for all non-VMS operating systems
*

s-asthan-vms-alpha.adb
        used for VMS on the Alpha
*

s-asthan-vms-ia64.adb
        used for VMS on the ia64
```

The dummy version `s-asthan.adb` simply raises exceptions noting that this operating system feature is not available, and the two remaining versions interface with the corresponding versions of VMS to provide VMS-compatible AST handling. The GNAT build script knows the architecture and operating system, and automatically selects the right version, renaming it if necessary to `s-asthan.adb` before the run-time build.

Another style for arranging alternative implementations is through Ada's access-to-subprogram facility. In case some functionality is to be conditionally included, you can declare an access-to-procedure variable *Ref* that is initialized to designate a 'do nothing' procedure, and then invoke *Ref.all* when appropriate. In some library package, set *Ref* to *Proc'Access* for some procedure *Proc* that performs the relevant processing. The initialization only occurs if the library package is included in the program. The same idea can also be implemented using tagged types and dispatching calls.

3.10.1.5 Preprocessing

Although it is quite possible to conditionalize code without the use of C-style preprocessing, as described earlier in this section, it is nevertheless convenient in some cases to use the C approach. Moreover, older Ada compilers have often provided some preprocessing capability, so legacy code may depend on this approach, even though it is not standard.

To accommodate such use, GNAT provides a preprocessor (modeled to a large extent on the various preprocessors that have been used with legacy code on other compilers, to enable easier transition).

The preprocessor may be used in two separate modes. It can be used quite separately from the compiler, to generate a separate output source file that is then fed to the compiler as a separate step. This is the *gnatprep* utility, whose use is fully described in [Preprocessing with gnatprep], page 46.

The preprocessing language allows such constructs as

```
#if DEBUG or else (PRIORITY > 4) then
   bunch of declarations
#else
   completely different bunch of declarations
#end if;
```

The values of the symbols *DEBUG* and *PRIORITY* can be defined either on the command line or in a separate file.

The other way of running the preprocessor is even closer to the C style and often more convenient. In this approach the preprocessing is integrated into the compilation process.

The compiler is fed the preprocessor input which includes #*if* lines etc, and then the compiler carries out the preprocessing internally and processes the resulting output. For more details on this approach, see [Integrated Preprocessing], page 50.

3.10.2 Preprocessing with *gnatprep*

This section discusses how to use GNAT's *gnatprep* utility for simple preprocessing. Although designed for use with GNAT, *gnatprep* does not depend on any special GNAT features. For further discussion of conditional compilation in general, see [Conditional Compilation], page 40.

3.10.2.1 Preprocessing Symbols

Preprocessing symbols are defined in definition files and referred to in sources to be preprocessed. A Preprocessing symbol is an identifier, following normal Ada (case-insensitive) rules for its syntax, with the restriction that all characters need to be in the ASCII set (no accented letters).

3.10.2.2 Using *gnatprep*

To call *gnatprep* use:

```
$ gnatprep ['switches'] 'infile' 'outfile' ['deffile']
```

where

*

  switches

          is an optional sequence of switches as described in the next section.

*

  infile

          is the full name of the input file, which is an Ada source file containing
          preprocessor directives.

*

  outfile

          is the full name of the output file, which is an Ada source in standard Ada
          form. When used with GNAT, this file name will normally have an ads or
          adb suffix.

*

  deffile

          is the full name of a text file containing definitions of preprocessing symbols
          to be referenced by the preprocessor. This argument is optional, and can
          be replaced by the use of the *-D* switch.

3.10.2.3 Switches for *gnatprep*

`--version`

          Display Copyright and version, then exit disregarding all other options.

`--help`

> If *–version* was not used, display usage, then exit disregarding all other options.

`-b`

> Causes both preprocessor lines and the lines deleted by preprocessing to be replaced by blank lines in the output source file, preserving line numbers in the output file.

`-c`

> Causes both preprocessor lines and the lines deleted by preprocessing to be retained in the output source as comments marked with the special string "–!
> ". This option will result in line numbers being preserved in the output file.

`-C`

> Causes comments to be scanned. Normally comments are ignored by gnatprep. If this option is specified, then comments are scanned and any $symbol substitutions performed as in program text. This is particularly useful when structured comments are used (e.g., when writing programs in the SPARK dialect of Ada). Note that this switch is not available when doing integrated preprocessing (it would be useless in this context since comments are ignored by the compiler in any case).

`-Dsymbol=value`

> Defines a new preprocessing symbol, associated with value. If no value is given on the command line, then symbol is considered to be *True*. This switch can be used in place of a definition file.

`-r`

> Causes a *Source_Reference* pragma to be generated that references the original input file, so that error messages will use the file name of this original file. The use of this switch implies that preprocessor lines are not to be removed from the file, so its use will force *-b* mode if *-c* has not been specified explicitly.

> Note that if the file to be preprocessed contains multiple units, then it will be necessary to *gnatchop* the output file from *gnatprep*. If a *Source_Reference* pragma is present in the preprocessed file, it will be respected by *gnatchop -r* so that the final chopped files will correctly refer to the original input source file for *gnatprep*.

`-s`

> Causes a sorted list of symbol names and values to be listed on the standard output file.

`-T`

> Use LF as line terminators when writing files. By default the line terminator of the host (LF under unix, CR/LF under Windows) is used.

`-u`

> Causes undefined symbols to be treated as having the value FALSE in the context of a preprocessor test. In the absence of this option, an undefined symbol in a *#if* or *#elsif* test will be treated as an error.

```
-v
```
Verbose mode: generates more output about work done.

Note: if neither -*b* nor -*c* is present, then preprocessor lines and deleted lines are completely removed from the output, unless -r is specified, in which case -b is assumed.

3.10.2.4 Form of Definitions File

The definitions file contains lines of the form:

```
symbol := value
```

where *symbol* is a preprocessing symbol, and *value* is one of the following:

* Empty, corresponding to a null substitution,
* A string literal using normal Ada syntax, or
* Any sequence of characters from the set {letters, digits, period, underline}.

Comment lines may also appear in the definitions file, starting with the usual --, and comments may be added to the definitions lines.

3.10.2.5 Form of Input Text for *gnatprep*

The input text may contain preprocessor conditional inclusion lines, as well as general symbol substitution sequences.

The preprocessor conditional inclusion commands have the form:

```
#if <expression> [then]
   lines
#elsif <expression> [then]
   lines
#elsif <expression> [then]
   lines
...
#else
   lines
#end if;
```

In this example, <expression> is defined by the following grammar:

```
<expression> ::=  <symbol>
<expression> ::=  <symbol> = "<value>"
<expression> ::=  <symbol> = <symbol>
<expression> ::=  <symbol> = <integer>
<expression> ::=  <symbol> > <integer>
<expression> ::=  <symbol> >= <integer>
<expression> ::=  <symbol> < <integer>
<expression> ::=  <symbol> <= <integer>
<expression> ::=  <symbol> 'Defined
<expression> ::=  not <expression>
<expression> ::=  <expression> and <expression>
<expression> ::=  <expression> or <expression>
<expression> ::=  <expression> and then <expression>
```

```
<expression> ::=  <expression> or else <expression>
<expression> ::=  ( <expression> )
```

Note the following restriction: it is not allowed to have "and" or "or" following "not" in the same expression without parentheses. For example, this is not allowed:

```
not X or Y
```

This can be expressed instead as one of the following forms:

```
(not X) or Y
not (X or Y)
```

For the first test (<expression> ::= <symbol>) the symbol must have either the value true or false, that is to say the right-hand of the symbol definition must be one of the (case-insensitive) literals *True* or *False*. If the value is true, then the corresponding lines are included, and if the value is false, they are excluded.

When comparing a symbol to an integer, the integer is any non negative literal integer as defined in the Ada Reference Manual, such as 3, 16#FF# or 2#11#. The symbol value must also be a non negative integer. Integer values in the range 0 .. 2**31-1 are supported.

The test (<expression> ::= <symbol>'Defined) is true only if the symbol has been defined in the definition file or by a *-D* switch on the command line. Otherwise, the test is false.

The equality tests are case insensitive, as are all the preprocessor lines.

If the symbol referenced is not defined in the symbol definitions file, then the effect depends on whether or not switch *-u* is specified. If so, then the symbol is treated as if it had the value false and the test fails. If this switch is not specified, then it is an error to reference an undefined symbol. It is also an error to reference a symbol that is defined with a value other than *True* or *False*.

The use of the *not* operator inverts the sense of this logical test. The *not* operator cannot be combined with the *or* or *and* operators, without parentheses. For example, "if not X or Y then" is not allowed, but "if (not X) or Y then" and "if not (X or Y) then" are.

The *then* keyword is optional as shown

The # must be the first non-blank character on a line, but otherwise the format is free form. Spaces or tabs may appear between the # and the keyword. The keywords and the symbols are case insensitive as in normal Ada code. Comments may be used on a preprocessor line, but other than that, no other tokens may appear on a preprocessor line. Any number of *elsif* clauses can be present, including none at all. The *else* is optional, as in Ada.

The # marking the start of a preprocessor line must be the first non-blank character on the line, i.e., it must be preceded only by spaces or horizontal tabs.

Symbol substitution outside of preprocessor lines is obtained by using the sequence:

```
$symbol
```

anywhere within a source line, except in a comment or within a string literal. The identifier following the *$* must match one of the symbols defined in the symbol definition file, and the result is to substitute the value of the symbol in place of *$symbol* in the output file.

Note that although the substitution of strings within a string literal is not possible, it is possible to have a symbol whose defined value is a string literal. So instead of setting XYZ to *hello* and writing:

```
    Header : String := "$XYZ";
```
you should set XYZ to "*hello*" and write:
```
    Header : String := $XYZ;
```
and then the substitution will occur as desired.

3.10.3 Integrated Preprocessing

GNAT sources may be preprocessed immediately before compilation. In this case, the actual text of the source is not the text of the source file, but is derived from it through a process called preprocessing. Integrated preprocessing is specified through switches *-gnatep* and/or *-gnateD*. *-gnatep* indicates, through a text file, the preprocessing data to be used. `-gnateD` specifies or modifies the values of preprocessing symbol. Note that integrated preprocessing applies only to Ada source files, it is not available for configuration pragma files.

Note that when integrated preprocessing is used, the output from the preprocessor is not written to any external file. Instead it is passed internally to the compiler. If you need to preserve the result of preprocessing in a file, then you should use *gnatprep* to perform the desired preprocessing in stand-alone mode.

It is recommended that *gnatmake* switch -s should be used when Integrated Preprocessing is used. The reason is that preprocessing with another Preprocessing Data file without changing the sources will not trigger recompilation without this switch.

Note that *gnatmake* switch -m will almost always trigger recompilation for sources that are preprocessed, because *gnatmake* cannot compute the checksum of the source after preprocessing.

The actual preprocessing function is described in detail in section [Preprocessing with gnatprep], page 46. This section only describes how integrated preprocessing is triggered and parameterized.

`-gnatep=`*file*

> This switch indicates to the compiler the file name (without directory information) of the preprocessor data file to use. The preprocessor data file should be found in the source directories. Alternatively when using project files, you can reference to the project file's directory via the `project name'Project_Dir` project attribute, e.g:

```
    project Prj is
        package Compiler is
            for Switches ("Ada") use
                ("-gnatep=" & Prj'Project_Dir & "prep.def");
        end Compiler;
    end Prj;
```

> A preprocessing data file is a text file with significant lines indicating how should be preprocessed either a specific source or all sources not mentioned in other lines. A significant line is a nonempty, non-comment line. Comments are similar to Ada comments.

> Each significant line starts with either a literal string or the character '*'. A literal string is the file name (without directory information) of the source to preprocess. A character '*' indicates the preprocessing for all the sources that

are not specified explicitly on other lines (order of the lines is not significant). It is an error to have two lines with the same file name or two lines starting with the character '*'.

After the file name or the character '*', another optional literal string indicating the file name of the definition file to be used for preprocessing ([Form of Definitions File], page 48). The definition files are found by the compiler in one of the source directories. In some cases, when compiling a source in a directory other than the current directory, if the definition file is in the current directory, it may be necessary to add the current directory as a source directory through switch -I., otherwise the compiler would not find the definition file.

Then, optionally, switches similar to those of *gnatprep* may be found. Those switches are:

-b

> Causes both preprocessor lines and the lines deleted by preprocessing to be replaced by blank lines, preserving the line number. This switch is always implied; however, if specified after *-c* it cancels the effect of *-c*.

-c

> Causes both preprocessor lines and the lines deleted by preprocessing to be retained as comments marked with the special string '--!'.

-Dsymbol=*value*

> Define or redefine a symbol, associated with value. A symbol is an Ada identifier, or an Ada reserved word, with the exception of *if, else, elsif, end, and, or* and *then. value* is either a literal string, an Ada identifier or any Ada reserved word. A symbol declared with this switch replaces a symbol with the same name defined in a definition file.

-s

> Causes a sorted list of symbol names and values to be listed on the standard output file.

-u

> Causes undefined symbols to be treated as having the value *FALSE* in the context of a preprocessor test. In the absence of this option, an undefined symbol in a *#if* or *#elsif* test will be treated as an error.

Examples of valid lines in a preprocessor data file:

```
"toto.adb"  "prep.def" -u
--  preprocess "toto.adb", using definition file "prep.def",
--  undefined symbol are False.

* -c -DVERSION=V101
--  preprocess all other sources without a definition file;
--  suppressed lined are commented; symbol VERSION has the value V101
```

```
"titi.adb" "prep2.def" -s
--  preprocess "titi.adb", using definition file "prep2.def";
--  list all symbols with their values.
```

-gnateDsymbol[=value]

Define or redefine a preprocessing symbol, associated with value. If no value is given on the command line, then the value of the symbol is *True*. A symbol is an identifier, following normal Ada (case-insensitive) rules for its syntax, and value is either an arbitrary string between double quotes or any sequence (including an empty sequence) of characters from the set (letters, digits, period, underline). Ada reserved words may be used as symbols, with the exceptions of *if, else, elsif, end, and, or* and *then*.

Examples:

```
-gnateDToto=Titi
-gnateDFoo
-gnateDFoo=\"Foo-Bar\"
```

A symbol declared with this switch on the command line replaces a symbol with the same name either in a definition file or specified with a switch -D in the preprocessor data file.

This switch is similar to switch *-D* of *gnatprep*.

-gnateG

When integrated preprocessing is performed and the preprocessor modifies the source text, write the result of this preprocessing into a file <source>.prep.

3.11 Mixed Language Programming

This section describes how to develop a mixed-language program, with a focus on combining Ada with C or C++.

3.11.1 Interfacing to C

Interfacing Ada with a foreign language such as C involves using compiler directives to import and/or export entity definitions in each language – using *extern* statements in C, for instance, and the *Import*, *Export*, and *Convention* pragmas in Ada. A full treatment of these topics is provided in Appendix B, section 1 of the Ada Reference Manual.

There are two ways to build a program using GNAT that contains some Ada sources and some foreign language sources, depending on whether or not the main subprogram is written in Ada. Here is a source example with the main subprogram in Ada:

```
/* file1.c */
#include <stdio.h>

void print_num (int num)
{
  printf ("num is %d.\\n", num);
  return;
}
```

```
/* file2.c */

/* num_from_Ada is declared in my_main.adb */
extern int num_from_Ada;

int get_num (void)
{
  return num_from_Ada;
}
--  my_main.adb
procedure My_Main is

    --  Declare then export an Integer entity called num_from_Ada
    My_Num : Integer := 10;
    pragma Export (C, My_Num, "num_from_Ada");

    --  Declare an Ada function spec for Get_Num, then use
    --  C function get_num for the implementation.
    function Get_Num return Integer;
    pragma Import (C, Get_Num, "get_num");

    --  Declare an Ada procedure spec for Print_Num, then use
    --  C function print_num for the implementation.
    procedure Print_Num (Num : Integer);
    pragma Import (C, Print_Num, "print_num";

begin
    Print_Num (Get_Num);
end My_Main;
```

To build this example:

* First compile the foreign language files to generate object files:

      $ gcc -c file1.c
      $ gcc -c file2.c

* Then, compile the Ada units to produce a set of object files and ALI files:

      $ gnatmake -c my_main.adb

* Run the Ada binder on the Ada main program:

      $ gnatbind my_main.ali

* Link the Ada main program, the Ada objects and the other language objects:

      $ gnatlink my_main.ali file1.o file2.o

The last three steps can be grouped in a single command:

      $ gnatmake my_main.adb -largs file1.o file2.o

If the main program is in a language other than Ada, then you may have more than one entry point into the Ada subsystem. You must use a special binder option to generate callable routines that initialize and finalize the Ada units ([Binding with Non-Ada Main

Programs], page 159). Calls to the initialization and finalization routines must be inserted in the main program, or some other appropriate point in the code. The call to initialize the Ada units must occur before the first Ada subprogram is called, and the call to finalize the Ada units must occur after the last Ada subprogram returns. The binder will place the initialization and finalization subprograms into the b~xxx.adb file where they can be accessed by your C sources. To illustrate, we have the following example:

```
/* main.c */
extern void adainit (void);
extern void adafinal (void);
extern int add (int, int);
extern int sub (int, int);

int main (int argc, char *argv[])
{
   int a = 21, b = 7;

   adainit();

   /* Should print "21 + 7 = 28" */
   printf ("%d + %d = %d\\n", a, b, add (a, b));

   /* Should print "21 - 7 = 14" */
   printf ("%d - %d = %d\\n", a, b, sub (a, b));

   adafinal();
}
--   unit1.ads
package Unit1 is
   function Add (A, B : Integer) return Integer;
   pragma Export (C, Add, "add");
end Unit1;
--   unit1.adb
package body Unit1 is
   function Add (A, B : Integer) return Integer is
   begin
      return A + B;
   end Add;
end Unit1;
--   unit2.ads
package Unit2 is
   function Sub (A, B : Integer) return Integer;
   pragma Export (C, Sub, "sub");
end Unit2;
--   unit2.adb
package body Unit2 is
   function Sub (A, B : Integer) return Integer is
```

```
      begin
         return A - B;
      end Sub;
   end Unit2;
```

The build procedure for this application is similar to the last example's:

* First, compile the foreign language files to generate object files:

      ```
      $ gcc -c main.c
      ```

* Next, compile the Ada units to produce a set of object files and ALI files:

      ```
      $ gnatmake -c unit1.adb
      $ gnatmake -c unit2.adb
      ```

* Run the Ada binder on every generated ALI file. Make sure to use the -n option to specify a foreign main program:

      ```
      $ gnatbind -n unit1.ali unit2.ali
      ```

* Link the Ada main program, the Ada objects and the foreign language objects. You need only list the last ALI file here:

      ```
      $ gnatlink unit2.ali main.o -o exec_file
      ```

   This procedure yields a binary executable called `exec_file`.

Depending on the circumstances (for example when your non-Ada main object does not provide symbol *main*), you may also need to instruct the GNAT linker not to include the standard startup objects by passing the -nostartfiles switch to *gnatlink*.

3.11.2 Calling Conventions

GNAT follows standard calling sequence conventions and will thus interface to any other language that also follows these conventions. The following Convention identifiers are recognized by GNAT:

Ada

> This indicates that the standard Ada calling sequence will be used and all Ada data items may be passed without any limitations in the case where GNAT is used to generate both the caller and callee. It is also possible to mix GNAT generated code and code generated by another Ada compiler. In this case, the data types should be restricted to simple cases, including primitive types. Whether complex data types can be passed depends on the situation. Probably it is safe to pass simple arrays, such as arrays of integers or floats. Records may or may not work, depending on whether both compilers lay them out identically. Complex structures involving variant records, access parameters, tasks, or protected types, are unlikely to be able to be passed.
>
> Note that in the case of GNAT running on a platform that supports HP Ada 83, a higher degree of compatibility can be guaranteed, and in particular records are laid out in an identical manner in the two compilers. Note also that if output from two different compilers is mixed, the program is responsible for dealing with elaboration issues. Probably the safest approach is to write the main program in the version of Ada other than GNAT, so that it takes care of its own elaboration requirements, and then call the GNAT-generated adainit procedure

to ensure elaboration of the GNAT components. Consult the documentation of the other Ada compiler for further details on elaboration.

However, it is not possible to mix the tasking run time of GNAT and HP Ada 83, All the tasking operations must either be entirely within GNAT compiled sections of the program, or entirely within HP Ada 83 compiled sections of the program.

Assembler

Specifies assembler as the convention. In practice this has the same effect as convention Ada (but is not equivalent in the sense of being considered the same convention).

Asm

Equivalent to Assembler.

COBOL

Data will be passed according to the conventions described in section B.4 of the Ada Reference Manual.

C

Data will be passed according to the conventions described in section B.3 of the Ada Reference Manual.

A note on interfacing to a C 'varargs' function:

> In C, *varargs* allows a function to take a variable number of arguments. There is no direct equivalent in this to Ada. One approach that can be used is to create a C wrapper for each different profile and then interface to this C wrapper. For example, to print an *int* value using *printf*, create a C function *printfi* that takes two arguments, a pointer to a string and an int, and calls *printf*. Then in the Ada program, use pragma *Import* to interface to *printfi*.

> It may work on some platforms to directly interface to a *varargs* function by providing a specific Ada profile for a particular call. However, this does not work on all platforms, since there is no guarantee that the calling sequence for a two argument normal C function is the same as for calling a *varargs* C function with the same two arguments.

Default

Equivalent to C.

External

Equivalent to C.

C_Plus_Plus (or CPP)

This stands for C++. For most purposes this is identical to C. See the separate description of the specialized GNAT pragmas relating to C++ interfacing for further details.

Fortran

Data will be passed according to the conventions described in section B.5 of the Ada Reference Manual.

Intrinsic

This applies to an intrinsic operation, as defined in the Ada Reference Manual. If a pragma Import (Intrinsic) applies to a subprogram, this means that the body of the subprogram is provided by the compiler itself, usually by means of an efficient code sequence, and that the user does not supply an explicit body for it. In an application program, the pragma may be applied to the following sets of names:

* Rotate_Left, Rotate_Right, Shift_Left, Shift_Right, Shift_Right_Arithmetic. The corresponding subprogram declaration must have two formal parameters. The first one must be a signed integer type or a modular type with a binary modulus, and the second parameter must be of type Natural. The return type must be the same as the type of the first argument. The size of this type can only be 8, 16, 32, or 64.

* Binary arithmetic operators: '+', '-', '*', '/'. The corresponding operator declaration must have parameters and result type that have the same root numeric type (for example, all three are long_float types). This simplifies the definition of operations that use type checking to perform dimensional checks:

```
type Distance is new Long_Float;
type Time     is new Long_Float;
type Velocity is new Long_Float;
function "/" (D : Distance; T : Time)
  return Velocity;
pragma Import (Intrinsic, "/");
```

This common idiom is often programmed with a generic definition and a explicit body. The pragma makes it simpler to introduce such declarat It incurs no overhead in compilation time or code size, because it is implemented as a single machine instruction.

* General subprogram entities. This is used to bind an Ada subprogram declaration to a compiler builtin by name with back-ends where such interfaces are available. A typical example is the set of __*builtin* functions exposed by the GCC back-end, as in the following example:

```
function builtin_sqrt (F : Float) return Float;
pragma Import (Intrinsic, builtin_sqrt, "__builtin_sqrtf");
```

Most of the GCC builtins are accessible this way, and as for other import conventions (e.g. C), it is the user's responsibility to ensure that the Ada subprogram profile matches the underlying builtin expectations.

Stdcall

This is relevant only to Windows implementations of GNAT, and specifies that the *Stdcall* calling sequence will be used, as defined by the NT API. Nevertheless, to ease building cross-platform bindings this convention will be handled as a *C* calling convention on non-Windows platforms.

DLL

> This is equivalent to *Stdcall*.

Win32

> This is equivalent to *Stdcall*.

Stubbed

> This is a special convention that indicates that the compiler should provide a stub body that raises *Program_Error*.

GNAT additionally provides a useful pragma *Convention_Identifier* that can be used to parameterize conventions and allow additional synonyms to be specified. For example if you have legacy code in which the convention identifier Fortran77 was used for Fortran, you can use the configuration pragma:

```
pragma Convention_Identifier (Fortran77, Fortran);
```

And from now on the identifier Fortran77 may be used as a convention identifier (for example in an *Import* pragma) with the same meaning as Fortran.

3.11.3 Building Mixed Ada and C++ Programs

A programmer inexperienced with mixed-language development may find that building an application containing both Ada and C++ code can be a challenge. This section gives a few hints that should make this task easier.

3.11.3.1 Interfacing to C++

GNAT supports interfacing with the G++ compiler (or any C++ compiler generating code that is compatible with the G++ Application Binary Interface —see http://www.codesourcery.com/archives/cxx-abi).

Interfacing can be done at 3 levels: simple data, subprograms, and classes. In the first two cases, GNAT offers a specific *Convention C_Plus_Plus* (or *CPP*) that behaves exactly like *Convention C*. Usually, C++ mangles the names of subprograms. To generate proper mangled names automatically, see [Generating Ada Bindings for C and C++ headers], page 69). This problem can also be addressed manually in two ways:

* by modifying the C++ code in order to force a C convention using the *extern "C"* syntax.

* by figuring out the mangled name (using e.g. *nm*) and using it as the Link_Name argument of the pragma import.

Interfacing at the class level can be achieved by using the GNAT specific pragmas such as *CPP_Constructor*. See the *GNAT_Reference_Manual* for additional information.

3.11.3.2 Linking a Mixed C++ & Ada Program

Usually the linker of the C++ development system must be used to link mixed applications because most C++ systems will resolve elaboration issues (such as calling constructors on global class instances) transparently during the link phase. GNAT has been adapted to ease the use of a foreign linker for the last phase. Three cases can be considered:

* Using GNAT and G++ (GNU C++ compiler) from the same GCC installation: The C++ linker can simply be called by using the C++ specific driver called *g++*.

Note that if the C++ code uses inline functions, you will need to compile your C++ code with the *-fkeep-inline-functions* switch in order to provide an existing function implementation that the Ada code can link with.

```
$ g++ -c -fkeep-inline-functions file1.C
$ g++ -c -fkeep-inline-functions file2.C
$ gnatmake ada_unit -largs file1.o file2.o --LINK=g++
```

* Using GNAT and G++ from two different GCC installations: If both compilers are on the :envvar'PATH', the previous method may be used. It is important to note that environment variables such as `C_INCLUDE_PATH`, `GCC_EXEC_PREFIX`, `BINUTILS_ROOT`, and `GCC_ROOT` will affect both compilers at the same time and may make one of the two compilers operate improperly if set during invocation of the wrong compiler. It is also very important that the linker uses the proper `libgcc.a` GCC library – that is, the one from the C++ compiler installation. The implicit link command as suggested in the *gnatmake* command from the former example can be replaced by an explicit link command with the full-verbosity option in order to verify which library is used:

```
$ gnatbind ada_unit
$ gnatlink -v -v ada_unit file1.o file2.o --LINK=c++
```

If there is a problem due to interfering environment variables, it can be worked around by using an intermediate script. The following example shows the proper script to use when GNAT has not been installed at its default location and g++ has been installed at its default location:

```
$ cat ./my_script
#!/bin/sh
unset BINUTILS_ROOT
unset GCC_ROOT
c++ $*
$ gnatlink -v -v ada_unit file1.o file2.o --LINK=./my_script
```

* Using a non-GNU C++ compiler: The commands previously described can be used to insure that the C++ linker is used. Nonetheless, you need to add a few more parameters to the link command line, depending on the exception mechanism used.

If the *setjmp/longjmp* exception mechanism is used, only the paths to the libgcc libraries are required:

```
$ cat ./my_script
#!/bin/sh
CC $* `gcc -print-file-name=libgcc.a` `gcc -print-file-name=libgcc_eh.a`
$ gnatlink ada_unit file1.o file2.o --LINK=./my_script
```

where CC is the name of the non-GNU C++ compiler.

If the *zero cost* exception mechanism is used, and the platform supports automatic registration of exception tables (e.g., Solaris), paths to more objects are required:

```
$ cat ./my_script
#!/bin/sh
CC `gcc -print-file-name=crtbegin.o` $* \\
```

```
`gcc -print-file-name=libgcc.a` `gcc -print-file-name=libgcc_eh.a` \\
`gcc -print-file-name=crtend.o`
$ gnatlink ada_unit file1.o file2.o --LINK=./my_script
```

If the "zero cost exception" mechanism is used, and the platform doesn't support automatic registration of exception tables (e.g., HP-UX or AIX), the simple approach described above will not work and a pre-linking phase using GNAT will be necessary.

Another alternative is to use the `gprbuild` multi-language builder which has a large knowledge base and knows how to link Ada and C++ code together automatically in most cases.

3.11.3.3 A Simple Example

The following example, provided as part of the GNAT examples, shows how to achieve procedural interfacing between Ada and C++ in both directions. The C++ class A has two methods. The first method is exported to Ada by the means of an extern C wrapper function. The second method calls an Ada subprogram. On the Ada side, The C++ calls are modelled by a limited record with a layout comparable to the C++ class. The Ada subprogram, in turn, calls the C++ method. So, starting from the C++ main program, the process passes back and forth between the two languages.

Here are the compilation commands:

```
$ gnatmake -c simple_cpp_interface
$ g++ -c cpp_main.C
$ g++ -c ex7.C
$ gnatbind -n simple_cpp_interface
$ gnatlink simple_cpp_interface -o cpp_main --LINK=g++ -lstdc++ ex7.o cpp_main.o
```

Here are the corresponding sources:

```
//cpp_main.C

#include "ex7.h"

extern "C" {
  void adainit (void);
  void adafinal (void);
  void method1 (A *t);
}

void method1 (A *t)
{
  t->method1 ();
}

int main ()
{
  A obj;
  adainit ();
  obj.method2 (3030);
  adafinal ();
```

```
}
//ex7.h

class Origin {
 public:
   int o_value;
};
class A : public Origin {
 public:
   void method1 (void);
   void method2 (int v);
   A();
   int   a_value;
};
//ex7.C

#include "ex7.h"
#include <stdio.h>

extern "C" { void ada_method2 (A *t, int v);}

void A::method1 (void)
{
  a_value = 2020;
  printf ("in A::method1, a_value = %d \\n",a_value);
}

void A::method2 (int v)
{
   ada_method2 (this, v);
   printf ("in A::method2, a_value = %d \\n",a_value);
}

A::A(void)
{
   a_value = 1010;
  printf ("in A::A, a_value = %d \\n",a_value);
}
-- simple_cpp_interface.ads
with System;
package Simple_Cpp_Interface is
   type A is limited
      record
         Vptr    : System.Address;
         O_Value : Integer;
         A_Value : Integer;
```

```
      end record;
   pragma Convention (C, A);

   procedure Method1 (This : in out A);
   pragma Import (C, Method1);

   procedure Ada_Method2 (This : in out A; V : Integer);
   pragma Export (C, Ada_Method2);

end Simple_Cpp_Interface;
-- simple_cpp_interface.adb
package body Simple_Cpp_Interface is

   procedure Ada_Method2 (This : in out A; V : Integer) is
   begin
      Method1 (This);
      This.A_Value := V;
   end Ada_Method2;

end Simple_Cpp_Interface;
```

3.11.3.4 Interfacing with C++ constructors

In order to interface with C++ constructors GNAT provides the *pragma CPP_Constructor*
(see the *GNAT_Reference_Manual* for additional information). In this section we present
some common uses of C++ constructors in mixed-languages programs in GNAT.

Let us assume that we need to interface with the following C++ class:

```
class Root {
public:
  int  a_value;
  int  b_value;
  virtual int Get_Value ();
  Root();                 // Default constructor
  Root(int v);            // 1st non-default constructor
  Root(int v, int w);     // 2nd non-default constructor
};
```

For this purpose we can write the following package spec (further information on how
to build this spec is available in [Interfacing with C++ at the Class Level], page 65 and
[Generating Ada Bindings for C and C++ headers], page 69).

```
with Interfaces.C; use Interfaces.C;
package Pkg_Root is
  type Root is tagged limited record
     A_Value : int;
     B_Value : int;
  end record;
  pragma Import (CPP, Root);
```

```
function Get_Value (Obj : Root) return int;
pragma Import (CPP, Get_Value);

function Constructor return Root;
pragma Cpp_Constructor (Constructor, "_ZN4RootC1Ev");

function Constructor (v : Integer) return Root;
pragma Cpp_Constructor (Constructor, "_ZN4RootC1Ei");

function Constructor (v, w : Integer) return Root;
pragma Cpp_Constructor (Constructor, "_ZN4RootC1Eii");
end Pkg_Root;
```

On the Ada side the constructor is represented by a function (whose name is arbitrary) that returns the classwide type corresponding to the imported C++ class. Although the constructor is described as a function, it is typically a procedure with an extra implicit argument (the object being initialized) at the implementation level. GNAT issues the appropriate call, whatever it is, to get the object properly initialized.

Constructors can only appear in the following contexts:

* On the right side of an initialization of an object of type T.

* On the right side of an initialization of a record component of type T.

* In an Ada 2005 limited aggregate.

* In an Ada 2005 nested limited aggregate.

* In an Ada 2005 limited aggregate that initializes an object built in place by an extended return statement.

In a declaration of an object whose type is a class imported from C++, either the default C++ constructor is implicitly called by GNAT, or else the required C++ constructor must be explicitly called in the expression that initializes the object. For example:

```
Obj1 : Root;
Obj2 : Root := Constructor;
Obj3 : Root := Constructor (v => 10);
Obj4 : Root := Constructor (30, 40);
```

The first two declarations are equivalent: in both cases the default C++ constructor is invoked (in the former case the call to the constructor is implicit, and in the latter case the call is explicit in the object declaration). *Obj3* is initialized by the C++ non-default constructor that takes an integer argument, and *Obj4* is initialized by the non-default C++ constructor that takes two integers.

Let us derive the imported C++ class in the Ada side. For example:

```
type DT is new Root with record
   C_Value : Natural := 2009;
end record;
```

In this case the components DT inherited from the C++ side must be initialized by a C++ constructor, and the additional Ada components of type DT are initialized by GNAT. The initialization of such an object is done either by default, or by means of a function returning an aggregate of type DT, or by means of an extension aggregate.

```
Obj5 : DT;
Obj6 : DT := Function_Returning_DT (50);
Obj7 : DT := (Constructor (30,40) with C_Value => 50);
```

The declaration of *Obj5* invokes the default constructors: the C++ default constructor of the parent type takes care of the initialization of the components inherited from Root, and GNAT takes care of the default initialization of the additional Ada components of type DT (that is, *C_Value* is initialized to value 2009). The order of invocation of the constructors is consistent with the order of elaboration required by Ada and C++. That is, the constructor of the parent type is always called before the constructor of the derived type.

Let us now consider a record that has components whose type is imported from C++. For example:

```
type Rec1 is limited record
   Data1 : Root := Constructor (10);
   Value : Natural := 1000;
end record;

type Rec2 (D : Integer := 20) is limited record
   Rec   : Rec1;
   Data2 : Root := Constructor (D, 30);
end record;
```

The initialization of an object of type *Rec2* will call the non-default C++ constructors specified for the imported components. For example:

```
Obj8 : Rec2 (40);
```

Using Ada 2005 we can use limited aggregates to initialize an object invoking C++ constructors that differ from those specified in the type declarations. For example:

```
Obj9 : Rec2 := (Rec => (Data1 => Constructor (15, 16),
                        others => <>),
                others => <>);
```

The above declaration uses an Ada 2005 limited aggregate to initialize *Obj9*, and the C++ constructor that has two integer arguments is invoked to initialize the *Data1* component instead of the constructor specified in the declaration of type *Rec1*. In Ada 2005 the box in the aggregate indicates that unspecified components are initialized using the expression (if any) available in the component declaration. That is, in this case discriminant *D* is initialized to value *20*, *Value* is initialized to value 1000, and the non-default C++ constructor that handles two integers takes care of initializing component *Data2* with values *20,30*.

In Ada 2005 we can use the extended return statement to build the Ada equivalent to C++ non-default constructors. For example:

```
function Constructor (V : Integer) return Rec2 is
begin
   return Obj : Rec2 := (Rec => (Data1  => Constructor (V, 20),
                                 others => <>),
                         others => <>) do
      --  Further actions required for construction of
      --  objects of type Rec2
      ...
```

```
        end record;
     end Constructor;
```

In this example the extended return statement construct is used to build in place the returned object whose components are initialized by means of a limited aggregate. Any further action associated with the constructor can be placed inside the construct.

3.11.3.5 Interfacing with C++ at the Class Level

In this section we demonstrate the GNAT features for interfacing with C++ by means of an example making use of Ada 2005 abstract interface types. This example consists of a classification of animals; classes have been used to model our main classification of animals, and interfaces provide support for the management of secondary classifications. We first demonstrate a case in which the types and constructors are defined on the C++ side and imported from the Ada side, and latter the reverse case.

The root of our derivation will be the *Animal* class, with a single private attribute (the *Age* of the animal), a constructor, and two public primitives to set and get the value of this attribute.

```
     class Animal {
      public:
        virtual void Set_Age (int New_Age);
        virtual int Age ();
        Animal() {Age_Count = 0;};
      private:
        int Age_Count;
     };
```

Abstract interface types are defined in C++ by means of classes with pure virtual functions and no data members. In our example we will use two interfaces that provide support for the common management of *Carnivore* and *Domestic* animals:

```
     class Carnivore {
     public:
        virtual int Number_Of_Teeth () = 0;
     };

     class Domestic {
     public:
        virtual void Set_Owner (char* Name) = 0;
     };
```

Using these declarations, we can now say that a *Dog* is an animal that is both Carnivore and Domestic, that is:

```
     class Dog : Animal, Carnivore, Domestic {
      public:
        virtual int  Number_Of_Teeth ();
        virtual void Set_Owner (char* Name);

        Dog(); // Constructor
      private:
```

```
      int  Tooth_Count;
      char *Owner;
};
```

In the following examples we will assume that the previous declarations are located in a file named *animals.h*. The following package demonstrates how to import these C++ declarations from the Ada side:

```
with Interfaces.C.Strings; use Interfaces.C.Strings;
package Animals is
  type Carnivore is limited interface;
  pragma Convention (C_Plus_Plus, Carnivore);
  function Number_Of_Teeth (X : Carnivore)
    return Natural is abstract;

  type Domestic is limited interface;
  pragma Convention (C_Plus_Plus, Domestic);
  procedure Set_Owner
    (X     : in out Domestic;
     Name : Chars_Ptr) is abstract;

  type Animal is tagged limited record
    Age : Natural;
  end record;
  pragma Import (C_Plus_Plus, Animal);

  procedure Set_Age (X : in out Animal; Age : Integer);
  pragma Import (C_Plus_Plus, Set_Age);

  function Age (X : Animal) return Integer;
  pragma Import (C_Plus_Plus, Age);

  function New_Animal return Animal;
  pragma CPP_Constructor (New_Animal);
  pragma Import (CPP, New_Animal, "_ZN6AnimalC1Ev");

  type Dog is new Animal and Carnivore and Domestic with record
    Tooth_Count : Natural;
    Owner       : String (1 .. 30);
  end record;
  pragma Import (C_Plus_Plus, Dog);

  function Number_Of_Teeth (A : Dog) return Natural;
  pragma Import (C_Plus_Plus, Number_Of_Teeth);

  procedure Set_Owner (A : in out Dog; Name : Chars_Ptr);
  pragma Import (C_Plus_Plus, Set_Owner);
```

```
      function New_Dog return Dog;
      pragma CPP_Constructor (New_Dog);
      pragma Import (CPP, New_Dog, "_ZN3DogC2Ev");
   end Animals;
```

Thanks to the compatibility between GNAT run-time structures and the C++ ABI, interfacing with these C++ classes is easy. The only requirement is that all the primitives and components must be declared exactly in the same order in the two languages.

Regarding the abstract interfaces, we must indicate to the GNAT compiler by means of a *pragma Convention (C_Plus_Plus)*, the convention used to pass the arguments to the called primitives will be the same as for C++. For the imported classes we use *pragma Import* with convention *C_Plus_Plus* to indicate that they have been defined on the C++ side; this is required because the dispatch table associated with these tagged types will be built in the C++ side and therefore will not contain the predefined Ada primitives which Ada would otherwise expect.

As the reader can see there is no need to indicate the C++ mangled names associated with each subprogram because it is assumed that all the calls to these primitives will be dispatching calls. The only exception is the constructor, which must be registered with the compiler by means of *pragma CPP_Constructor* and needs to provide its associated C++ mangled name because the Ada compiler generates direct calls to it.

With the above packages we can now declare objects of type Dog on the Ada side and dispatch calls to the corresponding subprograms on the C++ side. We can also extend the tagged type Dog with further fields and primitives, and override some of its C++ primitives on the Ada side. For example, here we have a type derivation defined on the Ada side that inherits all the dispatching primitives of the ancestor from the C++ side.

```
      with Animals; use Animals;
      package Vaccinated_Animals is
         type Vaccinated_Dog is new Dog with null record;
         function Vaccination_Expired (A : Vaccinated_Dog) return Boolean;
      end Vaccinated_Animals;
```

It is important to note that, because of the ABI compatibility, the programmer does not need to add any further information to indicate either the object layout or the dispatch table entry associated with each dispatching operation.

Now let us define all the types and constructors on the Ada side and export them to C++, using the same hierarchy of our previous example:

```
      with Interfaces.C.Strings;
      use Interfaces.C.Strings;
      package Animals is
         type Carnivore is limited interface;
         pragma Convention (C_Plus_Plus, Carnivore);
         function Number_Of_Teeth (X : Carnivore)
            return Natural is abstract;

         type Domestic is limited interface;
         pragma Convention (C_Plus_Plus, Domestic);
         procedure Set_Owner
```

```
     (X     : in out Domestic;
      Name : Chars_Ptr) is abstract;

   type Animal is tagged record
     Age : Natural;
   end record;
   pragma Convention (C_Plus_Plus, Animal);

   procedure Set_Age (X : in out Animal; Age : Integer);
   pragma Export (C_Plus_Plus, Set_Age);

   function Age (X : Animal) return Integer;
   pragma Export (C_Plus_Plus, Age);

   function New_Animal return Animal'Class;
   pragma Export (C_Plus_Plus, New_Animal);

   type Dog is new Animal and Carnivore and Domestic with record
     Tooth_Count : Natural;
     Owner       : String (1 .. 30);
   end record;
   pragma Convention (C_Plus_Plus, Dog);

   function Number_Of_Teeth (A : Dog) return Natural;
   pragma Export (C_Plus_Plus, Number_Of_Teeth);

   procedure Set_Owner (A : in out Dog; Name : Chars_Ptr);
   pragma Export (C_Plus_Plus, Set_Owner);

   function New_Dog return Dog'Class;
   pragma Export (C_Plus_Plus, New_Dog);
end Animals;
```

Compared with our previous example the only differences are the use of *pragma Convention* (instead of *pragma Import*), and the use of *pragma Export* to indicate to the GNAT compiler that the primitives will be available to C++. Thanks to the ABI compatibility, on the C++ side there is nothing else to be done; as explained above, the only requirement is that all the primitives and components are declared in exactly the same order.

For completeness, let us see a brief C++ main program that uses the declarations available in *animals.h* (presented in our first example) to import and use the declarations from the Ada side, properly initializing and finalizing the Ada run-time system along the way:

```
#include "animals.h"
#include <iostream>
using namespace std;

void Check_Carnivore (Carnivore *obj) {...}
void Check_Domestic  (Domestic *obj)   {...}
```

```
      void Check_Animal (Animal *obj)        {...}
      void Check_Dog (Dog *obj)              {...}

      extern "C" {
        void adainit (void);
        void adafinal (void);
        Dog* new_dog ();
      }

      void test ()
      {
        Dog *obj = new_dog();  // Ada constructor
        Check_Carnivore (obj); // Check secondary DT
        Check_Domestic (obj);  // Check secondary DT
        Check_Animal (obj);    // Check primary DT
        Check_Dog (obj);       // Check primary DT
      }

      int main ()
      {
        adainit ();  test();  adafinal ();
        return 0;
      }
```

3.11.4 Generating Ada Bindings for C and C++ headers

GNAT includes a binding generator for C and C++ headers which is intended to do 95% of the tedious work of generating Ada specs from C or C++ header files.

Note that this capability is not intended to generate 100% correct Ada specs, and will is some cases require manual adjustments, although it can often be used out of the box in practice.

Some of the known limitations include:

* only very simple character constant macros are translated into Ada constants. Function macros (macros with arguments) are partially translated as comments, to be completed manually if needed.

* some extensions (e.g. vector types) are not supported

* pointers to pointers or complex structures are mapped to System.Address

* identifiers with identical name (except casing) will generate compilation errors (e.g. *shm_get* vs *SHM_GET*).

The code generated is using the Ada 2005 syntax, which makes it easier to interface with other languages than previous versions of Ada.

3.11.4.1 Running the Binding Generator

The binding generator is part of the *gcc* compiler and can be invoked via the *-fdump-ada-spec* switch, which will generate Ada spec files for the header files specified on the command line, and all header files needed by these files transitively. For example:

```
$ g++ -c -fdump-ada-spec -C /usr/include/time.h
$ gcc -c -gnat05 *.ads
```

will generate, under GNU/Linux, the following files: `time_h.ads`, `bits_time_h.ads`, `stddef_h.ads`, `bits_types_h.ads` which correspond to the files `/usr/include/time.h`, `/usr/include/bits/time.h`, etc..., and will then compile in Ada 2005 mode these Ada specs.

The *-C* switch tells *gcc* to extract comments from headers, and will attempt to generate corresponding Ada comments.

If you want to generate a single Ada file and not the transitive closure, you can use instead the *-fdump-ada-spec-slim* switch.

You can optionally specify a parent unit, of which all generated units will be children, using *-fada-spec-parent=<unit>*.

Note that we recommend when possible to use the *g++* driver to generate bindings, even for most C headers, since this will in general generate better Ada specs. For generating bindings for C++ headers, it is mandatory to use the *g++* command, or *gcc -x c++* which is equivalent in this case. If *g++* cannot work on your C headers because of incompatibilities between C and C++, then you can fallback to *gcc* instead.

For an example of better bindings generated from the C++ front-end, the name of the parameters (when available) are actually ignored by the C front-end. Consider the following C header:

```
extern void foo (int variable);
```

with the C front-end, *variable* is ignored, and the above is handled as:

```
extern void foo (int);
```

generating a generic:

```
procedure foo (param1 : int);
```

with the C++ front-end, the name is available, and we generate:

```
procedure foo (variable : int);
```

In some cases, the generated bindings will be more complete or more meaningful when defining some macros, which you can do via the *-D* switch. This is for example the case with `Xlib.h` under GNU/Linux:

```
$ g++ -c -fdump-ada-spec -DXLIB_ILLEGAL_ACCESS -C /usr/include/X11/Xlib.h
```

The above will generate more complete bindings than a straight call without the *-DXLIB_ILLEGAL_ACCESS* switch.

In other cases, it is not possible to parse a header file in a stand-alone manner, because other include files need to be included first. In this case, the solution is to create a small header file including the needed *#include* and possible *#define* directives. For example, to generate Ada bindings for `readline/readline.h`, you need to first include `stdio.h`, so you can create a file with the following two lines in e.g. `readline1.h`:

```
#include <stdio.h>
#include <readline/readline.h>
```

and then generate Ada bindings from this file:

```
$ g++ -c -fdump-ada-spec readline1.h
```

3.11.4.2 Generating Bindings for C++ Headers

Generating bindings for C++ headers is done using the same options, always with the *g++* compiler. Note that generating Ada spec from C++ headers is a much more complex job and support for C++ headers is much more limited that support for C headers. As a result, you will need to modify the resulting bindings by hand more extensively when using C++ headers.

In this mode, C++ classes will be mapped to Ada tagged types, constructors will be mapped using the *CPP_Constructor* pragma, and when possible, multiple inheritance of abstract classes will be mapped to Ada interfaces (see the *Interfacing to C++* section in the *GNAT Reference Manual* for additional information on interfacing to C++).

For example, given the following C++ header file:

```
class Carnivore {
public:
    virtual int Number_Of_Teeth () = 0;
};

class Domestic {
public:
    virtual void Set_Owner (char* Name) = 0;
};

class Animal {
public:
  int Age_Count;
  virtual void Set_Age (int New_Age);
};

class Dog : Animal, Carnivore, Domestic {
 public:
  int  Tooth_Count;
  char *Owner;

  virtual int  Number_Of_Teeth ();
  virtual void Set_Owner (char* Name);

  Dog();
};
```

The corresponding Ada code is generated:

```
package Class_Carnivore is
   type Carnivore is limited interface;
   pragma Import (CPP, Carnivore);

   function Number_Of_Teeth (this : access Carnivore) return int is abstract;
end;
use Class_Carnivore;
```

```
package Class_Domestic is
  type Domestic is limited interface;
  pragma Import (CPP, Domestic);

  procedure Set_Owner
    (this : access Domestic;
     Name : Interfaces.C.Strings.chars_ptr) is abstract;
end;
use Class_Domestic;

package Class_Animal is
  type Animal is tagged limited record
    Age_Count : aliased int;
  end record;
  pragma Import (CPP, Animal);

  procedure Set_Age (this : access Animal; New_Age : int);
  pragma Import (CPP, Set_Age, "_ZN6Animal7Set_AgeEi");
end;
use Class_Animal;

package Class_Dog is
  type Dog is new Animal and Carnivore and Domestic with record
    Tooth_Count : aliased int;
    Owner : Interfaces.C.Strings.chars_ptr;
  end record;
  pragma Import (CPP, Dog);

  function Number_Of_Teeth (this : access Dog) return int;
  pragma Import (CPP, Number_Of_Teeth, "_ZN3Dog15Number_Of_TeethEv");

  procedure Set_Owner
    (this : access Dog; Name : Interfaces.C.Strings.chars_ptr);
  pragma Import (CPP, Set_Owner, "_ZN3Dog9Set_OwnerEPc");

  function New_Dog return Dog;
  pragma CPP_Constructor (New_Dog);
  pragma Import (CPP, New_Dog, "_ZN3DogC1Ev");
end;
use Class_Dog;
```

3.11.4.3 Switches

`-fdump-ada-spec`

> Generate Ada spec files for the given header files transitively (including all
> header files that these headers depend upon).

`-fdump-ada-spec-slim`
>   Generate Ada spec files for the header files specified on the command line only.

`-fada-spec-parent=`*unit*
>   Specifies that all files generated by *-fdump-ada-spec** are to be child units of the specified parent unit.

`-C`

>   Extract comments from headers and generate Ada comments in the Ada spec files.

3.11.5 Generating C Headers for Ada Specifications

GNAT includes a C header generator for Ada specifications which supports Ada types that have a direct mapping to C types. This includes in particular support for:

* Scalar types
* Constrained arrays
* Records (untagged)
* Composition of the above types
* Constant declarations
* Object declarations
* Subprogram declarations

3.11.5.1 Running the C Header Generator

The C header generator is part of the GNAT compiler and can be invoked via the *-gnatceg* combination of switches, which will generate a `.h` file corresponding to the given input file (Ada spec or body). Note that only spec files are processed in any case, so giving a spec or a body file as input is equivalent. For example:

```
$ gcc -c -gnatceg pack1.ads
```

will generate a self-contained file called `pack1.h` including common definitions from the Ada Standard package, followed by the definitions included in `pack1.ads`, as well as all the other units withed by this file.

For instance, given the following Ada files:

```
package Pack2 is
   type Int is range 1 .. 10;
end Pack2;

with Pack2;

package Pack1 is
   type Rec is record
      Field1, Field2 : Pack2.Int;
   end record;

   Global : Rec := (1, 2);

   procedure Proc1 (R : Rec);
```

```
        procedure Proc2 (R : in out Rec);
      end Pack1;
```

The above *gcc* command will generate the following `pack1.h` file:

```
/* Standard definitions skipped */
#ifndef PACK2_ADS
#define PACK2_ADS
typedef short_short_integer pack2__TintB;
typedef pack2__TintB pack2__int;
#endif /* PACK2_ADS */

#ifndef PACK1_ADS
#define PACK1_ADS
typedef struct _pack1__rec {
  pack2__int field1;
  pack2__int field2;
} pack1__rec;
extern pack1__rec pack1__global;
extern void pack1__proc1(const pack1__rec r);
extern void pack1__proc2(pack1__rec *r);
#endif /* PACK1_ADS */
```

You can then *include* `pack1.h` from a C source file and use the types, call subprograms, reference objects, and constants.

3.12 GNAT and Other Compilation Models

This section compares the GNAT model with the approaches taken in other environents, first the C/C++ model and then the mechanism that has been used in other Ada systems, in particular those traditionally used for Ada 83.

3.12.1 Comparison between GNAT and C/C++ Compilation Models

The GNAT model of compilation is close to the C and C++ models. You can think of Ada specs as corresponding to header files in C. As in C, you don't need to compile specs; they are compiled when they are used. The Ada *with* is similar in effect to the *#include* of a C header.

One notable difference is that, in Ada, you may compile specs separately to check them for semantic and syntactic accuracy. This is not always possible with C headers because they are fragments of programs that have less specific syntactic or semantic rules.

The other major difference is the requirement for running the binder, which performs two important functions. First, it checks for consistency. In C or C++, the only defense against assembling inconsistent programs lies outside the compiler, in a makefile, for example. The binder satisfies the Ada requirement that it be impossible to construct an inconsistent program when the compiler is used in normal mode.

The other important function of the binder is to deal with elaboration issues. There are also elaboration issues in C++ that are handled automatically. This automatic handling has the advantage of being simpler to use, but the C++ programmer has no control over elaboration. Where *gnatbind* might complain there was no valid order of elaboration, a C++ compiler would simply construct a program that malfunctioned at run time.

3.12.2 Comparison between GNAT and Conventional Ada Library Models

This section is intended for Ada programmers who have used an Ada compiler implementing the traditional Ada library model, as described in the Ada Reference Manual.

In GNAT, there is no 'library' in the normal sense. Instead, the set of source files themselves acts as the library. Compiling Ada programs does not generate any centralized information, but rather an object file and a ALI file, which are of interest only to the binder and linker. In a traditional system, the compiler reads information not only from the source file being compiled, but also from the centralized library. This means that the effect of a compilation depends on what has been previously compiled. In particular:

* When a unit is *with*ed, the unit seen by the compiler corresponds to the version of the unit most recently compiled into the library.

* Inlining is effective only if the necessary body has already been compiled into the library.

* Compiling a unit may obsolete other units in the library.

In GNAT, compiling one unit never affects the compilation of any other units because the compiler reads only source files. Only changes to source files can affect the results of a compilation. In particular:

* When a unit is *with*ed, the unit seen by the compiler corresponds to the source version of the unit that is currently accessible to the compiler.

* Inlining requires the appropriate source files for the package or subprogram bodies to be available to the compiler. Inlining is always effective, independent of the order in which units are compiled.

* Compiling a unit never affects any other compilations. The editing of sources may cause previous compilations to be out of date if they depended on the source file being modified.

The most important result of these differences is that order of compilation is never significant in GNAT. There is no situation in which one is required to do one compilation before another. What shows up as order of compilation requirements in the traditional Ada library becomes, in GNAT, simple source dependencies; in other words, there is only a set of rules saying what source files must be present when a file is compiled.

3.13 Using GNAT Files with External Tools

This section explains how files that are produced by GNAT may be used with tools designed for other languages.

3.13.1 Using Other Utility Programs with GNAT

The object files generated by GNAT are in standard system format and in particular the debugging information uses this format. This means programs generated by GNAT can be used with existing utilities that depend on these formats.

In general, any utility program that works with C will also often work with Ada programs generated by GNAT. This includes software utilities such as gprof (a profiling program), gdb (the FSF debugger), and utilities such as Purify.

3.13.2 The External Symbol Naming Scheme of GNAT

In order to interpret the output from GNAT, when using tools that are originally intended for use with other languages, it is useful to understand the conventions used to generate link names from the Ada entity names.

All link names are in all lowercase letters. With the exception of library procedure names, the mechanism used is simply to use the full expanded Ada name with dots replaced by double underscores. For example, suppose we have the following package spec:

```
package QRS is
    MN : Integer;
end QRS;
```

The variable *MN* has a full expanded Ada name of *QRS.MN*, so the corresponding link name is *qrs__mn*. Of course if a *pragma Export* is used this may be overridden:

```
package Exports is
    Var1 : Integer;
    pragma Export (Var1, C, External_Name => "var1_name");
    Var2 : Integer;
    pragma Export (Var2, C, Link_Name => "var2_link_name");
end Exports;
```

In this case, the link name for *Var1* is whatever link name the C compiler would assign for the C function *var1_name*. This typically would be either *var1_name* or *_var1_name*, depending on operating system conventions, but other possibilities exist. The link name for *Var2* is *var2_link_name*, and this is not operating system dependent.

One exception occurs for library level procedures. A potential ambiguity arises between the required name *_main* for the C main program, and the name we would otherwise assign to an Ada library level procedure called *Main* (which might well not be the main program).

To avoid this ambiguity, we attach the prefix *_ada_* to such names. So if we have a library level procedure such as:

```
procedure Hello (S : String);
```

the external name of this procedure will be *_ada_hello*.

4 Building Executable Programs with GNAT

This chapter describes first the gnatmake tool ([Building with gnatmake], page 77), which automatically determines the set of sources needed by an Ada compilation unit and executes the necessary (re)compilations, binding and linking. It also explains how to use each tool individually: the compiler (gcc, see [Compiling with gcc], page 87), binder (gnatbind, see [Binding with gnatbind], page 150), and linker (gnatlink, see [Linking with gnatlink], page 162) to build executable programs. Finally, this chapter provides examples of how to make use of the general GNU make mechanism in a GNAT context (see [Using the GNU make Utility], page 164).

4.1 Building with *gnatmake*

A typical development cycle when working on an Ada program consists of the following steps:

1. Edit some sources to fix bugs;

2. Add enhancements;

3. Compile all sources affected;

4. Rebind and relink; and

5. Test.

The third step in particular can be tricky, because not only do the modified files have to be compiled, but any files depending on these files must also be recompiled. The dependency rules in Ada can be quite complex, especially in the presence of overloading, *use* clauses, generics and inlined subprograms.

gnatmake automatically takes care of the third and fourth steps of this process. It determines which sources need to be compiled, compiles them, and binds and links the resulting object files.

Unlike some other Ada make programs, the dependencies are always accurately recomputed from the new sources. The source based approach of the GNAT compilation model makes this possible. This means that if changes to the source program cause corresponding changes in dependencies, they will always be tracked exactly correctly by *gnatmake*.

Note that for advanced forms of project structure, we recommend creating a project file as explained in the *GNAT_Project_Manager* chapter in the *GPRbuild User's Guide*, and using the *gprbuild* tool which supports building with project files and works similarly to *gnatmake*.

4.1.1 Running *gnatmake*

The usual form of the *gnatmake* command is

```
$ gnatmake [<switches>] <file_name> [<file_names>] [<mode_switches>]
```

The only required argument is one *file_name*, which specifies a compilation unit that is a main program. Several *file_names* can be specified: this will result in several executables being built. If *switches* are present, they can be placed before the first *file_name*, between *file_names* or after the last *file_name*. If *mode_switches* are present, they must always be placed after the last *file_name* and all *switches*.

If you are using standard file extensions (`.adb` and `.ads`), then the extension may be omitted from the *file_name* arguments. However, if you are using non-standard extensions, then it is required that the extension be given. A relative or absolute directory path can be specified in a *file_name*, in which case, the input source file will be searched for in the specified directory only. Otherwise, the input source file will first be searched in the directory where *gnatmake* was invoked and if it is not found, it will be search on the source path of the compiler as described in [Search Paths and the Run-Time Library (RTL)], page 89.

All *gnatmake* output (except when you specify *-M*) is sent to **stderr**. The output produced by the *-M* switch is sent to **stdout**.

4.1.2 Switches for *gnatmake*

You may specify any of the following switches to *gnatmake*:

`--version`

> Display Copyright and version, then exit disregarding all other options.

`--help`

> If `--version` was not used, display usage, then exit disregarding all other options.

`--GCC=compiler_name`

> Program used for compiling. The default is **gcc**. You need to use quotes around *compiler_name* if *compiler_name* contains spaces or other separator characters. As an example `--GCC="foo -x -y"` will instruct *gnatmake* to use **foo -x -y** as your compiler. A limitation of this syntax is that the name and path name of the executable itself must not include any embedded spaces. Note that switch `-c` is always inserted after your command name. Thus in the above example the compiler command that will be used by *gnatmake* will be **foo -c -x -y**. If several `--GCC=compiler_name` are used, only the last *compiler_name* is taken into account. However, all the additional switches are also taken into account. Thus, `--GCC="foo -x -y" --GCC="bar -z -t"` is equivalent to `--GCC="bar -x -y -z -t"`.

`--GNATBIND=binder_name`

> Program used for binding. The default is **gnatbind**. You need to use quotes around *binder_name* if *binder_name* contains spaces or other separator characters. As an example `--GNATBIND="bar -x -y"` will instruct *gnatmake* to use *bar -x -y* as your binder. Binder switches that are normally appended by *gnatmake* to **gnatbind** are now appended to the end of *bar -x -y*. A limitation of this syntax is that the name and path name of the executable itself must not include any embedded spaces.

`--GNATLINK=linker_name`

> Program used for linking. The default is **gnatlink**. You need to use quotes around *linker_name* if *linker_name* contains spaces or other separator characters. As an example `--GNATLINK="lan -x -y"` will instruct *gnatmake* to use **lan -x -y** as your linker. Linker switches that are normally appended by **gnatmake** to **gnatlink** are now appended to the end of **lan -x -y**. A limitation of this syntax is that the name and path name of the executable itself must not include any embedded spaces.

`--create-map-file`

> When linking an executable, create a map file. The name of the map file has the same name as the executable with extension ".map".

`--create-map-file=mapfile`

> When linking an executable, create a map file with the specified name.

`--create-missing-dirs`

> When using project files (`-Pproject`), automatically create missing object directories, library directories and exec directories.

`--single-compile-per-obj-dir`

> Disallow simultaneous compilations in the same object directory when project files are used.

`--subdirs=subdir`

> Actual object directory of each project file is the subdirectory subdir of the object directory specified or defaulted in the project file.

`--unchecked-shared-lib-imports`

> By default, shared library projects are not allowed to import static library projects. When this switch is used on the command line, this restriction is relaxed.

`--source-info=source info file`

> Specify a source info file. This switch is active only when project files are used. If the source info file is specified as a relative path, then it is relative to the object directory of the main project. If the source info file does not exist, then after the Project Manager has successfully parsed and processed the project files and found the sources, it creates the source info file. If the source info file already exists and can be read successfully, then the Project Manager will get all the needed information about the sources from the source info file and will not look for them. This reduces the time to process the project files, especially when looking for sources that take a long time. If the source info file exists but cannot be parsed successfully, the Project Manager will attempt to recreate it. If the Project Manager fails to create the source info file, a message is issued, but gnatmake does not fail. *gnatmake* "trusts" the source info file. This means that if the source files have changed (addition, deletion, moving to a different source directory), then the source info file need to be deleted and recreated.

`-a`

> Consider all files in the make process, even the GNAT internal system files (for example, the predefined Ada library files), as well as any locked files. Locked files are files whose ALI file is write-protected. By default, *gnatmake* does not check these files, because the assumption is that the GNAT internal files are properly up to date, and also that any write protected ALI files have been properly installed. Note that if there is an installation problem, such that one of these files is not up to date, it will be properly caught by the binder. You may have to specify this switch if you are working on GNAT itself. The switch `-a` is also useful in conjunction with `-f` if you need to recompile an entire

application, including run-time files, using special configuration pragmas, such as a *Normalize_Scalars* pragma.

By default `gnatmake -a` compiles all GNAT internal files with `gcc -c -gnatpg` rather than `gcc -c`.

-b

Bind only. Can be combined with *-c* to do compilation and binding, but no link. Can be combined with *-l* to do binding and linking. When not combined with *-c* all the units in the closure of the main program must have been previously compiled and must be up to date. The root unit specified by *file_name* may be given without extension, with the source extension or, if no GNAT Project File is specified, with the ALI file extension.

-c

Compile only. Do not perform binding, except when *-b* is also specified. Do not perform linking, except if both *-b* and *-l* are also specified. If the root unit specified by *file_name* is not a main unit, this is the default. Otherwise *gnatmake* will attempt binding and linking unless all objects are up to date and the executable is more recent than the objects.

-C

Use a temporary mapping file. A mapping file is a way to communicate to the compiler two mappings: from unit names to file names (without any directory information) and from file names to path names (with full directory information). A mapping file can make the compiler's file searches faster, especially if there are many source directories, or the sources are read over a slow network connection. If *-P* is used, a mapping file is always used, so *-C* is unnecessary; in this case the mapping file is initially populated based on the project file. If *-C* is used without *-P*, the mapping file is initially empty. Each invocation of the compiler will add any newly accessed sources to the mapping file.

-C=*file*

Use a specific mapping file. The file, specified as a path name (absolute or relative) by this switch, should already exist, otherwise the switch is ineffective. The specified mapping file will be communicated to the compiler. This switch is not compatible with a project file (-P'file') or with multiple compiling processes (-jnnn, when nnn is greater than 1).

-d

Display progress for each source, up to date or not, as a single line:

```
completed x out of y (zz%)
```

If the file needs to be compiled this is displayed after the invocation of the compiler. These lines are displayed even in quiet output mode.

-D *dir*

Put all object files and ALI file in directory *dir*. If the *-D* switch is not used, all object files and ALI files go in the current working directory.

This switch cannot be used when using a project file.

`-eInnn`

> Indicates that the main source is a multi-unit source and the rank of the unit in the source file is nnn. nnn needs to be a positive number and a valid index in the source. This switch cannot be used when *gnatmake* is invoked for several mains.

`-eL`

> Follow all symbolic links when processing project files. This should be used if your project uses symbolic links for files or directories, but is not needed in other cases.
>
> This also assumes that no directory matches the naming scheme for files (for instance that you do not have a directory called "sources.ads" when using the default GNAT naming scheme).
>
> When you do not have to use this switch (i.e., by default), gnatmake is able to save a lot of system calls (several per source file and object file), which can result in a significant speed up to load and manipulate a project file, especially when using source files from a remote system.

`-eS`

> Output the commands for the compiler, the binder and the linker on standard output, instead of standard error.

`-f`

> Force recompilations. Recompile all sources, even though some object files may be up to date, but don't recompile predefined or GNAT internal files or locked files (files with a write-protected ALI file), unless the *-a* switch is also specified.

`-F`

> When using project files, if some errors or warnings are detected during parsing and verbose mode is not in effect (no use of switch -v), then error lines start with the full path name of the project file, rather than its simple file name.

`-g`

> Enable debugging. This switch is simply passed to the compiler and to the linker.

`-i`

> In normal mode, *gnatmake* compiles all object files and ALI files into the current directory. If the *-i* switch is used, then instead object files and ALI files that already exist are overwritten in place. This means that once a large project is organized into separate directories in the desired manner, then *gnatmake* will automatically maintain and update this organization. If no ALI files are found on the Ada object path (see [Search Paths and the Run-Time Library (RTL)], page 89), the new object and ALI files are created in the directory containing the source being compiled. If another organization is desired, where objects and sources are kept in different directories, a useful technique is to create dummy ALI files in the desired directories. When detecting such a dummy file, *gnatmake* will be forced to recompile the corresponding source file, and it will

be put the resulting object and ALI files in the directory where it found the dummy file.

-jn

Use *n* processes to carry out the (re)compilations. On a multiprocessor machine compilations will occur in parallel. If *n* is 0, then the maximum number of parallel compilations is the number of core processors on the platform. In the event of compilation errors, messages from various compilations might get interspersed (but *gnatmake* will give you the full ordered list of failing compiles at the end). If this is problematic, rerun the make process with n set to 1 to get a clean list of messages.

-k

Keep going. Continue as much as possible after a compilation error. To ease the programmer's task in case of compilation errors, the list of sources for which the compile fails is given when *gnatmake* terminates.

If *gnatmake* is invoked with several **file_names** and with this switch, if there are compilation errors when building an executable, *gnatmake* will not attempt to build the following executables.

-l

Link only. Can be combined with *-b* to binding and linking. Linking will not be performed if combined with *-c* but not with *-b*. When not combined with *-b* all the units in the closure of the main program must have been previously compiled and must be up to date, and the main program needs to have been bound. The root unit specified by *file_name* may be given without extension, with the source extension or, if no GNAT Project File is specified, with the ALI file extension.

-m

Specify that the minimum necessary amount of recompilations be performed. In this mode *gnatmake* ignores time stamp differences when the only modifications to a source file consist in adding/removing comments, empty lines, spaces or tabs. This means that if you have changed the comments in a source file or have simply reformatted it, using this switch will tell *gnatmake* not to recompile files that depend on it (provided other sources on which these files depend have undergone no semantic modifications). Note that the debugging information may be out of date with respect to the sources if the *-m* switch causes a compilation to be switched, so the use of this switch represents a trade-off between compilation time and accurate debugging information.

-M

Check if all objects are up to date. If they are, output the object dependences to **stdout** in a form that can be directly exploited in a **Makefile**. By default, each source file is prefixed with its (relative or absolute) directory name. This name is whatever you specified in the various *-aI* and *-I* switches. If you use *gnatmake -M -q* (see below), only the source file names, without relative paths, are output. If you just specify the *-M* switch, dependencies of the GNAT internal system files are omitted. This is typically what you want. If you also specify the -a switch, dependencies of the GNAT internal files are also listed. Note that dependencies of the objects in external Ada libraries (see switch -aL*dir* in the following list) are never reported.

-n

> Don't compile, bind, or link. Checks if all objects are up to date. If they are not, the full name of the first file that needs to be recompiled is printed. Repeated use of this option, followed by compiling the indicated source file, will eventually result in recompiling all required units.

-o *exec_name*

> Output executable name. The name of the final executable program will be *exec_name*. If the -o switch is omitted the default name for the executable will be the name of the input file in appropriate form for an executable file on the host system.
>
> This switch cannot be used when invoking *gnatmake* with several file_names.

-p

> Same as --create-missing-dirs

-P*project*

> Use project file *project*. Only one such switch can be used.

-q

> Quiet. When this flag is not set, the commands carried out by *gnatmake* are displayed.

-s

> Recompile if compiler switches have changed since last compilation. All compiler switches but -I and -o are taken into account in the following way: orders between different 'first letter' switches are ignored, but orders between same switches are taken into account. For example, -O -O2 is different than -O2 -O, but -g -O is equivalent to -O -g.
>
> This switch is recommended when Integrated Preprocessing is used.

-u

> Unique. Recompile at most the main files. It implies -c. Combined with -f, it is equivalent to calling the compiler directly. Note that using -u with a project file and no main has a special meaning.

-U

> When used without a project file or with one or several mains on the command line, is equivalent to -u. When used with a project file and no main on the command line, all sources of all project files are checked and compiled if not up to date, and libraries are rebuilt, if necessary.

-v

> Verbose. Display the reason for all recompilations *gnatmake* decides are necessary, with the highest verbosity level.

-vl

        Verbosity level Low. Display fewer lines than in verbosity Medium.

-vm

        Verbosity level Medium. Potentially display fewer lines than in verbosity High.

-vh

        Verbosity level High. Equivalent to -v.

-vP*x*

        Indicate the verbosity of the parsing of GNAT project files. See [Switches Related to Project Files], page 333.

-x

        Indicate that sources that are not part of any Project File may be compiled. Normally, when using Project Files, only sources that are part of a Project File may be compile. When this switch is used, a source outside of all Project Files may be compiled. The ALI file and the object file will be put in the object directory of the main Project. The compilation switches used will only be those specified on the command line. Even when -*x* is used, mains specified on the command line need to be sources of a project file.

-X*name*=*value*

        Indicate that external variable *name* has the value *value*. The Project Manager will use this value for occurrences of *external(name)* when parsing the project file. [Switches Related to Project Files], page 333.

-z

        No main subprogram. Bind and link the program even if the unit name given on the command line is a package name. The resulting executable will execute the elaboration routines of the package and its closure, then the finalization routines.

GCC switches

Any uppercase or multi-character switch that is not a *gnatmake* switch is passed to *gcc* (e.g., -*O*, -*gnato*, etc.)

Source and library search path switches

-aI*dir*

        When looking for source files also look in directory *dir*. The order in which source files search is undertaken is described in [Search Paths and the Run-Time Library (RTL)], page 89.

-aL*dir*

        Consider *dir* as being an externally provided Ada library. Instructs *gnatmake* to skip compilation units whose .ALI files have been located in directory *dir*. This allows you to have missing bodies for the units in *dir* and to ignore out of date bodies for the same units. You still need to specify the location of the specs for these units by using the switches -aI*dir* or -I*dir*. Note: this switch is provided for compatibility with previous versions of *gnatmake*. The easier method of causing standard libraries to be excluded from consideration is to write-protect the corresponding ALI files.

-aO*dir*

When searching for library and object files, look in directory *dir*. The order in which library files are searched is described in [Search Paths for gnatbind], page 161.

-A*dir*

Equivalent to -aL*dir* -aI*dir*.

-I*dir*

Equivalent to -aO*dir* -aI*dir*.

-I-

Do not look for source files in the directory containing the source file named in the command line. Do not look for ALI or object files in the directory where *gnatmake* was invoked.

-L*dir*

Add directory *dir* to the list of directories in which the linker will search for libraries. This is equivalent to -largs -L*dir*. Furthermore, under Windows, the sources pointed to by the libraries path set in the registry are not searched for.

-nostdinc

Do not look for source files in the system default directory.

-nostdlib

Do not look for library files in the system default directory.

--RTS=*rts-path*

Specifies the default location of the runtime library. GNAT looks for the runtime in the following directories, and stops as soon as a valid runtime is found (adainclude or ada_source_path, and adalib or ada_object_path present):

* *<current directory>/$rts_path*
* *<default-search-dir>/$rts_path*
* *<default-search-dir>/rts-$rts_path*
* The selected path is handled like a normal RTS path.

4.1.3 Mode Switches for *gnatmake*

The mode switches (referred to as *mode_switches*) allow the inclusion of switches that are to be passed to the compiler itself, the binder or the linker. The effect of a mode switch is to cause all subsequent switches up to the end of the switch list, or up to the next mode switch, to be interpreted as switches to be passed on to the designated component of GNAT.

-cargs *switches*

Compiler switches. Here *switches* is a list of switches that are valid switches for *gcc*. They will be passed on to all compile steps performed by *gnatmake*.

`-bargs` *switches*

> Binder switches. Here *switches* is a list of switches that are valid switches for *gnatbind*. They will be passed on to all bind steps performed by *gnatmake*.

`-largs` *switches*

> Linker switches. Here *switches* is a list of switches that are valid switches for *gnatlink*. They will be passed on to all link steps performed by *gnatmake*.

`-margs` *switches*

> Make switches. The switches are directly interpreted by *gnatmake*, regardless of any previous occurrence of *-cargs*, *-bargs* or *-largs*.

4.1.4 Notes on the Command Line

This section contains some additional useful notes on the operation of the *gnatmake* command.

* If *gnatmake* finds no ALI files, it recompiles the main program and all other units required by the main program. This means that *gnatmake* can be used for the initial compile, as well as during subsequent steps of the development cycle.

* If you enter `gnatmake foo.adb`, where `foo` is a subunit or body of a generic unit, *gnatmake* recompiles `foo.adb` (because it finds no ALI) and stops, issuing a warning.

* In *gnatmake* the switch *-I* is used to specify both source and library file paths. Use *-aI* instead if you just want to specify source paths only and *-aO* if you want to specify library paths only.

* *gnatmake* will ignore any files whose ALI file is write-protected. This may conveniently be used to exclude standard libraries from consideration and in particular it means that the use of the *-f* switch will not recompile these files unless *-a* is also specified.

* *gnatmake* has been designed to make the use of Ada libraries particularly convenient. Assume you have an Ada library organized as follows: *obj-dir* contains the objects and ALI files for of your Ada compilation units, whereas *include-dir* contains the specs of these units, but no bodies. Then to compile a unit stored in *main.adb*, which uses this Ada library you would just type:

```
$ gnatmake -aI'include-dir'  -aL'obj-dir'  main
```

* Using *gnatmake* along with the *-m (minimal recompilation)* switch provides a mechanism for avoiding unnecessary recompilations. Using this switch, you can update the comments/format of your source files without having to recompile everything. Note, however, that adding or deleting lines in a source files may render its debugging info obsolete. If the file in question is a spec, the impact is rather limited, as that debugging info will only be useful during the elaboration phase of your program. For bodies the impact can be more significant. In all events, your debugger will warn you if a source file is more recent than the corresponding object, and alert you to the fact that the debugging information may be out of date.

4.1.5 How *gnatmake* Works

Generally *gnatmake* automatically performs all necessary recompilations and you don't need to worry about how it works. However, it may be useful to have some basic understanding of the *gnatmake* approach and in particular to understand how it uses the results of previous compilations without incorrectly depending on them.

First a definition: an object file is considered *up to date* if the corresponding ALI file exists and if all the source files listed in the dependency section of this ALI file have time stamps matching those in the ALI file. This means that neither the source file itself nor any files that it depends on have been modified, and hence there is no need to recompile this file.

gnatmake works by first checking if the specified main unit is up to date. If so, no compilations are required for the main unit. If not, *gnatmake* compiles the main program to build a new ALI file that reflects the latest sources. Then the ALI file of the main unit is examined to find all the source files on which the main program depends, and *gnatmake* recursively applies the above procedure on all these files.

This process ensures that *gnatmake* only trusts the dependencies in an existing ALI file if they are known to be correct. Otherwise it always recompiles to determine a new, guaranteed accurate set of dependencies. As a result the program is compiled 'upside down' from what may be more familiar as the required order of compilation in some other Ada systems. In particular, clients are compiled before the units on which they depend. The ability of GNAT to compile in any order is critical in allowing an order of compilation to be chosen that guarantees that *gnatmake* will recompute a correct set of new dependencies if necessary.

When invoking *gnatmake* with several *file_names*, if a unit is imported by several of the executables, it will be recompiled at most once.

Note: when using non-standard naming conventions ([Using Other File Names], page 14), changing through a configuration pragmas file the version of a source and invoking *gnatmake* to recompile may have no effect, if the previous version of the source is still accessible by *gnatmake*. It may be necessary to use the switch -f.

4.1.6 Examples of *gnatmake* Usage

gnatmake hello.adb

> Compile all files necessary to bind and link the main program `hello.adb` (containing unit *Hello*) and bind and link the resulting object files to generate an executable file `hello`.

gnatmake main1 main2 main3

> Compile all files necessary to bind and link the main programs `main1.adb` (containing unit *Main1*), `main2.adb` (containing unit *Main2*) and `main3.adb` (containing unit *Main3*) and bind and link the resulting object files to generate three executable files `main1`, `main2` and `main3`.

gnatmake -q Main_Unit -cargs -O2 -bargs -l

> Compile all files necessary to bind and link the main program unit *Main_Unit* (from file `main_unit.adb`). All compilations will be done with optimization level 2 and the order of elaboration will be listed by the binder. *gnatmake* will operate in quiet mode, not displaying commands it is executing.

4.2 Compiling with *gcc*

This section discusses how to compile Ada programs using the *gcc* command. It also describes the set of switches that can be used to control the behavior of the compiler.

4.2.1 Compiling Programs

The first step in creating an executable program is to compile the units of the program
using the *gcc* command. You must compile the following files:

*   the body file (`.adb`) for a library level subprogram or generic subprogram
*   the spec file (`.ads`) for a library level package or generic package that has no body
*   the body file (`.adb`) for a library level package or generic package that has a body

You need *not* compile the following files

*   the spec of a library unit which has a body
*   subunits

because they are compiled as part of compiling related units. GNAT package specs when
the corresponding body is compiled, and subunits when the parent is compiled.

If you attempt to compile any of these files, you will get one of the following error messages
(where *fff* is the name of the file you compiled):

```
cannot generate code for file 'fff' (package spec)
to check package spec, use -gnatc

cannot generate code for file 'fff' (missing subunits)
to check parent unit, use -gnatc

cannot generate code for file 'fff' (subprogram spec)
to check subprogram spec, use -gnatc

cannot generate code for file 'fff' (subunit)
to check subunit, use -gnatc
```

As indicated by the above error messages, if you want to submit one of these files to the
compiler to check for correct semantics without generating code, then use the *-gnatc* switch.

The basic command for compiling a file containing an Ada unit is:

```
$ gcc -c [switches] <file name>
```

where *file name* is the name of the Ada file (usually having an extension `.ads` for a spec or
`.adb` for a body). You specify the `-c` switch to tell *gcc* to compile, but not link, the file.
The result of a successful compilation is an object file, which has the same name as the
source file but an extension of `.o` and an Ada Library Information (ALI) file, which also
has the same name as the source file, but with `.ali` as the extension. GNAT creates these
two output files in the current directory, but you may specify a source file in any directory
using an absolute or relative path specification containing the directory information.

gcc is actually a driver program that looks at the extensions of the file arguments and
loads the appropriate compiler. For example, the GNU C compiler is `cc1`, and the Ada
compiler is `gnat1`. These programs are in directories known to the driver program (in some
configurations via environment variables you set), but need not be in your path. The *gcc*
driver also calls the assembler and any other utilities needed to complete the generation of
the required object files.

It is possible to supply several file names on the same *gcc* command. This causes *gcc* to
call the appropriate compiler for each file. For example, the following command lists two
separate files to be compiled:

```
$ gcc -c x.adb y.adb
```

calls *gnat1* (the Ada compiler) twice to compile `x.adb` and `y.adb`. The compiler generates two object files `x.o` and `y.o` and the two ALI files `x.ali` and `y.ali`.

Any switches apply to all the files listed, see [Compiler Switches], page 90 for a list of available *gcc* switches.

4.2.2 Search Paths and the Run-Time Library (RTL)

With the GNAT source-based library system, the compiler must be able to find source files for units that are needed by the unit being compiled. Search paths are used to guide this process.

The compiler compiles one source file whose name must be given explicitly on the command line. In other words, no searching is done for this file. To find all other source files that are needed (the most common being the specs of units), the compiler examines the following directories, in the following order:

* The directory containing the source file of the main unit being compiled (the file name on the command line).

* Each directory named by an *-I* switch given on the *gcc* command line, in the order given.

* Each of the directories listed in the text file whose name is given by the `ADA_PRJ_INCLUDE_FILE` environment variable. `ADA_PRJ_INCLUDE_FILE` is normally set by gnat-make or by the gnat driver when project files are used. It should not normally be set by other means.

* Each of the directories listed in the value of the `ADA_INCLUDE_PATH` environment variable. Construct this value exactly as the `PATH` environment variable: a list of directory names separated by colons (semicolons when working with the NT version).

* The content of the `ada_source_path` file which is part of the GNAT installation tree and is used to store standard libraries such as the GNAT Run Time Library (RTL) source files. [Installing a library], page 35

Specifying the switch *-I-* inhibits the use of the directory containing the source file named in the command line. You can still have this directory on your search path, but in this case it must be explicitly requested with a *-I* switch.

Specifying the switch *-nostdinc* inhibits the search of the default location for the GNAT Run Time Library (RTL) source files.

The compiler outputs its object files and ALI files in the current working directory. Caution: The object file can be redirected with the *-o* switch; however, *gcc* and *gnat1* have not been coordinated on this so the `ALI` file will not go to the right place. Therefore, you should avoid using the *-o* switch.

The packages *Ada*, *System*, and *Interfaces* and their children make up the GNAT RTL, together with the simple *System.IO* package used in the "*Hello World*" example. The sources for these units are needed by the compiler and are kept together in one directory. Not all of the bodies are needed, but all of the sources are kept together anyway. In a normal installation, you need not specify these directory names when compiling or binding. Either the environment variables or the built-in defaults cause these files to be found.

In addition to the language-defined hierarchies (*System*, *Ada* and *Interfaces*), the GNAT distribution provides a fourth hierarchy, consisting of child units of *GNAT*. This is a collection of generally useful types, subprograms, etc. See the *GNAT_Reference_Manual* for further details.

Besides simplifying access to the RTL, a major use of search paths is in compiling sources from multiple directories. This can make development environments much more flexible.

4.2.3 Order of Compilation Issues

If, in our earlier example, there was a spec for the *hello* procedure, it would be contained in the file `hello.ads`; yet this file would not have to be explicitly compiled. This is the result of the model we chose to implement library management. Some of the consequences of this model are as follows:

* There is no point in compiling specs (except for package specs with no bodies) because these are compiled as needed by clients. If you attempt a useless compilation, you will receive an error message. It is also useless to compile subunits because they are compiled as needed by the parent.

* There are no order of compilation requirements: performing a compilation never obsoletes anything. The only way you can obsolete something and require recompilations is to modify one of the source files on which it depends.

* There is no library as such, apart from the ALI files ([The Ada Library Information Files], page 31, for information on the format of these files). For now we find it convenient to create separate ALI files, but eventually the information therein may be incorporated into the object file directly.

* When you compile a unit, the source files for the specs of all units that it *with*s, all its subunits, and the bodies of any generics it instantiates must be available (reachable by the search-paths mechanism described above), or you will receive a fatal error message.

4.2.4 Examples

The following are some typical Ada compilation command line examples:

```
$ gcc -c xyz.adb
```

Compile body in file `xyz.adb` with all default options.

```
$ gcc -c -O2 -gnata xyz-def.adb
```

Compile the child unit package in file `xyz-def.adb` with extensive optimizations, and pragma *Assert/Debug* statements enabled.

```
$ gcc -c -gnatc abc-def.adb
```

Compile the subunit in file `abc-def.adb` in semantic-checking-only mode.

4.3 Compiler Switches

The *gcc* command accepts switches that control the compilation process. These switches are fully described in this section: first an alphabetical listing of all switches with a brief description, and then functionally grouped sets of switches with more detailed information.

More switches exist for GCC than those documented here, especially for specific targets. However, their use is not recommended as they may change code generation in ways that are incompatible with the Ada run-time library, or can cause inconsistencies between compilation units.

4.3.1 Alphabetical List of All Switches

`-b target`

> Compile your program to run on *target*, which is the name of a system configuration. You must have a GNAT cross-compiler built if *target* is not the same as your host system.

`-Bdir`

> Load compiler executables (for example, *gnat1*, the Ada compiler) from *dir* instead of the default location. Only use this switch when multiple versions of the GNAT compiler are available. See the "Options for Directory Search" section in the *Using the GNU Compiler Collection (GCC)* manual for further details. You would normally use the *-b* or *-V* switch instead.

`-c`

> Compile. Always use this switch when compiling Ada programs.
>
> Note: for some other languages when using *gcc*, notably in the case of C and C++, it is possible to use use *gcc* without a *-c* switch to compile and link in one step. In the case of GNAT, you cannot use this approach, because the binder must be run and *gcc* cannot be used to run the GNAT binder.

`-fcallgraph-info[=su,da]`

> Makes the compiler output callgraph information for the program, on a per-file basis. The information is generated in the VCG format. It can be decorated with additional, per-node and/or per-edge information, if a list of comma-separated markers is additionally specified. When the *su* marker is specified, the callgraph is decorated with stack usage information; it is equivalent to -*fstack-usage*. When the *da* marker is specified, the callgraph is decorated with information about dynamically allocated objects.

`-fdump-scos`

> Generates SCO (Source Coverage Obligation) information in the ALI file. This information is used by advanced coverage tools. See unit SCOs in the compiler sources for details in files `scos.ads` and `scos.adb`.

`-fdump-xref`

> Generates cross reference information in GLI files for C and C++ sources. The GLI files have the same syntax as the ALI files for Ada, and can be used for source navigation in IDEs and on the command line using e.g. gnatxref and the *–ext=gli* switch.

`-flto[=n]`

> Enables Link Time Optimization. This switch must be used in conjunction with the traditional -*Ox* switches and instructs the compiler to defer most optimizations until the link stage. The advantage of this approach is that the compiler can do a whole-program analysis and choose the best interprocedural optimization strategy based on a complete view of the program, instead

of a fragmentary view with the usual approach. This can also speed up the compilation of big programs and reduce the size of the executable, compared with a traditional per-unit compilation with inlining across modules enabled by the *-gnatn* switch. The drawback of this approach is that it may require more memory and that the debugging information generated by -g with it might be hardly usable. The switch, as well as the accompanying *-Ox* switches, must be specified both for the compilation and the link phases. If the *n* parameter is specified, the optimization and final code generation at link time are executed using *n* parallel jobs by means of an installed *make* program.

`-fno-inline`
Suppresses all inlining, unless requested with pragma *Inline_Always*. The effect is enforced regardless of other optimization or inlining switches. Note that inlining can also be suppressed on a finer-grained basis with pragma *No_Inline*.

`-fno-inline-functions`
Suppresses automatic inlining of subprograms, which is enabled if *-O3* is used.

`-fno-inline-small-functions`
Suppresses automatic inlining of small subprograms, which is enabled if *-O2* is used.

`-fno-inline-functions-called-once`
Suppresses inlining of subprograms local to the unit and called once from within it, which is enabled if *-O1* is used.

`-fno-ivopts`
Suppresses high-level loop induction variable optimizations, which are enabled if *-O1* is used. These optimizations are generally profitable but, for some specific cases of loops with numerous uses of the iteration variable that follow a common pattern, they may end up destroying the regularity that could be exploited at a lower level and thus producing inferior code.

`-fno-strict-aliasing`
Causes the compiler to avoid assumptions regarding non-aliasing of objects of different types. See [Optimization and Strict Aliasing], page 215 for details.

`-fno-strict-overflow`
Causes the compiler to avoid assumptions regarding the rules of signed integer overflow. These rules specify that signed integer overflow will result in a Constraint_Error exception at run time and are enforced in default mode by the compiler, so this switch should not be necessary in normal operating mode. It might be useful in conjunction with *-gnato0* for very peculiar cases of low-level programming.

`-fstack-check`
Activates stack checking. See [Stack Overflow Checking], page 230 for details.

`-fstack-usage`
Makes the compiler output stack usage information for the program, on a per-subprogram basis. See [Static Stack Usage Analysis], page 230 for details.

-g

> Generate debugging information. This information is stored in the object file and copied from there to the final executable file by the linker, where it can be read by the debugger. You must use the *-g* switch if you plan on using the debugger.

-gnat05

> Allow full Ada 2005 features.

-gnat12

> Allow full Ada 2012 features.

-gnat2005

> Allow full Ada 2005 features (same as *-gnat05*)

-gnat2012

> Allow full Ada 2012 features (same as *-gnat12*)

-gnat83

> Enforce Ada 83 restrictions.

-gnat95

> Enforce Ada 95 restrictions.
>
> Note: for compatibility with some Ada 95 compilers which support only the *overriding* keyword of Ada 2005, the *-gnatd.D* switch can be used along with *-gnat95* to achieve a similar effect with GNAT.
>
> *-gnatd.D* instructs GNAT to consider *overriding* as a keyword and handle its associated semantic checks, even in Ada 95 mode.

-gnata

> Assertions enabled. *Pragma Assert* and *pragma Debug* to be activated. Note that these pragmas can also be controlled using the configuration pragmas *Assertion_Policy* and *Debug_Policy*. It also activates pragmas *Check*, *Precondition*, and *Postcondition*. Note that these pragmas can also be controlled using the configuration pragma *Check_Policy*. In Ada 2012, it also activates all assertions defined in the RM as aspects: preconditions, postconditions, type invariants and (sub)type predicates. In all Ada modes, corresponding pragmas for type invariants and (sub)type predicates are also activated. The default is that all these assertions are disabled, and have no effect, other than being checked for syntactic validity, and in the case of subtype predicates, constructions such as membership tests still test predicates even if assertions are turned off.

-gnatA

> Avoid processing `gnat.adc`. If a `gnat.adc` file is present, it will be ignored.

-gnatb

> Generate brief messages to `stderr` even if verbose mode set.

-gnatB

> Assume no invalid (bad) values except for 'Valid attribute use ([Validity Checking], page 126).

-gnatc

> Check syntax and semantics only (no code generation attempted). When the compiler is invoked by *gnatmake*, if the switch *-gnatc* is only given to the compiler (after *-cargs* or in package Compiler of the project file, *gnatmake* will fail because it will not find the object file after compilation. If *gnatmake* is called with *-gnatc* as a builder switch (before *-cargs* or in package Builder of the project file) then *gnatmake* will not fail because it will not look for the object files after compilation, and it will not try to build and link. This switch may not be given if a previous *-gnatR* switch has been given, since *-gnatR* requires that the code generator be called to complete determination of representation information.

-gnatC

> Generate CodePeer intermediate format (no code generation attempted). This switch will generate an intermediate representation suitable for use by CodePeer (`.scil` files). This switch is not compatible with code generation (it will, among other things, disable some switches such as -gnatn, and enable others such as -gnata).

-gnatd

> Specify debug options for the compiler. The string of characters after the *-gnatd* specify the specific debug options. The possible characters are 0-9, a-z, A-Z, optionally preceded by a dot. See compiler source file `debug.adb` for details of the implemented debug options. Certain debug options are relevant to applications programmers, and these are documented at appropriate points in this users guide.

-gnatD

> Create expanded source files for source level debugging. This switch also suppress generation of cross-reference information (see *-gnatx*). Note that this switch is not allowed if a previous -gnatR switch has been given, since these two switches are not compatible.

-gnateA

> Check that the actual parameters of a subprogram call are not aliases of one another. To qualify as aliasing, the actuals must denote objects of a composite type, their memory locations must be identical or overlapping, and at least one of the corresponding formal parameters must be of mode OUT or IN OUT.

```
    type Rec_Typ is record
       Data : Integer := 0;
    end record;

    function Self (Val : Rec_Typ) return Rec_Typ is
    begin
```

```
            return Val;
         end Self;

         procedure Detect_Aliasing (Val_1 : in out Rec_Typ; Val_2 : Rec_Typ)
         begin
            null;
         end Detect_Aliasing;

         Obj : Rec_Typ;

         Detect_Aliasing (Obj, Obj);
         Detect_Aliasing (Obj, Self (Obj));
```

In the example above, the first call to *Detect_Aliasing* fails with a *Program_Error* at runtime because the actuals for *Val_1* and *Val_2* denote the same object. The second call executes without raising an exception because *Self(Obj)* produces an anonymous object which does not share the memory location of *Obj*.

`-gnatec=path`

Specify a configuration pragma file (the equal sign is optional) ([The Configuration Pragmas Files], page 29).

`-gnateC`

Generate CodePeer messages in a compiler-like format. This switch is only effective if *-gnatcC* is also specified and requires an installation of CodePeer.

`-gnated`

Disable atomic synchronization

`-gnateDsymbol[=value]`

Defines a symbol, associated with *value*, for preprocessing. ([Integrated Preprocessing], page 50).

`-gnateE`

Generate extra information in exception messages. In particular, display extra column information and the value and range associated with index and range check failures, and extra column information for access checks. In cases where the compiler is able to determine at compile time that a check will fail, it gives a warning, and the extra information is not produced at run time.

`-gnatef`

Display full source path name in brief error messages.

`-gnateF`

Check for overflow on all floating-point operations, including those for unconstrained predefined types. See description of pragma *Check_Float_Overflow* in GNAT RM.

`-gnateg -gnatceg`

The -gnatc switch must always be specified before this switch, e.g. -gnatceg. Generate a C header from the Ada input file. See [Generating C Headers for Ada Specifications], page 73 for more information.

`-gnateG`

> Save result of preprocessing in a text file.

`-gnateinnn`

> Set maximum number of instantiations during compilation of a single unit to nnn. This may be useful in increasing the default maximum of 8000 for the rare case when a single unit legitimately exceeds this limit.

`-gnateInnn`

> Indicates that the source is a multi-unit source and that the index of the unit to compile is nnn. nnn needs to be a positive number and need to be a valid index in the multi-unit source.

`-gnatel`

> This switch can be used with the static elaboration model to issue info messages showing where implicit pragma Elaborate and pragma Elaborate_All are generated. This is useful in diagnosing elaboration circularities caused by these implicit pragmas when using the static elaboration model. See See the section in this guide on elaboration checking for further details. These messages are not generated by default, and are intended only for temporary use when debugging circularity problems.

`-gnateL`

> This switch turns off the info messages about implicit elaboration pragmas.

`-gnatem=path`

> Specify a mapping file (the equal sign is optional) ([Units to Sources Mapping Files], page 149).

`-gnatep=file`

> Specify a preprocessing data file (the equal sign is optional) ([Integrated Preprocessing], page 50).

`-gnateP`

> Turn categorization dependency errors into warnings. Ada requires that units that WITH one another have compatible categories, for example a Pure unit cannot WITH a Preelaborate unit. If this switch is used, these errors become warnings (which can be ignored, or suppressed in the usual manner). This can be useful in some specialized circumstances such as the temporary use of special test software.

`-gnateS`

> Synonym of -fdump-scos, kept for backwards compatibility.

`-gnatet=path`

> Generate target dependent information. The format of the output file is described in the section about switch -gnateT.

`-gnateT=path`

> Read target dependent information, such as endianness or sizes and alignments of base type. If this switch is passed, the default target dependent information of the compiler is replaced by the one read from the input file. This is used by tools other than the compiler, e.g. to do semantic analysis of programs that will run on some other target than the machine on which the tool is run.
>
> The following target dependent values should be defined, where *Nat* denotes a natural integer value, *Pos* denotes a positive integer value, and fields marked with a question mark are boolean fields, where a value of 0 is False, and a value of 1 is True:

```
Bits_BE                    : Nat; -- Bits stored big-endian?
Bits_Per_Unit              : Pos; -- Bits in a storage unit
Bits_Per_Word              : Pos; -- Bits in a word
Bytes_BE                   : Nat; -- Bytes stored big-endian?
Char_Size                  : Pos; -- Standard.Character'Size
Double_Float_Alignment     : Nat; -- Alignment of double float
Double_Scalar_Alignment    : Nat; -- Alignment of double length scala
Double_Size                : Pos; -- Standard.Long_Float'Size
Float_Size                 : Pos; -- Standard.Float'Size
Float_Words_BE             : Nat; -- Float words stored big-endian?
Int_Size                   : Pos; -- Standard.Integer'Size
Long_Double_Size           : Pos; -- Standard.Long_Long_Float'Size
Long_Long_Size             : Pos; -- Standard.Long_Long_Integer'Size
Long_Size                  : Pos; -- Standard.Long_Integer'Size
Maximum_Alignment          : Pos; -- Maximum permitted alignment
Max_Unaligned_Field        : Pos; -- Maximum size for unaligned bit f
Pointer_Size               : Pos; -- System.Address'Size
Short_Enums                : Nat; -- Short foreign convention enums?
Short_Size                 : Pos; -- Standard.Short_Integer'Size
Strict_Alignment           : Nat; -- Strict alignment?
System_Allocator_Alignment : Nat; -- Alignment for malloc calls
Wchar_T_Size               : Pos; -- Interfaces.C.wchar_t'Size
Words_BE                   : Nat; -- Words stored big-endian?
```

> The format of the input file is as follows. First come the values of the variables defined above, with one line per value:

```
name  value
```

> where *name* is the name of the parameter, spelled out in full, and cased as in the above list, and *value* is an unsigned decimal integer. Two or more blanks separates the name from the value.
>
> All the variables must be present, in alphabetical order (i.e. the same order as the list above).
>
> Then there is a blank line to separate the two parts of the file. Then come the lines showing the floating-point types to be registered, with one line per registered mode:

```
name  digs float_rep size alignment
```

where *name* is the string name of the type (which can have single spaces embedded in the name (e.g. long double), *digs* is the number of digits for the floating-point type, *float_rep* is the float representation (I/V/A for IEEE-754-Binary, Vax_Native, AAMP), *size* is the size in bits, *alignment* is the alignment in bits. The name is followed by at least two blanks, fields are separated by at least one blank, and a LF character immediately follows the alignment field.

Here is an example of a target parameterization file:

```
Bits_BE                         0
Bits_Per_Unit                   8
Bits_Per_Word                  64
Bytes_BE                        0
Char_Size                       8
Double_Float_Alignment          0
Double_Scalar_Alignment         0
Double_Size                    64
Float_Size                     32
Float_Words_BE                  0
Int_Size                       64
Long_Double_Size              128
Long_Long_Size                 64
Long_Size                      64
Maximum_Alignment              16
Max_Unaligned_Field            64
Pointer_Size                   64
Short_Size                     16
Strict_Alignment                0
System_Allocator_Alignment     16
Wchar_T_Size                   32
Words_BE                        0

float           15  I   64  64
double          15  I   64  64
long double     18  I   80 128
TF              33  I  128 128
```

`-gnateu`

Ignore unrecognized validity, warning, and style switches that appear after this switch is given. This may be useful when compiling sources developed on a later version of the compiler with an earlier version. Of course the earlier version must support this switch.

`-gnateV`

Check that all actual parameters of a subprogram call are valid according to the rules of validity checking ([Validity Checking], page 126).

`-gnateY`

Ignore all STYLE_CHECKS pragmas. Full legality checks are still carried out, but the pragmas have no effect on what style checks are active. This allows all style checking options to be controlled from the command line.

`-gnatE`

Full dynamic elaboration checks.

`-gnatf`

Full errors. Multiple errors per line, all undefined references, do not attempt to suppress cascaded errors.

`-gnatF`

Externals names are folded to all uppercase.

`-gnatg`

Internal GNAT implementation mode. This should not be used for applications programs, it is intended only for use by the compiler and its run-time library. For documentation, see the GNAT sources. Note that *-gnatg* implies *-gnatw.ge* and *-gnatyg* so that all standard warnings and all standard style options are turned on. All warnings and style messages are treated as errors.

`-gnatG=nn`

List generated expanded code in source form.

`-gnath`

Output usage information. The output is written to `stdout`.

`-gnatic`

Identifier character set ($c = 1/2/3/4/8/9/p/f/n/w$). For details of the possible selections for c, see [Character Set Control], page 141.

`-gnatI`

Ignore representation clauses. When this switch is used, representation clauses are treated as comments. This is useful when initially porting code where you want to ignore rep clause problems, and also for compiling foreign code (particularly for use with ASIS). The representation clauses that are ignored are: enumeration_representation_clause, record_representation_clause, and attribute_definition_clause for the following attributes: Address, Alignment, Bit_Order, Component_Size, Machine_Radix, Object_Size, Size, Small, Stream_Size, and Value_Size. Note that this option should be used only for compiling – the code is likely to malfunction at run time.

Note that when *-gnatct* is used to generate trees for input into *ASIS* tools, these representation clauses are removed from the tree and ignored. This means that the tool will not see them.

`-gnatjnn`

Reformat error messages to fit on *nn* character lines

`-gnatk=n`

Limit file names to *n* (1-999) characters (k = krunch).

-gnatl

> Output full source listing with embedded error messages.

-gnatL

> Used in conjunction with -gnatG or -gnatD to intersperse original source lines (as comment lines with line numbers) in the expanded source output.

-gnatm=n

> Limit number of detected error or warning messages to n where n is in the range 1..999999. The default setting if no switch is given is 9999. If the number of warnings reaches this limit, then a message is output and further warnings are suppressed, but the compilation is continued. If the number of error messages reaches this limit, then a message is output and the compilation is abandoned. The equal sign here is optional. A value of zero means that no limit applies.

-gnatn[12]

> Activate inlining for subprograms for which pragma *Inline* is specified. This inlining is performed by the GCC back-end. An optional digit sets the inlining level: 1 for moderate inlining across modules or 2 for full inlining across modules. If no inlining level is specified, the compiler will pick it based on the optimization level.

-gnatN

> Activate front end inlining for subprograms for which pragma *Inline* is specified. This inlining is performed by the front end and will be visible in the *-gnatG* output.

> When using a gcc-based back end (in practice this means using any version of GNAT other than the JGNAT, .NET or GNAAMP versions), then the use of *-gnatN* is deprecated, and the use of *-gnatn* is preferred. Historically front end inlining was more extensive than the gcc back end inlining, but that is no longer the case.

-gnato0

> Suppresses overflow checking. This causes the behavior of the compiler to match the default for older versions where overflow checking was suppressed by default. This is equivalent to having *pragma Suppress (Overflow_Mode)* in a configuration pragma file.

-gnato??

> Set default mode for handling generation of code to avoid intermediate arithmetic overflow. Here *??* is two digits, a single digit, or nothing. Each digit is one of the digits *1* through *3*:

> | Digit | Interpretation |
> |---|---|
> | *1* | All intermediate overflows checked against base type (*STRICT*) |
> | *2* | Minimize intermediate overflows (*MINIMIZED*) |

       3   Eliminate intermediate overflows (*ELIMINATED*)

If only one digit appears, then it applies to all cases; if two digits are given, then the first applies outside assertions, pre/postconditions, and type invariants, and the second applies within assertions, pre/postconditions, and type invariants.

If no digits follow the *-gnato*, then it is equivalent to *-gnato11*, causing all intermediate overflows to be handled in strict mode.

This switch also causes arithmetic overflow checking to be performed (as though *pragma Unsuppress (Overflow_Mode)* had been specified).

The default if no option *-gnato* is given is that overflow handling is in *STRICT* mode (computations done using the base type), and that overflow checking is enabled.

Note that division by zero is a separate check that is not controlled by this switch (divide-by-zero checking is on by default).

See also [Specifying the Desired Mode], page 225.

-gnatp

Suppress all checks. See [Run-Time Checks], page 137 for details. This switch has no effect if cancelled by a subsequent *-gnat-p* switch.

-gnat-p

Cancel effect of previous *-gnatp* switch.

-gnatP

Enable polling. This is required on some systems (notably Windows NT) to obtain asynchronous abort and asynchronous transfer of control capability. See *Pragma_Polling* in the *GNAT_Reference_Manual* for full details.

-gnatq

Don't quit. Try semantics, even if parse errors.

-gnatQ

Don't quit. Generate `ALI` and tree files even if illegalities. Note that code generation is still suppressed in the presence of any errors, so even with *-gnatQ* no object file is generated.

-gnatr

Treat pragma Restrictions as Restriction_Warnings.

-gnatR[0/1/2/3[s]]

Output representation information for declared types and objects. Note that this switch is not allowed if a previous *-gnatD* switch has been given, since these two switches are not compatible.

-gnatRm[s]

Output convention and parameter passing mechanisms for all subprograms.

-gnats

Syntax check only.

`-gnatS`

> Print package Standard.

`-gnatt`

> Generate tree output file.

`-gnatTnnn`

> All compiler tables start at *nnn* times usual starting size.

`-gnatu`

> List units for this compilation.

`-gnatU`

> Tag all error messages with the unique string 'error:'

`-gnatv`

> Verbose mode. Full error output with source lines to `stdout`.

`-gnatV`

> Control level of validity checking ([Validity Checking], page 126).

`-gnatwxxx`

> Warning mode where *xxx* is a string of option letters that denotes the exact warnings that are enabled or disabled ([Warning Message Control], page 108).

`-gnatWe`

> Wide character encoding method (e=n/h/u/s/e/8).

`-gnatx`

> Suppress generation of cross-reference information.

`-gnatX`

> Enable GNAT implementation extensions and latest Ada version.

`-gnaty`

> Enable built-in style checks ([Style Checking], page 130).

`-gnatzm`

> Distribution stub generation and compilation (*m*=r/c for receiver/caller stubs).

`-Idir`

> Direct GNAT to search the *dir* directory for source files needed by the current compilation (see [Search Paths and the Run-Time Library (RTL)], page 89).

`-I-`

> Except for the source file named in the command line, do not look for source files in the directory containing the source file named in the command line (see [Search Paths and the Run-Time Library (RTL)], page 89).

`-o file`

> This switch is used in *gcc* to redirect the generated object file and its associated ALI file. Beware of this switch with GNAT, because it may cause the object file and ALI file to have different names which in turn may confuse the binder and the linker.

`-nostdinc`

Inhibit the search of the default location for the GNAT Run Time Library (RTL) source files.

`-nostdlib`

Inhibit the search of the default location for the GNAT Run Time Library (RTL) ALI files.

`-O[n]`

n controls the optimization level:

n	Effect
0	No optimization, the default setting if no *-O* appears
1	Normal optimization, the default if you specify *-O* without an operand. A compromise between code quality and compilation time.
2	Extensive optimization, may improve execution time, possibly at the cost o stantially increased compilation time.
3	Same as *-O2*, and also includes inline expansion for small subprograms in the unit.
s	Optimize space usage

See also [Optimization Levels], page 208.

`-pass-exit-codes`

Catch exit codes from the compiler and use the most meaningful as exit status.

`--RTS=rts-path`

Specifies the default location of the runtime library. Same meaning as the equivalent *gnatmake* flag ([Switches for gnatmake], page 78).

`-S`

Used in place of *-c* to cause the assembler source file to be generated, using `.s` as the extension, instead of the object file. This may be useful if you need to examine the generated assembly code.

`-fverbose-asm`

Used in conjunction with *-S* to cause the generated assembly code file to be annotated with variable names, making it significantly easier to follow.

`-v`

Show commands generated by the *gcc* driver. Normally used only for debugging purposes or if you need to be sure what version of the compiler you are executing.

`-V ver`

Execute *ver* version of the compiler. This is the *gcc* version, not the GNAT version.

-w

> Turn off warnings generated by the back end of the compiler. Use of this switch also causes the default for front end warnings to be set to suppress (as though *-gnatws* had appeared at the start of the options).

You may combine a sequence of GNAT switches into a single switch. For example, the combined switch

> -gnatofi3

is equivalent to specifying the following sequence of switches:

> -gnato -gnatf -gnati3

The following restrictions apply to the combination of switches in this manner:

* The switch *-gnatc* if combined with other switches must come first in the string.
* The switch *-gnats* if combined with other switches must come first in the string.
* The switches *-gnatzc* and *-gnatzr* may not be combined with any other switches, and only one of them may appear in the command line.
* The switch *-gnat-p* may not be combined with any other switch.
* Once a 'y' appears in the string (that is a use of the *-gnaty* switch), then all further characters in the switch are interpreted as style modifiers (see description of *-gnaty*).
* Once a 'd' appears in the string (that is a use of the *-gnatd* switch), then all further characters in the switch are interpreted as debug flags (see description of *-gnatd*).
* Once a 'w' appears in the string (that is a use of the *-gnatw* switch), then all further characters in the switch are interpreted as warning mode modifiers (see description of *-gnatw*).
* Once a 'V' appears in the string (that is a use of the *-gnatV* switch), then all further characters in the switch are interpreted as validity checking options ([Validity Checking], page 126).
* Option 'em', 'ec', 'ep', 'l=' and 'R' must be the last options in a combined list of options.

4.3.2 Output and Error Message Control

The standard default format for error messages is called 'brief format'. Brief format messages are written to `stderr` (the standard error file) and have the following form:

```
e.adb:3:04: Incorrect spelling of keyword "function"
e.adb:4:20: ";" should be "is"
```

The first integer after the file name is the line number in the file, and the second integer is the column number within the line. *GPS* can parse the error messages and point to the referenced character. The following switches provide control over the error message format:

-gnatv

> The *v* stands for verbose. The effect of this setting is to write long-format error messages to `stdout` (the standard output file. The same program compiled with the *-gnatv* switch would generate:

```
3. funcion X (Q : Integer)
   |
```

```
>>> Incorrect spelling of keyword "function"
4. return Integer;
                 |
>>> ";" should be "is"
```

The vertical bar indicates the location of the error, and the `>>>` prefix can be used to search for error messages. When this switch is used the only source lines output are those with errors.

-gnatl

The *l* stands for list. This switch causes a full listing of the file to be generated. In the case where a body is compiled, the corresponding spec is also listed, along with any subunits. Typical output from compiling a package body `p.adb` might look like:

```
Compiling: p.adb


    1. package body p is
    2.    procedure a;
    3.    procedure a is separate;
    4. begin
    5.    null
             |
       >>> missing ";"


    6. end;

Compiling: p.ads


    1. package p is
    2.    pragma Elaborate_Body
                                |
       >>> missing ";"


    3. end p;

Compiling: p-a.adb


    1. separate p
             |
       >>> missing "("


    2. procedure a is
    3. begin
    4.    null
             |
       >>> missing ";"


    5. end;
```

When you specify the *-gnatv* or *-gnatl* switches and standard output is redirected, a brief summary is written to **stderr** (standard error) giving the number of error messages and warning messages generated.

-gnatl=*fname*

This has the same effect as *-gnatl* except that the output is written to a file instead of to standard output. If the given name **fname** does not start with a period, then it is the full name of the file to be written. If **fname** is an extension, it is appended to the name of the file being compiled. For example, if file **xyz.adb** is compiled with *-gnatl=.lst*, then the output is written to file xyz.adb.lst.

-gnatU

This switch forces all error messages to be preceded by the unique string 'error:'. This means that error messages take a few more characters in space, but allows easy searching for and identification of error messages.

-gnatb

The *b* stands for brief. This switch causes GNAT to generate the brief format error messages to **stderr** (the standard error file) as well as the verbose format message or full listing (which as usual is written to **stdout** (the standard output file).

-gnatm=*n*

The *m* stands for maximum. *n* is a decimal integer in the range of 1 to 999999 and limits the number of error or warning messages to be generated. For example, using *-gnatm2* might yield

```
e.adb:3:04: Incorrect spelling of keyword "function"
e.adb:5:35: missing ".."
fatal error: maximum number of errors detected
compilation abandoned
```

The default setting if no switch is given is 9999. If the number of warnings reaches this limit, then a message is output and further warnings are suppressed, but the compilation is continued. If the number of error messages reaches this limit, then a message is output and the compilation is abandoned. A value of zero means that no limit applies.

Note that the equal sign is optional, so the switches *-gnatm2* and *-gnatm=2* are equivalent.

-gnatf

The *f* stands for full. Normally, the compiler suppresses error messages that are likely to be redundant. This switch causes all error messages to be generated. In particular, in the case of references to undefined variables. If a given variable is referenced several times, the normal format of messages is

```
e.adb:7:07: "V" is undefined (more references follow)
```

where the parenthetical comment warns that there are additional references to the variable *V*. Compiling the same program with the *-gnatf* switch yields

```
e.adb:7:07: "V" is undefined
e.adb:8:07: "V" is undefined
e.adb:8:12: "V" is undefined
e.adb:8:16: "V" is undefined
e.adb:9:07: "V" is undefined
e.adb:9:12: "V" is undefined
```

The *-gnatf* switch also generates additional information for some error messages. Some examples are:

* Details on possibly non-portable unchecked conversion

* List possible interpretations for ambiguous calls

* Additional details on incorrect parameters

`-gnatjnn`

In normal operation mode (or if *-gnatj0* is used), then error messages with continuation lines are treated as though the continuation lines were separate messages (and so a warning with two continuation lines counts as three warnings, and is listed as three separate messages).

If the *-gnatjnn* switch is used with a positive value for nn, then messages are output in a different manner. A message and all its continuation lines are treated as a unit, and count as only one warning or message in the statistics totals. Furthermore, the message is reformatted so that no line is longer than nn characters.

`-gnatq`

The *q* stands for quit (really 'don't quit'). In normal operation mode, the compiler first parses the program and determines if there are any syntax errors. If there are, appropriate error messages are generated and compilation is immediately terminated. This switch tells GNAT to continue with semantic analysis even if syntax errors have been found. This may enable the detection of more errors in a single run. On the other hand, the semantic analyzer is more likely to encounter some internal fatal error when given a syntactically invalid tree.

`-gnatQ`

In normal operation mode, the ALI file is not generated if any illegalities are detected in the program. The use of *-gnatQ* forces generation of the ALI file. This file is marked as being in error, so it cannot be used for binding purposes, but it does contain reasonably complete cross-reference information, and thus may be useful for use by tools (e.g., semantic browsing tools or integrated development environments) that are driven from the ALI file. This switch implies *-gnatq*, since the semantic phase must be run to get a meaningful ALI file.

In addition, if *-gnatt* is also specified, then the tree file is generated even if there are illegalities. It may be useful in this case to also specify *-gnatq* to ensure that full semantic processing occurs. The resulting tree file can be processed by ASIS, for the purpose of providing partial information about illegal units, but if the error causes the tree to be badly malformed, then ASIS may crash during the analysis.

When *-gnatQ* is used and the generated `ALI` file is marked as being in error, *gnatmake* will attempt to recompile the source when it finds such an `ALI` file, including with switch *-gnatc*.

Note that *-gnatQ* has no effect if *-gnats* is specified, since ALI files are never generated if *-gnats* is set.

4.3.3 Warning Message Control

In addition to error messages, which correspond to illegalities as defined in the Ada Reference Manual, the compiler detects two kinds of warning situations.

First, the compiler considers some constructs suspicious and generates a warning message to alert you to a possible error. Second, if the compiler detects a situation that is sure to raise an exception at run time, it generates a warning message. The following shows an example of warning messages:

```
e.adb:4:24: warning: creation of object may raise Storage_Error
e.adb:10:17: warning: static value out of range
e.adb:10:17: warning: "Constraint_Error" will be raised at run time
```

GNAT considers a large number of situations as appropriate for the generation of warning messages. As always, warnings are not definite indications of errors. For example, if you do an out-of-range assignment with the deliberate intention of raising a *Constraint_Error* exception, then the warning that may be issued does not indicate an error. Some of the situations for which GNAT issues warnings (at least some of the time) are given in the following list. This list is not complete, and new warnings are often added to subsequent versions of GNAT. The list is intended to give a general idea of the kinds of warnings that are generated.

* Possible infinitely recursive calls

* Out-of-range values being assigned

* Possible order of elaboration problems

* Size not a multiple of alignment for a record type

* Assertions (pragma Assert) that are sure to fail

* Unreachable code

* Address clauses with possibly unaligned values, or where an attempt is made to overlay a smaller variable with a larger one.

* Fixed-point type declarations with a null range

* Direct_IO or Sequential_IO instantiated with a type that has access values

* Variables that are never assigned a value

* Variables that are referenced before being initialized

* Task entries with no corresponding *accept* statement

* Duplicate accepts for the same task entry in a *select*

* Objects that take too much storage

* Unchecked conversion between types of differing sizes

* Missing *return* statement along some execution path in a function

* Incorrect (unrecognized) pragmas

* Incorrect external names
* Allocation from empty storage pool
* Potentially blocking operation in protected type
* Suspicious parenthesization of expressions
* Mismatching bounds in an aggregate
* Attempt to return local value by reference
* Premature instantiation of a generic body
* Attempt to pack aliased components
* Out of bounds array subscripts
* Wrong length on string assignment
* Violations of style rules if style checking is enabled
* Unused *with* clauses
* *Bit_Order* usage that does not have any effect
* *Standard.Duration* used to resolve universal fixed expression
* Dereference of possibly null value
* Declaration that is likely to cause storage error
* Internal GNAT unit *with*ed by application unit
* Values known to be out of range at compile time
* Unreferenced or unmodified variables. Note that a special exemption applies to variables which contain any of the substrings *DISCARD, DUMMY, IGNORE, JUNK, UNUSED*, in any casing. Such variables are considered likely to be intentionally used in a situation where otherwise a warning would be given, so warnings of this kind are always suppressed for such variables.
* Address overlays that could clobber memory
* Unexpected initialization when address clause present
* Bad alignment for address clause
* Useless type conversions
* Redundant assignment statements and other redundant constructs
* Useless exception handlers
* Accidental hiding of name by child unit
* Access before elaboration detected at compile time
* A range in a *for* loop that is known to be null or might be null

The following section lists compiler switches that are available to control the handling of warning messages. It is also possible to exercise much finer control over what warnings are issued and suppressed using the GNAT pragma Warnings (see the description of the pragma in the *GNAT_Reference_manual*).

`-gnatwa`

> *Activate most optional warnings.*
>
> This switch activates most optional warning messages. See the remaining list in this section for details on optional warning messages that can be individually controlled. The warnings that are not turned on by this switch are:

* `-gnatwd` (implicit dereferencing)
* `-gnatw.d` (tag warnings with -gnatw switch)
* `-gnatwh` (hiding)
* `-gnatw.h` (holes in record layouts)
* `-gnatw.k` (redefinition of names in standard)
* `-gnatwl` (elaboration warnings)
* `-gnatw.l` (inherited aspects)
* `-gnatw.n` (atomic synchronization)
* `-gnatwo` (address clause overlay)
* `-gnatw.o` (values set by out parameters ignored)
* `-gnatw.s` (overridden size clause)
* `-gnatwt` (tracking of deleted conditional code)
* `-gnatw.u` (unordered enumeration)
* `-gnatw.w` (use of Warnings Off)
* `-gnatw.y` (reasons for package needing body)

All other optional warnings are turned on.

`-gnatwA`

> *Suppress all optional errors.*
>
> This switch suppresses all optional warning messages, see remaining list in this section for details on optional warning messages that can be individually controlled. Note that unlike switch *-gnatws*, the use of switch *-gnatwA* does not suppress warnings that are normally given unconditionally and cannot be individually controlled (for example, the warning about a missing exit path in a function). Also, again unlike switch *-gnatws*, warnings suppressed by the use of switch *-gnatwA* can be individually turned back on. For example the use of switch *-gnatwA* followed by switch *-gnatwd* will suppress all optional warnings except the warnings for implicit dereferencing.

`-gnatw.a`

> *Activate warnings on failing assertions.*
>
> This switch activates warnings for assertions where the compiler can tell at compile time that the assertion will fail. Note that this warning is given even if assertions are disabled. The default is that such warnings are generated.

`-gnatw.A`

> *Suppress warnings on failing assertions.*
>
> This switch suppresses warnings for assertions where the compiler can tell at compile time that the assertion will fail.

`-gnatwb`

> *Activate warnings on bad fixed values.*
>
> This switch activates warnings for static fixed-point expressions whose value is not an exact multiple of Small. Such values are implementation dependent,

since an implementation is free to choose either of the multiples that surround the value. GNAT always chooses the closer one, but this is not required behavior, and it is better to specify a value that is an exact multiple, ensuring predictable execution. The default is that such warnings are not generated.

-gnatwB

Suppress warnings on bad fixed values.

This switch suppresses warnings for static fixed-point expressions whose value is not an exact multiple of Small.

-gnatw.b

Activate warnings on biased representation.

This switch activates warnings when a size clause, value size clause, component clause, or component size clause forces the use of biased representation for an integer type (e.g. representing a range of 10..11 in a single bit by using 0/1 to represent 10/11). The default is that such warnings are generated.

-gnatw.B

Suppress warnings on biased representation.

This switch suppresses warnings for representation clauses that force the use of biased representation.

-gnatwc

Activate warnings on conditionals.

This switch activates warnings for conditional expressions used in tests that are known to be True or False at compile time. The default is that such warnings are not generated. Note that this warning does not get issued for the use of boolean variables or constants whose values are known at compile time, since this is a standard technique for conditional compilation in Ada, and this would generate too many false positive warnings.

This warning option also activates a special test for comparisons using the operators '>=' and' <='. If the compiler can tell that only the equality condition is possible, then it will warn that the '>' or '<' part of the test is useless and that the operator could be replaced by '='. An example would be comparing a *Natural* variable <= 0.

This warning option also generates warnings if one or both tests is optimized away in a membership test for integer values if the result can be determined at compile time. Range tests on enumeration types are not included, since it is common for such tests to include an end point.

This warning can also be turned on using *-gnatwa*.

-gnatwC

Suppress warnings on conditionals.

This switch suppresses warnings for conditional expressions used in tests that are known to be True or False at compile time.

-gnatw.c

Activate warnings on missing component clauses.

This switch activates warnings for record components where a record representation clause is present and has component clauses for the majority, but not all, of the components. A warning is given for each component for which no component clause is present.

-gnatw.C

Suppress warnings on missing component clauses.

This switch suppresses warnings for record components that are missing a component clause in the situation described above.

-gnatwd

Activate warnings on implicit dereferencing.

If this switch is set, then the use of a prefix of an access type in an indexed component, slice, or selected component without an explicit *.all* will generate a warning. With this warning enabled, access checks occur only at points where an explicit *.all* appears in the source code (assuming no warnings are generated as a result of this switch). The default is that such warnings are not generated.

-gnatwD

Suppress warnings on implicit dereferencing.

This switch suppresses warnings for implicit dereferences in indexed components, slices, and selected components.

-gnatw.d

Activate tagging of warning and info messages.

If this switch is set, then warning messages are tagged, with one of the following strings:

- *[-gnatw?]* Used to tag warnings controlled by the switch *-gnatwx* where x is a letter a-z.
- *[-gnatw.?]* Used to tag warnings controlled by the switch *-gnatw.x* where x is a letter a-z.
- *[-gnatel]* Used to tag elaboration information (info) messages generated when the static model of elaboration is used and the *-gnatel* switch is set.
- *[restriction warning]* Used to tag warning messages for restriction violations, activated by use of the pragma *Restriction_Warnings*.
- *[warning-as-error]* Used to tag warning messages that have been converted to error messages by use of the pragma Warning_As_Error. Note that such warnings are prefixed by the string "error: " rather than "warning: ".
- *[enabled by default]* Used to tag all other warnings that are always given by default, unless warnings are completely suppressed using pragma *Warnings(Off)* or the switch *-gnatws*.

-gnatw.D

> *Deactivate tagging of warning and info messages messages.*
>
> If this switch is set, then warning messages return to the default mode in which warnings and info messages are not tagged as described above for *-gnatw.d*.

-gnatwe

> *Treat warnings and style checks as errors.*
>
> This switch causes warning messages and style check messages to be treated as errors. The warning string still appears, but the warning messages are counted as errors, and prevent the generation of an object file. Note that this is the only -gnatw switch that affects the handling of style check messages. Note also that this switch has no effect on info (information) messages, which are not treated as errors if this switch is present.

-gnatw.e

> *Activate every optional warning.*
>
> This switch activates all optional warnings, including those which are not activated by *-gnatwa*. The use of this switch is not recommended for normal use. If you turn this switch on, it is almost certain that you will get large numbers of useless warnings. The warnings that are excluded from *-gnatwa* are typically highly specialized warnings that are suitable for use only in code that has been specifically designed according to specialized coding rules.

-gnatwf

> *Activate warnings on unreferenced formals.*
>
> This switch causes a warning to be generated if a formal parameter is not referenced in the body of the subprogram. This warning can also be turned on using *-gnatwu*. The default is that these warnings are not generated.

-gnatwF

> *Suppress warnings on unreferenced formals.*
>
> This switch suppresses warnings for unreferenced formal parameters. Note that the combination *-gnatwu* followed by *-gnatwF* has the effect of warning on unreferenced entities other than subprogram formals.

-gnatwg

> *Activate warnings on unrecognized pragmas.*
>
> This switch causes a warning to be generated if an unrecognized pragma is encountered. Apart from issuing this warning, the pragma is ignored and has no effect. The default is that such warnings are issued (satisfying the Ada Reference Manual requirement that such warnings appear).

-gnatwG

> *Suppress warnings on unrecognized pragmas.*
>
> This switch suppresses warnings for unrecognized pragmas.

-gnatw.g

> *Warnings used for GNAT sources.*

This switch sets the warning categories that are used by the standard GNAT style. Currently this is equivalent to *-gnatwAao.sI.C.V.X* but more warnings may be added in the future without advanced notice.

-gnatwh

Activate warnings on hiding.

This switch activates warnings on hiding declarations that are considered potentially confusing. Not all cases of hiding cause warnings; for example an overriding declaration hides an implicit declaration, which is just normal code. The default is that warnings on hiding are not generated.

-gnatwH

Suppress warnings on hiding.

This switch suppresses warnings on hiding declarations.

-gnatw.h

Activate warnings on holes/gaps in records.

This switch activates warnings on component clauses in record representation clauses that leave holes (gaps) in the record layout. If this warning option is active, then record representation clauses should specify a contiguous layout, adding unused fill fields if needed.

-gnatw.H

Suppress warnings on holes/gaps in records.

This switch suppresses warnings on component clauses in record representation clauses that leave holes (haps) in the record layout.

-gnatwi

Activate warnings on implementation units.

This switch activates warnings for a *with* of an internal GNAT implementation unit, defined as any unit from the *Ada*, *Interfaces*, *GNAT*, or *System* hierarchies that is not documented in either the Ada Reference Manual or the GNAT Programmer's Reference Manual. Such units are intended only for internal implementation purposes and should not be *with*ed by user programs. The default is that such warnings are generated

-gnatwI

Disable warnings on implementation units.

This switch disables warnings for a *with* of an internal GNAT implementation unit.

-gnatw.i

Activate warnings on overlapping actuals.

This switch enables a warning on statically detectable overlapping actuals in a subprogram call, when one of the actuals is an in-out parameter, and the types of the actuals are not by-copy types. This warning is off by default.

`-gnatw.I`

Disable warnings on overlapping actuals.

This switch disables warnings on overlapping actuals in a call..

`-gnatwj`

Activate warnings on obsolescent features (Annex J).

If this warning option is activated, then warnings are generated for calls to subprograms marked with *pragma Obsolescent* and for use of features in Annex J of the Ada Reference Manual. In the case of Annex J, not all features are flagged. In particular use of the renamed packages (like *Text_IO*) and use of package *ASCII* are not flagged, since these are very common and would generate many annoying positive warnings. The default is that such warnings are not generated.

In addition to the above cases, warnings are also generated for GNAT features that have been provided in past versions but which have been superseded (typically by features in the new Ada standard). For example, *pragma Ravenscar* will be flagged since its function is replaced by *pragma Profile(Ravenscar)*, and *pragma Interface_Name* will be flagged since its function is replaced by *pragma Import*.

Note that this warning option functions differently from the restriction *No_Obsolescent_Features* in two respects. First, the restriction applies only to annex J features. Second, the restriction does flag uses of package *ASCII*.

`-gnatwJ`

Suppress warnings on obsolescent features (Annex J).

This switch disables warnings on use of obsolescent features.

`-gnatwk`

Activate warnings on variables that could be constants.

This switch activates warnings for variables that are initialized but never modified, and then could be declared constants. The default is that such warnings are not given.

`-gnatwK`

Suppress warnings on variables that could be constants.

This switch disables warnings on variables that could be declared constants.

`-gnatw.k`

Activate warnings on redefinition of names in standard.

This switch activates warnings for declarations that declare a name that is defined in package Standard. Such declarations can be confusing, especially since the names in package Standard continue to be directly visible, meaning that use visibiliy on such redeclared names does not work as expected. Names of discriminants and components in records are not included in this check.

`-gnatw.K`

Suppress warnings on redefinition of names in standard.

This switch activates warnings for declarations that declare a name that is defined in package Standard.

-gnatwl

Activate warnings for elaboration pragmas.

This switch activates warnings for possible elaboration problems, including suspicious use of *Elaborate* pragmas, when using the static elaboration model, and possible situations that may raise *Program_Error* when using the dynamic elaboration model. See the section in this guide on elaboration checking for further details. The default is that such warnings are not generated.

-gnatwL

Suppress warnings for elaboration pragmas.

This switch suppresses warnings for possible elaboration problems.

-gnatw.l

List inherited aspects.

This switch causes the compiler to list inherited invariants, preconditions, and postconditions from Type_Invariant'Class, Invariant'Class, Pre'Class, and Post'Class aspects. Also list inherited subtype predicates.

-gnatw.L

Suppress listing of inherited aspects.

This switch suppresses listing of inherited aspects.

-gnatwm

Activate warnings on modified but unreferenced variables.

This switch activates warnings for variables that are assigned (using an initialization value or with one or more assignment statements) but whose value is never read. The warning is suppressed for volatile variables and also for variables that are renamings of other variables or for which an address clause is given. The default is that these warnings are not given.

-gnatwM

Disable warnings on modified but unreferenced variables.

This switch disables warnings for variables that are assigned or initialized, but never read.

-gnatw.m

Activate warnings on suspicious modulus values.

This switch activates warnings for modulus values that seem suspicious. The cases caught are where the size is the same as the modulus (e.g. a modulus of 7 with a size of 7 bits), and modulus values of 32 or 64 with no size clause. The guess in both cases is that $2**x$ was intended rather than x. In addition expressions of the form $2*x$ for small x generate a warning (the almost certainly accurate guess being that $2**x$ was intended). The default is that these warnings are given.

`-gnatw.M`

>   *Disable warnings on suspicious modulus values.*
>
>   This switch disables warnings for suspicious modulus values.

`-gnatwn`

>   *Set normal warnings mode.*
>
>   This switch sets normal warning mode, in which enabled warnings are issued and treated as warnings rather than errors. This is the default mode. the switch *-gnatwn* can be used to cancel the effect of an explicit *-gnatws* or *-gnatwe*. It also cancels the effect of the implicit *-gnatwe* that is activated by the use of *-gnatg*.

`-gnatw.n`

>   *Activate warnings on atomic synchronization.*
>
>   This switch actives warnings when an access to an atomic variable requires the generation of atomic synchronization code. These warnings are off by default.

`-gnatw.N`

>   *Suppress warnings on atomic synchronization.*
>
>   This switch suppresses warnings when an access to an atomic variable requires the generation of atomic synchronization code.

`-gnatwo`

>   *Activate warnings on address clause overlays.*
>
>   This switch activates warnings for possibly unintended initialization effects of defining address clauses that cause one variable to overlap another. The default is that such warnings are generated.

`-gnatwO`

>   *Suppress warnings on address clause overlays.*
>
>   This switch suppresses warnings on possibly unintended initialization effects of defining address clauses that cause one variable to overlap another.

`-gnatw.o`

>   *Activate warnings on modified but unreferenced out parameters.*
>
>   This switch activates warnings for variables that are modified by using them as actuals for a call to a procedure with an out mode formal, where the resulting assigned value is never read. It is applicable in the case where there is more than one out mode formal. If there is only one out mode formal, the warning is issued by default (controlled by -gnatwu). The warning is suppressed for volatile variables and also for variables that are renamings of other variables or for which an address clause is given. The default is that these warnings are not given.

`-gnatw.O`

>   *Disable warnings on modified but unreferenced out parameters.*
>
>   This switch suppresses warnings for variables that are modified by using them as actuals for a call to a procedure with an out mode formal, where the resulting assigned value is never read.

`-gnatwp`

Activate warnings on ineffective pragma Inlines.

This switch activates warnings for failure of front end inlining (activated by *-gnatN*) to inline a particular call. There are many reasons for not being able to inline a call, including most commonly that the call is too complex to inline. The default is that such warnings are not given. Warnings on ineffective inlining by the gcc back-end can be activated separately, using the gcc switch -Winline.

`-gnatwP`

Suppress warnings on ineffective pragma Inlines.

This switch suppresses warnings on ineffective pragma Inlines. If the inlining mechanism cannot inline a call, it will simply ignore the request silently.

`-gnatw.p`

Activate warnings on parameter ordering.

This switch activates warnings for cases of suspicious parameter ordering when the list of arguments are all simple identifiers that match the names of the formals, but are in a different order. The warning is suppressed if any use of named parameter notation is used, so this is the appropriate way to suppress a false positive (and serves to emphasize that the "misordering" is deliberate). The default is that such warnings are not given.

`-gnatw.P`

Suppress warnings on parameter ordering.

This switch suppresses warnings on cases of suspicious parameter ordering.

`-gnatwq`

Activate warnings on questionable missing parentheses.

This switch activates warnings for cases where parentheses are not used and the result is potential ambiguity from a readers point of view. For example (not a > b) when a and b are modular means ((not a) > b) and very likely the programmer intended (not (a > b)). Similarly (-x mod 5) means (-(x mod 5)) and quite likely ((-x) mod 5) was intended. In such situations it seems best to follow the rule of always parenthesizing to make the association clear, and this warning switch warns if such parentheses are not present. The default is that these warnings are given.

`-gnatwQ`

Suppress warnings on questionable missing parentheses.

This switch suppresses warnings for cases where the association is not clear and the use of parentheses is preferred.

`-gnatwr`

Activate warnings on redundant constructs.

This switch activates warnings for redundant constructs. The following is the current list of constructs regarded as redundant:

   *   Assignment of an item to itself.

* Type conversion that converts an expression to its own type.

* Use of the attribute *Base* where *typ'Base* is the same as *typ*.

* Use of pragma *Pack* when all components are placed by a record representation clause.

* Exception handler containing only a reraise statement (raise with no operand) which has no effect.

* Use of the operator abs on an operand that is known at compile time to be non-negative

* Comparison of boolean expressions to an explicit True value.

The default is that warnings for redundant constructs are not given.

-gnatwR

Suppress warnings on redundant constructs.

This switch suppresses warnings for redundant constructs.

-gnatw.r

Activate warnings for object renaming function.

This switch activates warnings for an object renaming that renames a function call, which is equivalent to a constant declaration (as opposed to renaming the function itself). The default is that these warnings are given.

-gnatw.R

Suppress warnings for object renaming function.

This switch suppresses warnings for object renaming function.

-gnatws

Suppress all warnings.

This switch completely suppresses the output of all warning messages from the GNAT front end, including both warnings that can be controlled by switches described in this section, and those that are normally given unconditionally. The effect of this suppress action can only be cancelled by a subsequent use of the switch *-gnatwn*.

Note that switch *-gnatws* does not suppress warnings from the *gcc* back end. To suppress these back end warnings as well, use the switch *-w* in addition to *-gnatws*. Also this switch has no effect on the handling of style check messages.

-gnatw.s

Activate warnings on overridden size clauses.

This switch activates warnings on component clauses in record representation clauses where the length given overrides that specified by an explicit size clause for the component type. A warning is similarly given in the array case if a specified component size overrides an explicit size clause for the array component type.

-gnatw.S

Suppress warnings on overridden size clauses.

This switch suppresses warnings on component clauses in record representation clauses that override size clauses, and similar warnings when an array component size overrides a size clause.

-gnatwt

Activate warnings for tracking of deleted conditional code.

This switch activates warnings for tracking of code in conditionals (IF and CASE statements) that is detected to be dead code which cannot be executed, and which is removed by the front end. This warning is off by default. This may be useful for detecting deactivated code in certified applications.

-gnatwT

Suppress warnings for tracking of deleted conditional code.

This switch suppresses warnings for tracking of deleted conditional code.

-gnatw.t

Activate warnings on suspicious contracts.

This switch activates warnings on suspicious contracts. This includes warnings on suspicious postconditions (whether a pragma *Postcondition* or a *Post* aspect in Ada 2012) and suspicious contract cases (pragma or aspect *Contract_Cases*). A function postcondition or contract case is suspicious when no postcondition or contract case for this function mentions the result of the function. A procedure postcondition or contract case is suspicious when it only refers to the pre-state of the procedure, because in that case it should rather be expressed as a precondition. This switch also controls warnings on suspicious cases of expressions typically found in contracts like quantified expressions and uses of Update attribute. The default is that such warnings are generated.

-gnatw.T

Suppress warnings on suspicious contracts.

This switch suppresses warnings on suspicious contracts.

-gnatwu

Activate warnings on unused entities.

This switch activates warnings to be generated for entities that are declared but not referenced, and for units that are *with*ed and not referenced. In the case of packages, a warning is also generated if no entities in the package are referenced. This means that if a with'ed package is referenced but the only references are in *use* clauses or *renames* declarations, a warning is still generated. A warning is also generated for a generic package that is *with*ed but never instantiated. In the case where a package or subprogram body is compiled, and there is a *with* on the corresponding spec that is only referenced in the body, a warning is also generated, noting that the *with* can be moved to the body. The default is that such warnings are not generated. This switch also activates warnings on unreferenced formals (it includes the effect of *-gnatwf*).

-gnatwU

Suppress warnings on unused entities.

This switch suppresses warnings for unused entities and packages. It also turns off warnings on unreferenced formals (and thus includes the effect of -gnatwF).

-gnatw.u

Activate warnings on unordered enumeration types.

This switch causes enumeration types to be considered as conceptually unordered, unless an explicit pragma *Ordered* is given for the type. The effect is to generate warnings in clients that use explicit comparisons or subranges, since these constructs both treat objects of the type as ordered. (A *client* is defined as a unit that is other than the unit in which the type is declared, or its body or subunits.) Please refer to the description of pragma *Ordered* in the *GNAT Reference Manual* for further details. The default is that such warnings are not generated.

-gnatw.U

Deactivate warnings on unordered enumeration types.

This switch causes all enumeration types to be considered as ordered, so that no warnings are given for comparisons or subranges for any type.

-gnatwv

Activate warnings on unassigned variables.

This switch activates warnings for access to variables which may not be properly initialized. The default is that such warnings are generated.

-gnatwV

Suppress warnings on unassigned variables.

This switch suppresses warnings for access to variables which may not be properly initialized. For variables of a composite type, the warning can also be suppressed in Ada 2005 by using a default initialization with a box. For example, if Table is an array of records whose components are only partially uninitialized, then the following code:

```
Tab : Table := (others => <>);
```

will suppress warnings on subsequent statements that access components of variable Tab.

-gnatw.v

Activate info messages for non-default bit order.

This switch activates messages (labeled "info", they are not warnings, just informational messages) about the effects of non-default bit-order on records to which a component clause is applied. The effect of specifying non-default bit ordering is a bit subtle (and changed with Ada 2005), so these messages, which are given by default, are useful in understanding the exact consequences of using this feature.

-gnatw.V

Suppress info messages for non-default bit order.

This switch suppresses information messages for the effects of specifying non-default bit order on record components with component clauses.

-gnatww

Activate warnings on wrong low bound assumption.

This switch activates warnings for indexing an unconstrained string parameter with a literal or S'Length. This is a case where the code is assuming that the low bound is one, which is in general not true (for example when a slice is passed). The default is that such warnings are generated.

-gnatwW

Suppress warnings on wrong low bound assumption.

This switch suppresses warnings for indexing an unconstrained string parameter with a literal or S'Length. Note that this warning can also be suppressed in a particular case by adding an assertion that the lower bound is 1, as shown in the following example:

```
procedure K (S : String) is
   pragma Assert (S'First = 1);
   ...
```

-gnatw.w

Activate warnings on Warnings Off pragmas.

This switch activates warnings for use of *pragma Warnings (Off, entity)* where either the pragma is entirely useless (because it suppresses no warnings), or it could be replaced by *pragma Unreferenced* or *pragma Unmodified*. Also activates warnings for the case of Warnings (Off, String), where either there is no matching Warnings (On, String), or the Warnings (Off) did not suppress any warning. The default is that these warnings are not given.

-gnatw.W

Suppress warnings on unnecessary Warnings Off pragmas.

This switch suppresses warnings for use of *pragma Warnings (Off, ...)*.

-gnatwx

Activate warnings on Export/Import pragmas.

This switch activates warnings on Export/Import pragmas when the compiler detects a possible conflict between the Ada and foreign language calling sequences. For example, the use of default parameters in a convention C procedure is dubious because the C compiler cannot supply the proper default, so a warning is issued. The default is that such warnings are generated.

-gnatwX

Suppress warnings on Export/Import pragmas.

This switch suppresses warnings on Export/Import pragmas. The sense of this is that you are telling the compiler that you know what you are doing in writing the pragma, and it should not complain at you.

-gnatw.x

Activate warnings for No_Exception_Propagation mode.

This switch activates warnings for exception usage when pragma Restrictions (No_Exception_Propagation) is in effect. Warnings are given for implicit or explicit exception raises which are not covered by a local handler, and for exception handlers which do not cover a local raise. The default is that these warnings are not given.

`-gnatw.X`

Disable warnings for No_Exception_Propagation mode.

This switch disables warnings for exception usage when pragma Restrictions (No_Exception_Propagation) is in effect.

`-gnatwy`

Activate warnings for Ada compatibility issues.

For the most part, newer versions of Ada are upwards compatible with older versions. For example, Ada 2005 programs will almost always work when compiled as Ada 2012. However there are some exceptions (for example the fact that *some* is now a reserved word in Ada 2012). This switch activates several warnings to help in identifying and correcting such incompatibilities. The default is that these warnings are generated. Note that at one point Ada 2005 was called Ada 0Y, hence the choice of character.

`-gnatwY`

Disable warnings for Ada compatibility issues.

This switch suppresses the warnings intended to help in identifying incompatibilities between Ada language versions.

`-gnatw.y`

Activate information messages for why package spec needs body.

There are a number of cases in which a package spec needs a body. For example, the use of pragma Elaborate_Body, or the declaration of a procedure specification requiring a completion. This switch causes information messages to be output showing why a package specification requires a body. This can be useful in the case of a large package specification which is unexpectedly requiring a body. The default is that such information messages are not output.

`-gnatw.Y`

Disable information messages for why package spec needs body.

This switch suppresses the output of information messages showing why a package specification needs a body.

`-gnatwz`

Activate warnings on unchecked conversions.

This switch activates warnings for unchecked conversions where the types are known at compile time to have different sizes. The default is that such warnings are generated. Warnings are also generated for subprogram pointers with different conventions.

`-gnatwZ`

Suppress warnings on unchecked conversions.

This switch suppresses warnings for unchecked conversions where the types are known at compile time to have different sizes or conventions.

`-gnatw.z`

> *Activate warnings for size not a multiple of alignment.*
>
> This switch activates warnings for cases of record types with specified *Size* and *Alignment* attributes where the size is not a multiple of the alignment, resulting in an object size that is greater than the specified size. The default is that such warnings are generated.

`-gnatw.Z`

> *Suppress warnings for size not a multiple of alignment.*
>
> This switch suppresses warnings for cases of record types with specified *Size* and *Alignment* attributes where the size is not a multiple of the alignment, resulting in an object size that is greater than the specified size. The warning can also be suppressed by giving an explicit *Object_Size* value.

`-Wunused`

> The warnings controlled by the *-gnatw* switch are generated by the front end of the compiler. The *GCC* back end can provide additional warnings and they are controlled by the *-W* switch. For example, *-Wunused* activates back end warnings for entities that are declared but not referenced.

`-Wuninitialized`

> Similarly, *-Wuninitialized* activates the back end warning for uninitialized variables. This switch must be used in conjunction with an optimization level greater than zero.

`-Wstack-usage=len`

> Warn if the stack usage of a subprogram might be larger than *len* bytes. See [Static Stack Usage Analysis], page 230 for details.

`-Wall`

> This switch enables most warnings from the *GCC* back end. The code generator detects a number of warning situations that are missed by the *GNAT* front end, and this switch can be used to activate them. The use of this switch also sets the default front end warning mode to *-gnatwa*, that is, most front end warnings activated as well.

`-w`

> Conversely, this switch suppresses warnings from the *GCC* back end. The use of this switch also sets the default front end warning mode to *-gnatws*, that is, front end warnings suppressed as well.

`-Werror`

> This switch causes warnings from the *GCC* back end to be treated as errors. The warning string still appears, but the warning messages are counted as errors, and prevent the generation of an object file.

A string of warning parameters can be used in the same parameter. For example:

> `-gnatwaGe`

will turn on all optional warnings except for unrecognized pragma warnings, and also specify that warnings should be treated as errors.

When no switch *-gnatw* is used, this is equivalent to:

* -gnatw.a
* -gnatwB
* -gnatw.b
* -gnatwC
* -gnatw.C
* -gnatwD
* -gnatwF
* -gnatwg
* -gnatwH
* -gnatwi
* -gnatw.I
* -gnatwJ
* -gnatwK
* -gnatwL
* -gnatw.L
* -gnatwM
* -gnatw.m
* -gnatwn
* -gnatwo
* -gnatw.O
* -gnatwP
* -gnatw.P
* -gnatwq
* -gnatwR
* -gnatw.R
* -gnatw.S
* -gnatwT
* -gnatw.T
* -gnatwU
* -gnatwv
* -gnatww
* -gnatw.W
* -gnatwx
* -gnatw.X
* -gnatwy
* -gnatwz

4.3.4 Debugging and Assertion Control

`-gnata`

The *-gnata* option is equivalent to the following Assertion_Policy pragma:

```
pragma Assertion_Policy (Check);
```

Which is a shorthand for:

```
pragma Assertion_Policy
   (Assert                 => Check,
    Static_Predicate       => Check,
    Dynamic_Predicate      => Check,
    Pre                    => Check,
    Pre'Class              => Check,
    Post                   => Check,
    Post'Class             => Check,
    Type_Invariant         => Check,
    Type_Invariant'Class => Check);
```

The pragmas *Assert* and *Debug* normally have no effect and are ignored. This switch, where a stands for assert, causes pragmas *Assert* and *Debug* to be activated. This switch also causes preconditions, postconditions, subtype predicates, and type invariants to be activated.

The pragmas have the form:

```
pragma Assert (<Boolean-expression> [, <static-string-expression>])
pragma Debug (<procedure call>)
pragma Type_Invariant (<type-local-name>, <Boolean-expression>)
pragma Predicate (<type-local-name>, <Boolean-expression>)
pragma Precondition (<Boolean-expression>, <string-expression>)
pragma Postcondition (<Boolean-expression>, <string-expression>)
```

The aspects have the form:

```
with [Pre|Post|Type_Invariant|Dynamic_Predicate|Static_Predicate]
   => <Boolean-expression>;
```

The *Assert* pragma causes *Boolean-expression* to be tested. If the result is *True*, the pragma has no effect (other than possible side effects from evaluating the expression). If the result is *False*, the exception *Assert_Failure* declared in the package *System.Assertions* is raised (passing *static-string-expression*, if present, as the message associated with the exception). If no string expression is given, the default is a string containing the file name and line number of the pragma.

The *Debug* pragma causes *procedure* to be called. Note that *pragma Debug* may appear within a declaration sequence, allowing debugging procedures to be called between declarations.

For the aspect specification, the <*Boolean-expression*> is evaluated. If the result is *True*, the aspect has no effect. If the result is *False*, the exception *Assert_Failure* is raised.

4.3.5 Validity Checking

The Ada Reference Manual defines the concept of invalid values (see RM 13.9.1). The primary source of invalid values is uninitialized variables. A scalar variable that is left uninitialized may contain an invalid value; the concept of invalid does not apply to access or composite types.

It is an error to read an invalid value, but the RM does not require run-time checks to detect such errors, except for some minimal checking to prevent erroneous execution (i.e. unpredictable behavior). This corresponds to the *-gnatVd* switch below, which is the default. For example, by default, if the expression of a case statement is invalid, it will raise Constraint_Error rather than causing a wild jump, and if an array index on the left-hand side of an assignment is invalid, it will raise Constraint_Error rather than overwriting an arbitrary memory location.

The *-gnatVa* may be used to enable additional validity checks, which are not required by the RM. These checks are often very expensive (which is why the RM does not require them). These checks are useful in tracking down uninitialized variables, but they are not usually recommended for production builds, and in particular we do not recommend using these extra validity checking options in combination with optimization, since this can confuse the optimizer. If performance is a consideration, leading to the need to optimize, then the validity checking options should not be used.

The other *-gnatV*x switches below allow finer-grained control; you can enable whichever validity checks you desire. However, for most debugging purposes, *-gnatVa* is sufficient, and the default *-gnatVd* (i.e. standard Ada behavior) is usually sufficient for non-debugging use.

The *-gnatB* switch tells the compiler to assume that all values are valid (that is, within their declared subtype range) except in the context of a use of the Valid attribute. This means the compiler can generate more efficient code, since the range of values is better known at compile time. However, an uninitialized variable can cause wild jumps and memory corruption in this mode.

The *-gnatV*x switch allows control over the validity checking mode as described below. The x argument is a string of letters that indicate validity checks that are performed or not performed in addition to the default checks required by Ada as described above.

-gnatVa

> *All validity checks.*
>
> All validity checks are turned on. That is, *-gnatVa* is equivalent to *gnatVcdfimorst*.

-gnatVc

> *Validity checks for copies.*
>
> The right hand side of assignments, and the initializing values of object declarations are validity checked.

-gnatVd

> *Default (RM) validity checks.*
>
> Some validity checks are done by default following normal Ada semantics (RM 13.9.1 (9-11)). A check is done in case statements that the expression is within

the range of the subtype. If it is not, Constraint_Error is raised. For assignments to array components, a check is done that the expression used as index is within the range. If it is not, Constraint_Error is raised. Both these validity checks may be turned off using switch *-gnatVD*. They are turned on by default. If *-gnatVD* is specified, a subsequent switch *-gnatVd* will leave the checks turned on. Switch *-gnatVD* should be used only if you are sure that all such expressions have valid values. If you use this switch and invalid values are present, then the program is erroneous, and wild jumps or memory overwriting may occur.

`-gnatVe`

Validity checks for elementary components.

In the absence of this switch, assignments to record or array components are not validity checked, even if validity checks for assignments generally (*-gnatVc*) are turned on. In Ada, assignment of composite values do not require valid data, but assignment of individual components does. So for example, there is a difference between copying the elements of an array with a slice assignment, compared to assigning element by element in a loop. This switch allows you to turn off validity checking for components, even when they are assigned component by component.

`-gnatVf`

Validity checks for floating-point values.

In the absence of this switch, validity checking occurs only for discrete values. If *-gnatVf* is specified, then validity checking also applies for floating-point values, and NaNs and infinities are considered invalid, as well as out of range values for constrained types. Note that this means that standard IEEE infinity mode is not allowed. The exact contexts in which floating-point values are checked depends on the setting of other options. For example, *-gnatVif* or *-gnatVfi* (the order does not matter) specifies that floating-point parameters of mode *in* should be validity checked.

`-gnatVi`

Validity checks for 'in' mode parameters.

Arguments for parameters of mode *in* are validity checked in function and procedure calls at the point of call.

`-gnatVm`

Validity checks for 'in out' mode parameters.

Arguments for parameters of mode *in out* are validity checked in procedure calls at the point of call. The 'm' here stands for modify, since this concerns parameters that can be modified by the call. Note that there is no specific option to test *out* parameters, but any reference within the subprogram will be tested in the usual manner, and if an invalid value is copied back, any reference to it will be subject to validity checking.

`-gnatVn`

No validity checks.

This switch turns off all validity checking, including the default checking for case statements and left hand side subscripts. Note that the use of the switch -*gnatp* suppresses all run-time checks, including validity checks, and thus implies -*gnatVn*. When this switch is used, it cancels any other -*gnatV* previously issued.

`-gnatVo`

Validity checks for operator and attribute operands.

Arguments for predefined operators and attributes are validity checked. This includes all operators in package *Standard*, the shift operators defined as intrinsic in package *Interfaces* and operands for attributes such as *Pos*. Checks are also made on individual component values for composite comparisons, and on the expressions in type conversions and qualified expressions. Checks are also made on explicit ranges using .. (e.g., slices, loops etc).

`-gnatVp`

Validity checks for parameters.

This controls the treatment of parameters within a subprogram (as opposed to -*gnatVi* and -*gnatVm* which control validity testing of parameters on a call. If either of these call options is used, then normally an assumption is made within a subprogram that the input arguments have been validity checking at the point of call, and do not need checking again within a subprogram). If -*gnatVp* is set, then this assumption is not made, and parameters are not assumed to be valid, so their validity will be checked (or rechecked) within the subprogram.

`-gnatVr`

Validity checks for function returns.

The expression in *return* statements in functions is validity checked.

`-gnatVs`

Validity checks for subscripts.

All subscripts expressions are checked for validity, whether they appear on the right side or left side (in default mode only left side subscripts are validity checked).

`-gnatVt`

Validity checks for tests.

Expressions used as conditions in *if, while* or *exit* statements are checked, as well as guard expressions in entry calls.

The -*gnatV* switch may be followed by a string of letters to turn on a series of validity checking options. For example, `-gnatVcr` specifies that in addition to the default validity checking, copies and function return expressions are to be validity checked. In order to make it easier to specify the desired combination of effects, the upper case letters *CDFIMORST* may be used to turn off the corresponding lower case option. Thus `-gnatVaM` turns on all validity checking options except for checking of **in out** procedure arguments.

The specification of additional validity checking generates extra code (and in the case of -*gnatVa* the code expansion can be substantial). However, these additional checks can be very useful in detecting uninitialized variables, incorrect use of unchecked conversion, and other errors leading to invalid values. The use of pragma *Initialize_Scalars* is useful in conjunction with the extra validity checking, since this ensures that wherever possible uninitialized variables have invalid values.

See also the pragma *Validity_Checks* which allows modification of the validity checking mode at the program source level, and also allows for temporary disabling of validity checks.

4.3.6 Style Checking

The *-gnatyx* switch causes the compiler to enforce specified style rules. A limited set of style rules has been used in writing the GNAT sources themselves. This switch allows user programs to activate all or some of these checks. If the source program fails a specified style check, an appropriate message is given, preceded by the character sequence '(style)'. This message does not prevent successful compilation (unless the *-gnatwe* switch is used).

Note that this is by no means intended to be a general facility for checking arbitrary coding standards. It is simply an embedding of the style rules we have chosen for the GNAT sources. If you are starting a project which does not have established style standards, you may find it useful to adopt the entire set of GNAT coding standards, or some subset of them.

The string *x* is a sequence of letters or digits indicating the particular style checks to be performed. The following checks are defined:

-gnaty0

Specify indentation level.

If a digit from 1-9 appears in the string after *-gnaty* then proper indentation is checked, with the digit indicating the indentation level required. A value of zero turns off this style check. The general style of required indentation is as specified by the examples in the Ada Reference Manual. Full line comments must be aligned with the – starting on a column that is a multiple of the alignment level, or they may be aligned the same way as the following non-blank line (this is useful when full line comments appear in the middle of a statement, or they may be aligned with the source line on the previous non-blank line.

-gnatya

Check attribute casing.

Attribute names, including the case of keywords such as *digits* used as attributes names, must be written in mixed case, that is, the initial letter and any letter following an underscore must be uppercase. All other letters must be lowercase.

-gnatyA

Use of array index numbers in array attributes.

When using the array attributes First, Last, Range, or Length, the index number must be omitted for one-dimensional arrays and is required for multi-dimensional arrays.

-gnatyb

Blanks not allowed at statement end.

Trailing blanks are not allowed at the end of statements. The purpose of this rule, together with h (no horizontal tabs), is to enforce a canonical format for the use of blanks to separate source tokens.

-gnatyB

Check Boolean operators.

The use of AND/OR operators is not permitted except in the cases of modular operands, array operands, and simple stand-alone boolean variables or boolean constants. In all other cases *and then/or else* are required.

-gnatyc

Check comments, double space.

Comments must meet the following set of rules:

* The '–' that starts the column must either start in column one, or else at least one blank must precede this sequence.
* Comments that follow other tokens on a line must have at least one blank following the '–' at the start of the comment.
* Full line comments must have at least two blanks following the '–' that starts the comment, with the following exceptions.
* A line consisting only of the '–' characters, possibly preceded by blanks is permitted.
* A comment starting with '–x' where x is a special character is permitted. This allows proper processing of the output generated by specialized tools including *gnatprep* (where '–!' is used) and the SPARK annotation language (where '–#' is used). For the purposes of this rule, a special character is defined as being in one of the ASCII ranges $16\#21\#...16\#2F\#$ or $16\#3A\#...16\#3F\#$. Note that this usage is not permitted in GNAT implementation units (i.e., when *-gnatg* is used).
* A line consisting entirely of minus signs, possibly preceded by blanks, is permitted. This allows the construction of box comments where lines of minus signs are used to form the top and bottom of the box.
* A comment that starts and ends with '–' is permitted as long as at least one blank follows the initial '–'. Together with the preceding rule, this allows the construction of box comments, as shown in the following example:

```
----------------------------
-- This is a box comment --
-- with two text lines.   --
----------------------------
```

-gnatyC

Check comments, single space.

This is identical to c except that only one space is required following the – of a comment instead of two.

-gnatyd

Check no DOS line terminators present.

All lines must be terminated by a single ASCII.LF character (in particular the DOS line terminator sequence CR/LF is not allowed).

`-gnatye`

Check end/exit labels.

Optional labels on *end* statements ending subprograms and on *exit* statements exiting named loops, are required to be present.

`-gnatyf`

No form feeds or vertical tabs.

Neither form feeds nor vertical tab characters are permitted in the source text.

`-gnatyg`

GNAT style mode.

The set of style check switches is set to match that used by the GNAT sources. This may be useful when developing code that is eventually intended to be incorporated into GNAT. Currently this is equivalent to *-gnatwydISux*) but additional style switches may be added to this set in the future without advance notice.

`-gnatyh`

No horizontal tabs.

Horizontal tab characters are not permitted in the source text. Together with the b (no blanks at end of line) check, this enforces a canonical form for the use of blanks to separate source tokens.

`-gnatyi`

Check if-then layout.

The keyword *then* must appear either on the same line as corresponding *if*, or on a line on its own, lined up under the *if*.

`-gnatyI`

check mode IN keywords.

Mode *in* (the default mode) is not allowed to be given explicitly. *in out* is fine, but not *in* on its own.

`-gnatyk`

Check keyword casing.

All keywords must be in lower case (with the exception of keywords such as *digits* used as attribute names to which this check does not apply).

`-gnatyl`

Check layout.

Layout of statement and declaration constructs must follow the recommendations in the Ada Reference Manual, as indicated by the form of the syntax rules. For example an *else* keyword must be lined up with the corresponding *if* keyword.

There are two respects in which the style rule enforced by this check option are more liberal than those in the Ada Reference Manual. First in the case of record declarations, it is permissible to put the *record* keyword on the same line as the *type* keyword, and then the *end* in *end record* must line up under *type*. This is also permitted when the type declaration is split on two lines. For example, any of the following three layouts is acceptable:

```
type q is record
   a : integer;
   b : integer;
end record;

type q is
   record
      a : integer;
      b : integer;
   end record;

type q is
   record
      a : integer;
      b : integer;
end record;
```

Second, in the case of a block statement, a permitted alternative is to put the block label on the same line as the *declare* or *begin* keyword, and then line the *end* keyword up under the block label. For example both the following are permitted:

```
Block : declare
   A : Integer := 3;
begin
   Proc (A, A);
end Block;

Block :
   declare
      A : Integer := 3;
   begin
      Proc (A, A);
   end Block;
```

The same alternative format is allowed for loops. For example, both of the following are permitted:

```
Clear : while J < 10 loop
   A (J) := 0;
end loop Clear;

Clear :
   while J < 10 loop
```

```
              A (J) := 0;
            end loop Clear;
```

-gnatyL

> *Set maximum nesting level.*
>
> The maximum level of nesting of constructs (including subprograms, loops, blocks, packages, and conditionals) may not exceed the given value *nnn*. A value of zero disconnects this style check.

-gnatym

> *Check maximum line length.*
>
> The length of source lines must not exceed 79 characters, including any trailing blanks. The value of 79 allows convenient display on an 80 character wide device or window, allowing for possible special treatment of 80 character lines. Note that this count is of characters in the source text. This means that a tab character counts as one character in this count and a wide character sequence counts as a single character (however many bytes are needed in the encoding).

-gnatyM

> *Set maximum line length.*
>
> The length of lines must not exceed the given value *nnn*. The maximum value that can be specified is 32767. If neither style option for setting the line length is used, then the default is 255. This also controls the maximum length of lexical elements, where the only restriction is that they must fit on a single line.

-gnatyn

> *Check casing of entities in Standard.*
>
> Any identifier from Standard must be cased to match the presentation in the Ada Reference Manual (for example, *Integer* and *ASCII.NUL*).

-gnatyN

> *Turn off all style checks.*
>
> All style check options are turned off.

-gnatyo

> *Check order of subprogram bodies.*
>
> All subprogram bodies in a given scope (e.g., a package body) must be in alphabetical order. The ordering rule uses normal Ada rules for comparing strings, ignoring casing of letters, except that if there is a trailing numeric suffix, then the value of this suffix is used in the ordering (e.g., Junk2 comes before Junk10).

-gnatyO

> *Check that overriding subprograms are explicitly marked as such.*
>
> This applies to all subprograms of a derived type that override a primitive operation of the type, for both tagged and untagged types. In particular, the declaration of a primitive operation of a type extension that overrides an inherited operation must carry an overriding indicator. Another case is the declaration of a function that overrides a predefined operator (such as an equality operator).

`-gnatyp`

> *Check pragma casing.*
>
> Pragma names must be written in mixed case, that is, the initial letter and any letter following an underscore must be uppercase. All other letters must be lowercase. An exception is that SPARK_Mode is allowed as an alternative for Spark_Mode.

`-gnatyr`

> *Check references.*
>
> All identifier references must be cased in the same way as the corresponding declaration. No specific casing style is imposed on identifiers. The only requirement is for consistency of references with declarations.

`-gnatys`

> *Check separate specs.*
>
> Separate declarations ('specs') are required for subprograms (a body is not allowed to serve as its own declaration). The only exception is that parameterless library level procedures are not required to have a separate declaration. This exception covers the most frequent form of main program procedures.

`-gnatyS`

> *Check no statements after then/else.*
>
> No statements are allowed on the same line as a *then* or *else* keyword following the keyword in an *if* statement. *or else* and *and then* are not affected, and a special exception allows a pragma to appear after *else*.

`-gnatyt`

> *Check token spacing.*
>
> The following token spacing rules are enforced:
>   * The keywords *abs* and *not* must be followed by a space.
>   * The token => must be surrounded by spaces.
>   * The token <> must be preceded by a space or a left parenthesis.
>   * Binary operators other than ** must be surrounded by spaces. There is no restriction on the layout of the ** binary operator.
>   * Colon must be surrounded by spaces.
>   * Colon-equal (assignment, initialization) must be surrounded by spaces.
>   * Comma must be the first non-blank character on the line, or be immediately preceded by a non-blank character, and must be followed by a space.
>   * If the token preceding a left parenthesis ends with a letter or digit, then a space must separate the two tokens.
>   * If the token following a right parenthesis starts with a letter or digit, then a space must separate the two tokens.
>   * A right parenthesis must either be the first non-blank character on a line, or it must be preceded by a non-blank character.

> * A semicolon must not be preceded by a space, and must not be followed by a non-blank character.
> * A unary plus or minus may not be followed by a space.
> * A vertical bar must be surrounded by spaces.

Exactly one blank (and no other white space) must appear between a *not* token and a following *in* token.

`-gnatyu`

      Check unnecessary blank lines.

      Unnecessary blank lines are not allowed. A blank line is considered unnecessary if it appears at the end of the file, or if more than one blank line occurs in sequence.

`-gnatyx`

      Check extra parentheses.

      Unnecessary extra level of parentheses (C-style) are not allowed around conditions in *if* statements, *while* statements and *exit* statements.

`-gnatyy`

      Set all standard style check options.

      This is equivalent to *gnaty3aAbcefhiklmnprst*, that is all checking options enabled with the exception of *-gnatyB*, *-gnatyd*, *-gnatyI*, *-gnatyLnnn*, *-gnatyo*, *-gnatyO*, *-gnatyS*, *-gnatyu*, and *-gnatyx*.

`-gnaty-`

      Remove style check options.

      This causes any subsequent options in the string to act as canceling the corresponding style check option. To cancel maximum nesting level control, use *L* parameter witout any integer value after that, because any digit following - in the parameter string of the *-gnaty* option will be threated as canceling indentation check. The same is true for *M* parameter. *y* and *N* parameters are not allowed after -.

`-gnaty+`

      Enable style check options.

      This causes any subsequent options in the string to enable the corresponding style check option. That is, it cancels the effect of a previous -, if any.

In the above rules, appearing in column one is always permitted, that is, counts as meeting either a requirement for a required preceding space, or as meeting a requirement for no preceding space.

Appearing at the end of a line is also always permitted, that is, counts as meeting either a requirement for a following space, or as meeting a requirement for no following space.

If any of these style rules is violated, a message is generated giving details on the violation. The initial characters of such messages are always '*(style)*'. Note that these messages are treated as warning messages, so they normally do not prevent the generation of an object file. The *-gnatwe* switch can be used to treat warning messages, including style messages, as fatal errors.

The switch **-gnaty** on its own (that is not followed by any letters or digits) is equivalent to the use of *-gnatyy* as described above, that is all built-in standard style check options are enabled.

The switch **-gnatyN** clears any previously set style checks.

4.3.7 Run-Time Checks

By default, the following checks are suppressed: stack overflow checks, and checks for access before elaboration on subprogram calls. All other checks, including overflow checks, range checks and array bounds checks, are turned on by default. The following *gcc* switches refine this default behavior.

-gnatp

> This switch causes the unit to be compiled as though *pragma Suppress (All_checks)* had been present in the source. Validity checks are also eliminated (in other words *-gnatp* also implies *-gnatVn*. Use this switch to improve the performance of the code at the expense of safety in the presence of invalid data or program bugs.
>
> Note that when checks are suppressed, the compiler is allowed, but not required, to omit the checking code. If the run-time cost of the checking code is zero or near-zero, the compiler will generate it even if checks are suppressed. In particular, if the compiler can prove that a certain check will necessarily fail, it will generate code to do an unconditional 'raise', even if checks are suppressed. The compiler warns in this case. Another case in which checks may not be eliminated is when they are embedded in certain run time routines such as math library routines.
>
> Of course, run-time checks are omitted whenever the compiler can prove that they will not fail, whether or not checks are suppressed.
>
> Note that if you suppress a check that would have failed, program execution is erroneous, which means the behavior is totally unpredictable. The program might crash, or print wrong answers, or do anything else. It might even do exactly what you wanted it to do (and then it might start failing mysteriously next week or next year). The compiler will generate code based on the assumption that the condition being checked is true, which can result in erroneous execution if that assumption is wrong.
>
> The checks subject to suppression include all the checks defined by the Ada standard, the additional implementation defined checks *Alignment_Check*, *Duplicated_Tag_Check*, *Predicate_Check*, Container_Checks, Tampering_Check, and *Validity_Check*, as well as any checks introduced using *pragma Check_Name*. Note that *Atomic_Synchronization* is not automatically suppressed by use of this option.
>
> If the code depends on certain checks being active, you can use pragma *Unsuppress* either as a configuration pragma or as a local pragma to make sure that a specified check is performed even if *gnatp* is specified.
>
> The *-gnatp* switch has no effect if a subsequent *-gnat-p* switch appears.

`-gnat-p`

This switch cancels the effect of a previous *gnatp* switch.

`-gnato??`

This switch controls the mode used for computing intermediate arithmetic integer operations, and also enables overflow checking. For a full description of overflow mode and checking control, see the 'Overflow Check Handling in GNAT' appendix in this User's Guide.

Overflow checks are always enabled by this switch. The argument controls the mode, using the codes

1 = STRICT

In STRICT mode, intermediate operations are always done using the base type, and overflow checking ensures that the result is within the base type range.

2 = MINIMIZED

In MINIMIZED mode, overflows in intermediate operations are avoided where possible by using a larger integer type for the computation (typically *Long_Long_Integer*). Overflow checking ensures that the result fits in this larger integer type.

3 = ELIMINATED

In ELIMINATED mode, overflows in intermediate operations are avoided by using multi-precision arithmetic. In this case, overflow checking has no effect on intermediate operations (since overflow is impossible).

If two digits are present after *-gnato* then the first digit sets the mode for expressions outside assertions, and the second digit sets the mode for expressions within assertions. Here assertions is used in the technical sense (which includes for example precondition and postcondition expressions).

If one digit is present, the corresponding mode is applicable to both expressions within and outside assertion expressions.

If no digits are present, the default is to enable overflow checks and set STRICT mode for both kinds of expressions. This is compatible with the use of *-gnato* in previous versions of GNAT.

Note that the *-gnato??* switch does not affect the code generated for any floating-point operations; it applies only to integer semantics. For floating-point, GNAT has the *Machine_Overflows* attribute set to *False* and the normal mode of operation is to generate IEEE NaN and infinite values on overflow or invalid operations (such as dividing 0.0 by 0.0).

The reason that we distinguish overflow checking from other kinds of range constraint checking is that a failure of an overflow check, unlike for example the failure of a range check, can result in an incorrect value, but cannot cause random memory destruction (like an out of range subscript), or a wild jump (from an out of range case value). Overflow checking is also quite expensive in time and space, since in general it requires the use of double length arithmetic.

Note again that the default is *-gnato11* (equivalent to *-gnato1*), so overflow checking is performed in STRICT mode by default.

-gnatE

Enables dynamic checks for access-before-elaboration on subprogram calls and generic instantiations. Note that *-gnatE* is not necessary for safety, because in the default mode, GNAT ensures statically that the checks would not fail. For full details of the effect and use of this switch, [Compiling with gcc], page 87.

-fstack-check

Activates stack overflow checking. For full details of the effect and use of this switch see [Stack Overflow Checking], page 230.

The setting of these switches only controls the default setting of the checks. You may modify them using either *Suppress* (to remove checks) or *Unsuppress* (to add back suppressed checks) pragmas in the program source.

4.3.8 Using *gcc* for Syntax Checking

-gnats

The *s* stands for 'syntax'.

Run GNAT in syntax checking only mode. For example, the command

```
$ gcc -c -gnats x.adb
```

compiles file `x.adb` in syntax-check-only mode. You can check a series of files in a single command , and can use wild cards to specify such a group of files. Note that you must specify the *-c* (compile only) flag in addition to the *-gnats* flag.

You may use other switches in conjunction with *-gnats*. In particular, *-gnatl* and *-gnatv* are useful to control the format of any generated error messages.

When the source file is empty or contains only empty lines and/or comments, the output is a warning:

```
$ gcc -c -gnats -x ada toto.txt
toto.txt:1:01: warning: empty file, contains no compilation units
$
```

Otherwise, the output is simply the error messages, if any. No object file or ALI file is generated by a syntax-only compilation. Also, no units other than the one specified are accessed. For example, if a unit *X* *with*s a unit *Y*, compiling unit *X* in syntax check only mode does not access the source file containing unit *Y*.

Normally, GNAT allows only a single unit in a source file. However, this restriction does not apply in syntax-check-only mode, and it is possible to check a file containing multiple compilation units concatenated together. This is primarily used by the *gnatchop* utility ([Renaming Files with gnatchop], page 22).

4.3.9 Using *gcc* for Semantic Checking

-gnatc

The c stands for 'check'. Causes the compiler to operate in semantic check mode, with full checking for all illegalities specified in the Ada Reference Manual, but without generation of any object code (no object file is generated).

Because dependent files must be accessed, you must follow the GNAT semantic restrictions on file structuring to operate in this mode:

* The needed source files must be accessible (see [Search Paths and the Run-Time Library (RTL)], page 89).

* Each file must contain only one compilation unit.

* The file name and unit name must match ([File Naming Rules], page 13).

The output consists of error messages as appropriate. No object file is generated. An `ALI` file is generated for use in the context of cross-reference tools, but this file is marked as not being suitable for binding (since no object file is generated). The checking corresponds exactly to the notion of legality in the Ada Reference Manual.

Any unit can be compiled in semantics-checking-only mode, including units that would not normally be compiled (subunits, and specifications where a separate body is present).

4.3.10 Compiling Different Versions of Ada

The switches described in this section allow you to explicitly specify the version of the Ada language that your programs are written in. The default mode is Ada 2012, but you can also specify Ada 95, Ada 2005 mode, or indicate Ada 83 compatibility mode.

-gnat83 (Ada 83 Compatibility Mode)

> Although GNAT is primarily an Ada 95 / Ada 2005 compiler, this switch specifies that the program is to be compiled in Ada 83 mode. With *-gnat83*, GNAT rejects most post-Ada 83 extensions and applies Ada 83 semantics where this can be done easily. It is not possible to guarantee this switch does a perfect job; some subtle tests, such as are found in earlier ACVC tests (and that have been removed from the ACATS suite for Ada 95), might not compile correctly. Nevertheless, this switch may be useful in some circumstances, for example where, due to contractual reasons, existing code needs to be maintained using only Ada 83 features.

> With few exceptions (most notably the need to use <> on unconstrained generic formal parameters, the use of the new Ada 95 / Ada 2005 reserved words, and the use of packages with optional bodies), it is not necessary to specify the *-gnat83* switch when compiling Ada 83 programs, because, with rare exceptions, Ada 95 and Ada 2005 are upwardly compatible with Ada 83. Thus a correct Ada 83 program is usually also a correct program in these later versions of the language standard. For further information please refer to the *Compatibility_and_Porting_Guide* chapter in the *GNAT Reference Manual*.

-gnat95 (Ada 95 mode)

> This switch directs the compiler to implement the Ada 95 version of the language. Since Ada 95 is almost completely upwards compatible with Ada 83, Ada 83 programs may generally be compiled using this switch (see the description of the *-gnat83* switch for further information about Ada 83 mode). If an

Ada 2005 program is compiled in Ada 95 mode, uses of the new Ada 2005 features will cause error messages or warnings.

This switch also can be used to cancel the effect of a previous *-gnat83*, *-gnat05/2005*, or *-gnat12/2012* switch earlier in the command line.

-gnat05 or **-gnat2005** (Ada 2005 mode)

This switch directs the compiler to implement the Ada 2005 version of the language, as documented in the official Ada standards document. Since Ada 2005 is almost completely upwards compatible with Ada 95 (and thus also with Ada 83), Ada 83 and Ada 95 programs may generally be compiled using this switch (see the description of the *-gnat83* and *-gnat95* switches for further information).

-gnat12 or **-gnat2012** (Ada 2012 mode)

This switch directs the compiler to implement the Ada 2012 version of the language (also the default). Since Ada 2012 is almost completely upwards compatible with Ada 2005 (and thus also with Ada 83, and Ada 95), Ada 83 and Ada 95 programs may generally be compiled using this switch (see the description of the *-gnat83*, *-gnat95*, and *-gnat05/2005* switches for further information).

-gnatX (Enable GNAT Extensions)

This switch directs the compiler to implement the latest version of the language (currently Ada 2012) and also to enable certain GNAT implementation extensions that are not part of any Ada standard. For a full list of these extensions, see the GNAT reference manual.

4.3.11 Character Set Control

-gnat*ic*

Normally GNAT recognizes the Latin-1 character set in source program identifiers, as described in the Ada Reference Manual. This switch causes GNAT to recognize alternate character sets in identifiers. *c* is a single character indicating the character set, as follows:

1	ISO 8859-1 (Latin-1) identifiers
2	ISO 8859-2 (Latin-2) letters allowed in identifiers
3	ISO 8859-3 (Latin-3) letters allowed in identifiers
4	ISO 8859-4 (Latin-4) letters allowed in identifiers
5	ISO 8859-5 (Cyrillic) letters allowed in identifiers
9	ISO 8859-15 (Latin-9) letters allowed in identifiers
p	IBM PC letters (code page 437) allowed in identifiers

8	IBM PC letters (code page 850) allowed in identifiers
f	Full upper-half codes allowed in identifiers
n	No upper-half codes allowed in identifiers
w	Wide-character codes (that is, codes greater than 255) allowed in identifiers

See [Foreign Language Representation], page 10 for full details on the implementation of these character sets.

`-gnatWe`

Specify the method of encoding for wide characters. *e* is one of the following:

h	Hex encoding (brackets coding also recognized)
u	Upper half encoding (brackets encoding also recognized)
s	Shift/JIS encoding (brackets encoding also recognized)
e	EUC encoding (brackets encoding also recognized)
8	UTF-8 encoding (brackets encoding also recognized)
b	Brackets encoding only (default value)

For full details on these encoding methods see [Wide_Character Encodings], page 11. Note that brackets coding is always accepted, even if one of the other options is specified, so for example *-gnatW8* specifies that both brackets and UTF-8 encodings will be recognized. The units that are with'ed directly or indirectly will be scanned using the specified representation scheme, and so if one of the non-brackets scheme is used, it must be used consistently throughout the program. However, since brackets encoding is always recognized, it may be conveniently used in standard libraries, allowing these libraries to be used with any of the available coding schemes.

Note that brackets encoding only applies to program text. Within comments, brackets are considered to be normal graphic characters, and bracket sequences are never recognized as wide characters.

If no *-gnatW?* parameter is present, then the default representation is normally Brackets encoding only. However, if the first three characters of the file are 16#EF# 16#BB# 16#BF# (the standard byte order mark or BOM for UTF-8), then these three characters are skipped and the default representation for the file is set to UTF-8.

Note that the wide character representation that is specified (explicitly or by default) for the main program also acts as the default encoding used for Wide_Text_IO files if not specifically overridden by a WCEM form parameter.

When no -*gnatW?* is specified, then characters (other than wide characters represented using brackets notation) are treated as 8-bit Latin-1 codes. The codes recognized are the Latin-1 graphic characters, and ASCII format effectors (CR, LF, HT, VT). Other lower half control characters in the range 16#00#..16#1F# are not accepted in program text or in comments. Upper half control characters (16#80#..16#9F#) are rejected in program text, but allowed and ignored in comments. Note in particular that the Next Line (NEL) character whose encoding is 16#85# is not recognized as an end of line in this default mode. If your source program contains instances of the NEL character used as a line terminator, you must use UTF-8 encoding for the whole source program. In default mode, all lines must be ended by a standard end of line sequence (CR, CR/LF, or LF).

Note that the convention of simply accepting all upper half characters in comments means that programs that use standard ASCII for program text, but UTF-8 encoding for comments are accepted in default mode, providing that the comments are ended by an appropriate (CR, or CR/LF, or LF) line terminator. This is a common mode for many programs with foreign language comments.

4.3.12 File Naming Control

`-gnatkn`

> Activates file name 'krunching'. *n*, a decimal integer in the range 1-999, indicates the maximum allowable length of a file name (not including the `.ads` or `.adb` extension). The default is not to enable file name krunching.
>
> For the source file naming rules, [File Naming Rules], page 13.

4.3.13 Subprogram Inlining Control

`-gnatn[12]`

> The *n* here is intended to suggest the first syllable of the word 'inline'. GNAT recognizes and processes *Inline* pragmas. However, for the inlining to actually occur, optimization must be enabled and, in order to enable inlining of subprograms specified by pragma *Inline*, you must also specify this switch. In the absence of this switch, GNAT does not attempt inlining and does not need to access the bodies of subprograms for which *pragma Inline* is specified if they are not in the current unit.
>
> You can optionally specify the inlining level: 1 for moderate inlining across modules, which is a good compromise between compilation times and performances at run time, or 2 for full inlining across modules, which may bring about longer compilation times. If no inlining level is specified, the compiler will pick it based on the optimization level: 1 for -*O1*, -*O2* or -*Os* and 2 for -*O3*.
>
> If you specify this switch the compiler will access these bodies, creating an extra source dependency for the resulting object file, and where possible, the call will be inlined. For further details on when inlining is possible see [Inlining of Subprograms], page 211.

`-gnatN`

> This switch activates front-end inlining which also generates additional dependencies.

When using a gcc-based back end (in practice this means using any version of GNAT other than the JGNAT, .NET or GNAAMP versions), then the use of *-gnatN* is deprecated, and the use of *-gnatn* is preferred. Historically front end inlining was more extensive than the gcc back end inlining, but that is no longer the case.

4.3.14 Auxiliary Output Control

`-gnatt`

Causes GNAT to write the internal tree for a unit to a file (with the extension `.adt`. This not normally required, but is used by separate analysis tools. Typically these tools do the necessary compilations automatically, so you should not have to specify this switch in normal operation. Note that the combination of switches *-gnatct* generates a tree in the form required by ASIS applications.

`-gnatu`

Print a list of units required by this compilation on `stdout`. The listing includes all units on which the unit being compiled depends either directly or indirectly.

`-pass-exit-codes`

If this switch is not used, the exit code returned by *gcc* when compiling multiple files indicates whether all source files have been successfully used to generate object files or not.

When *-pass-exit-codes* is used, *gcc* exits with an extended exit status and allows an integrated development environment to better react to a compilation failure. Those exit status are:

5	There was an error in at least one source file.
3	At least one source file did not generate an object file.
2	The compiler died unexpectedly (internal error for example).
0	An object file has been generated for every source file.

4.3.15 Debugging Control

`-gnatdx`

Activate internal debugging switches. *x* is a letter or digit, or string of letters or digits, which specifies the type of debugging outputs desired. Normally these are used only for internal development or system debugging purposes. You can find full documentation for these switches in the body of the *Debug* unit in the compiler source file `debug.adb`.

`-gnatG[=nn]`

This switch causes the compiler to generate auxiliary output containing a pseudo-source listing of the generated expanded code. Like most Ada compilers, GNAT works by first transforming the high level Ada code into lower level constructs. For example, tasking operations are transformed into calls to the tasking run-time routines. A unique capability of GNAT is to list this expanded code in a form very close to normal Ada source. This is very useful in understanding the implications of various Ada usage on the efficiency of the generated code. There are many cases in Ada (e.g., the use of controlled types), where simple Ada statements can generate a lot of run-time code. By using *-gnatG* you can identify these cases, and consider whether it may be desirable to modify the coding approach to improve efficiency.

The optional parameter *nn* if present after -gnatG specifies an alternative maximum line length that overrides the normal default of 72. This value is in the range 40-999999, values less than 40 being silently reset to 40. The equal sign is optional.

The format of the output is very similar to standard Ada source, and is easily understood by an Ada programmer. The following special syntactic additions correspond to low level features used in the generated code that do not have any exact analogies in pure Ada source form. The following is a partial list of these special constructions. See the spec of package *Sprint* in file `sprint.ads` for a full list.

If the switch *-gnatL* is used in conjunction with *-gnatG*, then the original source lines are interspersed in the expanded source (as comment lines with the original line number).

new *xxx* [storage_pool = *yyy*]
> Shows the storage pool being used for an allocator.

at end *procedure-name*;
> Shows the finalization (cleanup) procedure for a scope.

(if *expr* then *expr* else *expr*)
> Conditional expression equivalent to the *x?y:z* construction in C.

***target*^(*source*)**
> A conversion with floating-point truncation instead of rounding.

***target*?(*source*)**
> A conversion that bypasses normal Ada semantic checking. In particular enumeration types and fixed-point types are treated simply as integers.

***target*?^(*source*)**
> Combines the above two cases.

x* #/ *y

x* #mod *y

x* # *y

x* #rem *y
> A division or multiplication of fixed-point values which are treated as integers without any kind of scaling.

free *expr* [storage_pool = *xxx*]
> Shows the storage pool associated with a *free* statement.

[subtype or type declaration]

> Used to list an equivalent declaration for an internally generated type that is referenced elsewhere in the listing.

freeze *type-name* [*actions*]

> Shows the point at which *type-name* is frozen, with possible associated actions to be performed at the freeze point.

reference *itype*

> Reference (and hence definition) to internal type *itype*.

function-name! (arg, arg, arg)

> Intrinsic function call.

label-name : label

> Declaration of label *labelname*.

#$ *subprogram-name*

> An implicit call to a run-time support routine (to meet the requirement of H.3.1(9) in a convenient manner).

expr && *expr* && *expr* ... && *expr*

> A multiple concatenation (same effect as *expr* & *expr* & *expr*, but handled more efficiently).

[constraint_error]

> Raise the *Constraint_Error* exception.

expression'reference

> A pointer to the result of evaluating {expression}.

target-type!(*source-expression*)

> An unchecked conversion of *source-expression* to *target-type*.

[*numerator/denominator*]

> Used to represent internal real literals (that) have no exact representation in base 2-16 (for example, the result of compile time evaluation of the expression 1.0/27.0).

-gnatD[=nn]

> When used in conjunction with *-gnatG*, this switch causes the expanded source, as described above for *-gnatG* to be written to files with names **xxx.dg**, where **xxx** is the normal file name, instead of to the standard output file. For example, if the source file name is **hello.adb**, then a file **hello.adb.dg** will be written. The debugging information generated by the *gcc -g* switch will refer to the generated **xxx.dg** file. This allows you to do source level debugging using the generated code which is sometimes useful for complex code, for example to find out exactly which part of a complex construction raised an exception. This switch also suppress generation of cross-reference information (see *-gnatx*) since otherwise the cross-reference information would refer to the **.dg** file, which would cause confusion since this is not the original source file.
>
> Note that *-gnatD* actually implies *-gnatG* automatically, so it is not necessary to give both options. In other words *-gnatD* is equivalent to *-gnatDG*).

If the switch *-gnatL* is used in conjunction with *-gnatDG*, then the original source lines are interspersed in the expanded source (as comment lines with the original line number).

The optional parameter *nn* if present after -gnatD specifies an alternative maximum line length that overrides the normal default of 72. This value is in the range 40-999999, values less than 40 being silently reset to 40. The equal sign is optional.

`-gnatr`

This switch causes pragma Restrictions to be treated as Restriction_Warnings so that violation of restrictions causes warnings rather than illegalities. This is useful during the development process when new restrictions are added or investigated. The switch also causes pragma Profile to be treated as Profile_Warnings, and pragma Restricted_Run_Time and pragma Ravenscar set restriction warnings rather than restrictions.

`-gnatR[0|1|2|3[s]]`

This switch controls output from the compiler of a listing showing representation information for declared types and objects. For *-gnatR0*, no information is output (equivalent to omitting the *-gnatR* switch). For *-gnatR1* (which is the default, so *-gnatR* with no parameter has the same effect), size and alignment information is listed for declared array and record types. For *-gnatR2*, size and alignment information is listed for all declared types and objects. The *Linker_Section* is also listed for any entity for which the *Linker_Section* is set explicitly or implicitly (the latter case occurs for objects of a type for which a *Linker_Section* is set).

Finally *-gnatR3* includes symbolic expressions for values that are computed at run time for variant records. These symbolic expressions have a mostly obvious format with #n being used to represent the value of the n'th discriminant. See source files `repinfo.ads/adb` in the *GNAT* sources for full details on the format of *-gnatR3* output. If the switch is followed by an s (e.g., *-gnatR2s*), then the output is to a file with the name `file.rep` where file is the name of the corresponding source file.

`-gnatRm[s]`

This form of the switch controls output of subprogram conventions and parameter passing mechanisms for all subprograms. A following *s* means output to a file as described above.

Note that it is possible for record components to have zero size. In this case, the component clause uses an obvious extension of permitted Ada syntax, for example *at 0 range 0 .. -1*.

Representation information requires that code be generated (since it is the code generator that lays out complex data structures). If an attempt is made to output representation information when no code is generated, for example when a subunit is compiled on its own, then no information can be generated and the compiler outputs a message to this effect.

`-gnatS`

> The use of the switch *-gnatS* for an Ada compilation will cause the compiler to output a representation of package Standard in a form very close to standard Ada. It is not quite possible to do this entirely in standard Ada (since new numeric base types cannot be created in standard Ada), but the output is easily readable to any Ada programmer, and is useful to determine the characteristics of target dependent types in package Standard.

`-gnatx`

> Normally the compiler generates full cross-referencing information in the `ALI` file. This information is used by a number of tools, including *gnatfind* and *gnatxref*. The *-gnatx* switch suppresses this information. This saves some space and may slightly speed up compilation, but means that these tools cannot be used.

4.3.16 Exception Handling Control

GNAT uses two methods for handling exceptions at run-time. The *setjmp/longjmp* method saves the context when entering a frame with an exception handler. Then when an exception is raised, the context can be restored immediately, without the need for tracing stack frames. This method provides very fast exception propagation, but introduces significant overhead for the use of exception handlers, even if no exception is raised.

The other approach is called 'zero cost' exception handling. With this method, the compiler builds static tables to describe the exception ranges. No dynamic code is required when entering a frame containing an exception handler. When an exception is raised, the tables are used to control a back trace of the subprogram invocation stack to locate the required exception handler. This method has considerably poorer performance for the propagation of exceptions, but there is no overhead for exception handlers if no exception is raised. Note that in this mode and in the context of mixed Ada and C/C++ programming, to propagate an exception through a C/C++ code, the C/C++ code must be compiled with the *-funwind-tables* GCC's option.

The following switches may be used to control which of the two exception handling methods is used.

`--RTS=sjlj`

> This switch causes the setjmp/longjmp run-time (when available) to be used for exception handling. If the default mechanism for the target is zero cost exceptions, then this switch can be used to modify this default, and must be used for all units in the partition. This option is rarely used. One case in which it may be advantageous is if you have an application where exception raising is common and the overall performance of the application is improved by favoring exception propagation.

`--RTS=zcx`

> This switch causes the zero cost approach to be used for exception handling. If this is the default mechanism for the target (see below), then this switch is unneeded. If the default mechanism for the target is setjmp/longjmp exceptions, then this switch can be used to modify this default, and must be used for all units in the partition. This option can only be used if the zero cost approach is available for the target in use, otherwise it will generate an error.

The same option *–RTS* must be used both for *gcc* and *gnatbind*. Passing this option to *gnatmake* ([Switches for gnatmake], page 78) will ensure the required consistency through the compilation and binding steps.

4.3.17 Units to Sources Mapping Files

`-gnatem=path`

A mapping file is a way to communicate to the compiler two mappings: from unit names to file names (without any directory information) and from file names to path names (with full directory information). These mappings are used by the compiler to short-circuit the path search.

The use of mapping files is not required for correct operation of the compiler, but mapping files can improve efficiency, particularly when sources are read over a slow network connection. In normal operation, you need not be concerned with the format or use of mapping files, and the *-gnatem* switch is not a switch that you would use explicitly. It is intended primarily for use by automatic tools such as *gnatmake* running under the project file facility. The description here of the format of mapping files is provided for completeness and for possible use by other tools.

A mapping file is a sequence of sets of three lines. In each set, the first line is the unit name, in lower case, with *%s* appended for specs and *%b* appended for bodies; the second line is the file name; and the third line is the path name.

Example:

```
main%b
main.2.ada
/gnat/project1/sources/main.2.ada
```

When the switch *-gnatem* is specified, the compiler will create in memory the two mappings from the specified file. If there is any problem (nonexistent file, truncated file or duplicate entries), no mapping will be created.

Several *-gnatem* switches may be specified; however, only the last one on the command line will be taken into account.

When using a project file, *gnatmake* creates a temporary mapping file and communicates it to the compiler using this switch.

4.3.18 Code Generation Control

The GCC technology provides a wide range of target dependent -m switches for controlling details of code generation with respect to different versions of architectures. This includes variations in instruction sets (e.g., different members of the power pc family), and different requirements for optimal arrangement of instructions (e.g., different members of the x86 family). The list of available *-m* switches may be found in the GCC documentation.

Use of these *-m* switches may in some cases result in improved code performance.

The GNAT technology is tested and qualified without any -m switches, so generally the most reliable approach is to avoid the use of these switches. However, we generally expect most of these switches to work successfully with GNAT, and many customers have reported successful use of these options.

Our general advice is to avoid the use of *-m* switches unless special needs lead to requirements in this area. In particular, there is no point in using *-m* switches to improve performance unless you actually see a performance improvement.

4.4 Binding with *gnatbind*

This chapter describes the GNAT binder, *gnatbind*, which is used to bind compiled GNAT objects.

Note: to invoke *gnatbind* with a project file, use the *gnat* driver (see *The_GNAT_Driver_and_Project_Files*).

The *gnatbind* program performs four separate functions:

* Checks that a program is consistent, in accordance with the rules in Chapter 10 of the Ada Reference Manual. In particular, error messages are generated if a program uses inconsistent versions of a given unit.

* Checks that an acceptable order of elaboration exists for the program and issues an error message if it cannot find an order of elaboration that satisfies the rules in Chapter 10 of the Ada Language Manual.

* Generates a main program incorporating the given elaboration order. This program is a small Ada package (body and spec) that must be subsequently compiled using the GNAT compiler. The necessary compilation step is usually performed automatically by *gnatlink*. The two most important functions of this program are to call the elaboration routines of units in an appropriate order and to call the main program.

* Determines the set of object files required by the given main program. This information is output in the forms of comments in the generated program, to be read by the *gnatlink* utility used to link the Ada application.

4.4.1 Running *gnatbind*

The form of the *gnatbind* command is

```
$ gnatbind ['switches'] 'mainprog'[.ali] ['switches']
```

where `mainprog.adb` is the Ada file containing the main program unit body. *gnatbind* constructs an Ada package in two files whose names are b~`mainprog.ads`, and b~`mainprog.adb`. For example, if given the parameter `hello.ali`, for a main program contained in file `hello.adb`, the binder output files would be b~`hello.ads` and b~`hello.adb`.

When doing consistency checking, the binder takes into consideration any source files it can locate. For example, if the binder determines that the given main program requires the package *Pack*, whose `.ALI` file is `pack.ali` and whose corresponding source spec file is `pack.ads`, it attempts to locate the source file `pack.ads` (using the same search path conventions as previously described for the *gcc* command). If it can locate this source file, it checks that the time stamps or source checksums of the source and its references to in `ALI` files match. In other words, any `ALI` files that mentions this spec must have resulted from compiling this version of the source file (or in the case where the source checksums match, a version close enough that the difference does not matter).

The effect of this consistency checking, which includes source files, is that the binder ensures that the program is consistent with the latest version of the source files that can be located at bind time. Editing a source file without compiling files that depend on the source file cause error messages to be generated by the binder.

For example, suppose you have a main program `hello.adb` and a package *P*, from file `p.ads` and you perform the following steps:

* Enter *gcc -c hello.adb* to compile the main program.

* Enter *gcc -c p.ads* to compile package *P*.

* Edit file `p.ads`.

* Enter *gnatbind hello.*

At this point, the file `p.ali` contains an out-of-date time stamp because the file `p.ads` has been edited. The attempt at binding fails, and the binder generates the following error messages:

```
error: "hello.adb" must be recompiled ("p.ads" has been modified)
error: "p.ads" has been modified and must be recompiled
```

Now both files must be recompiled as indicated, and then the bind can succeed, generating a main program. You need not normally be concerned with the contents of this file, but for reference purposes a sample binder output file is given in [Example of Binder Output File], page 263.

In most normal usage, the default mode of *gnatbind* which is to generate the main package in Ada, as described in the previous section. In particular, this means that any Ada programmer can read and understand the generated main program. It can also be debugged just like any other Ada code provided the *-g* switch is used for *gnatbind* and *gnatlink*.

4.4.2 Switches for *gnatbind*

The following switches are available with *gnatbind*; details will be presented in subsequent sections.

`--version`

Display Copyright and version, then exit disregarding all other options.

`--help`

If *–version* was not used, display usage, then exit disregarding all other options.

`-a`

Indicates that, if supported by the platform, the adainit procedure should be treated as an initialisation routine by the linker (a constructor). This is intended to be used by the Project Manager to automatically initialize shared Stand-Alone Libraries.

`-a0`

Specify directory to be searched for ALI files.

`-aI`

Specify directory to be searched for source file.

`-A[=filename]`

Output ALI list (to standard output or to the named file).

-b

> Generate brief messages to `stderr` even if verbose mode set.

-c

> Check only, no generation of binder output file.

-dnn[k|m]

> This switch can be used to change the default task stack size value to a specified size *nn*, which is expressed in bytes by default, or in kilobytes when suffixed with *k* or in megabytes when suffixed with *m*. In the absence of a [k|m] suffix, this switch is equivalent, in effect, to completing all task specs with

> > `pragma Storage_Size (nn);`

> When they do not already have such a pragma.

-Dnn[k|m]

> This switch can be used to change the default secondary stack size value to a specified size *nn*, which is expressed in bytes by default, or in kilobytes when suffixed with *k* or in megabytes when suffixed with *m*.

> The secondary stack is used to deal with functions that return a variable sized result, for example a function returning an unconstrained String. There are two ways in which this secondary stack is allocated.

> For most targets, the secondary stack is growing on demand and is allocated as a chain of blocks in the heap. The -D option is not very relevant. It only give some control over the size of the allocated blocks (whose size is the minimum of the default secondary stack size value, and the actual size needed for the current allocation request).

> For certain targets, notably VxWorks 653, the secondary stack is allocated by carving off a fixed ratio chunk of the primary task stack. The -D option is used to define the size of the environment task's secondary stack.

-e

> Output complete list of elaboration-order dependencies.

-Ea

> Store tracebacks in exception occurrences when the target supports it. The "a" is for "address"; tracebacks will contain hexadecimal addresses, unless symbolic tracebacks are enabled.

> See also the packages *GNAT.Traceback* and *GNAT.Traceback.Symbolic* for more information. Note that on x86 ports, you must not use *-fomit-frame-pointer gcc* option.

-Es

> Store tracebacks in exception occurrences when the target supports it. The "s" is for "symbolic"; symbolic tracebacks are enabled.

-E

> Currently the same as *-Ea*.

`-F`

Force the checks of elaboration flags. *gnatbind* does not normally generate checks of elaboration flags for the main executable, except when a Stand-Alone Library is used. However, there are cases when this cannot be detected by gnatbind. An example is importing an interface of a Stand-Alone Library through a pragma Import and only specifying through a linker switch this Stand-Alone Library. This switch is used to guarantee that elaboration flag checks are generated.

`-h`

Output usage (help) information.

`-H32`

Use 32-bit allocations for `__gnat_malloc` (and thus for access types). For further details see [Dynamic Allocation Control], page 159.

`-H64`

Use 64-bit allocations for `__gnat_malloc` (and thus for access types). For further details see [Dynamic Allocation Control], page 159.

`-I`

Specify directory to be searched for source and ALI files.

`-I-`

Do not look for sources in the current directory where *gnatbind* was invoked, and do not look for ALI files in the directory containing the ALI file named in the *gnatbind* command line.

`-l`

Output chosen elaboration order.

`-Lxxx`

Bind the units for library building. In this case the adainit and adafinal procedures ([Binding with Non-Ada Main Programs], page 159) are renamed to *xxx'init* and 'xxx'final. *Implies -n.* (:ref:'GNAT_and_Libraries, for more details.)

`-Mxyz`

Rename generated main program from main to xyz. This option is supported on cross environments only.

`-mn`

Limit number of detected errors or warnings to *n*, where *n* is in the range 1..999999. The default value if no switch is given is 9999. If the number of warnings reaches this limit, then a message is output and further warnings are suppressed, the bind continues in this case. If the number of errors reaches this limit, then a message is output and the bind is abandoned. A value of zero means that no limit is enforced. The equal sign is optional.

`-n`

No main program.

`-nostdinc`

>Do not look for sources in the system default directory.

`-nostdlib`

>Do not look for library files in the system default directory.

`--RTS=rts-path`

>Specifies the default location of the runtime library. Same meaning as the equivalent *gnatmake* flag ([Switches for gnatmake], page 78).

`-o file`

>Name the output file *file* (default is b~'xxx.adb'). Note that if this option is used, then linking must be done manually, gnatlink cannot be used.

`-O[=filename]`

>Output object list (to standard output or to the named file).

`-p`

>Pessimistic (worst-case) elaboration order.

`-P`

>Generate binder file suitable for CodePeer.

`-R`

>Output closure source list, which includes all non-run-time units that are included in the bind.

`-Ra`

>Like *-R* but the list includes run-time units.

`-s`

>Require all source files to be present.

`-Sxxx`

>Specifies the value to be used when detecting uninitialized scalar objects with pragma Initialize_Scalars. The *xxx* string specified with the switch is one of:
>
>>* `in` for an invalid value.
>>
>>If zero is invalid for the discrete type in question, then the scalar value is set to all zero bits. For signed discrete types, the largest possible negative value of the underlying scalar is set (i.e. a one bit followed by all zero bits). For unsigned discrete types, the underlying scalar value is set to all one bits. For floating-point types, a NaN value is set (see body of package System.Scalar_Values for exact values).
>>
>>* `lo` for low value.
>>
>>If zero is invalid for the discrete type in question, then the scalar value is set to all zero bits. For signed discrete types, the largest possible negative value of the underlying scalar is set (i.e. a one bit followed by all zero bits). For unsigned discrete types, the underlying scalar value is set to all zero bits. For floating-point, a small value is set (see body of package System.Scalar_Values for exact values).

* `hi` for high value.

  If zero is invalid for the discrete type in question, then the scalar value is set to all one bits. For signed discrete types, the largest possible positive value of the underlying scalar is set (i.e. a zero bit followed by all one bits). For unsigned discrete types, the underlying scalar value is set to all one bits. For floating-point, a large value is set (see body of package System.Scalar_Values for exact values).

* xx for hex value (two hex digits).

  The underlying scalar is set to a value consisting of repeated bytes, whose value corresponds to the given value. For example if BF is given, then a 32-bit scalar value will be set to the bit pattern `16#BFBFBFBF#`.

In addition, you can specify *-Sev* to indicate that the value is to be set at run time. In this case, the program will look for an environment variable of the form `GNAT_INIT_SCALARS=`*yy*, where *yy* is one of *in/lo/hi/'xx*' *with the same meanings as above. If no environment variable is found, or if it does not have a valid value, then the default is *in* (invalid values).

`-static`

Link against a static GNAT run time.

`-shared`

Link against a shared GNAT run time when available.

`-t`

Tolerate time stamp and other consistency errors.

`-Tn`

Set the time slice value to *n* milliseconds. If the system supports the specification of a specific time slice value, then the indicated value is used. If the system does not support specific time slice values, but does support some general notion of round-robin scheduling, then any nonzero value will activate round-robin scheduling.

A value of zero is treated specially. It turns off time slicing, and in addition, indicates to the tasking run time that the semantics should match as closely as possible the Annex D requirements of the Ada RM, and in particular sets the default scheduling policy to *FIFO_Within_Priorities*.

`-un`

Enable dynamic stack usage, with *n* results stored and displayed at program termination. A result is generated when a task terminates. Results that can't be stored are displayed on the fly, at task termination. This option is currently not supported on Itanium platforms. (See [Dynamic Stack Usage Analysis], page 231 for details.)

`-v`

Verbose mode. Write error messages, header, summary output to `stdout`.

`-Vkey=value`

> Store the given association of *key* to *value* in the bind environment. Values stored this way can be retrieved at run time using *GNAT.Bind_Environment*.

`-wx`

> Warning mode; *x* = s/e for suppress/treat as error.

`-Wxe`

> Override default wide character encoding for standard Text_IO files.

`-x`

> Exclude source files (check object consistency only).

`-Xnnn`

> Set default exit status value, normally 0 for POSIX compliance.

`-y`

> Enable leap seconds support in *Ada.Calendar* and its children.

`-z`

> No main subprogram.

You may obtain this listing of switches by running *gnatbind* with no arguments.

4.4.2.1 Consistency-Checking Modes

As described earlier, by default *gnatbind* checks that object files are consistent with one another and are consistent with any source files it can locate. The following switches control binder access to sources.

`-s`

> Require source files to be present. In this mode, the binder must be able to locate all source files that are referenced, in order to check their consistency. In normal mode, if a source file cannot be located it is simply ignored. If you specify this switch, a missing source file is an error.

`-Wxe`

> Override default wide character encoding for standard Text_IO files. Normally the default wide character encoding method used for standard [Wide_[Wide_]]Text_IO files is taken from the encoding specified for the main source input (see description of switch *-gnatWx* for the compiler). The use of this switch for the binder (which has the same set of possible arguments) overrides this default as specified.

`-x`

> Exclude source files. In this mode, the binder only checks that ALI files are consistent with one another. Source files are not accessed. The binder runs faster in this mode, and there is still a guarantee that the resulting program is self-consistent. If a source file has been edited since it was last compiled, and you specify this switch, the binder will not detect that the object file is out of date with respect to the source file. Note that this is the mode that

is automatically used by *gnatmake* because in this case the checking against sources has already been performed by *gnatmake* in the course of compilation (i.e., before binding).

4.4.2.2 Binder Error Message Control

The following switches provide control over the generation of error messages from the binder:

`-v`

> Verbose mode. In the normal mode, brief error messages are generated to `stderr`. If this switch is present, a header is written to `stdout` and any error messages are directed to `stdout`. All that is written to `stderr` is a brief summary message.

`-b`

> Generate brief error messages to `stderr` even if verbose mode is specified. This is relevant only when used with the *-v* switch.

`-mn`

> Limits the number of error messages to *n*, a decimal integer in the range 1-999. The binder terminates immediately if this limit is reached.

`-Mxxx`

> Renames the generated main program from *main* to *xxx*. This is useful in the case of some cross-building environments, where the actual main program is separate from the one generated by *gnatbind*.

`-ws`

> Suppress all warning messages.

`-we`

> Treat any warning messages as fatal errors.

`-t`

> The binder performs a number of consistency checks including:
>   * Check that time stamps of a given source unit are consistent
>   * Check that checksums of a given source unit are consistent
>   * Check that consistent versions of *GNAT* were used for compilation
>   * Check consistency of configuration pragmas as required

Normally failure of such checks, in accordance with the consistency requirements of the Ada Reference Manual, causes error messages to be generated which abort the binder and prevent the output of a binder file and subsequent link to obtain an executable.

The *-t* switch converts these error messages into warnings, so that binding and linking can continue to completion even in the presence of such errors. The result may be a failed link (due to missing symbols), or a non-functional executable which has undefined semantics.

> **Note:** This means that *-t* should be used only in unusual situations, with extreme care.

4.4.2.3 Elaboration Control

The following switches provide additional control over the elaboration order. For full details see [Elaboration Order Handling in GNAT], page 279.

`-p`

> Normally the binder attempts to choose an elaboration order that is likely to minimize the likelihood of an elaboration order error resulting in raising a *Program_Error* exception. This switch reverses the action of the binder, and requests that it deliberately choose an order that is likely to maximize the likelihood of an elaboration error. This is useful in ensuring portability and avoiding dependence on accidental fortuitous elaboration ordering.
>
> Normally it only makes sense to use the *-p* switch if dynamic elaboration checking is used (*-gnatE* switch used for compilation). This is because in the default static elaboration mode, all necessary *Elaborate* and *Elaborate_All* pragmas are implicitly inserted. These implicit pragmas are still respected by the binder in *-p* mode, so a safe elaboration order is assured.
>
> Note that *-p* is not intended for production use; it is more for debugging/experimental use.

4.4.2.4 Output Control

The following switches allow additional control over the output generated by the binder.

`-c`

> Check only. Do not generate the binder output file. In this mode the binder performs all error checks but does not generate an output file.

`-e`

> Output complete list of elaboration-order dependencies, showing the reason for each dependency. This output can be rather extensive but may be useful in diagnosing problems with elaboration order. The output is written to **stdout**.

`-h`

> Output usage information. The output is written to **stdout**.

`-K`

> Output linker options to **stdout**. Includes library search paths, contents of pragmas Ident and Linker_Options, and libraries added by *gnatbind*.

`-l`

> Output chosen elaboration order. The output is written to **stdout**.

`-O`

> Output full names of all the object files that must be linked to provide the Ada component of the program. The output is written to **stdout**. This list includes the files explicitly supplied and referenced by the user as well as implicitly referenced run-time unit files. The latter are omitted if the corresponding units

reside in shared libraries. The directory names for the run-time units depend on the system configuration.

-o *file*

Set name of output file to *file* instead of the normal b~'**mainprog**.adb' default. Note that *file* denote the Ada binder generated body filename. Note that if this option is used, then linking must be done manually. It is not possible to use gnatlink in this case, since it cannot locate the binder file.

-r

Generate list of *pragma Restrictions* that could be applied to the current unit. This is useful for code audit purposes, and also may be used to improve code generation in some cases.

4.4.2.5 Dynamic Allocation Control

The heap control switches – *-H32* and *-H64* – determine whether dynamic allocation uses 32-bit or 64-bit memory. They only affect compiler-generated allocations via __gnat_malloc; explicit calls to *malloc* and related functions from the C run-time library are unaffected.

-H32

Allocate memory on 32-bit heap

-H64

Allocate memory on 64-bit heap. This is the default unless explicitly overridden by a '*Size* clause on the access type.

These switches are only effective on VMS platforms.

4.4.2.6 Binding with Non-Ada Main Programs

The description so far has assumed that the main program is in Ada, and that the task of the binder is to generate a corresponding function *main* that invokes this Ada main program. GNAT also supports the building of executable programs where the main program is not in Ada, but some of the called routines are written in Ada and compiled using GNAT ([Mixed Language Programming], page 52). The following switch is used in this situation:

-n

No main program. The main program is not in Ada.

In this case, most of the functions of the binder are still required, but instead of generating a main program, the binder generates a file containing the following callable routines:

adainit

You must call this routine to initialize the Ada part of the program by calling the necessary elaboration routines. A call to *adainit* is required before the first call to an Ada subprogram.

Note that it is assumed that the basic execution environment must be setup to be appropriate for Ada execution at the point where the first Ada subprogram is called. In particular,

> if the Ada code will do any floating-point operations, then the FPU must be setup in an appropriate manner. For the case of the x86, for example, full precision mode is required. The procedure GNAT.Float_Control.Reset may be used to ensure that the FPU is in the right state.

adafinal

> You must call this routine to perform any library-level finalization required by the Ada subprograms. A call to *adafinal* is required after the last call to an Ada subprogram, and before the program terminates.

If the *-n* switch is given, more than one ALI file may appear on the command line for *gnatbind*. The normal *closure* calculation is performed for each of the specified units. Calculating the closure means finding out the set of units involved by tracing *with* references. The reason it is necessary to be able to specify more than one ALI file is that a given program may invoke two or more quite separate groups of Ada units.

The binder takes the name of its output file from the last specified ALI file, unless overridden by the use of the *-o file*.

The output is an Ada unit in source form that can be compiled with GNAT. This compilation occurs automatically as part of the *gnatlink* processing.

Currently the GNAT run time requires a FPU using 80 bits mode precision. Under targets where this is not the default it is required to call GNAT.Float_Control.Reset before using floating point numbers (this include float computation, float input and output) in the Ada code. A side effect is that this could be the wrong mode for the foreign code where floating point computation could be broken after this call.

4.4.2.7 Binding Programs with No Main Subprogram

It is possible to have an Ada program which does not have a main subprogram. This program will call the elaboration routines of all the packages, then the finalization routines.

The following switch is used to bind programs organized in this manner:

-z

> Normally the binder checks that the unit name given on the command line corresponds to a suitable main subprogram. When this switch is used, a list of ALI files can be given, and the execution of the program consists of elaboration of these units in an appropriate order. Note that the default wide character encoding method for standard Text_IO files is always set to Brackets if this switch is set (you can use the binder switch *-Wx* to override this default).

4.4.3 Command-Line Access

The package *Ada.Command_Line* provides access to the command-line arguments and program name. In order for this interface to operate correctly, the two variables

```
int gnat_argc;
char **gnat_argv;
```

are declared in one of the GNAT library routines. These variables must be set from the actual *argc* and *argv* values passed to the main program. With no *n* present, *gnatbind* generates the C main program to automatically set these variables. If the *n* switch is used, there is no automatic way to set these variables. If they are not set, the procedures in *Ada.Command_Line* will not be available, and any attempt to use them will raise *Constraint_Error*. If command line access is required, your main program must set *gnat_argc* and *gnat_argv* from the *argc* and *argv* values passed to it.

4.4.4 Search Paths for *gnatbind*

The binder takes the name of an ALI file as its argument and needs to locate source files as well as other ALI files to verify object consistency.

For source files, it follows exactly the same search rules as *gcc* (see [Search Paths and the Run-Time Library (RTL)], page 89). For ALI files the directories searched are:

* The directory containing the ALI file named in the command line, unless the switch *-I-* is specified.

* All directories specified by *-I* switches on the *gnatbind* command line, in the order given.

* Each of the directories listed in the text file whose name is given by the `ADA_PRJ_OBJECTS_FILE` environment variable.

  `ADA_PRJ_OBJECTS_FILE` is normally set by gnatmake or by the gnat driver when project files are used. It should not normally be set by other means.

* Each of the directories listed in the value of the `ADA_OBJECTS_PATH` environment variable. Construct this value exactly as the `PATH` environment variable: a list of directory names separated by colons (semicolons when working with the NT version of GNAT).

* The content of the `ada_object_path` file which is part of the GNAT installation tree and is used to store standard libraries such as the GNAT Run Time Library (RTL) unless the switch *-nostdlib* is specified. See [Installing a library], page 35

In the binder the switch *-I* is used to specify both source and library file paths. Use *-aI* instead if you want to specify source paths only, and *-aO* if you want to specify library paths only. This means that for the binder `-Idir` is equivalent to `-aIdir -aO'dir`. The binder generates the bind file (a C language source file) in the current working directory.

The packages *Ada*, *System*, and *Interfaces* and their children make up the GNAT Run-Time Library, together with the package GNAT and its children, which contain a set of useful additional library functions provided by GNAT. The sources for these units are needed by the compiler and are kept together in one directory. The ALI files and object files generated by compiling the RTL are needed by the binder and the linker and are kept together in one directory, typically different from the directory containing the sources. In a normal installation, you need not specify these directory names when compiling or binding. Either the environment variables or the built-in defaults cause these files to be found.

Besides simplifying access to the RTL, a major use of search paths is in compiling sources from multiple directories. This can make development environments much more flexible.

4.4.5 Examples of *gnatbind* Usage

Here are some examples of *gnatbind* invocations:

```
gnatbind hello
```

The main program *Hello* (source program in `hello.adb`) is bound using the standard switch settings. The generated main program is `b~hello.adb`. This is the normal, default use of the binder.

```
gnatbind hello -o mainprog.adb
```

The main program *Hello* (source program in `hello.adb`) is bound using the standard switch settings. The generated main program is `mainprog.adb` with the associated spec in `mainprog.ads`. Note that you must specify the body here not the spec. Note that if this option is used, then linking must be done manually, since gnatlink will not be able to find the generated file.

4.5 Linking with *gnatlink*

This chapter discusses *gnatlink*, a tool that links an Ada program and builds an executable file. This utility invokes the system linker (via the *gcc* command) with a correct list of object files and library references. *gnatlink* automatically determines the list of files and references for the Ada part of a program. It uses the binder file generated by the *gnatbind* to determine this list.

Note: to invoke *gnatlink* with a project file, use the *gnat* driver (see *The_GNAT_Driver_and_Project_Files*).

4.5.1 Running *gnatlink*

The form of the *gnatlink* command is

```
$ gnatlink ['switches'] 'mainprog'[.ali]
           ['non-Ada objects'] ['linker options']
```

The arguments of *gnatlink* (switches, main `ALI` file, non-Ada objects or linker options) may be in any order, provided that no non-Ada object may be mistaken for a main `ALI` file. Any file name `F` without the `.ali` extension will be taken as the main `ALI` file if a file exists whose name is the concatenation of `F` and `.ali`.

`mainprog.ali` references the ALI file of the main program. The `.ali` extension of this file can be omitted. From this reference, *gnatlink* locates the corresponding binder file `b~mainprog.adb` and, using the information in this file along with the list of non-Ada objects and linker options, constructs a linker command file to create the executable.

The arguments other than the *gnatlink* switches and the main `ALI` file are passed to the linker uninterpreted. They typically include the names of object files for units written in other languages than Ada and any library references required to resolve references in any of these foreign language units, or in *Import* pragmas in any Ada units.

linker options is an optional list of linker specific switches. The default linker called by gnatlink is *gcc* which in turn calls the appropriate system linker.

One useful option for the linker is *-s*: it reduces the size of the executable by removing all symbol table and relocation information from the executable.

Standard options for the linker such as *-lmy_lib* or *-Ldir* can be added as is. For options that are not recognized by *gcc* as linker options, use the *gcc* switches *-Xlinker* or *-Wl,*.

Refer to the GCC documentation for details.

Here is an example showing how to generate a linker map:

```
$ gnatlink my_prog -Wl,-Map,MAPFILE
```

Using *linker options* it is possible to set the program stack and heap size. See [Setting Stack Size from gnatlink], page 261 and [Setting Heap Size from gnatlink], page 261.

gnatlink determines the list of objects required by the Ada program and prepends them to the list of objects passed to the linker. *gnatlink* also gathers any arguments set by the use of *pragma Linker_Options* and adds them to the list of arguments presented to the linker.

4.5.2 Switches for *gnatlink*

The following switches are available with the *gnatlink* utility:

--version

> Display Copyright and version, then exit disregarding all other options.

--help

> If *–version* was not used, display usage, then exit disregarding all other options.

-f

> On some targets, the command line length is limited, and *gnatlink* will generate a separate file for the linker if the list of object files is too long. The *-f* switch forces this file to be generated even if the limit is not exceeded. This is useful in some cases to deal with special situations where the command line length is exceeded.

-g

> The option to include debugging information causes the Ada bind file (in other words, `b~mainprog.adb`) to be compiled with *-g*. In addition, the binder does not delete the `b~mainprog.adb`, `b~mainprog.o` and `b~mainprog.ali` files. Without *-g*, the binder removes these files by default.

-n

> Do not compile the file generated by the binder. This may be used when a link is rerun with different options, but there is no need to recompile the binder file.

-v

> Verbose mode. Causes additional information to be output, including a full list of the included object files. This switch option is most useful when you want to see what set of object files are being used in the link step.

-v -v

> Very verbose mode. Requests that the compiler operate in verbose mode when it compiles the binder file, and that the system linker run in verbose mode.

-o *exec-name*

> *exec-name* specifies an alternate name for the generated executable program. If this switch is omitted, the executable has the same name as the main unit. For example, *gnatlink try.ali* creates an executable called `try`.

-b *target*

> Compile your program to run on *target*, which is the name of a system configuration. You must have a GNAT cross-compiler built if *target* is not the same as your host system.

`-B`*dir*

> Load compiler executables (for example, *gnat1*, the Ada compiler) from *dir* instead of the default location. Only use this switch when multiple versions of the GNAT compiler are available. See the *Directory Options* section in *The_GNU_Compiler_Collection* for further details. You would normally use the *-b* or *-V* switch instead.

`-M`

> When linking an executable, create a map file. The name of the map file has the same name as the executable with extension ".map".

`-M=`*mapfile*

> When linking an executable, create a map file. The name of the map file is *mapfile*.

`--GCC=`*compiler_name*

> Program used for compiling the binder file. The default is `gcc`. You need to use quotes around *compiler_name* if *compiler_name* contains spaces or other separator characters. As an example `--GCC="foo -x -y"` will instruct *gnatlink* to use `foo -x -y` as your compiler. Note that switch `-c` is always inserted after your command name. Thus in the above example the compiler command that will be used by *gnatlink* will be `foo -c -x -y`. A limitation of this syntax is that the name and path name of the executable itself must not include any embedded spaces. If the compiler executable is different from the default one (gcc or <prefix>-gcc), then the back-end switches in the ALI file are not used to compile the binder generated source. For example, this is the case with `--GCC="foo -x -y"`. But the back end switches will be used for `--GCC="gcc -gnatv"`. If several `--GCC=compiler_name` are used, only the last *compiler_name* is taken into account. However, all the additional switches are also taken into account. Thus, `--GCC="foo -x -y" --GCC="bar -z -t"` is equivalent to `--GCC="bar -x -y -z -t"`.

`--LINK=`*name*

> *name* is the name of the linker to be invoked. This is especially useful in mixed language programs since languages such as C++ require their own linker to be used. When this switch is omitted, the default name for the linker is *gcc*. When this switch is used, the specified linker is called instead of *gcc* with exactly the same parameters that would have been passed to *gcc* so if the desired linker requires different parameters it is necessary to use a wrapper script that massages the parameters before invoking the real linker. It may be useful to control the exact invocation by using the verbose switch.

4.6 Using the GNU *make* Utility

This chapter offers some examples of makefiles that solve specific problems. It does not explain how to write a makefile, nor does it try to replace the *gnatmake* utility ([Building with gnatmake], page 77).

All the examples in this section are specific to the GNU version of make. Although *make* is a standard utility, and the basic language is the same, these examples use some advanced features found only in *GNU make*.

4.6.1 Using gnatmake in a Makefile

Complex project organizations can be handled in a very powerful way by using GNU make combined with gnatmake. For instance, here is a Makefile which allows you to build each subsystem of a big project into a separate shared library. Such a makefile allows you to significantly reduce the link time of very big applications while maintaining full coherence at each step of the build process.

The list of dependencies are handled automatically by *gnatmake*. The Makefile is simply used to call gnatmake in each of the appropriate directories.

Note that you should also read the example on how to automatically create the list of directories ([Automatically Creating a List of Directories], page 166) which might help you in case your project has a lot of subdirectories.

```
## This Makefile is intended to be used with the following directory
## configuration:
##   - The sources are split into a series of csc (computer software components)
##     Each of these csc is put in its own directory.
##     Their name are referenced by the directory names.
##     They will be compiled into shared library (although this would also work
##     with static libraries
##   - The main program (and possibly other packages that do not belong to any
##     csc is put in the top level directory (where the Makefile is).
##        toplevel_dir __ first_csc  (sources) __ lib (will contain the library)
##                       \\_ second_csc (sources) __ lib (will contain the library
##                       \\_ ...
## Although this Makefile is build for shared library, it is easy to modify
## to build partial link objects instead (modify the lines with -shared and
## gnatlink below)
##
## With this makefile, you can change any file in the system or add any new
## file, and everything will be recompiled correctly (only the relevant shared
## objects will be recompiled, and the main program will be re-linked).

# The list of computer software component for your project. This might be
# generated automatically.
CSC_LIST=aa bb cc

# Name of the main program (no extension)
MAIN=main

# If we need to build objects with -fPIC, uncomment the following line
#NEED_FPIC=-fPIC

# The following variable should give the directory containing libgnat.so
```

```
# You can get this directory through 'gnatls -v'. This is usually the last
# directory in the Object_Path.
GLIB=...


# The directories for the libraries
# (This macro expands the list of CSC to the list of shared libraries, you
# could simply use the expanded form:
# LIB_DIR=aa/lib/libaa.so bb/lib/libbb.so cc/lib/libcc.so
LIB_DIR=${foreach dir,${CSC_LIST},${dir}/lib/lib${dir}.so}

${MAIN}: objects ${LIB_DIR}
    gnatbind ${MAIN} ${CSC_LIST:%=-aO%/lib} -shared
    gnatlink ${MAIN} ${CSC_LIST:%=-l%}

objects::
    # recompile the sources
    gnatmake -c -i ${MAIN}.adb ${NEED_FPIC} ${CSC_LIST:%=-I%}

# Note: In a future version of GNAT, the following commands will be simplified
# by a new tool, gnatmlib
${LIB_DIR}:
    mkdir -p ${dir $@ }
    cd ${dir $@ } && gcc -shared -o ${notdir $@ } ../*.o -L${GLIB} -lgnat
    cd ${dir $@ } && cp -f ../*.ali .

# The dependencies for the modules
# Note that we have to force the expansion of *.o, since in some cases
# make won't be able to do it itself.
aa/lib/libaa.so: ${wildcard aa/*.o}
bb/lib/libbb.so: ${wildcard bb/*.o}
cc/lib/libcc.so: ${wildcard cc/*.o}

# Make sure all of the shared libraries are in the path before starting the
# program
run::
    LD_LIBRARY_PATH=`pwd`/aa/lib:`pwd`/bb/lib:`pwd`/cc/lib ./${MAIN}

clean::
    ${RM} -rf ${CSC_LIST:%=%/lib}
    ${RM} ${CSC_LIST:%=%/*.ali}
    ${RM} ${CSC_LIST:%=%/*.o}
    ${RM} *.o *.ali ${MAIN}
```

4.6.2 Automatically Creating a List of Directories

In most makefiles, you will have to specify a list of directories, and store it in a variable. For small projects, it is often easier to specify each of them by hand, since you then have full control over what is the proper order for these directories, which ones should be included.

However, in larger projects, which might involve hundreds of subdirectories, it might be more convenient to generate this list automatically.

The example below presents two methods. The first one, although less general, gives you more control over the list. It involves wildcard characters, that are automatically expanded by *make*. Its shortcoming is that you need to explicitly specify some of the organization of your project, such as for instance the directory tree depth, whether some directories are found in a separate tree, etc.

The second method is the most general one. It requires an external program, called *find*, which is standard on all Unix systems. All the directories found under a given root directory will be added to the list.

```
# The examples below are based on the following directory hierarchy:
# All the directories can contain any number of files
# ROOT_DIRECTORY ->  a  ->  aa  ->  aaa
#                       ->  ab
#                       ->  ac
#                 -> b ->  ba  ->  baa
#                       ->  bb
#                       ->  bc
# This Makefile creates a variable called DIRS, that can be reused any time
# you need this list (see the other examples in this section)

# The root of your project's directory hierarchy
ROOT_DIRECTORY=.

####
# First method: specify explicitly the list of directories
# This allows you to specify any subset of all the directories you need.
####

DIRS := a/aa/ a/ab/ b/ba/

####
# Second method: use wildcards
# Note that the argument(s) to wildcard below should end with a '/'.
# Since wildcards also return file names, we have to filter them out
# to avoid duplicate directory names.
# We thus use make's 'dir' and 'sort' functions.
# It sets DIRs to the following value (note that the directories aaa and baa
# are not given, unless you change the arguments to wildcard).
# DIRS= ./a/a/ ./b/ ./a/aa/ ./a/ab/ ./a/ac/ ./b/ba/ ./b/bb/ ./b/bc/
####
```

```
DIRS := ${sort ${dir ${wildcard ${ROOT_DIRECTORY}/*/
                    ${ROOT_DIRECTORY}/*/*/}}}

####
# Third method: use an external program
# This command is much faster if run on local disks, avoiding NFS slowdowns.
# This is the most complete command: it sets DIRs to the following value:
# DIRS= ./a ./a/aa ./a/aa/aaa ./a/ab ./a/ac ./b ./b/ba ./b/ba/baa ./b/bb ./b/bc
####

DIRS := ${shell find ${ROOT_DIRECTORY} -type d -print}
```

4.6.3 Generating the Command Line Switches

Once you have created the list of directories as explained in the previous section ([Automatically Creating a List of Directories], page 166), you can easily generate the command line arguments to pass to gnatmake.

For the sake of completeness, this example assumes that the source path is not the same as the object path, and that you have two separate lists of directories.

```
# see "Automatically creating a list of directories" to create
# these variables
SOURCE_DIRS=
OBJECT_DIRS=

GNATMAKE_SWITCHES := ${patsubst %,-aI%,${SOURCE_DIRS}}
GNATMAKE_SWITCHES += ${patsubst %,-aO%,${OBJECT_DIRS}}

all:
        gnatmake ${GNATMAKE_SWITCHES} main_unit
```

4.6.4 Overcoming Command Line Length Limits

One problem that might be encountered on big projects is that many operating systems limit the length of the command line. It is thus hard to give gnatmake the list of source and object directories.

This example shows how you can set up environment variables, which will make *gnatmake* behave exactly as if the directories had been specified on the command line, but have a much higher length limit (or even none on most systems).

It assumes that you have created a list of directories in your Makefile, using one of the methods presented in [Automatically Creating a List of Directories], page 166. For the sake of completeness, we assume that the object path (where the ALI files are found) is different from the sources patch.

Note a small trick in the Makefile below: for efficiency reasons, we create two temporary variables (SOURCE_LIST and OBJECT_LIST), that are expanded immediately by *make*. This way we overcome the standard make behavior which is to expand the variables only when they are actually used.

On Windows, if you are using the standard Windows command shell, you must replace colons with semicolons in the assignments to these variables.

```
# In this example, we create both ADA_INCLUDE_PATH and ADA_OBJECTS_PATH.
# This is the same thing as putting the -I arguments on the command line.
# (the equivalent of using -aI on the command line would be to define
#  only ADA_INCLUDE_PATH, the equivalent of -aO is ADA_OBJECTS_PATH).
# You can of course have different values for these variables.
#
# Note also that we need to keep the previous values of these variables, since
# they might have been set before running 'make' to specify where the GNAT
# library is installed.

# see "Automatically creating a list of directories" to create these
# variables
SOURCE_DIRS=
OBJECT_DIRS=

empty:=
space:=${empty} ${empty}
SOURCE_LIST := ${subst ${space},:,${SOURCE_DIRS}}
OBJECT_LIST := ${subst ${space},:,${OBJECT_DIRS}}
ADA_INCLUDE_PATH += ${SOURCE_LIST}
ADA_OBJECTS_PATH += ${OBJECT_LIST}
export ADA_INCLUDE_PATH
export ADA_OBJECTS_PATH

all:
        gnatmake main_unit
```

5 GNAT Utility Programs

This chapter describes a number of utility programs:

Other GNAT utilities are described elsewhere in this manual:

5.1 The File Cleanup Utility *gnatclean*

gnatclean is a tool that allows the deletion of files produced by the compiler, binder and linker, including ALI files, object files, tree files, expanded source files, library files, interface copy source files, binder generated files and executable files.

5.1.1 Running *gnatclean*

The *gnatclean* command has the form:

```
$ gnatclean switches 'names'
```

where *names* is a list of source file names. Suffixes `.ads` and `adb` may be omitted. If a project file is specified using switch `-P`, then *names* may be completely omitted.

In normal mode, *gnatclean* delete the files produced by the compiler and, if switch *-c* is not specified, by the binder and the linker. In informative-only mode, specified by switch *-n*, the list of files that would have been deleted in normal mode is listed, but no file is actually deleted.

5.1.2 Switches for *gnatclean*

gnatclean recognizes the following switches:

`--version`

> Display Copyright and version, then exit disregarding all other options.

`--help`

> If *–version* was not used, display usage, then exit disregarding all other options.

`--subdirs=subdir`

> Actual object directory of each project file is the subdirectory subdir of the object directory specified or defaulted in the project file.

`--unchecked-shared-lib-imports`

> By default, shared library projects are not allowed to import static library projects. When this switch is used on the command line, this restriction is relaxed.

-c

> Only attempt to delete the files produced by the compiler, not those produced
> by the binder or the linker. The files that are not to be deleted are library files,
> interface copy files, binder generated files and executable files.

-D dir

> Indicate that ALI and object files should normally be found in directory dir.

-F

> When using project files, if some errors or warnings are detected during parsing
> and verbose mode is not in effect (no use of switch -v), then error lines start
> with the full path name of the project file, rather than its simple file name.

-h

> Output a message explaining the usage of gnatclean.

-n

> Informative-only mode. Do not delete any files. Output the list of the files that
> would have been deleted if this switch was not specified.

-Pproject

> Use project file project. Only one such switch can be used. When cleaning a
> project file, the files produced by the compilation of the immediate sources or
> inherited sources of the project files are to be deleted. This is not depending
> on the presence or not of executable names on the command line.

-q

> Quiet output. If there are no errors, do not output anything, except in verbose
> mode (switch -v) or in informative-only mode (switch -n).

-r

> When a project file is specified (using switch -P), clean all imported and ex-
> tended project files, recursively. If this switch is not specified, only the files
> related to the main project file are to be deleted. This switch has no effect if
> no project file is specified.

-v

> Verbose mode.

-vPx

> Indicates the verbosity of the parsing of GNAT project files. [Switches Related
> to Project Files], page 333.

-Xname=value

> Indicates that external variable name has the value value. The Project Manager
> will use this value for occurrences of external(name) when parsing the project
> file. [Switches Related to Project Files], page 333.

-aOdir

> When searching for ALI and object files, look in directory dir.

`-Idir`

> Equivalent to `-aOdir`.

`-I-`

> Do not look for ALI or object files in the directory where *gnatclean* was invoked.

5.2 The GNAT Library Browser *gnatls*

gnatls is a tool that outputs information about compiled units. It gives the relationship between objects, unit names and source files. It can also be used to check the source dependencies of a unit as well as various characteristics.

Note: to invoke *gnatls* with a project file, use the *gnat* driver (see *The_GNAT_Driver_and_Project_Files*).

5.2.1 Running *gnatls*

The *gnatls* command has the form

```
$ gnatls switches 'object_or_ali_file'
```

The main argument is the list of object or `ali` files (see [The Ada Library Information Files], page 31) for which information is requested.

In normal mode, without additional option, *gnatls* produces a four-column listing. Each line represents information for a specific object. The first column gives the full path of the object, the second column gives the name of the principal unit in this object, the third column gives the status of the source and the fourth column gives the full path of the source representing this unit. Here is a simple example of use:

```
$ gnatls *.o
./demo1.o              demo1            DIF demo1.adb
./demo2.o              demo2            OK  demo2.adb
./hello.o              h1               OK  hello.adb
./instr-child.o        instr.child      MOK instr-child.adb
./instr.o              instr            OK  instr.adb
./tef.o                tef              DIF tef.adb
./text_io_example.o    text_io_example  OK  text_io_example.adb
./tgef.o               tgef             DIF tgef.adb
```

The first line can be interpreted as follows: the main unit which is contained in object file `demo1.o` is demo1, whose main source is in `demo1.adb`. Furthermore, the version of the source used for the compilation of demo1 has been modified (DIF). Each source file has a status qualifier which can be:

OK (unchanged)

> The version of the source file used for the compilation of the specified unit corresponds exactly to the actual source file.

MOK (slightly modified)

> The version of the source file used for the compilation of the specified unit differs from the actual source file but not enough to require recompilation. If you use gnatmake with the qualifier *-m (minimal recompilation)*, a file marked MOK will not be recompiled.

DIF (modified)
> No version of the source found on the path corresponds to the source used to build this object.

??? (file not found)
> No source file was found for this unit.

HID (hidden, unchanged version not first on PATH)
> The version of the source that corresponds exactly to the source used for compilation has been found on the path but it is hidden by another version of the same source that has been modified.

5.2.2 Switches for *gnatls*

gnatls recognizes the following switches:

`--version`
> Display Copyright and version, then exit disregarding all other options.

`*--help`
> If *–version* was not used, display usage, then exit disregarding all other options.

`-a`

> Consider all units, including those of the predefined Ada library. Especially useful with *-d*.

`-d`

> List sources from which specified units depend on.

`-h`

> Output the list of options.

`-o`

> Only output information about object files.

`-s`

> Only output information about source files.

`-u`

> Only output information about compilation units.

`-files=file`
> Take as arguments the files listed in text file *file*. Text file *file* may contain empty lines that are ignored. Each nonempty line should contain the name of an existing file. Several such switches may be specified simultaneously.

`-aOdir, -aIdir, -Idir, -I-, -nostdinc`
> Source path manipulation. Same meaning as the equivalent *gnatmake* flags ([Switches for gnatmake], page 78).

`-aPdir`

> Add *dir* at the beginning of the project search dir.

`--RTS=rts-path`'

> Specifies the default location of the runtime library. Same meaning as the equivalent *gnatmake* flag ([Switches for gnatmake], page 78).

`-v`

> Verbose mode. Output the complete source, object and project paths. Do not use the default column layout but instead use long format giving as much as information possible on each requested units, including special characteristics such as:
>
> * *Preelaborable*: The unit is preelaborable in the Ada sense.
> * *No_Elab_Code*: No elaboration code has been produced by the compiler for this unit.
> * *Pure*: The unit is pure in the Ada sense.
> * *Elaborate_Body*: The unit contains a pragma Elaborate_Body.
> * *Remote_Types*: The unit contains a pragma Remote_Types.
> * *Shared_Passive*: The unit contains a pragma Shared_Passive.
> * *Predefined*: This unit is part of the predefined environment and cannot be modified by the user.
> * *Remote_Call_Interface*: The unit contains a pragma Remote_Call_Interface.

5.2.3 Example of *gnatls* Usage

Example of using the verbose switch. Note how the source and object paths are affected by the -I switch.

```
$ gnatls -v -I.. demo1.o

GNATLS 5.03w (20041123-34)
Copyright 1997-2004 Free Software Foundation, Inc.

Source Search Path:
   <Current_Directory>
   ../
   /home/comar/local/adainclude/

Object Search Path:
   <Current_Directory>
   ../
   /home/comar/local/lib/gcc-lib/x86-linux/3.4.3/adalib/

Project Search Path:
   <Current_Directory>
   /home/comar/local/lib/gnat/

./demo1.o
   Unit =>
```

```
Name    => demo1
Kind    => subprogram body
Flags   => No_Elab_Code
Source => demo1.adb    modified
```

The following is an example of use of the dependency list. Note the use of the -s switch which gives a straight list of source files. This can be useful for building specialized scripts.

```
$ gnatls -d demo2.o
./demo2.o    demo2         OK demo2.adb
                           OK gen_list.ads
                           OK gen_list.adb
                           OK instr.ads
                           OK instr-child.ads


$ gnatls -d -s -a demo1.o
demo1.adb
/home/comar/local/adainclude/ada.ads
/home/comar/local/adainclude/a-finali.ads
/home/comar/local/adainclude/a-filico.ads
/home/comar/local/adainclude/a-stream.ads
/home/comar/local/adainclude/a-tags.ads
gen_list.ads
gen_list.adb
/home/comar/local/adainclude/gnat.ads
/home/comar/local/adainclude/g-io.ads
instr.ads
/home/comar/local/adainclude/system.ads
/home/comar/local/adainclude/s-exctab.ads
/home/comar/local/adainclude/s-finimp.ads
/home/comar/local/adainclude/s-finroo.ads
/home/comar/local/adainclude/s-secsta.ads
/home/comar/local/adainclude/s-stalib.ads
/home/comar/local/adainclude/s-stoele.ads
/home/comar/local/adainclude/s-stratt.ads
/home/comar/local/adainclude/s-tasoli.ads
/home/comar/local/adainclude/s-unstyp.ads
/home/comar/local/adainclude/unchconv.ads
```

5.3 The Cross-Referencing Tools *gnatxref* and *gnatfind*

The compiler generates cross-referencing information (unless you set the **-gnatx** switch), which are saved in the .ali files. This information indicates where in the source each entity is declared and referenced. Note that entities in package Standard are not included, but entities in all other predefined units are included in the output.

Before using any of these two tools, you need to compile successfully your application, so that GNAT gets a chance to generate the cross-referencing information.

The two tools *gnatxref* and *gnatfind* take advantage of this information to provide the user with the capability to easily locate the declaration and references to an entity. These tools are quite similar, the difference being that *gnatfind* is intended for locating definitions and/or references to a specified entity or entities, whereas *gnatxref* is oriented to generating a full report of all cross-references.

To use these tools, you must not compile your application using the *-gnatx* switch on the *gnatmake* command line (see [Building with gnatmake], page 77). Otherwise, cross-referencing information will not be generated.

Note: to invoke *gnatxref* or *gnatfind* with a project file, use the *gnat* driver (see *The_GNAT_Driver_and_Project_Files*).

5.3.1 *gnatxref* Switches

The command invocation for *gnatxref* is:

```
$ gnatxref ['switches'] 'sourcefile1' ['sourcefile2' ...]
```

where

sourcefile1 [, *sourcefile2* ...]

> identify the source files for which a report is to be generated. The 'with'ed units will be processed too. You must provide at least one file.

> These file names are considered to be regular expressions, so for instance specifying `source*.adb` is the same as giving every file in the current directory whose name starts with `source` and whose extension is `adb`.

> You shouldn't specify any directory name, just base names. *gnatxref* and *gnatfind* will be able to locate these files by themselves using the source path. If you specify directories, no result is produced.

The following switches are available for *gnatxref*:

`-version`

> Display Copyright and version, then exit disregarding all other options.

`-help`

> If *–version* was not used, display usage, then exit disregarding all other options.

`a`

> If this switch is present, *gnatfind* and *gnatxref* will parse the read-only files found in the library search path. Otherwise, these files will be ignored. This option can be used to protect Gnat sources or your own libraries from being parsed, thus making *gnatfind* and *gnatxref* much faster, and their output much smaller. Read-only here refers to access or permissions status in the file system for the current user.

`aIDIR`

> When looking for source files also look in directory DIR. The order in which source file search is undertaken is the same as for *gnatmake*.

`aODIR`

> When searching for library and object files, look in directory DIR. The order in which library files are searched is the same as for *gnatmake*.

`nostdinc`

Do not look for sources in the system default directory.

`nostdlib`

Do not look for library files in the system default directory.

`-ext=extension`

Specify an alternate ali file extension. The default is *ali* and other extensions (e.g. *gli* for C/C++ sources when using *-fdump-xref*) may be specified via this switch. Note that if this switch overrides the default, which means that only the new extension will be considered.

`-RTS=rts-path`

Specifies the default location of the runtime library. Same meaning as the equivalent *gnatmake* flag ([Switches for gnatmake], page 78).

`d`

If this switch is set *gnatxref* will output the parent type reference for each matching derived types.

`f`

If this switch is set, the output file names will be preceded by their directory (if the file was found in the search path). If this switch is not set, the directory will not be printed.

`g`

If this switch is set, information is output only for library-level entities, ignoring local entities. The use of this switch may accelerate *gnatfind* and *gnatxref*.

`IDIR`

Equivalent to `-aODIR -aIDIR`.

`pFILE`

Specify a project file to use (see the *GNAT_Project_Manager* chapter in the *GPRbuild User's Guide*). If you need to use the `.gpr` project files, you should use gnatxref through the GNAT driver (*gnat xref -Pproject*).

By default, *gnatxref* and *gnatfind* will try to locate a project file in the current directory.

If a project file is either specified or found by the tools, then the content of the source directory and object directory lines are added as if they had been specified respectively by `-aI` and `-aO`.

`u`

Output only unused symbols. This may be really useful if you give your main compilation unit on the command line, as *gnatxref* will then display every unused entity and 'with'ed package.

`v`

Instead of producing the default output, *gnatxref* will generate a **tags** file that can be used by vi. For examples how to use this feature, see [Examples of gnatxref Usage], page 183. The tags file is output to the standard output, thus you will have to redirect it to a file.

All these switches may be in any order on the command line, and may even appear after the file names. They need not be separated by spaces, thus you can say `gnatxref -ag` instead of `gnatxref -a -g`.

5.3.2 *gnatfind* Switches

The command invocation for *gnatfind* is:

```
$ gnatfind ['switches'] 'pattern'[:'sourcefile'[:'line'[:'column']]]
          ['file1' 'file2' ...]
```

with the following iterpretation of the command arguments:

pattern

> An entity will be output only if it matches the regular expression found in *pattern*, see [Regular Expressions in gnatfind and gnatxref], page 182.
>
> Omitting the pattern is equivalent to specifying *, which will match any entity. Note that if you do not provide a pattern, you have to provide both a sourcefile and a line.
>
> Entity names are given in Latin-1, with uppercase/lowercase equivalence for matching purposes. At the current time there is no support for 8-bit codes other than Latin-1, or for wide characters in identifiers.

sourcefile

> *gnatfind* will look for references, bodies or declarations of symbols referenced in `sourcefile`, at line *line* and column *column*. See [Examples of gnatfind Usage], page 185 for syntax examples.

line

> A decimal integer identifying the line number containing the reference to the entity (or entities) to be located.

column

> A decimal integer identifying the exact location on the line of the first character of the identifier for the entity reference. Columns are numbered from 1.

file1 file2 ...

> The search will be restricted to these source files. If none are given, then the search will be conducted for every library file in the search path. These files must appear only after the pattern or sourcefile.
>
> These file names are considered to be regular expressions, so for instance specifying `source*.adb` is the same as giving every file in the current directory whose name starts with `source` and whose extension is `adb`.
>
> The location of the spec of the entity will always be displayed, even if it isn't in one of `file1`, `file2`, ... The occurrences of the entity in the separate units of the ones given on the command line will also be displayed.
>
> Note that if you specify at least one file in this part, *gnatfind* may sometimes not be able to find the body of the subprograms.

At least one of 'sourcefile' or 'pattern' has to be present on the command line.

The following switches are available:

--version

>   Display Copyright and version, then exit disregarding all other options.

-help

>   If *–version* was not used, display usage, then exit disregarding all other options.

a

>   If this switch is present, *gnatfind* and *gnatxref* will parse the read-only files found in the library search path. Otherwise, these files will be ignored. This option can be used to protect Gnat sources or your own libraries from being parsed, thus making *gnatfind* and *gnatxref* much faster, and their output much smaller. Read-only here refers to access or permission status in the file system for the current user.

aI*DIR*

>   When looking for source files also look in directory DIR. The order in which source file search is undertaken is the same as for *gnatmake*.

aO*DIR*

>   When searching for library and object files, look in directory DIR. The order in which library files are searched is the same as for *gnatmake*.

nostdinc

>   Do not look for sources in the system default directory.

nostdlib

>   Do not look for library files in the system default directory.

-ext=*extension*

>   Specify an alternate ali file extension. The default is *ali* and other extensions (e.g. *gli* for C/C++ sources when using *-fdump-xref*) may be specified via this switch. Note that if this switch overrides the default, which means that only the new extension will be considered.

-RTS=*rts-path*

>   Specifies the default location of the runtime library. Same meaning as the equivalent *gnatmake* flag ([Switches for gnatmake], page 78).

d

>   If this switch is set, then *gnatfind* will output the parent type reference for each matching derived types.

e

>   By default, *gnatfind* accept the simple regular expression set for *pattern*. If this switch is set, then the pattern will be considered as full Unix-style regular expression.

f

> If this switch is set, the output file names will be preceded by their directory (if the file was found in the search path). If this switch is not set, the directory will not be printed.

g

> If this switch is set, information is output only for library-level entities, ignoring local entities. The use of this switch may accelerate *gnatfind* and *gnatxref*.

IDIR

> Equivalent to -aODIR -aIDIR.

pFILE

> Specify a project file (see the *GNAT_Project_Manager* chapter in the *GPRbuild User's Guide*). By default, *gnatxref* and *gnatfind* will try to locate a project file in the current directory.
>
> If a project file is either specified or found by the tools, then the content of the source directory and object directory lines are added as if they had been specified respectively by -aI and -aO.

r

> By default, *gnatfind* will output only the information about the declaration, body or type completion of the entities. If this switch is set, the *gnatfind* will locate every reference to the entities in the files specified on the command line (or in every file in the search path if no file is given on the command line).

s

> If this switch is set, then *gnatfind* will output the content of the Ada source file lines were the entity was found.

t

> If this switch is set, then *gnatfind* will output the type hierarchy for the specified type. It act like -d option but recursively from parent type to parent type. When this switch is set it is not possible to specify more than one file.

All these switches may be in any order on the command line, and may even appear after the file names. They need not be separated by spaces, thus you can say `gnatxref -ag` instead of `gnatxref -a -g`.

As stated previously, gnatfind will search in every directory in the search path. You can force it to look only in the current directory if you specify * at the end of the command line.

5.3.3 Project Files for *gnatxref* and *gnatfind*

Project files allow a programmer to specify how to compile its application, where to find sources, etc. These files are used primarily by GPS, but they can also be used by the two tools *gnatxref* and *gnatfind*.

A project file name must end with `.gpr`. If a single one is present in the current directory, then *gnatxref* and *gnatfind* will extract the information from it. If multiple project files are found, none of them is read, and you have to use the `-p` switch to specify the one you want to use.

The following lines can be included, even though most of them have default values which can be used in most cases. The lines can be entered in any order in the file. Except for `src_dir` and `obj_dir`, you can only have one instance of each line. If you have multiple instances, only the last one is taken into account.

*

  src_dir=DIR

> [default: "./"]. Specifies a directory where to look for source files. Multiple *src_dir* lines can be specified and they will be searched in the order they are specified.

*

  obj_dir=DIR

> [default: "./"]. Specifies a directory where to look for object and library files. Multiple *obj_dir* lines can be specified, and they will be searched in the order they are specified

*

  comp_opt=SWITCHES

> [default: ""]. Creates a variable which can be referred to subsequently by using the *${comp_opt}* notation. This is intended to store the default switches given to *gnatmake* and *gcc*.

*

  bind_opt=SWITCHES

> [default: ""]. Creates a variable which can be referred to subsequently by using the `$bind_opt` notation. This is intended to store the default switches given to *gnatbind*.

*

  link_opt=SWITCHES

> [default: ""]. Creates a variable which can be referred to subsequently by using the `$link_opt` notation. This is intended to store the default switches given to *gnatlink*.

*

  main=EXECUTABLE

> [default: ""]. Specifies the name of the executable for the application. This variable can be referred to in the following lines by using the *${main* notation.

*

  comp_cmd=COMMAND

> [default: "*gcc -c -I${src_dir} -g -gnatq*"]. Specifies the command used to compile a single file in the application.

*

make_cmd=COMMAND

> [default: *"gnatmake ${main} -aI${src_dir} -aO${obj_dir} -g -gnatq -cargs ${comp_opt} -bargs ${bind_opt} -largs ${link_opt}"*]. Specifies the command used to recompile the whole application.

*

run_cmd=COMMAND

> [default: *"${main}"*]. Specifies the command used to run the application.

*

debug_cmd=COMMAND

> [default: *"gdb ${main}"*]. Specifies the command used to debug the application

gnatxref and *gnatfind* only take into account the *src_dir* and *obj_dir* lines, and ignore the others.

5.3.4 Regular Expressions in *gnatfind* and *gnatxref*

As specified in the section about *gnatfind*, the pattern can be a regular expression. Two kinds of regular expressions are recognized:

*

Globbing pattern

> These are the most common regular expression. They are the same as are generally used in a Unix shell command line, or in a DOS session.
>
> Here is a more formal grammar:

```
regexp ::= term
term    ::= elmt            -- matches elmt
term    ::= elmt elmt       -- concatenation (elmt then elmt)
term    ::= *               -- any string of 0 or more characters
term    ::= ?               -- matches any character
term    ::= [char {char}]   -- matches any character listed
term    ::= [char - char]   -- matches any character in range
```

*

Full regular expression

> The second set of regular expressions is much more powerful. This is the type of regular expressions recognized by utilities such as `grep`.
>
> The following is the form of a regular expression, expressed in same BNF style as is found in the Ada Reference Manual:

```
regexp ::= term {| term}    -- alternation (term or term ...)

term ::= item {item}        -- concatenation (item then item)

item ::= elmt               -- match elmt
item ::= elmt *             -- zero or more elmt's
item ::= elmt +             -- one or more elmt's
item ::= elmt ?             -- matches elmt or nothing
```

```
elmt ::= nschar              -- matches given character
elmt ::= [nschar {nschar}]   -- matches any character listed
elmt ::= [^ nschar {nschar}] -- matches any character not listed
elmt ::= [char - char]       -- matches chars in given range
elmt ::= \\ char             -- matches given character
elmt ::= .                   -- matches any single character
elmt ::= ( regexp )          -- parens used for grouping

char  ::= any character, including special characters
nschar ::= any character except ()[].*+?^
```

Here are a few examples:

abcde|fghi

> will match any of the two strings abcde and
> fghi,

abc*d

> will match any string like abd, abcd, abccd,
> abcccd, and so on,

[a-z]+

> will match any string which has only lower-
> case characters in it (and at least one char-
> acter.

5.3.5 Examples of *gnatxref* Usage

5.3.5.1 General Usage

For the following examples, we will consider the following units:

```
main.ads:
1: with Bar;
2: package Main is
3:    procedure Foo (B : in Integer);
4:    C : Integer;
5: private
6:    D : Integer;
7: end Main;

main.adb:
1: package body Main is
2:    procedure Foo (B : in Integer) is
3:    begin
4:       C := B;
5:       D := B;
6:       Bar.Print (B);
7:       Bar.Print (C);
8:    end Foo;
```

```
9: end Main;

bar.ads:
1: package Bar is
2:      procedure Print (B : Integer);
3: end bar;
```

The first thing to do is to recompile your application (for instance, in that case just by doing a **gnatmake main**, so that GNAT generates the cross-referencing information. You can then issue any of the following commands:

* **gnatxref main.adb** *gnatxref* generates cross-reference information for main.adb and every unit 'with'ed by main.adb.

  The output would be:

```
            B                                               Type: Int
              Decl: bar.ads          2:22
            B                                               Type: Int
              Decl: main.ads         3:20
              Body: main.adb         2:20
              Ref:  main.adb         4:13       5:13       6:19
            Bar                                             Type: Uni
              Decl: bar.ads          1:9
              Ref:  main.adb         6:8        7:8
                    main.ads         1:6
            C                                               Type: Int
              Decl: main.ads         4:5
              Modi: main.adb         4:8
              Ref:  main.adb         7:19
            D                                               Type: Int
              Decl: main.ads         6:5
              Modi: main.adb         5:8
            Foo                                             Type: Uni
              Decl: main.ads         3:15
              Body: main.adb         2:15
            Main                                            Type: Un
              Decl: main.ads         2:9
              Body: main.adb         1:14
            Print                                           Type: Un
              Decl: bar.ads          2:15
              Ref:  main.adb         6:12       7:12
```

  This shows that the entity *Main* is declared in main.ads, line 2, column 9, its body is in main.adb, line 1, column 14 and is not referenced any where.

  The entity *Print* is declared in bar.ads, line 2, column 15 and it is referenced in main.adb, line 6 column 12 and line 7 column 12.

* **gnatxref package1.adb package2.ads** *gnatxref* will generates

> cross-reference information for package1.adb, package2.ads and any
> other package 'with'ed by any of these.

5.3.5.2 Using gnatxref with vi

gnatxref can generate a tags file output, which can be used directly from *vi*. Note that the standard version of *vi* will not work properly with overloaded symbols. Consider using another free implementation of *vi*, such as *vim*.

```
$ gnatxref -v gnatfind.adb > tags
```

The following command will generate the tags file for *gnatfind* itself (if the sources are in the search path!):

```
$ gnatxref -v gnatfind.adb > tags
```

From *vi*, you can then use the command `:tag entity` (replacing *entity* by whatever you are looking for), and vi will display a new file with the corresponding declaration of entity.

5.3.6 Examples of *gnatfind* Usage

* `gnatfind -f xyz:main.adb` Find declarations for all entities xyz referenced at least once in main.adb. The references are search in every library file in the search path.

  The directories will be printed as well (as the `-f` switch is set)

  The output will look like:

  ```
  directory/main.ads:106:14: xyz <= declaration
  directory/main.adb:24:10: xyz <= body
  directory/foo.ads:45:23: xyz <= declaration
  ```

  I.e., one of the entities xyz found in main.adb is declared at line 12 of main.ads (and its body is in main.adb), and another one is declared at line 45 of foo.ads

* `gnatfind -fs xyz:main.adb` This is the same command as the previous one, but *gnatfind* will display the content of the Ada source file lines.

  The output will look like:

  ```
  directory/main.ads:106:14: xyz <= declaration
     procedure xyz;
  directory/main.adb:24:10: xyz <= body
     procedure xyz is
  directory/foo.ads:45:23: xyz <= declaration
     xyz : Integer;
  ```

  This can make it easier to find exactly the location your are looking for.

* `gnatfind -r "*x*":main.ads:123 foo.adb` Find references to all entities containing an x that are referenced on line 123 of main.ads. The references will be searched only in main.ads and foo.adb.

* `gnatfind main.ads:123` Find declarations and bodies for all entities that are referenced on line 123 of main.ads.

  This is the same as `gnatfind "*":main.adb:123`

* `gnatfind mydir/main.adb:123:45` Find the declaration for the entity referenced at column 45 in line 123 of file main.adb in directory mydir. Note that it is usual to omit

the identifier name when the column is given, since the column position identifies a unique reference.

The column has to be the beginning of the identifier, and should not point to any character in the middle of the identifier.

5.4 The Ada to HTML Converter *gnathtml*

gnathtml is a Perl script that allows Ada source files to be browsed using standard Web browsers. For installation information, see [Installing gnathtml], page 187.

Ada reserved keywords are highlighted in a bold font and Ada comments in a blue font. Unless your program was compiled with the gcc *-gnatx* switch to suppress the generation of cross-referencing information, user defined variables and types will appear in a different color; you will be able to click on any identifier and go to its declaration.

5.4.1 Invoking *gnathtml*

The command line is as follows:

$ perl gnathtml.pl ['switches'] 'ada-files'

You can specify as many Ada files as you want. *gnathtml* will generate an html file for every ada file, and a global file called index.htm. This file is an index of every identifier defined in the files.

The following switches are available:

83

> Only the Ada 83 subset of keywords will be highlighted.

cc *color*

> This option allows you to change the color used for comments. The default value is green. The color argument can be any name accepted by html.

d

> If the Ada files depend on some other files (for instance through *with* clauses, the latter files will also be converted to html. Only the files in the user project will be converted to html, not the files in the run-time library itself.

D

> This command is the same as *-d* above, but *gnathtml* will also look for files in the run-time library, and generate html files for them.

ext *extension*

> This option allows you to change the extension of the generated HTML files. If you do not specify an extension, it will default to htm.

f

> By default, gnathtml will generate html links only for global entities ('with'ed units, global variables and types,...). If you specify *-f* on the command line, then links will be generated for local entities too.

l *number*

> If this switch is provided and *number* is not 0, then *gnathtml* will number the html files every *number* line.

I `dir`

> Specify a directory to search for library files (`.ALI` files) and source files. You can provide several -I switches on the command line, and the directories will be parsed in the order of the command line.

o `dir`

> Specify the output directory for html files. By default, gnathtml will saved the generated html files in a subdirectory named `html/`.

p `file`

> If you are using Emacs and the most recent Emacs Ada mode, which provides a full Integrated Development Environment for compiling, checking, running and debugging applications, you may use `.gpr` files to give the directories where Emacs can find sources and object files.
>
> Using this switch, you can tell gnathtml to use these files. This allows you to get an html version of your application, even if it is spread over multiple directories.

sc `color`

> This switch allows you to change the color used for symbol definitions. The default value is red. The color argument can be any name accepted by html.

t `file`

> This switch provides the name of a file. This file contains a list of file names to be converted, and the effect is exactly as though they had appeared explicitly on the command line. This is the recommended way to work around the command line length limit on some systems.

5.4.2 Installing *gnathtml*

Perl needs to be installed on your machine to run this script. *Perl* is freely available for almost every architecture and operating system via the Internet.

On Unix systems, you may want to modify the first line of the script *gnathtml*, to explicitly specify where Perl is located. The syntax of this line is:

```
#!full_path_name_to_perl
```

Alternatively, you may run the script using the following command line:

```
$ perl gnathtml.pl ['switches'] 'files'
```

6 GNAT and Program Execution

This chapter covers several topics:

6.1 Running and Debugging Ada Programs

This section discusses how to debug Ada programs.

An incorrect Ada program may be handled in three ways by the GNAT compiler:

* The illegality may be a violation of the static semantics of Ada. In that case GNAT diagnoses the constructs in the program that are illegal. It is then a straightforward matter for the user to modify those parts of the program.

* The illegality may be a violation of the dynamic semantics of Ada. In that case the program compiles and executes, but may generate incorrect results, or may terminate abnormally with some exception.

* When presented with a program that contains convoluted errors, GNAT itself may terminate abnormally without providing full diagnostics on the incorrect user program.

6.1.1 The GNAT Debugger GDB

GDB is a general purpose, platform-independent debugger that can be used to debug mixed-language programs compiled with *gcc*, and in particular is capable of debugging Ada programs compiled with GNAT. The latest versions of *GDB* are Ada-aware and can handle complex Ada data structures.

See *Debugging with GDB*, for full details on the usage of *GDB*, including a section on its usage on programs. This manual should be consulted for full details. The section that follows is a brief introduction to the philosophy and use of *GDB*.

When GNAT programs are compiled, the compiler optionally writes debugging information into the generated object file, including information on line numbers, and on declared types and variables. This information is separate from the generated code. It makes the object files considerably larger, but it does not add to the size of the actual executable that will be loaded into memory, and has no impact on run-time performance. The generation of debug information is triggered by the use of the -g switch in the *gcc* or *gnatmake* command used to carry out the compilations. It is important to emphasize that the use of these options does not change the generated code.

The debugging information is written in standard system formats that are used by many tools, including debuggers and profilers. The format of the information is typically designed to describe C types and semantics, but GNAT implements a translation scheme which allows full details about Ada types and variables to be encoded into these standard C formats.

Details of this encoding scheme may be found in the file exp_dbug.ads in the GNAT source distribution. However, the details of this encoding are, in general, of no interest to a user, since *GDB* automatically performs the necessary decoding.

When a program is bound and linked, the debugging information is collected from the object files, and stored in the executable image of the program. Again, this process significantly increases the size of the generated executable file, but it does not increase the size of the executable program itself. Furthermore, if this program is run in the normal manner, it runs exactly as if the debug information were not present, and takes no more actual memory.

However, if the program is run under control of *GDB*, the debugger is activated. The image of the program is loaded, at which point it is ready to run. If a run command is given, then the program will run exactly as it would have if *GDB* were not present. This is a crucial part of the *GDB* design philosophy. *GDB* is entirely non-intrusive until a breakpoint is encountered. If no breakpoint is ever hit, the program will run exactly as it would if no debugger were present. When a breakpoint is hit, *GDB* accesses the debugging information and can respond to user commands to inspect variables, and more generally to report on the state of execution.

6.1.2 Running GDB

This section describes how to initiate the debugger.

The debugger can be launched from a *GPS* menu or directly from the command line. The description below covers the latter use. All the commands shown can be used in the *GPS* debug console window, but there are usually more GUI-based ways to achieve the same effect.

The command to run *GDB* is

```
$ gdb program
```

where *program* is the name of the executable file. This activates the debugger and results in a prompt for debugger commands. The simplest command is simply *run*, which causes the program to run exactly as if the debugger were not present. The following section describes some of the additional commands that can be given to *GDB*.

6.1.3 Introduction to GDB Commands

GDB contains a large repertoire of commands. See *Debugging with GDB* for extensive documentation on the use of these commands, together with examples of their use. Furthermore, the command *help* invoked from within GDB activates a simple help facility which summarizes the available commands and their options. In this section we summarize a few of the most commonly used commands to give an idea of what *GDB* is about. You should create a simple program with debugging information and experiment with the use of these *GDB* commands on the program as you read through the following section.

*

set args 'arguments'

> The *arguments* list above is a list of arguments to be passed to the program on a subsequent run command, just as though the arguments had been entered on a normal invocation of the program. The *set args* command is not needed if the program does not require arguments.

*

run

> The *run* command causes execution of the program to start from the beginning. If the program is already running, that is to say if you are currently positioned at a breakpoint, then a prompt will ask for confirmation that you want to abandon the current execution and restart.

*

breakpoint 'location'

> The breakpoint command sets a breakpoint, that is to say a point at which execution will halt and *GDB* will await further commands. *location* is either a line number within a file, given in the format *file:linenumber*, or it is the name of a subprogram. If you request that a breakpoint be set on a subprogram that is overloaded, a prompt will ask you to specify on which of those subprograms you want to breakpoint. You can also specify that all of them should be breakpointed. If the program is run and execution encounters the breakpoint, then the program stops and *GDB* signals that the breakpoint was encountered by printing the line of code before which the program is halted.

*

catch exception 'name'

> This command causes the program execution to stop whenever exception *name* is raised. If *name* is omitted, then the execution is suspended when any exception is raised.

*

print 'expression'

> This will print the value of the given expression. Most simple Ada expression formats are properly handled by *GDB*, so the expression can contain function calls, variables, operators, and attribute references.

*

continue

> Continues execution following a breakpoint, until the next breakpoint or the termination of the program.

*

step

> Executes a single line after a breakpoint. If the next statement is a subprogram call, execution continues into (the first statement of) the called subprogram.

*

next

> Executes a single line. If this line is a subprogram call, executes and returns from the call.

*

    list

          Lists a few lines around the current source location. In practice, it is usually more convenient to have a separate edit window open with the relevant source file displayed. Successive applications of this command print subsequent lines. The command can be given an argument which is a line number, in which case it displays a few lines around the specified one.

*

    backtrace

          Displays a backtrace of the call chain. This command is typically used after a breakpoint has occurred, to examine the sequence of calls that leads to the current breakpoint. The display includes one line for each activation record (frame) corresponding to an active subprogram.

*

    up

          At a breakpoint, *GDB* can display the values of variables local to the current frame. The command *up* can be used to examine the contents of other active frames, by moving the focus up the stack, that is to say from callee to caller, one frame at a time.

*

    down

          Moves the focus of *GDB* down from the frame currently being examined to the frame of its callee (the reverse of the previous command),

*

    frame 'n'

          Inspect the frame with the given number. The value 0 denotes the frame of the current breakpoint, that is to say the top of the call stack.

*

    kill

          Kills the child process in which the program is running under GDB. This may be useful for several purposes:

        * It allows you to recompile and relink your program, since on many systems you cannot regenerate an executable file while it is running in a process.

        * You can run your program outside the debugger, on systems that do not permit executing a program outside GDB while breakpoints are set within GDB.

        * It allows you to debug a core dump rather than a running process.

The above list is a very short introduction to the commands that *GDB* provides. Important additional capabilities, including conditional breakpoints, the ability to execute command sequences on a breakpoint, the ability to debug at the machine instruction level and many other features are described in detail in *Debugging with GDB*. Note that most commands can be abbreviated (for example, c for continue, bt for backtrace).

6.1.4 Using Ada Expressions

GDB supports a fairly large subset of Ada expression syntax, with some extensions. The philosophy behind the design of this subset is

* That *GDB* should provide basic literals and access to operations for arithmetic, dereferencing, field selection, indexing, and subprogram calls, leaving more sophisticated computations to subprograms written into the program (which therefore may be called from *GDB*).

* That type safety and strict adherence to Ada language restrictions are not particularly relevant in a debugging context.

* That brevity is important to the *GDB* user.

Thus, for brevity, the debugger acts as if there were implicit *with* and *use* clauses in effect for all user-written packages, thus making it unnecessary to fully qualify most names with their packages, regardless of context. Where this causes ambiguity, *GDB* asks the user's intent.

For details on the supported Ada syntax, see *Debugging with GDB*.

6.1.5 Calling User-Defined Subprograms

An important capability of *GDB* is the ability to call user-defined subprograms while debugging. This is achieved simply by entering a subprogram call statement in the form:

```
call subprogram-name (parameters)
```

The keyword *call* can be omitted in the normal case where the *subprogram-name* does not coincide with any of the predefined *GDB* commands.

The effect is to invoke the given subprogram, passing it the list of parameters that is supplied. The parameters can be expressions and can include variables from the program being debugged. The subprogram must be defined at the library level within your program, and *GDB* will call the subprogram within the environment of your program execution (which means that the subprogram is free to access or even modify variables within your program).

The most important use of this facility is in allowing the inclusion of debugging routines that are tailored to particular data structures in your program. Such debugging routines can be written to provide a suitably high-level description of an abstract type, rather than a low-level dump of its physical layout. After all, the standard *GDB* *print* command only knows the physical layout of your types, not their abstract meaning. Debugging routines can provide information at the desired semantic level and are thus enormously useful.

For example, when debugging GNAT itself, it is crucial to have access to the contents of the tree nodes used to represent the program internally. But tree nodes are represented simply by an integer value (which in turn is an index into a table of nodes). Using the *print* command on a tree node would simply print this integer value, which is not very useful. But the PN routine (defined in file treepr.adb in the GNAT sources) takes a tree node as input, and displays a useful high level representation of the tree node, which includes the syntactic category of the node, its position in the source, the integers that denote descendant nodes and parent node, as well as varied semantic information. To study this example in more detail, you might want to look at the body of the PN procedure in the stated file.

Another useful application of this capability is to deal with situations of complex data which are not handled suitably by GDB. For example, if you specify Convention Fortran for a multi-dimensional array, GDB does not know that the ordering of array elements has been switched and will not properly address the array elements. In such a case, instead of trying to print the elements directly from GDB, you can write a callable procedure that prints the elements in the desired format.

6.1.6 Using the *next* Command in a Function

When you use the *next* command in a function, the current source location will advance to the next statement as usual. A special case arises in the case of a *return* statement.

Part of the code for a return statement is the 'epilogue' of the function. This is the code that returns to the caller. There is only one copy of this epilogue code, and it is typically associated with the last return statement in the function if there is more than one return. In some implementations, this epilogue is associated with the first statement of the function.

The result is that if you use the *next* command from a return statement that is not the last return statement of the function you may see a strange apparent jump to the last return statement or to the start of the function. You should simply ignore this odd jump. The value returned is always that from the first return statement that was stepped through.

6.1.7 Stopping When Ada Exceptions Are Raised

You can set catchpoints that stop the program execution when your program raises selected exceptions.

*

    catch exception

            Set a catchpoint that stops execution whenever (any task in the) program raises any exception.

*

    catch exception 'name'

            Set a catchpoint that stops execution whenever (any task in the) program raises the exception *name*.

*

    catch exception unhandled

            Set a catchpoint that stops executing whenever (any task in the) program raises an exception for which there is no handler.

*

    info exceptions, info exceptions 'regexp'

            The *info exceptions* command permits the user to examine all defined exceptions within Ada programs. With a regular expression, *regexp*, as argument, prints out only those exceptions whose name matches *regexp*.

6.1.8 Ada Tasks

GDB allows the following task-related commands:

*

> *info tasks*

>> This command shows a list of current Ada tasks, as in the following example:

```
(gdb) info tasks
    ID       TID P-ID   Thread Pri State                 Name
     1   8088000   0   807e000  15 Child Activation Wait main_task
     2   80a4000   1   80ae000  15 Accept/Select Wait    b
     3   809a800   1   80a4800  15 Child Activation Wait a
 *   4   80ae800   3   80b8000  15 Running               c
```

>> In this listing, the asterisk before the first task indicates it to be the currently running task. The first column lists the task ID that is used to refer to tasks in the following commands.

> * *break 'linespec' task 'taskid', break 'linespec' task 'taskid' if ...*

>> These commands are like the *break ... thread .... linespec* specifies source lines.

>> Use the qualifier `task taskid` with a breakpoint command to specify that you only want *GDB* to stop the program when a particular Ada task reaches this breakpoint. *taskid* is one of the numeric task identifiers assigned by *GDB*, shown in the first column of the `info tasks` display.

>> If you do not specify `task taskid` when you set a breakpoint, the breakpoint applies to *all* tasks of your program.

>> You can use the *task* qualifier on conditional breakpoints as well; in this case, place `task taskid` before the breakpoint condition (before the *if*).

> * *task 'taskno'*

>> This command allows switching to the task referred by *taskno*. In particular, this allows browsing of the backtrace of the specified task. It is advisable to switch back to the original task before continuing execution otherwise the scheduling of the program may be perturbed.

For more detailed information on the tasking support, see *Debugging with GDB*.

6.1.9 Debugging Generic Units

GNAT always uses code expansion for generic instantiation. This means that each time an instantiation occurs, a complete copy of the original code is made, with appropriate substitutions of formals by actuals.

It is not possible to refer to the original generic entities in *GDB*, but it is always possible to debug a particular instance of a generic, by using the appropriate expanded names. For example, if we have

```
procedure g is

   generic package k is
      procedure kp (v1 : in out integer);
   end k;

   package body k is
      procedure kp (v1 : in out integer) is
      begin
         v1 := v1 + 1;
      end kp;
   end k;

   package k1 is new k;
   package k2 is new k;

   var : integer := 1;

begin
   k1.kp (var);
   k2.kp (var);
   k1.kp (var);
   k2.kp (var);
end;
```

Then to break on a call to procedure kp in the k2 instance, simply use the command:

```
(gdb) break g.k2.kp
```

When the breakpoint occurs, you can step through the code of the instance in the normal manner and examine the values of local variables, as for other units.

6.1.10 Remote Debugging with gdbserver

On platforms where gdbserver is supported, it is possible to use this tool to debug your application remotely. This can be useful in situations where the program needs to be run on a target host that is different from the host used for development, particularly when the target has a limited amount of resources (either CPU and/or memory).

To do so, start your program using gdbserver on the target machine. gdbserver then automatically suspends the execution of your program at its entry point, waiting for a debugger to connect to it. The following commands starts an application and tells gdbserver to wait for a connection with the debugger on localhost port 4444.

```
$ gdbserver localhost:4444 program
Process program created; pid = 5685
Listening on port 4444
```

Once gdbserver has started listening, we can tell the debugger to establish a connection with this gdbserver, and then start the same debugging session as if the program was being debugged on the same host, directly under the control of GDB.

```
$ gdb program
```

```
(gdb) target remote targethost:4444
Remote debugging using targethost:4444
0x00007f29936d0af0 in ?? () from /lib64/ld-linux-x86-64.so.
(gdb) b foo.adb:3
Breakpoint 1 at 0x401f0c: file foo.adb, line 3.
(gdb) continue
Continuing.

Breakpoint 1, foo () at foo.adb:4
4          end foo;
```

It is also possible to use gdbserver to attach to an already running program, in which case the execution of that program is simply suspended until the connection between the debugger and gdbserver is established.

For more information on how to use gdbserver, see the *Using the gdbserver Program* section in *Debugging with GDB*. GNAT provides support for gdbserver on x86-linux, x86-windows and x86_64-linux.

6.1.11 GNAT Abnormal Termination or Failure to Terminate

When presented with programs that contain serious errors in syntax or semantics, GNAT may on rare occasions experience problems in operation, such as aborting with a segmentation fault or illegal memory access, raising an internal exception, terminating abnormally, or failing to terminate at all. In such cases, you can activate various features of GNAT that can help you pinpoint the construct in your program that is the likely source of the problem.

The following strategies are presented in increasing order of difficulty, corresponding to your experience in using GNAT and your familiarity with compiler internals.

* Run *gcc* with the *-gnatf*. This first switch causes all errors on a given line to be reported. In its absence, only the first error on a line is displayed.

  The *-gnatdO* switch causes errors to be displayed as soon as they are encountered, rather than after compilation is terminated. If GNAT terminates prematurely or goes into an infinite loop, the last error message displayed may help to pinpoint the culprit.

* Run *gcc* with the *-v (verbose)* switch. In this mode, *gcc* produces ongoing information about the progress of the compilation and provides the name of each procedure as code is generated. This switch allows you to find which Ada procedure was being compiled when it encountered a code generation problem.

* Run *gcc* with the *-gnatdc* switch. This is a GNAT specific switch that does for the front-end what *-v* does for the back end. The system prints the name of each unit, either a compilation unit or nested unit, as it is being analyzed.

* Finally, you can start *gdb* directly on the *gnat1* executable. *gnat1* is the front-end of GNAT, and can be run independently (normally it is just called from *gcc*). You can use *gdb* on *gnat1* as you would on a C program (but [The GNAT Debugger GDB], page 188 for caveats). The *where* command is the first line of attack; the variable *lineno* (seen by *print lineno*), used by the second phase of *gnat1* and by the *gcc* backend, indicates the source line at which the execution stopped, and *input_file name* indicates the name of the source file.

6.1.12 Naming Conventions for GNAT Source Files

In order to examine the workings of the GNAT system, the following brief description of its organization may be helpful:

* Files with prefix `sc` contain the lexical scanner.

* All files prefixed with `par` are components of the parser. The numbers correspond to chapters of the Ada Reference Manual. For example, parsing of select statements can be found in `par-ch9.adb`.

* All files prefixed with `sem` perform semantic analysis. The numbers correspond to chapters of the Ada standard. For example, all issues involving context clauses can be found in `sem_ch10.adb`. In addition, some features of the language require sufficient special processing to justify their own semantic files: sem_aggr for aggregates, sem_disp for dynamic dispatching, etc.

* All files prefixed with `exp` perform normalization and expansion of the intermediate representation (abstract syntax tree, or AST). these files use the same numbering scheme as the parser and semantics files. For example, the construction of record initialization procedures is done in `exp_ch3.adb`.

* The files prefixed with `bind` implement the binder, which verifies the consistency of the compilation, determines an order of elaboration, and generates the bind file.

* The files `atree.ads` and `atree.adb` detail the low-level data structures used by the front-end.

* The files `sinfo.ads` and `sinfo.adb` detail the structure of the abstract syntax tree as produced by the parser.

* The files `einfo.ads` and `einfo.adb` detail the attributes of all entities, computed during semantic analysis.

* Library management issues are dealt with in files with prefix `lib`.

* Ada files with the prefix `a-` are children of *Ada*, as defined in Annex A.

* Files with prefix `i-` are children of *Interfaces*, as defined in Annex B.

* Files with prefix `s-` are children of *System*. This includes both language-defined children and GNAT run-time routines.

* Files with prefix `g-` are children of *GNAT*. These are useful general-purpose packages, fully documented in their specs. All the other `.c` files are modifications of common *gcc* files.

6.1.13 Getting Internal Debugging Information

Most compilers have internal debugging switches and modes. GNAT does also, except GNAT internal debugging switches and modes are not secret. A summary and full description of all the compiler and binder debug flags are in the file `debug.adb`. You must obtain the sources of the compiler to see the full detailed effects of these flags.

The switches that print the source of the program (reconstructed from the internal tree) are of general interest for user programs, as are the options to print the full internal tree, and the entity table (the symbol table information). The reconstructed source provides a readable version of the program after the front-end has completed analysis and expansion, and is useful when studying the performance of specific constructs. For example, constraint checks are indicated, complex aggregates are replaced with loops and assignments, and tasking primitives are replaced with run-time calls.

6.1.14 Stack Traceback

Traceback is a mechanism to display the sequence of subprogram calls that leads to a specified execution point in a program. Often (but not always) the execution point is an instruction at which an exception has been raised. This mechanism is also known as *stack unwinding* because it obtains its information by scanning the run-time stack and recovering the activation records of all active subprograms. Stack unwinding is one of the most important tools for program debugging.

The first entry stored in traceback corresponds to the deepest calling level, that is to say the subprogram currently executing the instruction from which we want to obtain the traceback.

Note that there is no runtime performance penalty when stack traceback is enabled, and no exception is raised during program execution.

6.1.14.1 Non-Symbolic Traceback

Note: this feature is not supported on all platforms. See `GNAT.Traceback` spec in `g-traceb.ads` for a complete list of supported platforms.

Tracebacks From an Unhandled Exception

A runtime non-symbolic traceback is a list of addresses of call instructions. To enable this feature you must use the *-E gnatbind*'s option. With this option a stack traceback is stored as part of exception information. You can retrieve this information using the *addr2line* tool.

Here is a simple example:

```
procedure STB is

    procedure P1 is
    begin
       raise Constraint_Error;
    end P1;

    procedure P2 is
    begin
        P1;
    end P2;

begin
    P2;
end STB;
$ gnatmake stb -bargs -E
$ stb

Execution terminated by unhandled exception
Exception name: CONSTRAINT_ERROR
Message: stb.adb:5
```

```
         Call stack traceback locations:
         0x401373 0x40138b 0x40139c 0x401335 0x4011c4 0x4011f1 0x77e892a4
```

As we see the traceback lists a sequence of addresses for the unhandled exception *CON-STRAINT_ERROR* raised in procedure P1. It is easy to guess that this exception come from procedure P1. To translate these addresses into the source lines where the calls appear, the *addr2line* tool, described below, is invaluable. The use of this tool requires the program to be compiled with debug information.

```
         $ gnatmake -g stb -bargs -E
         $ stb

         Execution terminated by unhandled exception
         Exception name: CONSTRAINT_ERROR
         Message: stb.adb:5
         Call stack traceback locations:
         0x401373 0x40138b 0x40139c 0x401335 0x4011c4 0x4011f1 0x77e892a4

         $ addr2line --exe=stb 0x401373 0x40138b 0x40139c 0x401335 0x4011c4
             0x4011f1 0x77e892a4

         00401373 at d:/stb/stb.adb:5
         0040138B at d:/stb/stb.adb:10
         0040139C at d:/stb/stb.adb:14
         00401335 at d:/stb/b~stb.adb:104
         004011C4 at /build/.../crt1.c:200
         004011F1 at /build/.../crt1.c:222
         77E892A4 in ?? at ??:0
```

The *addr2line* tool has several other useful options:

      `--functions`   to get the function name corresponding to any location

      `--demangle=gnat`   to use the gnat decoding mode for the function names. N binutils version 2.9.x the option is simply `--demangle`.

```
         $ addr2line --exe=stb --functions --demangle=gnat 0x401373 0x40138b
             0x40139c 0x401335 0x4011c4 0x4011f1

         00401373 in stb.p1 at d:/stb/stb.adb:5
         0040138B in stb.p2 at d:/stb/stb.adb:10
         0040139C in stb at d:/stb/stb.adb:14
         00401335 in main at d:/stb/b~stb.adb:104
         004011C4 in <__mingw_CRTStartup> at /build/.../crt1.c:200
         004011F1 in <mainCRTStartup> at /build/.../crt1.c:222
```

From this traceback we can see that the exception was raised in `stb.adb` at line 5, which was reached from a procedure call in `stb.adb` at line 10, and so on. The `b~std.adb` is the binder file, which contains the call to the main program. [Running gnatbind], page 150. The remaining entries are assorted runtime routines, and the output will vary from platform to platform.

It is also possible to use *GDB* with these traceback addresses to debug the program. For example, we can break at a given code location, as reported in the stack traceback:

```
$ gdb -nw stb
```

Furthermore, this feature is not implemented inside Windows DLL. Only the non-symbolic traceback is reported in this case.

```
(gdb) break *0x401373
Breakpoint 1 at 0x401373: file stb.adb, line 5.
```

It is important to note that the stack traceback addresses do not change when debug information is included. This is particularly useful because it makes it possible to release software without debug information (to minimize object size), get a field report that includes a stack traceback whenever an internal bug occurs, and then be able to retrieve the sequence of calls with the same program compiled with debug information.

Tracebacks From Exception Occurrences

Non-symbolic tracebacks are obtained by using the -*E* binder argument. The stack traceback is attached to the exception information string, and can be retrieved in an exception handler within the Ada program, by means of the Ada facilities defined in *Ada.Exceptions*. Here is a simple example:

```
with Ada.Text_IO;
with Ada.Exceptions;

procedure STB is

    use Ada;
    use Ada.Exceptions;

    procedure P1 is
       K : Positive := 1;
    begin
       K := K - 1;
    exception
       when E : others =>
          Text_IO.Put_Line (Exception_Information (E));
    end P1;

    procedure P2 is
    begin
       P1;
    end P2;

begin
    P2;
end STB;
```

This program will output:

```
$ stb
```

```
Exception name: CONSTRAINT_ERROR
Message: stb.adb:12
Call stack traceback locations:
0x4015e4 0x401633 0x401644 0x401461 0x4011c4 0x4011f1 0x77e892a4
```

Tracebacks From Anywhere in a Program

It is also possible to retrieve a stack traceback from anywhere in a program. For this you
need to use the *GNAT.Traceback* API. This package includes a procedure called *Call_Chain*
that computes a complete stack traceback, as well as useful display procedures described
below. It is not necessary to use the *-E gnatbind* option in this case, because the stack
traceback mechanism is invoked explicitly.

In the following example we compute a traceback at a specific location in the program, and
we display it using *GNAT.Debug_Utilities.Image* to convert addresses to strings:

```
with Ada.Text_IO;
with GNAT.Traceback;
with GNAT.Debug_Utilities;

procedure STB is

   use Ada;
   use GNAT;
   use GNAT.Traceback;

   procedure P1 is
      TB  : Tracebacks_Array (1 .. 10);
      --  We are asking for a maximum of 10 stack frames.
      Len : Natural;
      --  Len will receive the actual number of stack frames returned.
   begin
      Call_Chain (TB, Len);

      Text_IO.Put ("In STB.P1 : ");

      for K in 1 .. Len loop
         Text_IO.Put (Debug_Utilities.Image (TB (K)));
         Text_IO.Put (' ');
      end loop;

      Text_IO.New_Line;
   end P1;

   procedure P2 is
   begin
      P1;
   end P2;
```

```
begin
   P2;
end STB;
$ gnatmake -g stb
$ stb

In STB.P1 : 16#0040_F1E4# 16#0040_14F2# 16#0040_170B# 16#0040_171C#
16#0040_1461# 16#0040_11C4# 16#0040_11F1# 16#77E8_92A4#
```

You can then get further information by invoking the *addr2line* tool as described earlier (note that the hexadecimal addresses need to be specified in C format, with a leading '0x').

6.1.14.2 Symbolic Traceback

A symbolic traceback is a stack traceback in which procedure names are associated with each code location.

Note that this feature is not supported on all platforms. See `GNAT.Traceback.Symbolic` spec in **g-trasym.ads** for a complete list of currently supported platforms.

Note that the symbolic traceback requires that the program be compiled with debug information. If it is not compiled with debug information only the non-symbolic information will be valid.

Tracebacks From Exception Occurrences

Here is an example:

```
with Ada.Text_IO;
with GNAT.Traceback.Symbolic;

procedure STB is

   procedure P1 is
   begin
      raise Constraint_Error;
   end P1;

   procedure P2 is
   begin
      P1;
   end P2;

   procedure P3 is
   begin
      P2;
   end P3;

begin
   P3;
```

```
exception
   when E : others =>
       Ada.Text_IO.Put_Line (GNAT.Traceback.Symbolic.Symbolic_Traceback
end STB;
$ gnatmake -g .\stb -bargs -E
$ stb

0040149F in stb.p1 at stb.adb:8
004014B7 in stb.p2 at stb.adb:13
004014CF in stb.p3 at stb.adb:18
004015DD in ada.stb at stb.adb:22
00401461 in main at b~stb.adb:168
004011C4 in __mingw_CRTStartup at crt1.c:200
004011F1 in mainCRTStartup at crt1.c:222
77E892A4 in ?? at ??:0
```

In the above example the .\ syntax in the *gnatmake* command is currently required by
addr2line for files that are in the current working directory. Moreover, the exact sequence of
linker options may vary from platform to platform. The above *-largs* section is for Windows
platforms. By contrast, under Unix there is no need for the *-largs* section. Differences across
platforms are due to details of linker implementation.

Tracebacks From Anywhere in a Program

It is possible to get a symbolic stack traceback from anywhere in a program, just as for
non-symbolic tracebacks. The first step is to obtain a non-symbolic traceback, and then
call *Symbolic_Traceback* to compute the symbolic information. Here is an example:

```
with Ada.Text_IO;
with GNAT.Traceback;
with GNAT.Traceback.Symbolic;

procedure STB is

   use Ada;
   use GNAT.Traceback;
   use GNAT.Traceback.Symbolic;

   procedure P1 is
      TB  : Tracebacks_Array (1 .. 10);
      --  We are asking for a maximum of 10 stack frames.
      Len : Natural;
      --  Len will receive the actual number of stack frames returned.
   begin
      Call_Chain (TB, Len);
      Text_IO.Put_Line (Symbolic_Traceback (TB (1 .. Len)));
   end P1;

   procedure P2 is
```

```
        begin
           P1;
        end P2;

     begin
        P2;
     end STB;
```

Automatic Symbolic Tracebacks

Symbolic tracebacks may also be enabled by using the -Es switch to gnatbind (as in *gprbuild -g ... -bargs -Es*). This will cause the Exception_Information to contain a symbolic traceback, which will also be printed if an unhandled exception terminates the program.

6.2 Code Coverage and Profiling

This section describes how to use the *gcov* coverage testing tool and the *gprof* profiler tool on Ada programs.

6.2.1 Code Coverage of Ada Programs with gcov

gcov is a test coverage program: it analyzes the execution of a given program on selected tests, to help you determine the portions of the program that are still untested.

gcov is part of the GCC suite, and is described in detail in the GCC User's Guide. You can refer to this documentation for a more complete description.

This chapter provides a quick startup guide, and details some GNAT-specific features.

6.2.1.1 Quick startup guide

In order to perform coverage analysis of a program using *gcov*, several steps are needed:

1. Instrument the code during the compilation process,
2. Execute the instrumented program, and
3. Invoke the *gcov* tool to generate the coverage results.

The code instrumentation needed by gcov is created at the object level. The source code is not modified in any way, because the instrumentation code is inserted by gcc during the compilation process. To compile your code with code coverage activated, you need to recompile your whole project using the switches *-fprofile-arcs* and *-ftest-coverage*, and link it using *-fprofile-arcs*.

```
$ gnatmake -P my_project.gpr -f -cargs -fprofile-arcs -ftest-coverage \\
    -largs -fprofile-arcs
```

This compilation process will create `.gcno` files together with the usual object files.

Once the program is compiled with coverage instrumentation, you can run it as many times as needed – on portions of a test suite for example. The first execution will produce `.gcda` files at the same location as the `.gcno` files. Subsequent executions will update those files, so that a cumulative result of the covered portions of the program is generated.

Finally, you need to call the *gcov* tool. The different options of *gcov* are described in the GCC User's Guide, section 'Invoking gcov'.

This will create annotated source files with a `.gcov` extension: `my_main.adb` file will be analyzed in `my_main.adb.gcov`.

6.2.1.2 GNAT specifics

Because of Ada semantics, portions of the source code may be shared among several object files. This is the case for example when generics are involved, when inlining is active or when declarations generate initialisation calls. In order to take into account this shared code, you need to call *gcov* on all source files of the tested program at once.

The list of source files might exceed the system's maximum command line length. In order to bypass this limitation, a new mechanism has been implemented in *gcov*: you can now list all your project's files into a text file, and provide this file to gcov as a parameter, preceded by a `@` (e.g. `gcov @mysrclist.txt`).

Note that on AIX compiling a static library with *-fprofile-arcs* is not supported as there can be unresolved symbols during the final link.

6.2.2 Profiling an Ada Program with gprof

This section is not meant to be an exhaustive documentation of *gprof*. Full documentation for it can be found in the *GNU Profiler User's Guide* documentation that is part of this GNAT distribution.

Profiling a program helps determine the parts of a program that are executed most often, and are therefore the most time-consuming.

gprof is the standard GNU profiling tool; it has been enhanced to better handle Ada programs and multitasking. It is currently supported on the following platforms

* linux x86/x86_64

* solaris sparc/sparc64/x86

* windows x86

In order to profile a program using *gprof*, several steps are needed:

1. Instrument the code, which requires a full recompilation of the project with the proper switches.

2. Execute the program under the analysis conditions, i.e. with the desired input.

3. Analyze the results using the *gprof* tool.

The following sections detail the different steps, and indicate how to interpret the results.

6.2.2.1 Compilation for profiling

In order to profile a program the first step is to tell the compiler to generate the necessary profiling information. The compiler switch to be used is `-pg`, which must be added to other compilation switches. This switch needs to be specified both during compilation and link stages, and can be specified once when using gnatmake:

```
$ gnatmake -f -pg -P my_project
```

Note that only the objects that were compiled with the `-pg` switch will be profiled; if you need to profile your whole project, use the `-f` gnatmake switch to force full recompilation.

6.2.2.2 Program execution

Once the program has been compiled for profiling, you can run it as usual.

The only constraint imposed by profiling is that the program must terminate normally. An interrupted program (via a Ctrl-C, kill, etc.) will not be properly analyzed.

Once the program completes execution, a data file called `gmon.out` is generated in the directory where the program was launched from. If this file already exists, it will be overwritten.

6.2.2.3 Running gprof

The *gprof* tool is called as follow:

```
$ gprof my_prog gmon.out
```

or simply:

```
$  gprof my_prog
```

The complete form of the gprof command line is the following:

```
$ gprof [switches] [executable [data-file]]
```

gprof supports numerous switches. The order of these switch does not matter. The full list of options can be found in the GNU Profiler User's Guide documentation that comes with this documentation.

The following is the subset of those switches that is most relevant:

`--demangle[=style]`, `--no-demangle`

These options control whether symbol names should be demangled when printing output. The default is to demangle C++ symbols. The `--no-demangle` option may be used to turn off demangling. Different compilers have different mangling styles. The optional demangling style argument can be used to choose an appropriate demangling style for your compiler, in particular Ada symbols generated by GNAT can be demangled using `--demangle=gnat`.

`-e function_name`

The `-e function` option tells *gprof* not to print information about the function *function_name* (and its children...) in the call graph. The function will still be listed as a child of any functions that call it, but its index number will be shown as `[not printed]`. More than one `-e` option may be given; only one *function_name* may be indicated with each `-e` option.

`-E function_name`

The `-E function` option works like the `-e` option, but execution time spent in the function (and children who were not called from anywhere else), will not be used to compute the percentages-of-time for the call graph. More than one `-E` option may be given; only one *function_name* may be indicated with each `-E` option.

`-f function_name`

The `-f function` option causes *gprof* to limit the call graph to the function *function_name* and its children (and their children...). More than one `-f` option may be given; only one *function_name* may be indicated with each `-f` option.

```
-F function_name
```
> The `-F function` option works like the `-f` option, but only time spent in the function and its children (and their children...) will be used to determine total-time and percentages-of-time for the call graph. More than one `-F` option may be given; only one *function_name* may be indicated with each `-F` option. The `-F` option overrides the `-E` option.

6.2.2.4 Interpretation of profiling results

The results of the profiling analysis are represented by two arrays: the 'flat profile' and the 'call graph'. Full documentation of those outputs can be found in the GNU Profiler User's Guide.

The flat profile shows the time spent in each function of the program, and how many time it has been called. This allows you to locate easily the most time-consuming functions.

The call graph shows, for each subprogram, the subprograms that call it, and the subprograms that it calls. It also provides an estimate of the time spent in each of those callers/called subprograms.

6.3 Improving Performance

This section presents several topics related to program performance. It first describes some of the tradeoffs that need to be considered and some of the techniques for making your program run faster.

It then documents the unused subprogram/data elimination feature, which can reduce the size of program executables.

6.3.1 Performance Considerations

The GNAT system provides a number of options that allow a trade-off between
* performance of the generated code
* speed of compilation
* minimization of dependences and recompilation
* the degree of run-time checking.

The defaults (if no options are selected) aim at improving the speed of compilation and minimizing dependences, at the expense of performance of the generated code:
* no optimization
* no inlining of subprogram calls
* all run-time checks enabled except overflow and elaboration checks

These options are suitable for most program development purposes. This section describes how you can modify these choices, and also provides some guidelines on debugging optimized code.

6.3.1.1 Controlling Run-Time Checks

By default, GNAT generates all run-time checks, except stack overflow checks, and checks for access before elaboration on subprogram calls. The latter are not required in default mode, because all necessary checking is done at compile time.

The gnat switch, *-gnatp* allows this default to be modified. See [Run-Time Checks], page 137.

Our experience is that the default is suitable for most development purposes.

Elaboration checks are off by default, and also not needed by default, since GNAT uses a static elaboration analysis approach that avoids the need for run-time checking. This manual contains a full chapter discussing the issue of elaboration checks, and if the default is not satisfactory for your use, you should read this chapter.

For validity checks, the minimal checks required by the Ada Reference Manual (for case statements and assignments to array elements) are on by default. These can be suppressed by use of the *-gnatVn* switch. Note that in Ada 83, there were no validity checks, so if the Ada 83 mode is acceptable (or when comparing GNAT performance with an Ada 83 compiler), it may be reasonable to routinely use *-gnatVn*. Validity checks are also suppressed entirely if *-gnatp* is used.

Note that the setting of the switches controls the default setting of the checks. They may be modified using either *pragma Suppress* (to remove checks) or *pragma Unsuppress* (to add back suppressed checks) in the program source.

6.3.1.2 Use of Restrictions

The use of pragma Restrictions allows you to control which features are permitted in your program. Apart from the obvious point that if you avoid relatively expensive features like finalization (enforceable by the use of pragma Restrictions (No_Finalization), the use of this pragma does not affect the generated code in most cases.

One notable exception to this rule is that the possibility of task abort results in some distributed overhead, particularly if finalization or exception handlers are used. The reason is that certain sections of code have to be marked as non-abortable.

If you use neither the *abort* statement, nor asynchronous transfer of control (*select ... then abort*), then this distributed overhead is removed, which may have a general positive effect in improving overall performance. Especially code involving frequent use of tasking constructs and controlled types will show much improved performance. The relevant restrictions pragmas are

```
pragma Restrictions (No_Abort_Statements);
pragma Restrictions (Max_Asynchronous_Select_Nesting => 0);
```

It is recommended that these restriction pragmas be used if possible. Note that this also means that you can write code without worrying about the possibility of an immediate abort at any point.

6.3.1.3 Optimization Levels

Without any optimization option, the compiler's goal is to reduce the cost of compilation and to make debugging produce the expected results. Statements are independent: if you stop the program with a breakpoint between statements, you can then assign a new value to any variable or change the program counter to any other statement in the subprogram and get exactly the results you would expect from the source code.

Turning on optimization makes the compiler attempt to improve the performance and/or code size at the expense of compilation time and possibly the ability to debug the program.

If you use multiple -O options, with or without level numbers, the last such option is the one that is effective.

The default is optimization off. This results in the fastest compile times, but GNAT makes absolutely no attempt to optimize, and the generated programs are considerably larger and slower than when optimization is enabled. You can use the *-O* switch (the permitted forms are *-O0, -O1 -O2, -O3*, and *-Os*) to *gcc* to control the optimization level:

    *

      -O0

> No optimization (the default); generates unoptimized code but has the fastest compilation time.

> Note that many other compilers do fairly extensive optimization even if 'no optimization' is specified. With gcc, it is very unusual to use -O0 for production if execution time is of any concern, since -O0 really does mean no optimization at all. This difference between gcc and other compilers should be kept in mind when doing performance comparisons.

    *

      -O1

> Moderate optimization; optimizes reasonably well but does not degrade compilation time significantly.

    *

      -O2

> Full optimization; generates highly optimized code and has the slowest compilation time.

    *

      -O3

> Full optimization as in *-O2*; also uses more aggressive automatic inlining of subprograms within a unit ([Inlining of Subprograms], page 211) and attempts to vectorize loops.

    *

      -Os

> Optimize space usage (code and data) of resulting program.

Higher optimization levels perform more global transformations on the program and apply more expensive analysis algorithms in order to generate faster and more compact code. The price in compilation time, and the resulting improvement in execution time, both depend on the particular application and the hardware environment. You should experiment to find the best level for your application.

Since the precise set of optimizations done at each level will vary from release to release (and sometime from target to target), it is best to think of the optimization settings in general terms. See the *Options That Control Optimization* section in *Using the GNU Compiler Collection (GCC)* for details about the *-O* settings and a number of *-f* options that individually enable or disable specific optimizations.

Unlike some other compilation systems, *gcc* has been tested extensively at all optimization levels. There are some bugs which appear only with optimization turned on, but there have also been bugs which show up only in *unoptimized* code. Selecting a lower level of optimization does not improve the reliability of the code generator, which in practice is highly reliable at all optimization levels.

Note regarding the use of *-O3*: The use of this optimization level is generally discouraged with GNAT, since it often results in larger executables which may run more slowly. See further discussion of this point in [Inlining of Subprograms], page 211.

6.3.1.4 Debugging Optimized Code

Although it is possible to do a reasonable amount of debugging at nonzero optimization levels, the higher the level the more likely that source-level constructs will have been eliminated by optimization. For example, if a loop is strength-reduced, the loop control variable may be completely eliminated and thus cannot be displayed in the debugger. This can only happen at *-O2* or *-O3*. Explicit temporary variables that you code might be eliminated at level *-O1* or higher.

The use of the *-g* switch, which is needed for source-level debugging, affects the size of the program executable on disk, and indeed the debugging information can be quite large. However, it has no effect on the generated code (and thus does not degrade performance)

Since the compiler generates debugging tables for a compilation unit before it performs optimizations, the optimizing transformations may invalidate some of the debugging data. You therefore need to anticipate certain anomalous situations that may arise while debugging optimized code. These are the most common cases:

* *The 'hopping Program Counter':* Repeated *step* or *next* commands show the PC bouncing back and forth in the code. This may result from any of the following optimizations:

    - *Common subexpression elimination:* using a single instance of code for a quantity that the source computes several times. As a result you may not be able to stop on what looks like a statement.

    - *Invariant code motion:* moving an expression that does not change within a loop, to the beginning of the loop.

    - *Instruction scheduling:* moving instructions so as to overlap loads and stores (typically) with other code, or in general to move computations of values closer to their uses. Often this causes you to pass an assignment statement without the assignment happening and then later bounce back to the statement when the value is actually needed. Placing a breakpoint on a line of code and then stepping over it may, therefore, not always cause all the expected side-effects.

* *The 'big leap':* More commonly known as *cross-jumping*, in which two identical pieces of code are merged and the program counter suddenly jumps to a statement that is not supposed to be executed, simply because it (and the code following) translates to the same thing as the code that *was* supposed to be executed. This effect is typically seen in sequences that end in a jump, such as a *goto*, a *return*, or a *break* in a C *switch* statement.

* *The 'roving variable':* The symptom is an unexpected value in a variable. There are various reasons for this effect:

    - In a subprogram prologue, a parameter may not yet have been moved to its 'home'.

- A variable may be dead, and its register re-used. This is probably the most common cause.
- As mentioned above, the assignment of a value to a variable may have been moved.
- A variable may be eliminated entirely by value propagation or other means. In this case, GCC may incorrectly generate debugging information for the variable

In general, when an unexpected value appears for a local variable or parameter you should first ascertain if that value was actually computed by your program, as opposed to being incorrectly reported by the debugger. Record fields or array elements in an object designated by an access value are generally less of a problem, once you have ascertained that the access value is sensible. Typically, this means checking variables in the preceding code and in the calling subprogram to verify that the value observed is explainable from other values (one must apply the procedure recursively to those other values); or re-running the code and stopping a little earlier (perhaps before the call) and stepping to better see how the variable obtained the value in question; or continuing to step *from* the point of the strange value to see if code motion had simply moved the variable's assignments later.

In light of such anomalies, a recommended technique is to use *-O0* early in the software development cycle, when extensive debugging capabilities are most needed, and then move to *-O1* and later *-O2* as the debugger becomes less critical. Whether to use the *-g* switch in the release version is a release management issue. Note that if you use *-g* you can then use the *strip* program on the resulting executable, which removes both debugging information and global symbols.

6.3.1.5 Inlining of Subprograms

A call to a subprogram in the current unit is inlined if all the following conditions are met:

* The optimization level is at least *-O1*.
* The called subprogram is suitable for inlining: It must be small enough and not contain something that *gcc* cannot support in inlined subprograms.
* Any one of the following applies: *pragma Inline* is applied to the subprogram and the *-gnatn* switch is specified; the subprogram is local to the unit and called once from within it; the subprogram is small and optimization level *-O2* is specified; optimization level *-O3* is specified.

Calls to subprograms in *with*ed units are normally not inlined. To achieve actual inlining (that is, replacement of the call by the code in the body of the subprogram), the following conditions must all be true:

* The optimization level is at least *-O1*.
* The called subprogram is suitable for inlining: It must be small enough and not contain something that *gcc* cannot support in inlined subprograms.
* The call appears in a body (not in a package spec).
* There is a *pragma Inline* for the subprogram.
* The *-gnatn* switch is used on the command line.

Even if all these conditions are met, it may not be possible for the compiler to inline the call, due to the length of the body, or features in the body that make it impossible for the compiler to do the inlining.

Note that specifying the *-gnatn* switch causes additional compilation dependencies. Consider the following:

```
package R is
   procedure Q;
   pragma Inline (Q);
end R;
package body R is
   ...
end R;

with R;
procedure Main is
begin
   ...
   R.Q;
end Main;
```

With the default behavior (no *-gnatn* switch specified), the compilation of the *Main* procedure depends only on its own source, `main.adb`, and the spec of the package in file `r.ads`. This means that editing the body of *R* does not require recompiling *Main*.

On the other hand, the call *R.Q* is not inlined under these circumstances. If the *-gnatn* switch is present when *Main* is compiled, the call will be inlined if the body of *Q* is small enough, but now *Main* depends on the body of *R* in `r.adb` as well as on the spec. This means that if this body is edited, the main program must be recompiled. Note that this extra dependency occurs whether or not the call is in fact inlined by *gcc*.

The use of front end inlining with *-gnatN* generates similar additional dependencies.

Note: The *-fno-inline* switch overrides all other conditions and ensures that no inlining occurs, unless requested with pragma Inline_Always for gcc back-ends. The extra dependences resulting from *-gnatn* will still be active, even if this switch is used to suppress the resulting inlining actions.

Note: The *-fno-inline-functions* switch can be used to prevent automatic inlining of subprograms if *-O3* is used.

Note: The *-fno-inline-small-functions* switch can be used to prevent automatic inlining of small subprograms if *-O2* is used.

Note: The *-fno-inline-functions-called-once* switch can be used to prevent inlining of subprograms local to the unit and called once from within it if *-O1* is used.

Note regarding the use of *-O3*: *-gnatn* is made up of two sub-switches *-gnatn1* and *-gnatn2* that can be directly specified in lieu of it, *-gnatn* being translated into one of them based on the optimization level. With *-O2* or below, *-gnatn* is equivalent to *-gnatn1* which activates pragma *Inline* with moderate inlining across modules. With *-O3*, *-gnatn* is equivalent to *-gnatn2* which activates pragma *Inline* with full inlining across modules. If you have used pragma *Inline* in appropriate cases, then it is usually much better to use *-O2* and *-gnatn* and avoid the use of *-O3* which has the additional effect of inlining subprograms you did not think should be inlined. We have found that the use of *-O3* may slow down the compilation and increase the code size by performing excessive inlining, leading to increased instruction cache pressure from the increased code size and thus minor performance improvements. So the bottom line here is that you should not automatically assume that *-O3* is better than *-O2*, and indeed you should use *-O3* only if tests show that it actually improves performance for your program.

6.3.1.6 Floating_Point_Operations

On almost all targets, GNAT maps Float and Long_Float to the 32-bit and 64-bit standard IEEE floating-point representations, and operations will use standard IEEE arithmetic as provided by the processor. On most, but not all, architectures, the attribute Machine_Overflows is False for these types, meaning that the semantics of overflow is implementation-defined. In the case of GNAT, these semantics correspond to the normal IEEE treatment of infinities and NaN (not a number) values. For example, 1.0 / 0.0 yields plus infinitiy and 0.0 / 0.0 yields a NaN. By avoiding explicit overflow checks, the performance is greatly improved on many targets. However, if required, floating-point overflow can be enabled by the use of the pragma Check_Float_Overflow.

Another consideration that applies specifically to x86 32-bit architectures is which form of floating-point arithmetic is used. By default the operations use the old style x86 floating-point, which implements an 80-bit extended precision form (on these architectures the type Long_Long_Float corresponds to that form). In addition, generation of efficient code in this mode means that the extended precision form will be used for intermediate results. This may be helpful in improving the final precision of a complex expression. However it means that the results obtained on the x86 will be different from those on other architectures, and for some algorithms, the extra intermediate precision can be detrimental.

In addition to this old-style floating-point, all modern x86 chips implement an alternative floating-point operation model referred to as SSE2. In this model there is no extended form, and furthermore execution performance is significantly enhanced. To force GNAT to use this more modern form, use both of the switches:

        -msse2 -mfpmath=sse

A unit compiled with these switches will automatically use the more efficient SSE2 instruction set for Float and Long_Float operations. Note that the ABI has the same form for both floating-point models, so it is permissible to mix units compiled with and without these switches.

6.3.1.7 Vectorization of loops

You can take advantage of the auto-vectorizer present in the *gcc* back end to vectorize loops with GNAT. The corresponding command line switch is *-ftree-vectorize* but, as it is enabled by default at *-O3* and other aggressive optimizations helpful for vectorization also are enabled by default at this level, using *-O3* directly is recommended.

You also need to make sure that the target architecture features a supported SIMD instruction set. For example, for the x86 architecture, you should at least specify *-msse2* to get significant vectorization (but you don't need to specify it for x86-64 as it is part of the base 64-bit architecture). Similarly, for the PowerPC architecture, you should specify *-maltivec*.

The preferred loop form for vectorization is the *for* iteration scheme. Loops with a *while* iteration scheme can also be vectorized if they are very simple, but the vectorizer will quickly give up otherwise. With either iteration scheme, the flow of control must be straight, in particular no *exit* statement may appear in the loop body. The loop may however contain a single nested loop, if it can be vectorized when considered alone:

```
A : array (1..4, 1..4) of Long_Float;
S : array (1..4) of Long_Float;

procedure Sum is
begin
   for I in A'Range(1) loop
      for J in A'Range(2) loop
         S (I) := S (I) + A (I, J);
      end loop;
   end loop;
end Sum;
```

The vectorizable operations depend on the targeted SIMD instruction set, but the adding and some of the multiplying operators are generally supported, as well as the logical operators for modular types. Note that compiling with -*gnatp* might well reveal cases where some checks do thwart vectorization.

Type conversions may also prevent vectorization if they involve semantics that are not directly supported by the code generator or the SIMD instruction set. A typical example is direct conversion from floating-point to integer types. The solution in this case is to use the following idiom:

```
Integer (S'Truncation (F))
```

if S is the subtype of floating-point object F.

In most cases, the vectorizable loops are loops that iterate over arrays. All kinds of array types are supported, i.e. constrained array types with static bounds:

```
type Array_Type is array (1 .. 4) of Long_Float;
```

constrained array types with dynamic bounds:

```
type Array_Type is array (1 .. Q.N) of Long_Float;

type Array_Type is array (Q.K .. 4) of Long_Float;

type Array_Type is array (Q.K .. Q.N) of Long_Float;
```

or unconstrained array types:

```
type Array_Type is array (Positive range <>) of Long_Float;
```

The quality of the generated code decreases when the dynamic aspect of the array type increases, the worst code being generated for unconstrained array types. This is so because, the less information the compiler has about the bounds of the array, the more fallback code it needs to generate in order to fix things up at run time.

It is possible to specify that a given loop should be subject to vectorization preferably to other optimizations by means of pragma *Loop_Optimize*:

```
pragma Loop_Optimize (Vector);
```

placed immediately within the loop will convey the appropriate hint to the compiler for this loop.

It is also possible to help the compiler generate better vectorized code for a given loop by asserting that there are no loop-carried dependencies in the loop. Consider for example the procedure:

```
type Arr is array (1 .. 4) of Long_Float;

procedure Add (X, Y : not null access Arr; R : not null access Arr) is
begin
  for I in Arr'Range loop
    R(I) := X(I) + Y(I);
  end loop;
end;
```

By default, the compiler cannot unconditionally vectorize the loop because assigning to a component of the array designated by R in one iteration could change the value read from the components of the array designated by X or Y in a later iteration. As a result, the compiler will generate two versions of the loop in the object code, one vectorized and the other not vectorized, as well as a test to select the appropriate version at run time. This can be overcome by another hint:

```
pragma Loop_Optimize (Ivdep);
```

placed immediately within the loop will tell the compiler that it can safely omit the non-vectorized version of the loop as well as the run-time test.

6.3.1.8 Other Optimization Switches

Since *GNAT* uses the *gcc* back end, all the specialized *gcc* optimization switches are potentially usable. These switches have not been extensively tested with GNAT but can generally be expected to work. Examples of switches in this category are *-funroll-loops* and the various target-specific *-m* options (in particular, it has been observed that *-march=xxx* can significantly improve performance on appropriate machines). For full details of these switches, see the *Submodel Options* section in the *Hardware Models and Configurations* chapter of *Using the GNU Compiler Collection (GCC)*.

6.3.1.9 Optimization and Strict Aliasing

The strong typing capabilities of Ada allow an optimizer to generate efficient code in situations where other languages would be forced to make worst case assumptions preventing such optimizations. Consider the following example:

```
procedure R is
    type Int1 is new Integer;
    type Int2 is new Integer;
    type Int1A is access Int1;
    type Int2A is access Int2;
    Int1V : Int1A;
    Int2V : Int2A;
    ...

begin
    ...
    for J in Data'Range loop
        if Data (J) = Int1V.all then
           Int2V.all := Int2V.all + 1;
        end if;
```

```
            end loop;
            . . .
         end R;
```

In this example, since the variable *Int1V* can only access objects of type *Int1*, and *Int2V* can only access objects of type *Int2*, there is no possibility that the assignment to *Int2V.all* affects the value of *Int1V.all*. This means that the compiler optimizer can "know" that the value *Int1V.all* is constant for all iterations of the loop and avoid the extra memory reference required to dereference it each time through the loop.

This kind of optimization, called strict aliasing analysis, is triggered by specifying an optimization level of *-O2* or higher or *-Os* and allows *GNAT* to generate more efficient code when access values are involved.

However, although this optimization is always correct in terms of the formal semantics of the Ada Reference Manual, difficulties can arise if features like *Unchecked_Conversion* are used to break the typing system. Consider the following complete program example:

```
         package p1 is
            type int1 is new integer;
            type int2 is new integer;
            type a1 is access int1;
            type a2 is access int2;
         end p1;

         with p1; use p1;
         package p2 is
            function to_a2 (Input : a1) return a2;
         end p2;

         with Unchecked_Conversion;
         package body p2 is
            function to_a2 (Input : a1) return a2 is
               function to_a2u is
                  new Unchecked_Conversion (a1, a2);
            begin
               return to_a2u (Input);
            end to_a2;
         end p2;

         with p2; use p2;
         with p1; use p1;
         with Text_IO; use Text_IO;
         procedure m is
            v1 : a1 := new int1;
            v2 : a2 := to_a2 (v1);
         begin
            v1.all := 1;
            v2.all := 0;
            put_line (int1'image (v1.all));
```

```
end;
```

This program prints out 0 in -*O0* or -*O1* mode, but it prints out 1 in -*O2* mode. That's because in strict aliasing mode, the compiler can and does assume that the assignment to *v2.all* could not affect the value of *v1.all*, since different types are involved.

This behavior is not a case of non-conformance with the standard, since the Ada RM specifies that an unchecked conversion where the resulting bit pattern is not a correct value of the target type can result in an abnormal value and attempting to reference an abnormal value makes the execution of a program erroneous. That's the case here since the result does not point to an object of type *int2*. This means that the effect is entirely unpredictable.

However, although that explanation may satisfy a language lawyer, in practice an applications programmer expects an unchecked conversion involving pointers to create true aliases and the behavior of printing 1 seems plain wrong. In this case, the strict aliasing optimization is unwelcome.

Indeed the compiler recognizes this possibility, and the unchecked conversion generates a warning:

```
p2.adb:5:07: warning: possible aliasing problem with type "a2"
p2.adb:5:07: warning: use -fno-strict-aliasing switch for references
p2.adb:5:07: warning:  or use "pragma No_Strict_Aliasing (a2);"
```

Unfortunately the problem is recognized when compiling the body of package *p2*, but the actual "bad" code is generated while compiling the body of *m* and this latter compilation does not see the suspicious *Unchecked_Conversion*.

As implied by the warning message, there are approaches you can use to avoid the unwanted strict aliasing optimization in a case like this.

One possibility is to simply avoid the use of -*O2*, but that is a bit drastic, since it throws away a number of useful optimizations that do not involve strict aliasing assumptions.

A less drastic approach is to compile the program using the option -*fno-strict-aliasing*. Actually it is only the unit containing the dereferencing of the suspicious pointer that needs to be compiled. So in this case, if we compile unit *m* with this switch, then we get the expected value of zero printed. Analyzing which units might need the switch can be painful, so a more reasonable approach is to compile the entire program with options -*O2* and -*fno-strict-aliasing*. If the performance is satisfactory with this combination of options, then the advantage is that the entire issue of possible "wrong" optimization due to strict aliasing is avoided.

To avoid the use of compiler switches, the configuration pragma *No_Strict_Aliasing* with no parameters may be used to specify that for all access types, the strict aliasing optimization should be suppressed.

However, these approaches are still overkill, in that they causes all manipulations of all access values to be deoptimized. A more refined approach is to concentrate attention on the specific access type identified as problematic.

First, if a careful analysis of uses of the pointer shows that there are no possible problematic references, then the warning can be suppressed by bracketing the instantiation of *Unchecked_Conversion* to turn the warning off:

```
pragma Warnings (Off);
function to_a2u is
```

```
        new Unchecked_Conversion (a1, a2);
     pragma Warnings (On);
```

Of course that approach is not appropriate for this particular example, since indeed there is a problematic reference. In this case we can take one of two other approaches.

The first possibility is to move the instantiation of unchecked conversion to the unit in which the type is declared. In this example, we would move the instantiation of *Unchecked_Conversion* from the body of package *p2* to the spec of package *p1*. Now the warning disappears. That's because any use of the access type knows there is a suspicious unchecked conversion, and the strict aliasing optimization is automatically suppressed for the type.

If it is not practical to move the unchecked conversion to the same unit in which the destination access type is declared (perhaps because the source type is not visible in that unit), you may use pragma *No_Strict_Aliasing* for the type. This pragma must occur in the same declarative sequence as the declaration of the access type:

```
        type a2 is access int2;
        pragma No_Strict_Aliasing (a2);
```

Here again, the compiler now knows that the strict aliasing optimization should be suppressed for any reference to type *a2* and the expected behavior is obtained.

Finally, note that although the compiler can generate warnings for simple cases of unchecked conversions, there are tricker and more indirect ways of creating type incorrect aliases which the compiler cannot detect. Examples are the use of address overlays and unchecked conversions involving composite types containing access types as components. In such cases, no warnings are generated, but there can still be aliasing problems. One safe coding practice is to forbid the use of address clauses for type overlaying, and to allow unchecked conversion only for primitive types. This is not really a significant restriction since any possible desired effect can be achieved by unchecked conversion of access values.

The aliasing analysis done in strict aliasing mode can certainly have significant benefits. We have seen cases of large scale application code where the time is increased by up to 5% by turning this optimization off. If you have code that includes significant usage of unchecked conversion, you might want to just stick with *-O1* and avoid the entire issue. If you get adequate performance at this level of optimization level, that's probably the safest approach. If tests show that you really need higher levels of optimization, then you can experiment with *-O2* and *-O2 -fno-strict-aliasing* to see how much effect this has on size and speed of the code. If you really need to use *-O2* with strict aliasing in effect, then you should review any uses of unchecked conversion of access types, particularly if you are getting the warnings described above.

6.3.1.10 Aliased Variables and Optimization

There are scenarios in which programs may use low level techniques to modify variables that otherwise might be considered to be unassigned. For example, a variable can be passed to a procedure by reference, which takes the address of the parameter and uses the address to modify the variable's value, even though it is passed as an IN parameter. Consider the following example:

```
        procedure P is
           Max_Length : constant Natural := 16;
```

```
                    type Char_Ptr is access all Character;

                    procedure Get_String(Buffer: Char_Ptr; Size : Integer);
                    pragma Import (C, Get_String, "get_string");

                    Name : aliased String (1 .. Max_Length) := (others => ' ');
                    Temp : Char_Ptr;

                    function Addr (S : String) return Char_Ptr is
                       function To_Char_Ptr is
                          new Ada.Unchecked_Conversion (System.Address, Char_Ptr);
                    begin
                       return To_Char_Ptr (S (S'First)'Address);
                    end;

                 begin
                    Temp := Addr (Name);
                    Get_String (Temp, Max_Length);
                 end;
```

where Get_String is a C function that uses the address in Temp to modify the variable
Name. This code is dubious, and arguably erroneous, and the compiler would be entitled
to assume that *Name* is never modified, and generate code accordingly.

However, in practice, this would cause some existing code that seems to work with no
optimization to start failing at high levels of optimzization.

What the compiler does for such cases is to assume that marking a variable as aliased
indicates that some "funny business" may be going on. The optimizer recognizes the aliased
keyword and inhibits optimizations that assume the value cannot be assigned. This means
that the above example will in fact "work" reliably, that is, it will produce the expected
results.

6.3.1.11 Atomic Variables and Optimization

There are two considerations with regard to performance when atomic variables are used.

First, the RM only guarantees that access to atomic variables be atomic, it has nothing to
say about how this is achieved, though there is a strong implication that this should not be
achieved by explicit locking code. Indeed GNAT will never generate any locking code for
atomic variable access (it will simply reject any attempt to make a variable or type atomic
if the atomic access cannot be achieved without such locking code).

That being said, it is important to understand that you cannot assume that the entire
variable will always be accessed. Consider this example:

```
            type R is record
               A,B,C,D : Character;
            end record;
            for R'Size use 32;
            for R'Alignment use 4;
```

```
RV : R;
pragma Atomic (RV);
X : Character;
...
X := RV.B;
```

You cannot assume that the reference to *RV.B* will read the entire 32-bit variable with a single load instruction. It is perfectly legitimate if the hardware allows it to do a byte read of just the B field. This read is still atomic, which is all the RM requires. GNAT can and does take advantage of this, depending on the architecture and optimization level. Any assumption to the contrary is non-portable and risky. Even if you examine the assembly language and see a full 32-bit load, this might change in a future version of the compiler.

If your application requires that all accesses to *RV* in this example be full 32-bit loads, you need to make a copy for the access as in:

```
declare
    RV_Copy : constant R := RV;
begin
    X := RV_Copy.B;
end;
```

Now the reference to RV must read the whole variable. Actually one can imagine some compiler which figures out that the whole copy is not required (because only the B field is actually accessed), but GNAT certainly won't do that, and we don't know of any compiler that would not handle this right, and the above code will in practice work portably across all architectures (that permit the Atomic declaration).

The second issue with atomic variables has to do with the possible requirement of generating synchronization code. For more details on this, consult the sections on the pragmas Enable/Disable_Atomic_Synchronization in the GNAT Reference Manual. If performance is critical, and such synchronization code is not required, it may be useful to disable it.

6.3.1.12 Passive Task Optimization

A passive task is one which is sufficiently simple that in theory a compiler could recognize it an implement it efficiently without creating a new thread. The original design of Ada 83 had in mind this kind of passive task optimization, but only a few Ada 83 compilers attempted it. The problem was that it was difficult to determine the exact conditions under which the optimization was possible. The result is a very fragile optimization where a very minor change in the program can suddenly silently make a task non-optimizable.

With the revisiting of this issue in Ada 95, there was general agreement that this approach was fundamentally flawed, and the notion of protected types was introduced. When using protected types, the restrictions are well defined, and you KNOW that the operations will be optimized, and furthermore this optimized performance is fully portable.

Although it would theoretically be possible for GNAT to attempt to do this optimization, but it really doesn't make sense in the context of Ada 95, and none of the Ada 95 compilers implement this optimization as far as we know. In particular GNAT never attempts to perform this optimization.

In any new Ada 95 code that is written, you should always use protected types in place of tasks that might be able to be optimized in this manner. Of course this does not help if you have legacy Ada 83 code that depends on this optimization, but it is unusual to encounter a case where the performance gains from this optimization are significant.

Your program should work correctly without this optimization. If you have performance problems, then the most practical approach is to figure out exactly where these performance problems arise, and update those particular tasks to be protected types. Note that typically clients of the tasks who call entries, will not have to be modified, only the task definition itself.

6.3.2 *Text_IO* Suggestions

The *Ada.Text_IO* package has fairly high overheads due in part to the requirement of maintaining page and line counts. If performance is critical, a recommendation is to use *Stream_IO* instead of *Text_IO* for volume output, since this package has less overhead.

If *Text_IO* must be used, note that by default output to the standard output and standard error files is unbuffered (this provides better behavior when output statements are used for debugging, or if the progress of a program is observed by tracking the output, e.g. by using the Unix *tail -f* command to watch redirected output.

If you are generating large volumes of output with *Text_IO* and performance is an important factor, use a designated file instead of the standard output file, or change the standard output file to be buffered using *Interfaces.C_Streams.setvbuf*.

6.3.3 Reducing Size of Executables with Unused Subprogram/Data Elimination

This section describes how you can eliminate unused subprograms and data from your executable just by setting options at compilation time.

6.3.3.1 About unused subprogram/data elimination

By default, an executable contains all code and data of its composing objects (directly linked or coming from statically linked libraries), even data or code never used by this executable.

This feature will allow you to eliminate such unused code from your executable, making it smaller (in disk and in memory).

This functionality is available on all Linux platforms except for the IA-64 architecture and on all cross platforms using the ELF binary file format. In both cases GNU binutils version 2.16 or later are required to enable it.

6.3.3.2 Compilation options

The operation of eliminating the unused code and data from the final executable is directly performed by the linker.

In order to do this, it has to work with objects compiled with the following options: *-ffunction-sections -fdata-sections*.

These options are usable with C and Ada files. They will place respectively each function or data in a separate section in the resulting object file.

Once the objects and static libraries are created with these options, the linker can perform the dead code elimination. You can do this by setting the *-Wl,-gc-sections* option to gcc command or in the *-largs* section of *gnatmake*. This will perform a garbage collection of code and data never referenced.

If the linker performs a partial link (-*r* linker option), then you will need to provide the entry point using the -*e* / –*entry* linker option.

Note that objects compiled without the -*ffunction-sections* and -*fdata-sections* options can still be linked with the executable. However, no dead code elimination will be performed on those objects (they will be linked as is).

The GNAT static library is now compiled with -ffunction-sections and -fdata-sections on some platforms. This allows you to eliminate the unused code and data of the GNAT library from your executable.

6.3.3.3 Example of unused subprogram/data elimination

Here is a simple example:

```
with Aux;

procedure Test is
begin
   Aux.Used (10);
end Test;

package Aux is
   Used_Data   : Integer;
   Unused_Data : Integer;

   procedure Used   (Data : Integer);
   procedure Unused (Data : Integer);
end Aux;

package body Aux is
   procedure Used (Data : Integer) is
   begin
      Used_Data := Data;
   end Used;

   procedure Unused (Data : Integer) is
   begin
      Unused_Data := Data;
   end Unused;
end Aux;
```

Unused and *Unused_Data* are never referenced in this code excerpt, and hence they may be safely removed from the final executable.

```
$ gnatmake test

$ nm test | grep used
020015f0 T aux__unused
02005d88 B aux__unused_data
020015cc T aux__used
02005d84 B aux__used_data
```

```
$ gnatmake test -cargs -fdata-sections -ffunction-sections \\
      -largs -Wl,--gc-sections

$ nm test | grep used
02005350 T aux__used
0201ffe0 B aux__used_data
```

It can be observed that the procedure *Unused* and the object *Unused_Data* are removed by
the linker when using the appropriate options.

6.4 Overflow Check Handling in GNAT

This section explains how to control the handling of overflow checks.

6.4.1 Background

Overflow checks are checks that the compiler may make to ensure that intermediate results
are not out of range. For example:

```
A : Integer;
...
A := A + 1;
```

If *A* has the value *Integer'Last*, then the addition may cause overflow since the result is
out of range of the type *Integer*. In this case *Constraint_Error* will be raised if checks are
enabled.

A trickier situation arises in examples like the following:

```
A, C : Integer;
...
A := (A + 1) + C;
```

where *A* is *Integer'Last* and *C* is *-1*. Now the final result of the expression on the right
hand side is *Integer'Last* which is in range, but the question arises whether the intermediate
addition of *(A + 1)* raises an overflow error.

The (perhaps surprising) answer is that the Ada language definition does not answer this
question. Instead it leaves it up to the implementation to do one of two things if overflow
checks are enabled.

  * raise an exception (*Constraint_Error*), or
  * yield the correct mathematical result which is then used in subsequent operations.

If the compiler chooses the first approach, then the assignment of this example will indeed
raise *Constraint_Error* if overflow checking is enabled, or result in erroneous execution if
overflow checks are suppressed.

But if the compiler chooses the second approach, then it can perform both additions yielding
the correct mathematical result, which is in range, so no exception will be raised, and the
right result is obtained, regardless of whether overflow checks are suppressed.

Note that in the first example an exception will be raised in either case, since if the compiler
gives the correct mathematical result for the addition, it will be out of range of the target
type of the assignment, and thus fails the range check.

This lack of specified behavior in the handling of overflow for intermediate results is a source of non-portability, and can thus be problematic when programs are ported. Most typically this arises in a situation where the original compiler did not raise an exception, and then the application is moved to a compiler where the check is performed on the intermediate result and an unexpected exception is raised.

Furthermore, when using Ada 2012's preconditions and other assertion forms, another issue arises. Consider:

```
procedure P (A, B : Integer) with
   Pre => A + B <= Integer'Last;
```

One often wants to regard arithmetic in a context like this from a mathematical point of view. So for example, if the two actual parameters for a call to *P* are both *Integer'Last*, then the precondition should be regarded as False. If we are executing in a mode with run-time checks enabled for preconditions, then we would like this precondition to fail, rather than raising an exception because of the intermediate overflow.

However, the language definition leaves the specification of whether the above condition fails (raising *Assert_Error*) or causes an intermediate overflow (raising *Constraint_Error*) up to the implementation.

The situation is worse in a case such as the following:

```
procedure Q (A, B, C : Integer) with
   Pre => A + B + C <= Integer'Last;
```

Consider the call

```
Q (A => Integer'Last, B => 1, C => -1);
```

From a mathematical point of view the precondition is True, but at run time we may (but are not guaranteed to) get an exception raised because of the intermediate overflow (and we really would prefer this precondition to be considered True at run time).

6.4.2 Management of Overflows in GNAT

To deal with the portability issue, and with the problem of mathematical versus run-time interpretation of the expressions in assertions, GNAT provides comprehensive control over the handling of intermediate overflow. GNAT can operate in three modes, and furthemore, permits separate selection of operating modes for the expressions within assertions (here the term 'assertions' is used in the technical sense, which includes preconditions and so forth) and for expressions appearing outside assertions.

The three modes are:

* *Use base type for intermediate operations* (*STRICT*)

   In this mode, all intermediate results for predefined arithmetic operators are computed using the base type, and the result must be in range of the base type. If this is not the case then either an exception is raised (if overflow checks are enabled) or the execution is erroneous (if overflow checks are suppressed). This is the normal default mode.

* *Most intermediate overflows avoided* (*MINIMIZED*)

   In this mode, the compiler attempts to avoid intermediate overflows by using a larger integer type, typically *Long_Long_Integer*, as the type in which arithmetic is performed for predefined arithmetic operators. This may be slightly more expensive at run time (compared to suppressing intermediate overflow checks), though the cost is negligible on modern 64-bit machines. For the examples given earlier, no intermediate overflows would have resulted in exceptions, since the intermediate results are all in the range of *Long_Long_Integer* (typically 64-bits on nearly all implementations of GNAT). In addition, if checks are enabled, this reduces the number of checks that must be made, so this choice may actually result in an improvement in space and time behavior.

However, there are cases where *Long_Long_Integer* is not large enough, consider the following example:

```
procedure R (A, B, C, D : Integer) with
    Pre => (A**2 * B**2) / (C**2 * D**2) <= 10;
```

where $A = B = C = D = Integer'Last$. Now the intermediate results are out of the range of *Long_Long_Integer* even though the final result is in range and the precondition is True (from a mathematical point of view). In such a case, operating in this mode, an overflow occurs for the intermediate computation (which is why this mode says *most* intermediate overflows are avoided). In this case, an exception is raised if overflow checks are enabled, and the execution is erroneous if overflow checks are suppressed.

* *All intermediate overflows avoided (ELIMINATED)*

In this mode, the compiler avoids all intermediate overflows by using arbitrary precision arithmetic as required. In this mode, the above example with $A**2 * B**2$ would not cause intermediate overflow, because the intermediate result would be evaluated using sufficient precision, and the result of evaluating the precondition would be True.

This mode has the advantage of avoiding any intermediate overflows, but at the expense of significant run-time overhead, including the use of a library (included automatically in this mode) for multiple-precision arithmetic.

This mode provides cleaner semantics for assertions, since now the run-time behavior emulates true arithmetic behavior for the predefined arithmetic operators, meaning that there is never a conflict between the mathematical view of the assertion, and its run-time behavior.

Note that in this mode, the behavior is unaffected by whether or not overflow checks are suppressed, since overflow does not occur. It is possible for gigantic intermediate expressions to raise *Storage_Error* as a result of attempting to compute the results of such expressions (e.g. *Integer'Last ** Integer'Last*) but overflow is impossible.

Note that these modes apply only to the evaluation of predefined arithmetic, membership, and comparison operators for signed integer aritmetic.

For fixed-point arithmetic, checks can be suppressed. But if checks are enabled then fixed-point values are always checked for overflow against the base type for intermediate expressions (that is such checks always operate in the equivalent of *STRICT* mode).

For floating-point, on nearly all architectures, *Machine_Overflows* is False, and IEEE infinities are generated, so overflow exceptions are never raised. If you want to avoid infinities, and check that final results of expressions are in range, then you can declare a constrained floating-point type, and range checks will be carried out in the normal manner (with infinite values always failing all range checks).

6.4.3 Specifying the Desired Mode

The desired mode of for handling intermediate overflow can be specified using either the *Overflow_Mode* pragma or an equivalent compiler switch. The pragma has the form

```
pragma Overflow_Mode ([General =>] MODE [, [Assertions =>] MODE]);
```

where *MODE* is one of

*   *STRICT*: intermediate overflows checked (using base type)
*   *MINIMIZED*: minimize intermediate overflows
*   *ELIMINATED*: eliminate intermediate overflows

The case is ignored, so *MINIMIZED*, *Minimized* and *minimized* all have the same effect.

If only the *General* parameter is present, then the given *MODE* applies to expressions both within and outside assertions. If both arguments are present, then *General* applies to expressions outside assertions, and *Assertions* applies to expressions within assertions. For example:

```
pragma Overflow_Mode
  (General => Minimized, Assertions => Eliminated);
```

specifies that general expressions outside assertions be evaluated in 'minimize intermediate overflows' mode, and expressions within assertions be evaluated in 'eliminate intermediate overflows' mode. This is often a reasonable choice, avoiding excessive overhead outside assertions, but assuring a high degree of portability when importing code from another compiler, while incurring the extra overhead for assertion expressions to ensure that the behavior at run time matches the expected mathematical behavior.

The *Overflow_Mode* pragma has the same scoping and placement rules as pragma *Suppress*, so it can occur either as a configuration pragma, specifying a default for the whole program, or in a declarative scope, where it applies to the remaining declarations and statements in that scope.

Note that pragma *Overflow_Mode* does not affect whether overflow checks are enabled or suppressed. It only controls the method used to compute intermediate values. To control whether overflow checking is enabled or suppressed, use pragma *Suppress* or *Unsuppress* in the usual manner

Additionally, a compiler switch *-gnato?* or *-gnato??* can be used to control the checking mode default (which can be subsequently overridden using pragmas).

Here ? is one of the digits 1 through 3:

1   use base type for intermediate operations (*STRICT*)

2   minimize intermediate overflows (*MINIMIZED*)

3   eliminate intermediate overflows (*ELIMINATED*)

As with the pragma, if only one digit appears then it applies to all cases; if two digits are given, then the first applies outside assertions, and the second within assertions. Thus the equivalent of the example pragma above would be *-gnato23*.

If no digits follow the *-gnato*, then it is equivalent to *-gnato11*, causing all intermediate operations to be computed using the base type (*STRICT* mode).

6.4.4 Default Settings

The default mode for overflow checks is

                    General => Strict

which causes all computations both inside and outside assertions to use the base type.

This retains compatibility with previous versions of GNAT which suppressed overflow checks by default and always used the base type for computation of intermediate results.

The switch *-gnato* (with no digits following) is equivalent to

                    General => Strict

which causes overflow checking of all intermediate overflows both inside and outside assertions against the base type.

The pragma *Suppress (Overflow_Check)* disables overflow checking, but it has no effect on the method used for computing intermediate results.

The pragma *Unsuppress (Overflow_Check)* enables overflow checking, but it has no effect on the method used for computing intermediate results.

6.4.5 Implementation Notes

In practice on typical 64-bit machines, the *MINIMIZED* mode is reasonably efficient, and can be generally used. It also helps to ensure compatibility with code imported from some other compiler to GNAT.

Setting all intermediate overflows checking (*CHECKED* mode) makes sense if you want to make sure that your code is compatible with any other possible Ada implementation. This may be useful in ensuring portability for code that is to be exported to some other compiler than GNAT.

The Ada standard allows the reassociation of expressions at the same precedence level if no parentheses are present. For example, $A+B+C$ parses as though it were $(A+B)+C$, but the compiler can reintepret this as $A+(B+C)$, possibly introducing or eliminating an overflow exception. The GNAT compiler never takes advantage of this freedom, and the expression $A+B+C$ will be evaluated as $(A+B)+C$. If you need the other order, you can write the parentheses explicitly $A+(B+C)$ and GNAT will respect this order.

The use of *ELIMINATED* mode will cause the compiler to automatically include an appropriate arbitrary precision integer arithmetic package. The compiler will make calls to this package, though only in cases where it cannot be sure that *Long_Long_Integer* is sufficient to guard against intermediate overflows. This package does not use dynamic alllocation, but it does use the secondary stack, so an appropriate secondary stack package must be present (this is always true for standard full Ada, but may require specific steps for restricted run times such as ZFP).

Although *ELIMINATED* mode causes expressions to use arbitrary precision arithmetic, avoiding overflow, the final result must be in an appropriate range. This is true even if the final result is of type *[Long_[Long_]]Integer'Base*, which still has the same bounds as its associated constrained type at run-time.

Currently, the *ELIMINATED* mode is only available on target platforms for which *Long_Long_Integer* is 64-bits (nearly all GNAT platforms).

6.5 Performing Dimensionality Analysis in GNAT

The GNAT compiler supports dimensionality checking. The user can specify physical units for objects, and the compiler will verify that uses of these objects are compatible with their dimensions, in a fashion that is familiar to engineering practice. The dimensions of algebraic expressions (including powers with static exponents) are computed from their constituents.

This feature depends on Ada 2012 aspect specifications, and is available from version 7.0.1 of GNAT onwards. The GNAT-specific aspect *Dimension_System* allows you to define a system of units; the aspect *Dimension* then allows the user to declare dimensioned quantities within a given system. (These aspects are described in the *Implementation Defined Aspects* chapter of the *GNAT Reference Manual*).

The major advantage of this model is that it does not require the declaration of multiple operators for all possible combinations of types: it is only necessary to use the proper subtypes in object declarations.

The simplest way to impose dimensionality checking on a computation is to make use of the package *System.Dim.Mks*, which is part of the GNAT library. This package defines a floating-point type *MKS_Type*, for which a sequence of dimension names are specified, together with their conventional abbreviations. The following should be read together with the full specification of the package, in file `s-dimmks.ads`.

```
type Mks_Type is new Long_Long_Float
  with
  Dimension_System => (
    (Unit_Name => Meter,    Unit_Symbol => 'm',   Dim_Symbol => 'L'),
    (Unit_Name => Kilogram, Unit_Symbol => "kg",  Dim_Symbol => 'M'),
    (Unit_Name => Second,   Unit_Symbol => 's',   Dim_Symbol => 'T'),
    (Unit_Name => Ampere,   Unit_Symbol => 'A',   Dim_Symbol => 'I'),
    (Unit_Name => Kelvin,   Unit_Symbol => 'K',   Dim_Symbol => "Theta"),
    (Unit_Name => Mole,     Unit_Symbol => "mol", Dim_Symbol => 'N'),
    (Unit_Name => Candela,  Unit_Symbol => "cd",  Dim_Symbol => 'J'));
```

The package then defines a series of subtypes that correspond to these conventional units. For example:

```
subtype Length is Mks_Type
  with
  Dimension => (Symbol => 'm', Meter => 1, others => 0);
```

and similarly for *Mass*, *Time*, *Electric_Current*, *Thermodynamic_Temperature*, *Amount_Of_Substance*, and *Luminous_Intensity* (the standard set of units of the SI system).

The package also defines conventional names for values of each unit, for example:

as well as useful multiples of these units:

```
cm  : constant Length := 1.0E-02;
g   : constant Mass   := 1.0E-03;
min : constant Time   := 60.0;
day : constant Time   := 60.0 * 24.0 * min;
...
```

Using this package, you can then define a derived unit by providing the aspect that specifies its dimensions within the MKS system, as well as the string to be used for output of a value of that unit:

```
subtype Acceleration is Mks_Type
  with Dimension => ("m/sec^2",
                       Meter => 1,
                       Second => -2,
                       others => 0);
```

Here is a complete example of use:

```
with System.Dim.MKS; use System.Dim.Mks;
with System.Dim.Mks_IO; use System.Dim.Mks_IO;
with Text_IO; use Text_IO;
procedure Free_Fall is
  subtype Acceleration is Mks_Type
    with Dimension => ("m/sec^2", 1, 0, -2, others => 0);
  G : constant acceleration := 9.81 * m / (s ** 2);
  T : Time := 10.0*s;
  Distance : Length;

begin
  Put ("Gravitational constant: ");
  Put (G, Aft => 2, Exp => 0); Put_Line ("");
  Distance := 0.5 * G * T ** 2;
  Put ("distance travelled in 10 seconds of free fall ");
  Put (Distance, Aft => 2, Exp => 0);
  Put_Line ("");
end Free_Fall;
```

Execution of this program yields:

```
Gravitational constant:  9.81 m/sec^2
distance travelled in 10 seconds of free fall 490.50 m
```

However, incorrect assignments such as:

```
Distance := 5.0;
Distance := 5.0 * kg:
```

are rejected with the following diagnoses:

```
Distance := 5.0;
   >>> dimensions mismatch in assignment
   >>> left-hand side has dimension [L]
   >>> right-hand side is dimensionless

Distance := 5.0 * kg:
   >>> dimensions mismatch in assignment
   >>> left-hand side has dimension [L]
   >>> right-hand side has dimension [M]
```

The dimensions of an expression are properly displayed, even if there is no explicit subtype for it. If we add to the program:

```
Put ("Final velocity: ");
Put (G * T, Aft =>2, Exp =>0);
Put_Line ("");
```

then the output includes:

```
Final velocity: 98.10 m.s**(-1)
```

6.6 Stack Related Facilities

This section describes some useful tools associated with stack checking and analysis. In particular, it deals with dynamic and static stack usage measurements.

6.6.1 Stack Overflow Checking

For most operating systems, *gcc* does not perform stack overflow checking by default. This means that if the main environment task or some other task exceeds the available stack space, then unpredictable behavior will occur. Most native systems offer some level of protection by adding a guard page at the end of each task stack. This mechanism is usually not enough for dealing properly with stack overflow situations because a large local variable could "jump" above the guard page. Furthermore, when the guard page is hit, there may not be any space left on the stack for executing the exception propagation code. Enabling stack checking avoids such situations.

To activate stack checking, compile all units with the gcc option *-fstack-check*. For example:

```
$ gcc -c -fstack-check package1.adb
```

Units compiled with this option will generate extra instructions to check that any use of the stack (for procedure calls or for declaring local variables in declare blocks) does not exceed the available stack space. If the space is exceeded, then a *Storage_Error* exception is raised.

For declared tasks, the stack size is controlled by the size given in an applicable *Storage_Size* pragma or by the value specified at bind time with **-d** ([Switches for gnatbind], page 151) or is set to the default size as defined in the GNAT runtime otherwise.

For the environment task, the stack size depends on system defaults and is unknown to the compiler. Stack checking may still work correctly if a fixed size stack is allocated, but this cannot be guaranteed. To ensure that a clean exception is signalled for stack overflow, set the environment variable `GNAT_STACK_LIMIT` to indicate the maximum stack area that can be used, as in:

```
$ SET GNAT_STACK_LIMIT 1600
```

The limit is given in kilobytes, so the above declaration would set the stack limit of the environment task to 1.6 megabytes. Note that the only purpose of this usage is to limit the amount of stack used by the environment task. If it is necessary to increase the amount of stack for the environment task, then this is an operating systems issue, and must be addressed with the appropriate operating systems commands.

6.6.2 Static Stack Usage Analysis

A unit compiled with **-fstack-usage** will generate an extra file that specifies the maximum amount of stack used, on a per-function basis. The file has the same basename as the target object file with a `.su` extension. Each line of this file is made up of three fields:

   * The name of the function.

* A number of bytes.
* One or more qualifiers: *static, dynamic, bounded.*

The second field corresponds to the size of the known part of the function frame.

The qualifier *static* means that the function frame size is purely static. It usually means that all local variables have a static size. In this case, the second field is a reliable measure of the function stack utilization.

The qualifier *dynamic* means that the function frame size is not static. It happens mainly when some local variables have a dynamic size. When this qualifier appears alone, the second field is not a reliable measure of the function stack analysis. When it is qualified with *bounded*, it means that the second field is a reliable maximum of the function stack utilization.

A unit compiled with -Wstack-usage will issue a warning for each subprogram whose stack usage might be larger than the specified amount of bytes. The wording is in keeping with the qualifier documented above.

6.6.3 Dynamic Stack Usage Analysis

It is possible to measure the maximum amount of stack used by a task, by adding a switch to *gnatbind*, as:

```
$ gnatbind -u0 file
```

With this option, at each task termination, its stack usage is output on stderr. It is not always convenient to output the stack usage when the program is still running. Hence, it is possible to delay this output until program termination. for a given number of tasks specified as the argument of the -u option. For instance:

```
$ gnatbind -u100 file
```

will buffer the stack usage information of the first 100 tasks to terminate and output this info at program termination. Results are displayed in four columns:

```
Index | Task Name | Stack Size | Stack Usage
```

where:

* *Index* is a number associated with each task.
* *Task Name* is the name of the task analyzed.
* *Stack Size* is the maximum size for the stack.
* *Stack Usage* is the measure done by the stack analyzer. In order to prevent overflow, the stack is not entirely analyzed, and it's not possible to know exactly how much has actually been used.

The environment task stack, e.g., the stack that contains the main unit, is only processed when the environment variable GNAT_STACK_LIMIT is set.

The package *GNAT.Task_Stack_Usage* provides facilities to get stack usage reports at run-time. See its body for the details.

6.7 Memory Management Issues

This section describes some useful memory pools provided in the GNAT library and in particular the GNAT Debug Pool facility, which can be used to detect incorrect uses of access values (including 'dangling references').

6.7.1 Some Useful Memory Pools

The *System.Pool_Global* package offers the Unbounded_No_Reclaim_Pool storage pool. Allocations use the standard system call *malloc* while deallocations use the standard system call *free*. No reclamation is performed when the pool goes out of scope. For performance reasons, the standard default Ada allocators/deallocators do not use any explicit storage pools but if they did, they could use this storage pool without any change in behavior. That is why this storage pool is used when the user manages to make the default implicit allocator explicit as in this example:

```
type T1 is access Something;
 -- no Storage pool is defined for T2

type T2 is access Something_Else;
for T2'Storage_Pool use T1'Storage_Pool;
-- the above is equivalent to
for T2'Storage_Pool use System.Pool_Global.Global_Pool_Object;
```

The *System.Pool_Local* package offers the Unbounded_Reclaim_Pool storage pool. The allocation strategy is similar to *Pool_Local*'s except that the all storage allocated with this pool is reclaimed when the pool object goes out of scope. This pool provides a explicit mechanism similar to the implicit one provided by several Ada 83 compilers for allocations performed through a local access type and whose purpose was to reclaim memory when exiting the scope of a given local access. As an example, the following program does not leak memory even though it does not perform explicit deallocation:

```
with System.Pool_Local;
procedure Pooloc1 is
   procedure Internal is
      type A is access Integer;
      X : System.Pool_Local.Unbounded_Reclaim_Pool;
      for A'Storage_Pool use X;
      v : A;
   begin
      for I in  1 .. 50 loop
         v := new Integer;
      end loop;
   end Internal;
begin
   for I in  1 .. 100 loop
      Internal;
   end loop;
end Pooloc1;
```

The *System.Pool_Size* package implements the Stack_Bounded_Pool used when *Storage_Size* is specified for an access type. The whole storage for the pool is allocated at once, usually on the stack at the point where the access type is elaborated. It is automatically reclaimed when exiting the scope where the access type is defined. This package is not intended to be used directly by the user and it is implicitly used for each such declaration:

```
type T1 is access Something;
for T1'Storage_Size use 10_000;
```

6.7.2 The GNAT Debug Pool Facility

The use of unchecked deallocation and unchecked conversion can easily lead to incorrect memory references. The problems generated by such references are usually difficult to tackle because the symptoms can be very remote from the origin of the problem. In such cases, it is very helpful to detect the problem as early as possible. This is the purpose of the Storage Pool provided by *GNAT.Debug_Pools*.

In order to use the GNAT specific debugging pool, the user must associate a debug pool object with each of the access types that may be related to suspected memory problems. See Ada Reference Manual 13.11.

```
type Ptr is access Some_Type;
Pool : GNAT.Debug_Pools.Debug_Pool;
for Ptr'Storage_Pool use Pool;
```

GNAT.Debug_Pools is derived from a GNAT-specific kind of pool: the *Checked_Pool*. Such pools, like standard Ada storage pools, allow the user to redefine allocation and deallocation strategies. They also provide a checkpoint for each dereference, through the use of the primitive operation *Dereference* which is implicitly called at each dereference of an access value.

Once an access type has been associated with a debug pool, operations on values of the type may raise four distinct exceptions, which correspond to four potential kinds of memory corruption:

* *GNAT.Debug_Pools.Accessing_Not_Allocated_Storage*
* *GNAT.Debug_Pools.Accessing_Deallocated_Storage*
* *GNAT.Debug_Pools.Freeing_Not_Allocated_Storage*
* *GNAT.Debug_Pools.Freeing_Deallocated_Storage*

For types associated with a Debug_Pool, dynamic allocation is performed using the standard GNAT allocation routine. References to all allocated chunks of memory are kept in an internal dictionary. Several deallocation strategies are provided, whereupon the user can choose to release the memory to the system, keep it allocated for further invalid access checks, or fill it with an easily recognizable pattern for debug sessions. The memory pattern is the old IBM hexadecimal convention: *16#DEADBEEF#*.

See the documentation in the file g-debpoo.ads for more information on the various strategies.

Upon each dereference, a check is made that the access value denotes a properly allocated memory location. Here is a complete example of use of *Debug_Pools*, that includes typical instances of memory corruption:

```
with Gnat.Io; use Gnat.Io;
with Unchecked_Deallocation;
with Unchecked_Conversion;
with GNAT.Debug_Pools;
with System.Storage_Elements;
with Ada.Exceptions; use Ada.Exceptions;
```

```
procedure Debug_Pool_Test is

   type T is access Integer;
   type U is access all T;

   P : GNAT.Debug_Pools.Debug_Pool;
   for T'Storage_Pool use P;

   procedure Free is new Unchecked_Deallocation (Integer, T);
   function UC is new Unchecked_Conversion (U, T);
   A, B : aliased T;

   procedure Info is new GNAT.Debug_Pools.Print_Info(Put_Line);

begin
   Info (P);
   A := new Integer;
   B := new Integer;
   B := A;
   Info (P);
   Free (A);
   begin
      Put_Line (Integer'Image(B.all));
   exception
      when E : others => Put_Line ("raised: " & Exception_Name (E));
   end;
   begin
      Free (B);
   exception
      when E : others => Put_Line ("raised: " & Exception_Name (E));
   end;
   B := UC(A'Access);
   begin
      Put_Line (Integer'Image(B.all));
   exception
      when E : others => Put_Line ("raised: " & Exception_Name (E));
   end;
   begin
      Free (B);
   exception
      when E : others => Put_Line ("raised: " & Exception_Name (E));
   end;
   Info (P);
end Debug_Pool_Test;
```

The debug pool mechanism provides the following precise diagnostics on the execution of this erroneous program:

```
Debug Pool info:
  Total allocated bytes :  0
  Total deallocated bytes :  0
  Current Water Mark:  0
  High Water Mark:  0

Debug Pool info:
  Total allocated bytes :  8
  Total deallocated bytes :  0
  Current Water Mark:  8
  High Water Mark:  8

raised: GNAT.DEBUG_POOLS.ACCESSING_DEALLOCATED_STORAGE
raised: GNAT.DEBUG_POOLS.FREEING_DEALLOCATED_STORAGE
raised: GNAT.DEBUG_POOLS.ACCESSING_NOT_ALLOCATED_STORAGE
raised: GNAT.DEBUG_POOLS.FREEING_NOT_ALLOCATED_STORAGE
Debug Pool info:
  Total allocated bytes :  8
  Total deallocated bytes :  4
  Current Water Mark:  4
  High Water Mark:  8
```

7 Platform-Specific Information

This appendix contains information relating to the implementation of run-time libraries on various platforms and also covers topics related to the GNAT implementation on Windows and Mac OS.

7.1 Run-Time Libraries

The GNAT run-time implementation may vary with respect to both the underlying threads library and the exception handling scheme. For threads support, one or more of the following are supplied:

* **native threads library**, a binding to the thread package from the underlying operating system

* **pthreads library** (Sparc Solaris only), a binding to the Solaris POSIX thread package

For exception handling, either or both of two models are supplied:

* **Zero-Cost Exceptions** ("ZCX"), which uses binder-generated tables that are interrogated at run time to locate a handler.

* **setjmp / longjmp** ('SJLJ'), which uses dynamically-set data to establish the set of handlers

Most programs should experience a substantial speed improvement by being compiled with a ZCX run-time. This is especially true for tasking applications or applications with many exception handlers.}

This section summarizes which combinations of threads and exception support are supplied on various GNAT platforms. It then shows how to select a particular library either permanently or temporarily, explains the properties of (and tradeoffs among) the various threads libraries, and provides some additional information about several specific platforms.

7.1.1 Summary of Run-Time Configurations

Platform	Run-Time	Tasking	Exceptions
ppc-aix	rts-native (default)	native AIX threads	ZCX
rts-sjlj	native AIX threads	SJLJ	
sparc-solaris	rts-native (default)	native Solaris threads library	ZCX
rts-pthread	pthread library	ZCX	
rts-sjlj	native Solaris threads library	SJLJ	
sparc64-solaris	rts-native (default)	native Solaris threads library	ZCX
x86-linux	rts-native (default)	pthread library	ZCX

rts-sjlj	pthread library	SJLJ	
x86-lynx	rts-native (default)	native LynxOS threads	SJLJ
x86-solaris	rts-native (default)	native Solaris threads library	ZCX
rts-sjlj	native Solaris threads library	SJLJ	
x86-windows	rts-native (default)	native Win32 threads	ZCX
rts-sjlj	native Win32 threads	SJLJ	
x86_64-linux	rts-native (default)	pthread library	ZCX
rts-sjlj	pthread library	SJLJ	

7.2 Specifying a Run-Time Library

The `adainclude` subdirectory containing the sources of the GNAT run-time library, and the `adalib` subdirectory containing the `ALI` files and the static and/or shared GNAT library, are located in the gcc target-dependent area:

```
target=$prefix/lib/gcc/gcc-*dumpmachine*/gcc-*dumpversion*/
```

As indicated above, on some platforms several run-time libraries are supplied. These libraries are installed in the target dependent area and contain a complete source and binary subdirectory. The detailed description below explains the differences between the different libraries in terms of their thread support.

The default run-time library (when GNAT is installed) is *rts-native*. This default run time is selected by the means of soft links. For example on x86-linux:

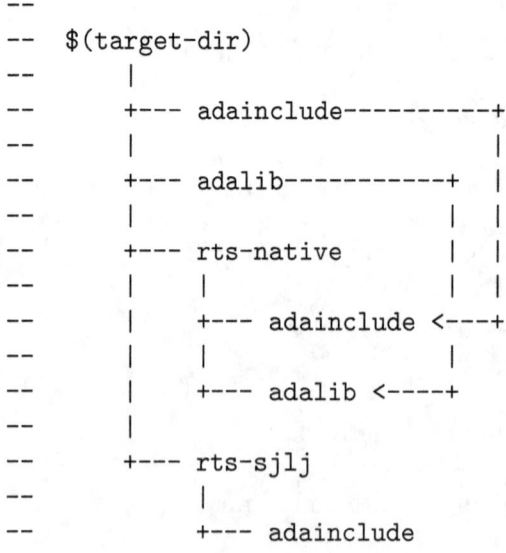

```
--
--    $(target-dir)
--       |
--       +--- adainclude----------+
--       |                        |
--       +--- adalib-----------+  |
--       |                     |  |
--       +--- rts-native       |  |
--       |    |                |  |
--       |    +--- adainclude <---+
--       |    |                |
--       |    +--- adalib <----+
--       |
--       +--- rts-sjlj
--            |
--            +--- adainclude
```

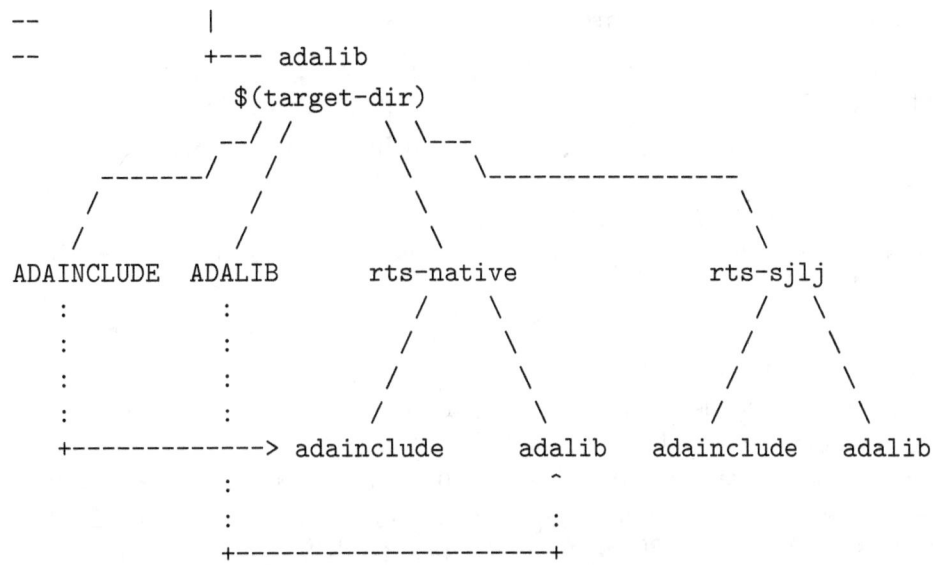

```
  --              |
  --          +--- adalib
              $(target-dir)
              __/ /       \ \___
        _____/   /         \   _____
       /         /           \                    \
      /         /             \                     \
 ADAINCLUDE  ADALIB        rts-native            rts-sjlj
      :         :            /  \                  /  \
      :         :           /    \                /    \
      :         :          /      \              /      \
      :         :         /        \            /        \
   +------------> adainclude      adalib    adainclude   adalib
      :                              ^
      :                              :
   +---------------------+
```

                  Run-Time Library Directory Structure
          (Upper-case names and dotted/dashed arrows represent soft links)

If the *rts-sjlj* library is to be selected on a permanent basis, these soft links can be modified
with the following commands:

```
$ cd $target
$ rm -f adainclude adalib
$ ln -s rts-sjlj/adainclude adainclude
$ ln -s rts-sjlj/adalib adalib
```

Alternatively, you can specify `rts-sjlj/adainclude` in the file `$target/ada_source_path`
and `rts-sjlj/adalib` in `$target/ada_object_path`.

Selecting another run-time library temporarily can be achieved by using the *–RTS* switch,
e.g., *–RTS=sjlj*

7.2.1 Choosing the Scheduling Policy

When using a POSIX threads implementation, you have a choice of several scheduling
policies: *SCHED_FIFO*, *SCHED_RR* and *SCHED_OTHER*.

Typically, the default is *SCHED_OTHER*, while using *SCHED_FIFO* or *SCHED_RR* requires special (e.g., root) privileges.

By default, GNAT uses the *SCHED_OTHER* policy. To specify *SCHED_FIFO*, you can
use one of the following:

* *pragma Time_Slice (0.0)*
* the corresponding binder option *-T0*
* *pragma Task_Dispatching_Policy (FIFO_Within_Priorities)*

To specify *SCHED_RR*, you should use *pragma Time_Slice* with a value greater than 0.0,
or else use the corresponding *-T* binder option.

7.2.2 Solaris-Specific Considerations

This section addresses some topics related to the various threads libraries on Sparc Solaris.

7.2.3 Solaris Threads Issues

GNAT under Solaris/Sparc 32 bits comes with an alternate tasking run-time library based on POSIX threads — *rts-pthread*.

This run-time library has the advantage of being mostly shared across all POSIX-compliant thread implementations, and it also provides under Solaris 8 the *PTHREAD_PRIO_INHERIT* and *PTHREAD_PRIO_PROTECT* semantics that can be selected using the predefined pragma *Locking_Policy* with respectively *Inheritance_Locking* and *Ceiling_Locking* as the policy.

As explained above, the native run-time library is based on the Solaris thread library (*libthread*) and is the default library.

When the Solaris threads library is used (this is the default), programs compiled with GNAT can automatically take advantage of and can thus execute on multiple processors. The user can alternatively specify a processor on which the program should run to emulate a single-processor system. The multiprocessor / uniprocessor choice is made by setting the environment variable `GNAT_PROCESSOR` to one of the following:

`GNAT_PROCESSOR` **Value**	**Effect**
-2	Use the default configuration (run the program on all ava the same as having *GNAT_PROCESSOR* unset
-1	Let the run-time implementation choose one processor and processor
0 .. Last_Proc	Run the program on the specified processor. *_SC_NPROCESSORS_CONF - 1* (where *_SC_NPROCES.* variable).

7.2.4 AIX-Specific Considerations

On AIX, the resolver library initializes some internal structure on the first call to *get*by** functions, which are used to implement *GNAT.Sockets.Get_Host_By_Name* and *GNAT.Sockets.Get_Host_By_Address*. If such initialization occurs within an Ada task, and the stack size for the task is the default size, a stack overflow may occur.

To avoid this overflow, the user should either ensure that the first call to *GNAT.Sockets.Get_Host_By_Name* or *GNAT.Sockets.Get_Host_By_Addrss* occurs in the environment task, or use *pragma Storage_Size* to specify a sufficiently large size for the stack of the task that contains this call.

7.3 Microsoft Windows Topics

This section describes topics that are specific to the Microsoft Windows platforms.

7.3.1 Using GNAT on Windows

One of the strengths of the GNAT technology is that its tool set (*gcc, gnatbind, gnatlink, gnatmake*, the *gdb* debugger, etc.) is used in the same way regardless of the platform.

On Windows this tool set is complemented by a number of Microsoft-specific tools that have been provided to facilitate interoperability with Windows when this is required. With these tools:

*   You can build applications using the *CONSOLE* or *WINDOWS* subsystems.

*   You can use any Dynamically Linked Library (DLL) in your Ada code (both relocatable and non-relocatable DLLs are supported).

*   You can build Ada DLLs for use in other applications. These applications can be written in a language other than Ada (e.g., C, C++, etc). Again both relocatable and non-relocatable Ada DLLs are supported.

*   You can include Windows resources in your Ada application.

*   You can use or create COM/DCOM objects.

Immediately below are listed all known general GNAT-for-Windows restrictions. Other restrictions about specific features like Windows Resources and DLLs are listed in separate sections below.

*   It is not possible to use *GetLastError* and *SetLastError* when tasking, protected records, or exceptions are used. In these cases, in order to implement Ada semantics, the GNAT run-time system calls certain Win32 routines that set the last error variable to 0 upon success. It should be possible to use *GetLastError* and *SetLastError* when tasking, protected record, and exception features are not used, but it is not guaranteed to work.

*   It is not possible to link against Microsoft C++ libraries except for import libraries. Interfacing must be done by the mean of DLLs.

*   It is possible to link against Microsoft C libraries. Yet the preferred solution is to use C/C++ compiler that comes with GNAT, since it doesn't require having two different development environments and makes the inter-language debugging experience smoother.

*   When the compilation environment is located on FAT32 drives, users may experience recompilations of the source files that have not changed if Daylight Saving Time (DST) state has changed since the last time files were compiled. NTFS drives do not have this problem.

*   No components of the GNAT toolset use any entries in the Windows registry. The only entries that can be created are file associations and PATH settings, provided the user has chosen to create them at installation time, as well as some minimal book-keeping information needed to correctly uninstall or integrate different GNAT products.

7.3.2 Using a network installation of GNAT

Make sure the system on which GNAT is installed is accessible from the current machine, i.e., the install location is shared over the network. Shared resources are accessed on Windows by means of UNC paths, which have the format *server**sharename**path*

In order to use such a network installation, simply add the UNC path of the `bin` directory of your GNAT installation in front of your PATH. For example, if GNAT is installed in \GNAT directory of a share location called `c-drive` on a machine `LOKI`, the following command will make it available:

```
$ path \\loki\c-drive\gnat\bin;%path%`
```

Be aware that every compilation using the network installation results in the transfer of large amounts of data across the network and will likely cause serious performance penalty.

7.3.3 CONSOLE and WINDOWS subsystems

There are two main subsystems under Windows. The *CONSOLE* subsystem (which is the default subsystem) will always create a console when launching the application. This is not something desirable when the application has a Windows GUI. To get rid of this console the application must be using the *WINDOWS* subsystem. To do so the *-mwindows* linker option must be specified.

```
$ gnatmake winprog -largs -mwindows
```

7.3.4 Temporary Files

It is possible to control where temporary files gets created by setting the TMP environment variable. The file will be created:

* Under the directory pointed to by the TMP environment variable if this directory exists.

* Under c:\temp, if the TMP environment variable is not set (or not pointing to a directory) and if this directory exists.

* Under the current working directory otherwise.

This allows you to determine exactly where the temporary file will be created. This is particularly useful in networked environments where you may not have write access to some directories.

7.3.5 Disabling Command Line Argument Expansion

By default, an executable compiled for the **Windows** platform will do the following post-processing on the arguments passed on the command line:

* If the argument contains the characters * and/or ?, then file expansion will be attempted. For example, if the current directory contains a.txt and b.txt, then when calling:

```
$ my_ada_program *.txt
```

The following arguments will effectively be passed to the main program (for example when using Ada.Command_Line.Argument):

```
Ada.Command_Line.Argument (1) -> "a.txt"
Ada.Command_Line.Argument (2) -> "b.txt"
```

* Filename expansion can be disabled for a given argument by using single quotes. Thus, calling:

```
$ my_ada_program '*.txt'
```

will result in:

```
Ada.Command_Line.Argument (1) -> "*.txt"
```

Note that if the program is launched from a shell such as **Cygwin Bash** then quote removal might be performed by the shell.

In some contexts it might be useful to disable this feature (for example if the program performs its own argument expansion). In order to do this, a C symbol needs to be defined and set to 0. You can do this by adding the following code fragment in one of your **Ada** units:

```
Do_Argv_Expansion : Integer := 0;
pragma Export (C, Do_Argv_Expansion, "__gnat_do_argv_expansion");
```

The results of previous examples will be respectively:

```
Ada.Command_Line.Argument (1) -> "*.txt"
```

and:

```
Ada.Command_Line.Argument (1) -> "'*.txt'"
```

7.3.6 Mixed-Language Programming on Windows

Developing pure Ada applications on Windows is no different than on other GNAT-supported platforms. However, when developing or porting an application that contains a mix of Ada and C/C++, the choice of your Windows C/C++ development environment conditions your overall interoperability strategy.

If you use *gcc* or Microsoft C to compile the non-Ada part of your application, there are no Windows-specific restrictions that affect the overall interoperability with your Ada code. If you do want to use the Microsoft tools for your C++ code, you have two choices:

*   Encapsulate your C++ code in a DLL to be linked with your Ada application. In this case, use the Microsoft or whatever environment to build the DLL and use GNAT to build your executable ([Using DLLs with GNAT], page 245).

*   Or you can encapsulate your Ada code in a DLL to be linked with the other part of your application. In this case, use GNAT to build the DLL ([Building DLLs with GNAT Project files], page 248) and use the Microsoft or whatever environment to build your executable.

In addition to the description about C main in [Mixed Language Programming], page 52 section, if the C main uses a stand-alone library it is required on x86-windows to setup the SEH context. For this the C main must looks like this:

```
/* main.c */
extern void adainit (void);
extern void adafinal (void);
extern void __gnat_initialize(void*);
extern void call_to_ada (void);

int main (int argc, char *argv[])
{
  int SEH [2];

  /* Initialize the SEH context */
  __gnat_initialize (&SEH);

  adainit();

  /* Then call Ada services in the stand-alone library */
```

```
            call_to_ada();

            adafinal();
      }
```

Note that this is not needed on x86_64-windows where the Windows native SEH support is used.

7.3.6.1 Windows Calling Conventions

This section pertain only to Win32. On Win64 there is a single native calling convention. All convention specifiers are ignored on this platform.

When a subprogram F (caller) calls a subprogram G (callee), there are several ways to push G's parameters on the stack and there are several possible scenarios to clean up the stack upon G's return. A calling convention is an agreed upon software protocol whereby the responsibilities between the caller (F) and the callee (G) are clearly defined. Several calling conventions are available for Windows:

*   *C* (Microsoft defined)
*   *Stdcall* (Microsoft defined)
*   *Win32* (GNAT specific)
*   *DLL* (GNAT specific)

7.3.6.2 *C* Calling Convention

This is the default calling convention used when interfacing to C/C++ routines compiled with either *gcc* or Microsoft Visual C++.

In the *C* calling convention subprogram parameters are pushed on the stack by the caller from right to left. The caller itself is in charge of cleaning up the stack after the call. In addition, the name of a routine with *C* calling convention is mangled by adding a leading underscore.

The name to use on the Ada side when importing (or exporting) a routine with *C* calling convention is the name of the routine. For instance the C function:

```
int get_val (long);
```

should be imported from Ada as follows:

```
function Get_Val (V : Interfaces.C.long) return Interfaces.C.int;
pragma Import (C, Get_Val, External_Name => "get_val");
```

Note that in this particular case the *External_Name* parameter could have been omitted since, when missing, this parameter is taken to be the name of the Ada entity in lower case. When the *Link_Name* parameter is missing, as in the above example, this parameter is set to be the *External_Name* with a leading underscore.

When importing a variable defined in C, you should always use the *C* calling convention unless the object containing the variable is part of a DLL (in which case you should use the *Stdcall* calling convention, [Stdcall Calling Convention], page 243).

7.3.6.3 *Stdcall* Calling Convention

This convention, which was the calling convention used for Pascal programs, is used by Microsoft for all the routines in the Win32 API for efficiency reasons. It must be used to import any routine for which this convention was specified.

In the *Stdcall* calling convention subprogram parameters are pushed on the stack by the caller from right to left. The callee (and not the caller) is in charge of cleaning the stack on routine exit. In addition, the name of a routine with *Stdcall* calling convention is mangled by adding a leading underscore (as for the *C* calling convention) and a trailing @*nn*, where *nn* is the overall size (in bytes) of the parameters passed to the routine.

The name to use on the Ada side when importing a C routine with a *Stdcall* calling convention is the name of the C routine. The leading underscore and trailing @*nn* are added automatically by the compiler. For instance the Win32 function:

```
APIENTRY int get_val (long);
```

should be imported from Ada as follows:

```
function Get_Val (V : Interfaces.C.long) return Interfaces.C.int;
pragma Import (Stdcall, Get_Val);
--  On the x86 a long is 4 bytes, so the Link_Name is "_get_val@4"
```

As for the *C* calling convention, when the *External_Name* parameter is missing, it is taken to be the name of the Ada entity in lower case. If instead of writing the above import pragma you write:

```
function Get_Val (V : Interfaces.C.long) return Interfaces.C.int;
pragma Import (Stdcall, Get_Val, External_Name => "retrieve_val");
```

then the imported routine is _*retrieve_val*@4. However, if instead of specifying the *External_Name* parameter you specify the *Link_Name* as in the following example:

```
function Get_Val (V : Interfaces.C.long) return Interfaces.C.int;
pragma Import (Stdcall, Get_Val, Link_Name => "retrieve_val");
```

then the imported routine is *retrieve_val*, that is, there is no decoration at all. No leading underscore and no Stdcall suffix @*nn*.

This is especially important as in some special cases a DLL's entry point name lacks a trailing @*nn* while the exported name generated for a call has it.

It is also possible to import variables defined in a DLL by using an import pragma for a variable. As an example, if a DLL contains a variable defined as:

```
int my_var;
```

then, to access this variable from Ada you should write:

```
My_Var : Interfaces.C.int;
pragma Import (Stdcall, My_Var);
```

Note that to ease building cross-platform bindings this convention will be handled as a *C* calling convention on non-Windows platforms.

7.3.6.4 *Win32* Calling Convention

This convention, which is GNAT-specific is fully equivalent to the *Stdcall* calling convention described above.

7.3.6.5 *DLL* Calling Convention

This convention, which is GNAT-specific is fully equivalent to the *Stdcall* calling convention described above.

7.3.6.6 Introduction to Dynamic Link Libraries (DLLs)

A Dynamically Linked Library (DLL) is a library that can be shared by several applications running under Windows. A DLL can contain any number of routines and variables.

One advantage of DLLs is that you can change and enhance them without forcing all the applications that depend on them to be relinked or recompiled. However, you should be aware than all calls to DLL routines are slower since, as you will understand below, such calls are indirect.

To illustrate the remainder of this section, suppose that an application wants to use the services of a DLL `API.dll`. To use the services provided by `API.dll` you must statically link against the DLL or an import library which contains a jump table with an entry for each routine and variable exported by the DLL. In the Microsoft world this import library is called `API.lib`. When using GNAT this import library is called either `libAPI.dll.a`, `libapi.dll.a`, `libAPI.a` or `libapi.a` (names are case insensitive).

After you have linked your application with the DLL or the import library and you run your application, here is what happens:

* Your application is loaded into memory.

* The DLL `API.dll` is mapped into the address space of your application. This means that:

    - The DLL will use the stack of the calling thread.

    - The DLL will use the virtual address space of the calling process.

    - The DLL will allocate memory from the virtual address space of the calling process.

    - Handles (pointers) can be safely exchanged between routines in the DLL routines and routines in the application using the DLL.

* The entries in the jump table (from the import library `libAPI.dll.a` or `API.lib` or automatically created when linking against a DLL) which is part of your application are initialized with the addresses of the routines and variables in `API.dll`.

* If present in `API.dll`, routines *DllMain* or *DllMainCRTStartup* are invoked. These routines typically contain the initialization code needed for the well-being of the routines and variables exported by the DLL.

There is an additional point which is worth mentioning. In the Windows world there are two kind of DLLs: relocatable and non-relocatable DLLs. Non-relocatable DLLs can only be loaded at a very specific address in the target application address space. If the addresses of two non-relocatable DLLs overlap and these happen to be used by the same application, a conflict will occur and the application will run incorrectly. Hence, when possible, it is always preferable to use and build relocatable DLLs. Both relocatable and non-relocatable DLLs are supported by GNAT. Note that the *-s* linker option (see GNU Linker User's Guide) removes the debugging symbols from the DLL but the DLL can still be relocated.

As a side note, an interesting difference between Microsoft DLLs and Unix shared libraries, is the fact that on most Unix systems all public routines are exported by default in a Unix shared library, while under Windows it is possible (but not required) to list exported routines in a definition file (see [The Definition File], page 247).

7.3.6.7 Using DLLs with GNAT

To use the services of a DLL, say `API.dll`, in your Ada application you must have:

* The Ada spec for the routines and/or variables you want to access in `API.dll`. If not available this Ada spec must be built from the C/C++ header files provided with the DLL.

* The import library (`libAPI.dll.a` or `API.lib`). As previously mentioned an import library is a statically linked library containing the import table which will be filled at load time to point to the actual `API.dll` routines. Sometimes you don't have an import library for the DLL you want to use. The following sections will explain how to build one. Note that this is optional.

* The actual DLL, `API.dll`.

Once you have all the above, to compile an Ada application that uses the services of `API.dll` and whose main subprogram is *My_Ada_App*, you simply issue the command

```
$ gnatmake my_ada_app -largs -lAPI
```

The argument *-largs -lAPI* at the end of the *gnatmake* command tells the GNAT linker to look for an import library. The linker will look for a library name in this specific order:

* `libAPI.dll.a`
* `API.dll.a`
* `libAPI.a`
* `API.lib`
* `libAPI.dll`
* `API.dll`

The first three are the GNU style import libraries. The third is the Microsoft style import libraries. The last two are the actual DLL names.

Note that if the Ada package spec for `API.dll` contains the following pragma

```
pragma Linker_Options ("-lAPI");
```

you do not have to add *-largs -lAPI* at the end of the *gnatmake* command.

If any one of the items above is missing you will have to create it yourself. The following sections explain how to do so using as an example a fictitious DLL called `API.dll`.

7.3.6.8 Creating an Ada Spec for the DLL Services

A DLL typically comes with a C/C++ header file which provides the definitions of the routines and variables exported by the DLL. The Ada equivalent of this header file is a package spec that contains definitions for the imported entities. If the DLL you intend to use does not come with an Ada spec you have to generate one such spec yourself. For example if the header file of `API.dll` is a file `api.h` containing the following two definitions:

```
int some_var;
int get (char *);
```

then the equivalent Ada spec could be:

```
with Interfaces.C.Strings;
package API is
```

```
   use Interfaces;

   Some_Var : C.int;
   function Get (Str : C.Strings.Chars_Ptr) return C.int;

private
   pragma Import (C, Get);
   pragma Import (DLL, Some_Var);
end API;
```

7.3.6.9 Creating an Import Library

If a Microsoft-style import library `API.lib` or a GNAT-style import library `libAPI.dll.a` or `libAPI.a` is available with `API.dll` you can skip this section. You can also skip this section if `API.dll` or `libAPI.dll` is built with GNU tools as in this case it is possible to link directly against the DLL. Otherwise read on.

The Definition File

As previously mentioned, and unlike Unix systems, the list of symbols that are exported from a DLL must be provided explicitly in Windows. The main goal of a definition file is precisely that: list the symbols exported by a DLL. A definition file (usually a file with a *.def* suffix) has the following structure:

```
[LIBRARY 'name']
[DESCRIPTION 'string']
EXPORTS
   'symbol1'
   'symbol2'
   ...
```

LIBRARY 'name'
> This section, which is optional, gives the name of the DLL.

DESCRIPTION 'string'
> This section, which is optional, gives a description string that will be embedded in the import library.

EXPORTS
> This section gives the list of exported symbols (procedures, functions or variables). For instance in the case of `API.dll` the *EXPORTS* section of `API.def` looks like:
> ```
> EXPORTS
>    some_var
>    get
> ```

Note that you must specify the correct suffix (`@nn`) (see [Windows Calling Conventions], page 243) for a Stdcall calling convention function in the exported symbols list.

There can actually be other sections in a definition file, but these sections are not relevant to the discussion at hand.

Creating a Definition File Automatically

You can automatically create the definition file `API.def` (see [The Definition File], page 247) from a DLL. For that use the *dlltool* program as follows:

```
$ dlltool API.dll -z API.def --export-all-symbols
```

Note that if some routines in the DLL have the *Stdcall* convention ([Windows Calling Conventions], page 243) with stripped `@nn` suffix then you'll have to edit `api.def` to add it, and specify *-k* to *gnatdll* when creating the import library.

Here are some hints to find the right `@nn` suffix.

- If you have the Microsoft import library (.lib), it is possible to get the right symbols by using Microsoft *dumpbin* tool (see the corresponding Microsoft documentation for further details).

```
$ dumpbin /exports api.lib
```

- If you have a message about a missing symbol at link time the compiler tells you what symbol is expected. You just have to go back to the definition file and add the right suffix.

GNAT-Style Import Library

To create a static import library from `API.dll` with the GNAT tools you should create the .def file, then use *gnatdll* tool (see [Using gnatdll], page 253) as follows:

```
$ gnatdll -e API.def -d API.dll
```

gnatdll takes as input a definition file `API.def` and the name of the DLL containing the services listed in the definition file `API.dll`. The name of the static import library generated is computed from the name of the definition file as follows: if the definition file name is *xyz'.def'*, the import library name will be *lib"xyz'.a'*. Note that in the previous example option *-e* could have been removed because the name of the definition file (before the '.def' suffix) is the same as the name of the DLL ([Using gnatdll], page 253 for more information about *gnatdll*).

Microsoft-Style Import Library

A Microsoft import library is needed only if you plan to make an Ada DLL available to applications developed with Microsoft tools ([Mixed-Language Programming on Windows], page 242).

To create a Microsoft-style import library for `API.dll` you should create the .def file, then build the actual import library using Microsoft's *lib* utility:

```
$ lib -machine:IX86 -def:API.def -out:API.lib
```

If you use the above command the definition file `API.def` must contain a line giving the name of the DLL:

```
LIBRARY        "API"
```

See the Microsoft documentation for further details about the usage of *lib*.

7.3.6.10 Building DLLs with GNAT Project files

There is nothing specific to Windows in the build process. See the *Library Projects* section in the *GNAT Project Manager* chapter of the *GPRbuild User's Guide*.

Due to a system limitation, it is not possible under Windows to create threads when inside the *DllMain* routine which is used for auto-initialization of shared libraries, so it is not possible to have library level tasks in SALs.

7.3.6.11 Building DLLs with GNAT

This section explain how to build DLLs using the GNAT built-in DLL support. With the following procedure it is straight forward to build and use DLLs with GNAT.

* Building object files. The first step is to build all objects files that are to be included into the DLL. This is done by using the standard *gnatmake* tool.

* Building the DLL. To build the DLL you must use *gcc*'s *-shared* and *-shared-libgcc* options. It is quite simple to use this method:

      $ gcc -shared -shared-libgcc -o api.dll obj1.o obj2.o ...

  It is important to note that in this case all symbols found in the object files are automatically exported. It is possible to restrict the set of symbols to export by passing to *gcc* a definition file (see [The Definition File], page 247). For example:

      $ gcc -shared -shared-libgcc -o api.dll api.def obj1.o obj2.o ...

  If you use a definition file you must export the elaboration procedures for every package that required one. Elaboration procedures are named using the package name followed by "_E".

* Preparing DLL to be used. For the DLL to be used by client programs the bodies must be hidden from it and the .ali set with read-only attribute. This is very important otherwise GNAT will recompile all packages and will not actually use the code in the DLL. For example:

      $ mkdir apilib
      $ copy *.ads *.ali api.dll apilib
      $ attrib +R apilib*.ali

At this point it is possible to use the DLL by directly linking against it. Note that you must use the GNAT shared runtime when using GNAT shared libraries. This is achieved by using *-shared* binder's option.

      $ gnatmake main -Iapilib -bargs -shared -largs -Lapilib -lAPI

7.3.6.12 Building DLLs with gnatdll

Note that it is preferred to use GNAT Project files ([Building DLLs with GNAT Project files], page 248) or the built-in GNAT DLL support ([Building DLLs with GNAT], page 249) or to build DLLs.

This section explains how to build DLLs containing Ada code using *gnatdll*. These DLLs will be referred to as Ada DLLs in the remainder of this section.

The steps required to build an Ada DLL that is to be used by Ada as well as non-Ada applications are as follows:

*   You need to mark each Ada *entity* exported by the DLL with a *C* or *Stdcall* calling convention to avoid any Ada name mangling for the entities exported by the DLL (see [Exporting Ada Entities], page 250). You can skip this step if you plan to use the Ada DLL only from Ada applications.

*   Your Ada code must export an initialization routine which calls the routine *adainit* generated by *gnatbind* to perform the elaboration of the Ada code in the DLL ([Ada DLLs and Elaboration], page 252). The initialization routine exported by the Ada DLL must be invoked by the clients of the DLL to initialize the DLL.

*   When useful, the DLL should also export a finalization routine which calls routine *adafinal* generated by *gnatbind* to perform the finalization of the Ada code in the DLL ([Ada DLLs and Finalization], page 252). The finalization routine exported by the Ada DLL must be invoked by the clients of the DLL when the DLL services are no further needed.

*   You must provide a spec for the services exported by the Ada DLL in each of the programming languages to which you plan to make the DLL available.

*   You must provide a definition file listing the exported entities ([The Definition File], page 247).

*   Finally you must use *gnatdll* to produce the DLL and the import library ([Using gnat-dll], page 253).

Note that a relocatable DLL stripped using the *strip* binutils tool will not be relocatable anymore. To build a DLL without debug information pass *-largs -s* to *gnatdll*. This restriction does not apply to a DLL built using a Library Project. See the *Library Projects* section in the *GNAT Project Manager* chapter of the *GPRbuild User's Guide*.

7.3.6.13 Limitations When Using Ada DLLs from Ada

When using Ada DLLs from Ada applications there is a limitation users should be aware of. Because on Windows the GNAT run time is not in a DLL of its own, each Ada DLL includes a part of the GNAT run time. Specifically, each Ada DLL includes the services of the GNAT run time that are necessary to the Ada code inside the DLL. As a result, when an Ada program uses an Ada DLL there are two independent GNAT run times: one in the Ada DLL and one in the main program.

It is therefore not possible to exchange GNAT run-time objects between the Ada DLL and the main Ada program. Example of GNAT run-time objects are file handles (e.g., *Text_IO.File_Type*), tasks types, protected objects types, etc.

It is completely safe to exchange plain elementary, array or record types, Windows object handles, etc.

7.3.6.14 Exporting Ada Entities

Building a DLL is a way to encapsulate a set of services usable from any application. As a result, the Ada entities exported by a DLL should be exported with the *C* or *Stdcall* calling conventions to avoid any Ada name mangling. As an example here is an Ada package *API*, spec and body, exporting two procedures, a function, and a variable:

```
with Interfaces.C; use Interfaces;
package API is
```

```
      Count : C.int := 0;
      function Factorial (Val : C.int) return C.int;

      procedure Initialize_API;
      procedure Finalize_API;
      --   Initialization & Finalization routines. More in the next section
   private
      pragma Export (C, Initialize_API);
      pragma Export (C, Finalize_API);
      pragma Export (C, Count);
      pragma Export (C, Factorial);
   end API;

   package body API is
      function Factorial (Val : C.int) return C.int is
         Fact : C.int := 1;
      begin
         Count := Count + 1;
         for K in 1 .. Val loop
            Fact := Fact * K;
         end loop;
         return Fact;
      end Factorial;

      procedure Initialize_API is
         procedure Adainit;
         pragma Import (C, Adainit);
      begin
         Adainit;
      end Initialize_API;

      procedure Finalize_API is
         procedure Adafinal;
         pragma Import (C, Adafinal);
      begin
         Adafinal;
      end Finalize_API;
   end API;
```

If the Ada DLL you are building will only be used by Ada applications you do not have to export Ada entities with a *C* or *Stdcall* convention. As an example, the previous package could be written as follows:

```
   package API is
      Count : Integer := 0;
      function Factorial (Val : Integer) return Integer;

      procedure Initialize_API;
      procedure Finalize_API;
```

```
                 --  Initialization and Finalization routines.
         end API;

         package body API is
            function Factorial (Val : Integer) return Integer is
               Fact : Integer := 1;
            begin
               Count := Count + 1;
               for K in 1 .. Val loop
                  Fact := Fact * K;
               end loop;
               return Fact;
            end Factorial;


            ...
            --  The remainder of this package body is unchanged.
         end API;
```

Note that if you do not export the Ada entities with a *C* or *Stdcall* convention you will have to provide the mangled Ada names in the definition file of the Ada DLL ([Creating the Definition File], page 253).

7.3.6.15 Ada DLLs and Elaboration

The DLL that you are building contains your Ada code as well as all the routines in the Ada library that are needed by it. The first thing a user of your DLL must do is elaborate the Ada code ([Elaboration Order Handling in GNAT], page 279).

To achieve this you must export an initialization routine (*Initialize_API* in the previous example), which must be invoked before using any of the DLL services. This elaboration routine must call the Ada elaboration routine *adainit* generated by the GNAT binder ([Binding with Non-Ada Main Programs], page 159). See the body of *Initialize_Api* for an example. Note that the GNAT binder is automatically invoked during the DLL build process by the *gnatdll* tool ([Using gnatdll], page 253).

When a DLL is loaded, Windows systematically invokes a routine called *DllMain*. It would therefore be possible to call *adainit* directly from *DllMain* without having to provide an explicit initialization routine. Unfortunately, it is not possible to call *adainit* from the *DllMain* if your program has library level tasks because access to the *DllMain* entry point is serialized by the system (that is, only a single thread can execute 'through' it at a time), which means that the GNAT run time will deadlock waiting for the newly created task to complete its initialization.

7.3.6.16 Ada DLLs and Finalization

When the services of an Ada DLL are no longer needed, the client code should invoke the DLL finalization routine, if available. The DLL finalization routine is in charge of releasing all resources acquired by the DLL. In the case of the Ada code contained in the DLL, this is achieved by calling routine *adafinal* generated by the GNAT binder ([Binding with Non-Ada Main Programs], page 159). See the body of *Finalize_Api* for an example. As already pointed out the GNAT binder is automatically invoked during the DLL build process by the *gnatdll* tool ([Using gnatdll], page 253).

7.3.6.17 Creating a Spec for Ada DLLs

To use the services exported by the Ada DLL from another programming language (e.g., C), you have to translate the specs of the exported Ada entities in that language. For instance in the case of *API.dll*, the corresponding C header file could look like:

```
extern int *_imp__count;
#define count (*_imp__count)
int factorial (int);
```

It is important to understand that when building an Ada DLL to be used by other Ada applications, you need two different specs for the packages contained in the DLL: one for building the DLL and the other for using the DLL. This is because the *DLL* calling convention is needed to use a variable defined in a DLL, but when building the DLL, the variable must have either the *Ada* or *C* calling convention. As an example consider a DLL comprising the following package *API*:

```
package API is
    Count : Integer := 0;
    ...
    --  Remainder of the package omitted.
end API;
```

After producing a DLL containing package *API*, the spec that must be used to import *API.Count* from Ada code outside of the DLL is:

```
package API is
    Count : Integer;
    pragma Import (DLL, Count);
end API;
```

7.3.6.18 Creating the Definition File

The definition file is the last file needed to build the DLL. It lists the exported symbols. As an example, the definition file for a DLL containing only package *API* (where all the entities are exported with a *C* calling convention) is:

```
EXPORTS
    count
    factorial
    finalize_api
    initialize_api
```

If the *C* calling convention is missing from package *API*, then the definition file contains the mangled Ada names of the above entities, which in this case are:

```
EXPORTS
    api__count
    api__factorial
    api__finalize_api
    api__initialize_api
```

7.3.6.19 Using *gnatdll*

gnatdll is a tool to automate the DLL build process once all the Ada and non-Ada sources that make up your DLL have been compiled. *gnatdll* is actually in charge of two distinct tasks: build the static import library for the DLL and the actual DLL. The form of the *gnatdll* command is

$$\texttt{\$ gnatdll ['switches'] 'list-of-files' [-largs 'opts']}$$

where *list-of-files* is a list of ALI and object files. The object file list must be the exact list of objects corresponding to the non-Ada sources whose services are to be included in the DLL. The ALI file list must be the exact list of ALI files for the corresponding Ada sources whose services are to be included in the DLL. If *list-of-files* is missing, only the static import library is generated.

You may specify any of the following switches to *gnatdll*:

`-a[address]`

> Build a non-relocatable DLL at *address*. If *address* is not specified the default address *0x11000000* will be used. By default, when this switch is missing, *gnatdll* builds relocatable DLL. We advise the reader to build relocatable DLL.

`-b address`

> Set the relocatable DLL base address. By default the address is *0x11000000*.

`-bargs opts`

> Binder options. Pass *opts* to the binder.

`-d dllfile`

> *dllfile* is the name of the DLL. This switch must be present for *gnatdll* to do anything. The name of the generated import library is obtained algorithmically from *dllfile* as shown in the following example: if *dllfile* is *xyz.dll*, the import library name is *libxyz.dll.a*. The name of the definition file to use (if not specified by option *-e*) is obtained algorithmically from *dllfile* as shown in the following example: if *dllfile* is *xyz.dll*, the definition file used is *xyz.def*.

`-e deffile`

> *deffile* is the name of the definition file.

`-g`

> Generate debugging information. This information is stored in the object file and copied from there to the final DLL file by the linker, where it can be read by the debugger. You must use the *-g* switch if you plan on using the debugger or the symbolic stack traceback.

`-h`

> Help mode. Displays *gnatdll* switch usage information.

`-Idir`

> Direct *gnatdll* to search the *dir* directory for source and object files needed to build the DLL. ([Search Paths and the Run-Time Library (RTL)], page 89).

`-k`

> Removes the `@nn` suffix from the import library's exported names, but keeps them for the link names. You must specify this option if you want to use a *Stdcall* function in a DLL for which the `@nn` suffix has been removed. This is the case for most of the Windows NT DLL for example. This option has no effect when *-n* option is specified.

`-l` *file*

> The list of ALI and object files used to build the DLL are listed in *file*, instead of being given in the command line. Each line in *file* contains the name of an ALI or object file.

`-n`

> No Import. Do not create the import library.

`-q`

> Quiet mode. Do not display unnecessary messages.

`-v`

> Verbose mode. Display extra information.

`-largs` *opts*

> Linker options. Pass *opts* to the linker.

gnatdll Example

As an example the command to build a relocatable DLL from `api.adb` once `api.adb` has been compiled and `api.def` created is

```
$ gnatdll -d api.dll api.ali
```

The above command creates two files: `libapi.dll.a` (the import library) and `api.dll` (the actual DLL). If you want to create only the DLL, just type:

```
$ gnatdll -d api.dll -n api.ali
```

Alternatively if you want to create just the import library, type:

```
$ gnatdll -d api.dll
```

gnatdll behind the Scenes

This section details the steps involved in creating a DLL. *gnatdll* does these steps for you. Unless you are interested in understanding what goes on behind the scenes, you should skip this section.

We use the previous example of a DLL containing the Ada package *API*, to illustrate the steps necessary to build a DLL. The starting point is a set of objects that will make up the DLL and the corresponding ALI files. In the case of this example this means that `api.o` and `api.ali` are available. To build a relocatable DLL, *gnatdll* does the following:

* *gnatdll* builds the base file (`api.base`). A base file gives the information necessary to generate relocation information for the DLL.

```
$ gnatbind -n api
$ gnatlink api -o api.jnk -mdll -Wl,--base-file,api.base
```

In addition to the base file, the *gnatlink* command generates an output file `api.jnk` which can be discarded. The *-mdll* switch asks *gnatlink* to generate the routines *DllMain* and *DllMainCRTStartup* that are called by the Windows loader when the DLL is loaded into memory.

* *gnatdll* uses *dlltool* (see [Using dlltool], page 256) to build the export table (`api.exp`). The export table contains the relocation information in a form which can be used during the final link to ensure that the Windows loader is able to place the DLL anywhere in memory.

```
$ dlltool --dllname api.dll --def api.def --base-file api.base \\
              --output-exp api.exp
```

* *gnatdll* builds the base file using the new export table. Note that *gnatbind* must be called once again since the binder generated file has been deleted during the previous call to *gnatlink*.

```
$ gnatbind -n api
$ gnatlink api -o api.jnk api.exp -mdll
      -Wl,--base-file,api.base
```

* *gnatdll* builds the new export table using the new base file and generates the DLL import library libAPI.dll.a.

```
$ dlltool --dllname api.dll --def api.def --base-file api.base \\
              --output-exp api.exp --output-lib libAPI.a
```

* Finally *gnatdll* builds the relocatable DLL using the final export table.

```
$ gnatbind -n api
$ gnatlink api api.exp -o api.dll -mdll
```

Using *dlltool*

dlltool is the low-level tool used by *gnatdll* to build DLLs and static import libraries. This section summarizes the most common *dlltool* switches. The form of the *dlltool* command is

```
$ dlltool ['switches']
```

dlltool switches include:

--base-file *basefile*

> Read the base file *basefile* generated by the linker. This switch is used to create a relocatable DLL.

--def *deffile*

> Read the definition file.

--dllname *name*

> Gives the name of the DLL. This switch is used to embed the name of the DLL in the static import library generated by *dlltool* with switch *–output-lib*.

-k

> Kill @*nn* from exported names ([Windows Calling Conventions], page 243 for a discussion about *Stdcall*-style symbols.

--help

> Prints the *dlltool* switches with a concise description.

--output-exp *exportfile*

> Generate an export file *exportfile*. The export file contains the export table (list of symbols in the DLL) and is used to create the DLL.

--output-lib *libfile*

> Generate a static import library *libfile*.

-v

> Verbose mode.

`--as` *assembler-name*

> Use *assembler-name* as the assembler. The default is *as*.

7.3.6.20 GNAT and Windows Resources

Resources are an easy way to add Windows specific objects to your application. The objects that can be added as resources include:

*   menus
*   accelerators
*   dialog boxes
*   string tables
*   bitmaps
*   cursors
*   icons
*   fonts
*   version information

For example, a version information resource can be defined as follow and embedded into an executable or DLL:

A version information resource can be used to embed information into an executable or a DLL. These information can be viewed using the file properties from the Windows Explorer. Here is an example of a version information resource:

```
1 VERSIONINFO
FILEVERSION     1,0,0,0
PRODUCTVERSION  1,0,0,0
BEGIN
  BLOCK "StringFileInfo"
  BEGIN
    BLOCK "080904E4"
    BEGIN
      VALUE "CompanyName", "My Company Name"
      VALUE "FileDescription", "My application"
      VALUE "FileVersion", "1.0"
      VALUE "InternalName", "my_app"
      VALUE "LegalCopyright", "My Name"
      VALUE "OriginalFilename", "my_app.exe"
      VALUE "ProductName", "My App"
      VALUE "ProductVersion", "1.0"
    END
  END

  BLOCK "VarFileInfo"
  BEGIN
    VALUE "Translation", 0x809, 1252
  END
END
```

The value *0809* (langID) is for the U.K English language and *04E4* (charsetID), which is equal to *1252* decimal, for multilingual.

This section explains how to build, compile and use resources. Note that this section does not cover all resource objects, for a complete description see the corresponding Microsoft documentation.

7.3.6.21 Building Resources

A resource file is an ASCII file. By convention resource files have an `.rc` extension. The easiest way to build a resource file is to use Microsoft tools such as *imagedit.exe* to build bitmaps, icons and cursors and *dlgedit.exe* to build dialogs. It is always possible to build an `.rc` file yourself by writing a resource script.

It is not our objective to explain how to write a resource file. A complete description of the resource script language can be found in the Microsoft documentation.

7.3.6.22 Compiling Resources

This section describes how to build a GNAT-compatible (COFF) object file containing the resources. This is done using the Resource Compiler *windres* as follows:

```
$ windres -i myres.rc -o myres.o
```

By default *windres* will run *gcc* to preprocess the `.rc` file. You can specify an alternate preprocessor (usually named `cpp.exe`) using the *windres –preprocessor* parameter. A list of all possible options may be obtained by entering the command *windres –help*.

It is also possible to use the Microsoft resource compiler *rc.exe* to produce a `.res` file (binary resource file). See the corresponding Microsoft documentation for further details. In this case you need to use *windres* to translate the `.res` file to a GNAT-compatible object file as follows:

```
$ windres -i myres.res -o myres.o
```

7.3.6.23 Using Resources

To include the resource file in your program just add the GNAT-compatible object file for the resource(s) to the linker arguments. With *gnatmake* this is done by using the *-largs* option:

```
$ gnatmake myprog -largs myres.o
```

7.3.6.24 Using GNAT DLLs from Microsoft Visual Studio Applications

This section describes a common case of mixed GNAT/Microsoft Visual Studio application development, where the main program is developed using MSVS, and is linked with a DLL developed using GNAT. Such a mixed application should be developed following the general guidelines outlined above; below is the cookbook-style sequence of steps to follow:

1. First develop and build the GNAT shared library using a library project (let's assume the project is *mylib.gpr*, producing the library *libmylib.dll*):

```
$ gprbuild -p mylib.gpr
```

2. Produce a .def file for the symbols you need to interface with, either by hand or automatically with possibly some manual adjustments (see [Creating Definition File Automatically], page 247):

```
$ dlltool libmylib.dll -z libmylib.def --export-all-symbols
```
3. Make sure that MSVS command-line tools are accessible on the path.
4. Create the Microsoft-style import library (see [MSVS-Style Import Library], page 248):
```
$ lib -machine:IX86 -def:libmylib.def -out:libmylib.lib
```
If you are using a 64-bit toolchain, the above becomes...
```
$ lib -machine:X64 -def:libmylib.def -out:libmylib.lib
```
5. Build the C main
```
$ cl /O2 /MD main.c libmylib.lib
```
6. Before running the executable, make sure you have set the PATH to the DLL, or copy the DLL into into the directory containing the .exe.

7.3.6.25 Debugging a DLL

Debugging a DLL is similar to debugging a standard program. But we have to deal with two different executable parts: the DLL and the program that uses it. We have the following four possibilities:

* The program and the DLL are built with *GCC/GNAT*.
* The program is built with foreign tools and the DLL is built with *GCC/GNAT*.
* The program is built with *GCC/GNAT* and the DLL is built with foreign tools.

In this section we address only cases one and two above. There is no point in trying to debug a DLL with *GNU/GDB*, if there is no GDB-compatible debugging information in it. To do so you must use a debugger compatible with the tools suite used to build the DLL.

7.3.6.26 Program and DLL Both Built with GCC/GNAT

This is the simplest case. Both the DLL and the program have *GDB* compatible debugging information. It is then possible to break anywhere in the process. Let's suppose here that the main procedure is named *ada_main* and that in the DLL there is an entry point named *ada_dll*.

The DLL ([Introduction to Dynamic Link Libraries (DLLs)], page 244) and program must have been built with the debugging information (see GNAT -g switch). Here are the step-by-step instructions for debugging it:

* Launch *GDB* on the main program.
```
$ gdb -nw ada_main
```
* Start the program and stop at the beginning of the main procedure
```
(gdb) start
```
This step is required to be able to set a breakpoint inside the DLL. As long as the program is not run, the DLL is not loaded. This has the consequence that the DLL debugging information is also not loaded, so it is not possible to set a breakpoint in the DLL.

* Set a breakpoint inside the DLL
```
(gdb) break ada_dll
(gdb) cont
```

At this stage a breakpoint is set inside the DLL. From there on you can use the standard approach to debug the whole program ([Running and Debugging Ada Programs], page 188).

7.3.6.27 Program Built with Foreign Tools and DLL Built with GCC/GNAT

In this case things are slightly more complex because it is not possible to start the main program and then break at the beginning to load the DLL and the associated DLL debugging information. It is not possible to break at the beginning of the program because there is no *GDB* debugging information, and therefore there is no direct way of getting initial control. This section addresses this issue by describing some methods that can be used to break somewhere in the DLL to debug it.

First suppose that the main procedure is named *main* (this is for example some C code built with Microsoft Visual C) and that there is a DLL named *test.dll* containing an Ada entry point named *ada_dll*.

The DLL (see [Introduction to Dynamic Link Libraries (DLLs)], page 244) must have been built with debugging information (see GNAT *-g* option).

Debugging the DLL Directly

* Find out the executable starting address
    ```
    $ objdump --file-header main.exe
    ```
  The starting address is reported on the last line. For example:
    ```
    main.exe:     file format pei-i386
    architecture: i386, flags 0x0000010a:
    EXEC_P, HAS_DEBUG, D_PAGED
    start address 0x00401010
    ```
* Launch the debugger on the executable.
    ```
    $ gdb main.exe
    ```
* Set a breakpoint at the starting address, and launch the program.
    ```
    $ (gdb) break *0x00401010
    $ (gdb) run
    ```
  The program will stop at the given address.
* Set a breakpoint on a DLL subroutine.
    ```
    (gdb) break ada_dll.adb:45
    ```
  Or if you want to break using a symbol on the DLL, you need first to select the Ada language (language used by the DLL).
    ```
    (gdb) set language ada
    (gdb) break ada_dll
    ```
* Continue the program.
    ```
    (gdb) cont
    ```
  This will run the program until it reaches the breakpoint that has been set. From that point you can use the standard way to debug a program as described in ([Running and Debugging Ada Programs], page 188).

It is also possible to debug the DLL by attaching to a running process.

Attaching to a Running Process

With *GDB* it is always possible to debug a running process by attaching to it. It is possible to debug a DLL this way. The limitation of this approach is that the DLL must run long enough to perform the attach operation. It may be useful for instance to insert a time wasting loop in the code of the DLL to meet this criterion.

* Launch the main program `main.exe`.

        $ main

* Use the Windows *Task Manager* to find the process ID. Let's say that the process PID for `main.exe` is 208.

* Launch gdb.

        $ gdb

* Attach to the running process to be debugged.

        (gdb) attach 208

* Load the process debugging information.

        (gdb) symbol-file main.exe

* Break somewhere in the DLL.

        (gdb) break ada_dll

* Continue process execution.

        (gdb) cont

This last step will resume the process execution, and stop at the breakpoint we have set. From there you can use the standard approach to debug a program as described in [Running and Debugging Ada Programs], page 188.

7.3.6.28 Setting Stack Size from *gnatlink*

It is possible to specify the program stack size at link time. On modern versions of Windows, starting with XP, this is mostly useful to set the size of the main stack (environment task). The other task stacks are set with pragma Storage_Size or with the *gnatbind -d* command.

Since older versions of Windows (2000, NT4, etc.) do not allow setting the reserve size of individual tasks, the link-time stack size applies to all tasks, and pragma Storage_Size has no effect. In particular, Stack Overflow checks are made against this link-time specified size.

This setting can be done with *gnatlink* using either of the following:

* *-Xlinker* linker option

        $ gnatlink hello -Xlinker --stack=0x10000,0x1000

This sets the stack reserve size to 0x10000 bytes and the stack commit size to 0x1000 bytes.

* *-Wl* linker option

        $ gnatlink hello -Wl,--stack=0x1000000

This sets the stack reserve size to 0x1000000 bytes. Note that with *-Wl* option it is not possible to set the stack commit size because the coma is a separator for this option.

7.3.6.29 Setting Heap Size from *gnatlink*

Under Windows systems, it is possible to specify the program heap size from *gnatlink* using either of the following:

* *-Xlinker* linker option

        $ gnatlink hello -Xlinker --heap=0x10000,0x1000

This sets the heap reserve size to 0x10000 bytes and the heap commit size to 0x1000 bytes.

* *-Wl* linker option

        $ gnatlink hello -Wl,--heap=0x1000000

This sets the heap reserve size to 0x1000000 bytes. Note that with *-Wl* option it is not possible to set the heap commit size because the coma is a separator for this option.

7.3.7 Windows Specific Add-Ons

This section describes the Windows specific add-ons.

7.3.7.1 Win32Ada

Win32Ada is a binding for the Microsoft Win32 API. This binding can be easily installed from the provided installer. To use the Win32Ada binding you need to use a project file, and adding a single with_clause will give you full access to the Win32Ada binding sources and ensure that the proper libraries are passed to the linker.

```
with "win32ada";
project P is
    for Sources use ...;
end P;
```

To build the application you just need to call gprbuild for the application's project, here p.gpr:

```
gprbuild p.gpr
```

7.3.7.2 wPOSIX

wPOSIX is a minimal POSIX binding whose goal is to help with building cross-platforms applications. This binding is not complete though, as the Win32 API does not provide the necessary support for all POSIX APIs.

To use the wPOSIX binding you need to use a project file, and adding a single with_clause will give you full access to the wPOSIX binding sources and ensure that the proper libraries are passed to the linker.

```
with "wposix";
project P is
    for Sources use ...;
end P;
```

To build the application you just need to call gprbuild for the application's project, here p.gpr:

```
gprbuild p.gpr
```

7.4 Mac OS Topics

This section describes topics that are specific to Apple's OS X platform.

7.4.1 Codesigning the Debugger

The Darwin Kernel requires the debugger to have special permissions before it is allowed to control other processes. These permissions are granted by codesigning the GDB executable. Without these permissions, the debugger will report error messages such as:

```
Starting program: /x/y/foo
Unable to find Mach task port for process-id 28885: (os/kern) failure (0x5).
(please check gdb is codesigned - see taskgated(8))
```

Codesigning requires a certificate. The following procedure explains how to create one:

* Start the Keychain Access application (in /Applications/Utilities/Keychain Access.app)

* Select the Keychain Access -> Certificate Assistant -> Create a Certificate... menu

* Then:

  * Choose a name for the new certificate (this procedure will use "gdb-cert" as an example)

  * Set "Identity Type" to "Self Signed Root"

  * Set "Certificate Type" to "Code Signing"

  * Activate the "Let me override defaults" option

* Click several times on "Continue" until the "Specify a Location For The Certificate" screen appears, then set "Keychain" to "System"

* Click on "Continue" until the certificate is created

* Finally, in the view, double-click on the new certificate, and set "When using this certificate" to "Always Trust"

* Exit the Keychain Access application and restart the computer (this is unfortunately required)

Once a certificate has been created, the debugger can be codesigned as follow. In a Terminal, run the following command:

```
$ codesign -f -s  "gdb-cert"  <gnat_install_prefix>/bin/gdb
```

where "gdb-cert" should be replaced by the actual certificate name chosen above, and <gnat_install_prefix> should be replaced by the location where you installed GNAT. Also, be sure that users are in the Unix group _developer.

8 Example of Binder Output File

This Appendix displays the source code for the output file generated by *gnatbind* for a simple 'Hello World' program. Comments have been added for clarification purposes.

```
--  The package is called Ada_Main unless this name is actually used
--  as a unit name in the partition, in which case some other unique
--  name is used.

pragma Ada_95;
with System;
package ada_main is
   pragma Warnings (Off);

   --  The main program saves the parameters (argument count,
   --  argument values, environment pointer) in global variables
   --  for later access by other units including
   --  Ada.Command_Line.

   gnat_argc : Integer;
   gnat_argv : System.Address;
   gnat_envp : System.Address;

   --  The actual variables are stored in a library routine. This
   --  is useful for some shared library situations, where there
   --  are problems if variables are not in the library.

   pragma Import (C, gnat_argc);
   pragma Import (C, gnat_argv);
   pragma Import (C, gnat_envp);

   --  The exit status is similarly an external location

   gnat_exit_status : Integer;
   pragma Import (C, gnat_exit_status);

   GNAT_Version : constant String :=
                   "GNAT Version: Pro 7.4.0w (20141119-49)" & ASCII.NUL;
   pragma Export (C, GNAT_Version, "__gnat_version");

   Ada_Main_Program_Name : constant String := "_ada_hello" & ASCII.NUL;
   pragma Export (C, Ada_Main_Program_Name, "__gnat_ada_main_program_name");

   --  This is the generated adainit routine that performs
   --  initialization at the start of execution. In the case
   --  where Ada is the main program, this main program makes
   --  a call to adainit at program startup.
```

```
procedure adainit;
pragma Export (C, adainit, "adainit");

--  This is the generated adafinal routine that performs
--  finalization at the end of execution. In the case where
--  Ada is the main program, this main program makes a call
--  to adafinal at program termination.

procedure adafinal;
pragma Export (C, adafinal, "adafinal");

--  This routine is called at the start of execution. It is
--  a dummy routine that is used by the debugger to breakpoint
--  at the start of execution.

--  This is the actual generated main program (it would be
--  suppressed if the no main program switch were used). As
--  required by standard system conventions, this program has
--  the external name main.

function main
  (argc : Integer;
   argv : System.Address;
   envp : System.Address)
   return Integer;
pragma Export (C, main, "main");

--  The following set of constants give the version
--  identification values for every unit in the bound
--  partition. This identification is computed from all
--  dependent semantic units, and corresponds to the
--  string that would be returned by use of the
--  Body_Version or Version attributes.

--  The following Export pragmas export the version numbers
--  with symbolic names ending in B (for body) or S
--  (for spec) so that they can be located in a link. The
--  information provided here is sufficient to track down
--  the exact versions of units used in a given build.

type Version_32 is mod 2 ** 32;
u00001 : constant Version_32 := 16#8ad6e54a#;
pragma Export (C, u00001, "helloB");
u00002 : constant Version_32 := 16#fbff4c67#;
pragma Export (C, u00002, "system__standard_libraryB");
u00003 : constant Version_32 := 16#1ec6fd90#;
pragma Export (C, u00003, "system__standard_libraryS");
```

```
u00004 : constant Version_32 := 16#3ffc8e18#;
pragma Export (C, u00004, "adaS");
u00005 : constant Version_32 := 16#28f088c2#;
pragma Export (C, u00005, "ada__text_ioB");
u00006 : constant Version_32 := 16#f372c8ac#;
pragma Export (C, u00006, "ada__text_ioS");
u00007 : constant Version_32 := 16#2c143749#;
pragma Export (C, u00007, "ada__exceptionsB");
u00008 : constant Version_32 := 16#f4f0cce8#;
pragma Export (C, u00008, "ada__exceptionsS");
u00009 : constant Version_32 := 16#a46739c0#;
pragma Export (C, u00009, "ada__exceptions__last_chance_handlerB");
u00010 : constant Version_32 := 16#3aac8c92#;
pragma Export (C, u00010, "ada__exceptions__last_chance_handlerS");
u00011 : constant Version_32 := 16#1d274481#;
pragma Export (C, u00011, "systemS");
u00012 : constant Version_32 := 16#a207fefe#;
pragma Export (C, u00012, "system__soft_linksB");
u00013 : constant Version_32 := 16#467d9556#;
pragma Export (C, u00013, "system__soft_linksS");
u00014 : constant Version_32 := 16#b01dad17#;
pragma Export (C, u00014, "system__parametersB");
u00015 : constant Version_32 := 16#630d49fe#;
pragma Export (C, u00015, "system__parametersS");
u00016 : constant Version_32 := 16#b19b6653#;
pragma Export (C, u00016, "system__secondary_stackB");
u00017 : constant Version_32 := 16#b6468be8#;
pragma Export (C, u00017, "system__secondary_stackS");
u00018 : constant Version_32 := 16#39a03df9#;
pragma Export (C, u00018, "system__storage_elementsB");
u00019 : constant Version_32 := 16#30e40e85#;
pragma Export (C, u00019, "system__storage_elementsS");
u00020 : constant Version_32 := 16#41837d1e#;
pragma Export (C, u00020, "system__stack_checkingB");
u00021 : constant Version_32 := 16#93982f69#;
pragma Export (C, u00021, "system__stack_checkingS");
u00022 : constant Version_32 := 16#393398c1#;
pragma Export (C, u00022, "system__exception_tableB");
u00023 : constant Version_32 := 16#b33e2294#;
pragma Export (C, u00023, "system__exception_tableS");
u00024 : constant Version_32 := 16#ce4af020#;
pragma Export (C, u00024, "system__exceptionsB");
u00025 : constant Version_32 := 16#75442977#;
pragma Export (C, u00025, "system__exceptionsS");
u00026 : constant Version_32 := 16#37d758f1#;
pragma Export (C, u00026, "system__exceptions__machineS");
u00027 : constant Version_32 := 16#b895431d#;
```

```
pragma Export (C, u00027, "system__exceptions_debugB");
u00028 : constant Version_32 := 16#aec55d3f#;
pragma Export (C, u00028, "system__exceptions_debugS");
u00029 : constant Version_32 := 16#570325c8#;
pragma Export (C, u00029, "system__img_intB");
u00030 : constant Version_32 := 16#1ffca443#;
pragma Export (C, u00030, "system__img_intS");
u00031 : constant Version_32 := 16#b98c3e16#;
pragma Export (C, u00031, "system__tracebackB");
u00032 : constant Version_32 := 16#831a9d5a#;
pragma Export (C, u00032, "system__tracebackS");
u00033 : constant Version_32 := 16#9ed49525#;
pragma Export (C, u00033, "system__traceback_entriesB");
u00034 : constant Version_32 := 16#1d7cb2f1#;
pragma Export (C, u00034, "system__traceback_entriesS");
u00035 : constant Version_32 := 16#8c33a517#;
pragma Export (C, u00035, "system__wch_conB");
u00036 : constant Version_32 := 16#065a6653#;
pragma Export (C, u00036, "system__wch_conS");
u00037 : constant Version_32 := 16#9721e840#;
pragma Export (C, u00037, "system__wch_stwB");
u00038 : constant Version_32 := 16#2b4b4a52#;
pragma Export (C, u00038, "system__wch_stwS");
u00039 : constant Version_32 := 16#92b797cb#;
pragma Export (C, u00039, "system__wch_cnvB");
u00040 : constant Version_32 := 16#09eddca0#;
pragma Export (C, u00040, "system__wch_cnvS");
u00041 : constant Version_32 := 16#6033a23f#;
pragma Export (C, u00041, "interfacesS");
u00042 : constant Version_32 := 16#ece6fdb6#;
pragma Export (C, u00042, "system__wch_jisB");
u00043 : constant Version_32 := 16#899dc581#;
pragma Export (C, u00043, "system__wch_jisS");
u00044 : constant Version_32 := 16#10558b11#;
pragma Export (C, u00044, "ada__streamsB");
u00045 : constant Version_32 := 16#2e6701ab#;
pragma Export (C, u00045, "ada__streamsS");
u00046 : constant Version_32 := 16#db5c917c#;
pragma Export (C, u00046, "ada__io_exceptionsS");
u00047 : constant Version_32 := 16#12c8cd7d#;
pragma Export (C, u00047, "ada__tagsB");
u00048 : constant Version_32 := 16#ce72c228#;
pragma Export (C, u00048, "ada__tagsS");
u00049 : constant Version_32 := 16#c3335bfd#;
pragma Export (C, u00049, "system__htableB");
u00050 : constant Version_32 := 16#99e5f76b#;
pragma Export (C, u00050, "system__htableS");
```

```
u00051 : constant Version_32 := 16#089f5cd0#;
pragma Export (C, u00051, "system__string_hashB");
u00052 : constant Version_32 := 16#3bbb9c15#;
pragma Export (C, u00052, "system__string_hashS");
u00053 : constant Version_32 := 16#807fe041#;
pragma Export (C, u00053, "system__unsigned_typesS");
u00054 : constant Version_32 := 16#d27be59e#;
pragma Export (C, u00054, "system__val_lluB");
u00055 : constant Version_32 := 16#fa8db733#;
pragma Export (C, u00055, "system__val_lluS");
u00056 : constant Version_32 := 16#27b600b2#;
pragma Export (C, u00056, "system__val_utilB");
u00057 : constant Version_32 := 16#b187f27f#;
pragma Export (C, u00057, "system__val_utilS");
u00058 : constant Version_32 := 16#d1060688#;
pragma Export (C, u00058, "system__case_utilB");
u00059 : constant Version_32 := 16#392e2d56#;
pragma Export (C, u00059, "system__case_utilS");
u00060 : constant Version_32 := 16#84a27f0d#;
pragma Export (C, u00060, "interfaces__c_streamsB");
u00061 : constant Version_32 := 16#8bb5f2c0#;
pragma Export (C, u00061, "interfaces__c_streamsS");
u00062 : constant Version_32 := 16#6db6928f#;
pragma Export (C, u00062, "system__crtlS");
u00063 : constant Version_32 := 16#4e6a342b#;
pragma Export (C, u00063, "system__file_ioB");
u00064 : constant Version_32 := 16#ba56a5e4#;
pragma Export (C, u00064, "system__file_ioS");
u00065 : constant Version_32 := 16#b7ab275c#;
pragma Export (C, u00065, "ada__finalizationB");
u00066 : constant Version_32 := 16#19f764ca#;
pragma Export (C, u00066, "ada__finalizationS");
u00067 : constant Version_32 := 16#95817ed8#;
pragma Export (C, u00067, "system__finalization_rootB");
u00068 : constant Version_32 := 16#52d53711#;
pragma Export (C, u00068, "system__finalization_rootS");
u00069 : constant Version_32 := 16#769e25e6#;
pragma Export (C, u00069, "interfaces__cB");
u00070 : constant Version_32 := 16#4a38bedb#;
pragma Export (C, u00070, "interfaces__cS");
u00071 : constant Version_32 := 16#07e6ee66#;
pragma Export (C, u00071, "system__os_libB");
u00072 : constant Version_32 := 16#d7b69782#;
pragma Export (C, u00072, "system__os_libS");
u00073 : constant Version_32 := 16#1a817b8e#;
pragma Export (C, u00073, "system__stringsB");
u00074 : constant Version_32 := 16#639855e7#;
```

```
pragma Export (C, u00074, "system__stringsS");
u00075 : constant Version_32 := 16#e0b8de29#;
pragma Export (C, u00075, "system__file_control_blockS");
u00076 : constant Version_32 := 16#b5b2aca1#;
pragma Export (C, u00076, "system__finalization_mastersB");
u00077 : constant Version_32 := 16#69316dc1#;
pragma Export (C, u00077, "system__finalization_mastersS");
u00078 : constant Version_32 := 16#57a37a42#;
pragma Export (C, u00078, "system__address_imageB");
u00079 : constant Version_32 := 16#bccbd9bb#;
pragma Export (C, u00079, "system__address_imageS");
u00080 : constant Version_32 := 16#7268f812#;
pragma Export (C, u00080, "system__img_boolB");
u00081 : constant Version_32 := 16#e8fe356a#;
pragma Export (C, u00081, "system__img_boolS");
u00082 : constant Version_32 := 16#d7aac20c#;
pragma Export (C, u00082, "system__ioB");
u00083 : constant Version_32 := 16#8365b3ce#;
pragma Export (C, u00083, "system__ioS");
u00084 : constant Version_32 := 16#6d4d969a#;
pragma Export (C, u00084, "system__storage_poolsB");
u00085 : constant Version_32 := 16#e87cc305#;
pragma Export (C, u00085, "system__storage_poolsS");
u00086 : constant Version_32 := 16#e34550ca#;
pragma Export (C, u00086, "system__pool_globalB");
u00087 : constant Version_32 := 16#c88d2d16#;
pragma Export (C, u00087, "system__pool_globalS");
u00088 : constant Version_32 := 16#9d39c675#;
pragma Export (C, u00088, "system__memoryB");
u00089 : constant Version_32 := 16#445a22b5#;
pragma Export (C, u00089, "system__memoryS");
u00090 : constant Version_32 := 16#6a859064#;
pragma Export (C, u00090, "system__storage_pools__subpoolsB");
u00091 : constant Version_32 := 16#e3b008dc#;
pragma Export (C, u00091, "system__storage_pools__subpoolsS");
u00092 : constant Version_32 := 16#63f11652#;
pragma Export (C, u00092, "system__storage_pools__subpools__finalizationB");
u00093 : constant Version_32 := 16#fe2f4b3a#;
pragma Export (C, u00093, "system__storage_pools__subpools__finalizationS");

--   BEGIN ELABORATION ORDER
--   ada%s
--   interfaces%s
--   system%s
--   system.case_util%s
--   system.case_util%b
--   system.htable%s
```

```
--    system.img_bool%s
--    system.img_bool%b
--    system.img_int%s
--    system.img_int%b
--    system.io%s
--    system.io%b
--    system.parameters%s
--    system.parameters%b
--    system.crtl%s
--    interfaces.c_streams%s
--    interfaces.c_streams%b
--    system.standard_library%s
--    system.exceptions_debug%s
--    system.exceptions_debug%b
--    system.storage_elements%s
--    system.storage_elements%b
--    system.stack_checking%s
--    system.stack_checking%b
--    system.string_hash%s
--    system.string_hash%b
--    system.htable%b
--    system.strings%s
--    system.strings%b
--    system.os_lib%s
--    system.traceback_entries%s
--    system.traceback_entries%b
--    ada.exceptions%s
--    system.soft_links%s
--    system.unsigned_types%s
--    system.val_llu%s
--    system.val_util%s
--    system.val_util%b
--    system.val_llu%b
--    system.wch_con%s
--    system.wch_con%b
--    system.wch_cnv%s
--    system.wch_jis%s
--    system.wch_jis%b
--    system.wch_cnv%b
--    system.wch_stw%s
--    system.wch_stw%b
--    ada.exceptions.last_chance_handler%s
--    ada.exceptions.last_chance_handler%b
--    system.address_image%s
--    system.exception_table%s
--    system.exception_table%b
--    ada.io_exceptions%s
```

```
--    ada.tags%s
--    ada.streams%s
--    ada.streams%b
--    interfaces.c%s
--    system.exceptions%s
--    system.exceptions%b
--    system.exceptions.machine%s
--    system.finalization_root%s
--    system.finalization_root%b
--    ada.finalization%s
--    ada.finalization%b
--    system.storage_pools%s
--    system.storage_pools%b
--    system.finalization_masters%s
--    system.storage_pools.subpools%s
--    system.storage_pools.subpools.finalization%s
--    system.storage_pools.subpools.finalization%b
--    system.memory%s
--    system.memory%b
--    system.standard_library%b
--    system.pool_global%s
--    system.pool_global%b
--    system.file_control_block%s
--    system.file_io%s
--    system.secondary_stack%s
--    system.file_io%b
--    system.storage_pools.subpools%b
--    system.finalization_masters%b
--    interfaces.c%b
--    ada.tags%b
--    system.soft_links%b
--    system.os_lib%b
--    system.secondary_stack%b
--    system.address_image%b
--    system.traceback%s
--    ada.exceptions%b
--    system.traceback%b
--    ada.text_io%s
--    ada.text_io%b
--    hello%b
--    END ELABORATION ORDER

end ada_main;

pragma Ada_95;
--   The following source file name pragmas allow the generated file
--   names to be unique for different main programs. They are needed
```

```
--  since the package name will always be Ada_Main.

pragma Source_File_Name (ada_main, Spec_File_Name => "b~hello.ads");
pragma Source_File_Name (ada_main, Body_File_Name => "b~hello.adb");

pragma Suppress (Overflow_Check);
with Ada.Exceptions;

--  Generated package body for Ada_Main starts here

package body ada_main is
   pragma Warnings (Off);

   --  These values are reference counter associated to units which have
   --  been elaborated. It is also used to avoid elaborating the
   --  same unit twice.

   E72 : Short_Integer; pragma Import (Ada, E72, "system__os_lib_E");
   E13 : Short_Integer; pragma Import (Ada, E13, "system__soft_links_E");
   E23 : Short_Integer; pragma Import (Ada, E23, "system__exception_table_E");
   E46 : Short_Integer; pragma Import (Ada, E46, "ada__io_exceptions_E");
   E48 : Short_Integer; pragma Import (Ada, E48, "ada__tags_E");
   E45 : Short_Integer; pragma Import (Ada, E45, "ada__streams_E");
   E70 : Short_Integer; pragma Import (Ada, E70, "interfaces__c_E");
   E25 : Short_Integer; pragma Import (Ada, E25, "system__exceptions_E");
   E68 : Short_Integer; pragma Import (Ada, E68, "system__finalization_root_E");
   E66 : Short_Integer; pragma Import (Ada, E66, "ada__finalization_E");
   E85 : Short_Integer; pragma Import (Ada, E85, "system__storage_pools_E");
   E77 : Short_Integer; pragma Import (Ada, E77, "system__finalization_masters_E");
   E91 : Short_Integer; pragma Import (Ada, E91, "system__storage_pools__subpools_E
   E87 : Short_Integer; pragma Import (Ada, E87, "system__pool_global_E");
   E75 : Short_Integer; pragma Import (Ada, E75, "system__file_control_block_E");
   E64 : Short_Integer; pragma Import (Ada, E64, "system__file_io_E");
   E17 : Short_Integer; pragma Import (Ada, E17, "system__secondary_stack_E");
   E06 : Short_Integer; pragma Import (Ada, E06, "ada__text_io_E");

   Local_Priority_Specific_Dispatching : constant String := "";
   Local_Interrupt_States : constant String := "";

   Is_Elaborated : Boolean := False;

   procedure finalize_library is
   begin
      E06 := E06 - 1;
      declare
         procedure F1;
         pragma Import (Ada, F1, "ada__text_io__finalize_spec");
```

```
      begin
         F1;
      end;
      E77 := E77 - 1;
      E91 := E91 - 1;
      declare
         procedure F2;
         pragma Import (Ada, F2, "system__file_io__finalize_body");
      begin
         E64 := E64 - 1;
         F2;
      end;
      declare
         procedure F3;
         pragma Import (Ada, F3, "system__file_control_block__finalize_spec");
      begin
         E75 := E75 - 1;
         F3;
      end;
      E87 := E87 - 1;
      declare
         procedure F4;
         pragma Import (Ada, F4, "system__pool_global__finalize_spec");
      begin
         F4;
      end;
      declare
         procedure F5;
         pragma Import (Ada, F5, "system__storage_pools__subpools__finalize_spe
      begin
         F5;
      end;
      declare
         procedure F6;
         pragma Import (Ada, F6, "system__finalization_masters__finalize_spec")
      begin
         F6;
      end;
      declare
         procedure Reraise_Library_Exception_If_Any;
         pragma Import (Ada, Reraise_Library_Exception_If_Any, "__gnat_reraise_
      begin
         Reraise_Library_Exception_If_Any;
      end;
   end finalize_library;


      -------------
```

```
-- adainit --
-------------

procedure adainit is

   Main_Priority : Integer;
   pragma Import (C, Main_Priority, "__gl_main_priority");
   Time_Slice_Value : Integer;
   pragma Import (C, Time_Slice_Value, "__gl_time_slice_val");
   WC_Encoding : Character;
   pragma Import (C, WC_Encoding, "__gl_wc_encoding");
   Locking_Policy : Character;
   pragma Import (C, Locking_Policy, "__gl_locking_policy");
   Queuing_Policy : Character;
   pragma Import (C, Queuing_Policy, "__gl_queuing_policy");
   Task_Dispatching_Policy : Character;
   pragma Import (C, Task_Dispatching_Policy, "__gl_task_dispatching_policy");
   Priority_Specific_Dispatching : System.Address;
   pragma Import (C, Priority_Specific_Dispatching, "__gl_priority_specific_disp
   Num_Specific_Dispatching : Integer;
   pragma Import (C, Num_Specific_Dispatching, "__gl_num_specific_dispatching");
   Main_CPU : Integer;
   pragma Import (C, Main_CPU, "__gl_main_cpu");
   Interrupt_States : System.Address;
   pragma Import (C, Interrupt_States, "__gl_interrupt_states");
   Num_Interrupt_States : Integer;
   pragma Import (C, Num_Interrupt_States, "__gl_num_interrupt_states");
   Unreserve_All_Interrupts : Integer;
   pragma Import (C, Unreserve_All_Interrupts, "__gl_unreserve_all_interrupts");
   Detect_Blocking : Integer;
   pragma Import (C, Detect_Blocking, "__gl_detect_blocking");
   Default_Stack_Size : Integer;
   pragma Import (C, Default_Stack_Size, "__gl_default_stack_size");
   Leap_Seconds_Support : Integer;
   pragma Import (C, Leap_Seconds_Support, "__gl_leap_seconds_support");

   procedure Runtime_Initialize;
   pragma Import (C, Runtime_Initialize, "__gnat_runtime_initialize");

   Finalize_Library_Objects : No_Param_Proc;
   pragma Import (C, Finalize_Library_Objects, "__gnat_finalize_library_objects")

-- Start of processing for adainit

begin

   -- Record various information for this partition.  The values
```

```
--   are derived by the binder from information stored in the ali
--   files by the compiler.

if Is_Elaborated then
   return;
end if;
Is_Elaborated := True;
Main_Priority := -1;
Time_Slice_Value := -1;
WC_Encoding := 'b';
Locking_Policy := ' ';
Queuing_Policy := ' ';
Task_Dispatching_Policy := ' ';
Priority_Specific_Dispatching :=
   Local_Priority_Specific_Dispatching'Address;
Num_Specific_Dispatching := 0;
Main_CPU := -1;
Interrupt_States := Local_Interrupt_States'Address;
Num_Interrupt_States := 0;
Unreserve_All_Interrupts := 0;
Detect_Blocking := 0;
Default_Stack_Size := -1;
Leap_Seconds_Support := 0;

Runtime_Initialize;

Finalize_Library_Objects := finalize_library'access;

--   Now we have the elaboration calls for all units in the partition.
--   The Elab_Spec and Elab_Body attributes generate references to the
--   implicit elaboration procedures generated by the compiler for
--   each unit that requires elaboration. Increment a counter of
--   reference for each unit.

System.Soft_Links'Elab_Spec;
System.Exception_Table'Elab_Body;
E23 := E23 + 1;
Ada.Io_Exceptions'Elab_Spec;
E46 := E46 + 1;
Ada.Tags'Elab_Spec;
Ada.Streams'Elab_Spec;
E45 := E45 + 1;
Interfaces.C'Elab_Spec;
System.Exceptions'Elab_Spec;
E25 := E25 + 1;
System.Finalization_Root'Elab_Spec;
E68 := E68 + 1;
```

```
      Ada.Finalization'Elab_Spec;
      E66 := E66 + 1;
      System.Storage_Pools'Elab_Spec;
      E85 := E85 + 1;
      System.Finalization_Masters'Elab_Spec;
      System.Storage_Pools.Subpools'Elab_Spec;
      System.Pool_Global'Elab_Spec;
      E87 := E87 + 1;
      System.File_Control_Block'Elab_Spec;
      E75 := E75 + 1;
      System.File_Io'Elab_Body;
      E64 := E64 + 1;
      E91 := E91 + 1;
      System.Finalization_Masters'Elab_Body;
      E77 := E77 + 1;
      E70 := E70 + 1;
      Ada.Tags'Elab_Body;
      E48 := E48 + 1;
      System.Soft_Links'Elab_Body;
      E13 := E13 + 1;
      System.Os_Lib'Elab_Body;
      E72 := E72 + 1;
      System.Secondary_Stack'Elab_Body;
      E17 := E17 + 1;
      Ada.Text_Io'Elab_Spec;
      Ada.Text_Io'Elab_Body;
      E06 := E06 + 1;
   end adainit;


   --------------
   -- adafinal --
   --------------

   procedure adafinal is
      procedure s_stalib_adafinal;
      pragma Import (C, s_stalib_adafinal, "system__standard_library__adafinal");

      procedure Runtime_Finalize;
      pragma Import (C, Runtime_Finalize, "__gnat_runtime_finalize");

   begin
      if not Is_Elaborated then
         return;
      end if;
      Is_Elaborated := False;
      Runtime_Finalize;
      s_stalib_adafinal;
```

```
end adafinal;

--  We get to the main program of the partition by using
--  pragma Import because if we try to with the unit and
--  call it Ada style, then not only do we waste time
--  recompiling it, but also, we don't really know the right
--  switches (e.g.@: identifier character set) to be used
--  to compile it.

procedure Ada_Main_Program;
pragma Import (Ada, Ada_Main_Program, "_ada_hello");

----------
-- main --
----------

--  main is actually a function, as in the ANSI C standard,
--  defined to return the exit status. The three parameters
--  are the argument count, argument values and environment
--  pointer.

function main
   (argc : Integer;
    argv : System.Address;
    envp : System.Address)
    return Integer
is
      --  The initialize routine performs low level system
      --  initialization using a standard library routine which
      --  sets up signal handling and performs any other
      --  required setup. The routine can be found in file
      --  a-init.c.

   procedure initialize;
   pragma Import (C, initialize, "__gnat_initialize");

      --  The finalize routine performs low level system
      --  finalization using a standard library routine. The
      --  routine is found in file a-final.c and in the standard
      --  distribution is a dummy routine that does nothing, so
      --  really this is a hook for special user finalization.

   procedure finalize;
   pragma Import (C, finalize, "__gnat_finalize");

      --  The following is to initialize the SEH exceptions
```

```
      SEH : aliased array (1 .. 2) of Integer;

      Ensure_Reference : aliased System.Address := Ada_Main_Program_Name'Address;
      pragma Volatile (Ensure_Reference);

   --  Start of processing for main

begin
      --  Save global variables

      gnat_argc := argc;
      gnat_argv := argv;
      gnat_envp := envp;

      --  Call low level system initialization

      Initialize (SEH'Address);

      --  Call our generated Ada initialization routine

      adainit;

      --  Now we call the main program of the partition

      Ada_Main_Program;

      --  Perform Ada finalization

      adafinal;

      --  Perform low level system finalization

      Finalize;

      --  Return the proper exit status
      return (gnat_exit_status);
   end;

--  This section is entirely comments, so it has no effect on the
--  compilation of the Ada_Main package. It provides the list of
--  object files and linker options, as well as some standard
--  libraries needed for the link. The gnatlink utility parses
--  this b~hello.adb file to read these comment lines to generate
--  the appropriate command line arguments for the call to the
--  system linker. The BEGIN/END lines are used for sentinels for
--  this parsing operation.
```

```
--   The exact file names will of course depend on the environment,
--   host/target and location of files on the host system.

-- BEGIN Object file/option list
   --    ./hello.o
   --    -L./
   --    -L/usr/local/gnat/lib/gcc-lib/i686-pc-linux-gnu/2.8.1/adalib/
   --    /usr/local/gnat/lib/gcc-lib/i686-pc-linux-gnu/2.8.1/adalib/libgnat.a
-- END Object file/option list
```

```
end ada_main;
```

The Ada code in the above example is exactly what is generated by the binder. We have added comments to more clearly indicate the function of each part of the generated *Ada_Main* package.

The code is standard Ada in all respects, and can be processed by any tools that handle Ada. In particular, it is possible to use the debugger in Ada mode to debug the generated *Ada_Main* package. For example, suppose that for reasons that you do not understand, your program is crashing during elaboration of the body of *Ada.Text_IO*. To locate this bug, you can place a breakpoint on the call:

```
Ada.Text_Io'Elab_Body;
```

and trace the elaboration routine for this package to find out where the problem might be (more usually of course you would be debugging elaboration code in your own application).

9 Elaboration Order Handling in GNAT

This appendix describes the handling of elaboration code in Ada and in GNAT, and discusses how the order of elaboration of program units can be controlled in GNAT, either automatically or with explicit programming features.

9.1 Elaboration Code

Ada provides rather general mechanisms for executing code at elaboration time, that is to say before the main program starts executing. Such code arises in three contexts:

* *Initializers for variables*

    Variables declared at the library level, in package specs or bodies, can require initialization that is performed at elaboration time, as in:

    ```
    Sqrt_Half : Float := Sqrt (0.5);
    ```

* *Package initialization code*

    Code in a *BEGIN-END* section at the outer level of a package body is executed as part of the package body elaboration code.

* *Library level task allocators*

    Tasks that are declared using task allocators at the library level start executing immediately and hence can execute at elaboration time.

Subprogram calls are possible in any of these contexts, which means that any arbitrary part of the program may be executed as part of the elaboration code. It is even possible to write a program which does all its work at elaboration time, with a null main program, although stylistically this would usually be considered an inappropriate way to structure a program.

An important concern arises in the context of elaboration code: we have to be sure that it is executed in an appropriate order. What we have is a series of elaboration code sections, potentially one section for each unit in the program. It is important that these execute in the correct order. Correctness here means that, taking the above example of the declaration of *Sqrt_Half*, if some other piece of elaboration code references *Sqrt_Half*, then it must run after the section of elaboration code that contains the declaration of *Sqrt_Half*.

There would never be any order of elaboration problem if we made a rule that whenever you *with* a unit, you must elaborate both the spec and body of that unit before elaborating the unit doing the *with*ing:

```
with Unit_1;
package Unit_2 is ...
```

would require that both the body and spec of *Unit_1* be elaborated before the spec of *Unit_2*. However, a rule like that would be far too restrictive. In particular, it would make it impossible to have routines in separate packages that were mutually recursive.

You might think that a clever enough compiler could look at the actual elaboration code and determine an appropriate correct order of elaboration, but in the general case, this is not possible. Consider the following example.

In the body of *Unit_1*, we have a procedure *Func_1* that references the variable *Sqrt_1*, which is declared in the elaboration code of the body of *Unit_1*:

```
Sqrt_1 : Float := Sqrt (0.1);
```

The elaboration code of the body of *Unit_1* also contains:

```
if expression_1 = 1 then
    Q := Unit_2.Func_2;
end if;
```

Unit_2 is exactly parallel, it has a procedure *Func_2* that references the variable *Sqrt_2*, which is declared in the elaboration code of the body *Unit_2*:

```
Sqrt_2 : Float := Sqrt (0.1);
```

The elaboration code of the body of *Unit_2* also contains:

```
if expression_2 = 2 then
    Q := Unit_1.Func_1;
end if;
```

Now the question is, which of the following orders of elaboration is acceptable:

```
Spec of Unit_1
Spec of Unit_2
Body of Unit_1
Body of Unit_2
```

or

```
Spec of Unit_2
Spec of Unit_1
Body of Unit_2
Body of Unit_1
```

If you carefully analyze the flow here, you will see that you cannot tell at compile time the answer to this question. If *expression_1* is not equal to 1, and *expression_2* is not equal to 2, then either order is acceptable, because neither of the function calls is executed. If both tests evaluate to true, then neither order is acceptable and in fact there is no correct order.

If one of the two expressions is true, and the other is false, then one of the above orders is correct, and the other is incorrect. For example, if *expression_1* /= 1 and *expression_2* = 2, then the call to *Func_1* will occur, but not the call to *Func_2*. This means that it is essential to elaborate the body of *Unit_1* before the body of *Unit_2*, so the first order of elaboration is correct and the second is wrong.

By making *expression_1* and *expression_2* depend on input data, or perhaps the time of day, we can make it impossible for the compiler or binder to figure out which of these expressions will be true, and hence it is impossible to guarantee a safe order of elaboration at run time.

9.2 Checking the Elaboration Order

In some languages that involve the same kind of elaboration problems, e.g., Java and C++, the programmer needs to take these ordering problems into account, and it is common to write a program in which an incorrect elaboration order gives surprising results, because it references variables before they are initialized. Ada is designed to be a safe language, and a programmer-beware approach is clearly not sufficient. Consequently, the language provides three lines of defense:

* *Standard rules*

  Some standard rules restrict the possible choice of elaboration order. In particular, if you *with* a unit, then its spec is always elaborated before the unit doing the *with*. Similarly, a parent spec is always elaborated before the child spec, and finally a spec is always elaborated before its corresponding body.

* *Dynamic elaboration checks*

  Dynamic checks are made at run time, so that if some entity is accessed before it is elaborated (typically by means of a subprogram call) then the exception (*Program_Error*) is raised.

* *Elaboration control*

  Facilities are provided for the programmer to specify the desired order of elaboration.

Let's look at these facilities in more detail. First, the rules for dynamic checking. One possible rule would be simply to say that the exception is raised if you access a variable which has not yet been elaborated. The trouble with this approach is that it could require expensive checks on every variable reference. Instead Ada has two rules which are a little more restrictive, but easier to check, and easier to state:

* *Restrictions on calls*

  A subprogram can only be called at elaboration time if its body has been elaborated. The rules for elaboration given above guarantee that the spec of the subprogram has been elaborated before the call, but not the body. If this rule is violated, then the exception *Program_Error* is raised.

* *Restrictions on instantiations*

  A generic unit can only be instantiated if the body of the generic unit has been elaborated. Again, the rules for elaboration given above guarantee that the spec of the generic unit has been elaborated before the instantiation, but not the body. If this rule is violated, then the exception *Program_Error* is raised.

The idea is that if the body has been elaborated, then any variables it references must have been elaborated; by checking for the body being elaborated we guarantee that none of its references causes any trouble. As we noted above, this is a little too restrictive, because a subprogram that has no non-local references in its body may in fact be safe to call. However, it really would be unsafe to rely on this, because it would mean that the caller was aware of details of the implementation in the body. This goes against the basic tenets of Ada.

A plausible implementation can be described as follows. A Boolean variable is associated with each subprogram and each generic unit. This variable is initialized to False, and is set to True at the point body is elaborated. Every call or instantiation checks the variable, and raises *Program_Error* if the variable is False.

Note that one might think that it would be good enough to have one Boolean variable for each package, but that would not deal with cases of trying to call a body in the same package as the call that has not been elaborated yet. Of course a compiler may be able to do enough analysis to optimize away some of the Boolean variables as unnecessary, and *GNAT* indeed does such optimizations, but still the easiest conceptual model is to think of there being one variable per subprogram.

9.3 Controlling the Elaboration Order

In the previous section we discussed the rules in Ada which ensure that *Program_Error* is raised if an incorrect elaboration order is chosen. This prevents erroneous executions, but we need mechanisms to specify a correct execution and avoid the exception altogether. To achieve this, Ada provides a number of features for controlling the order of elaboration. We discuss these features in this section.

First, there are several ways of indicating to the compiler that a given unit has no elaboration problems:

* *packages that do not require a body*

  A library package that does not require a body does not permit a body (this rule was introduced in Ada 95). Thus if we have a such a package, as in:

  ```
  package Definitions is
     generic
        type m is new integer;
     package Subp is
        type a is array (1 .. 10) of m;
        type b is array (1 .. 20) of m;
     end Subp;
  end Definitions;
  ```

  A package that *withs Definitions* may safely instantiate *Definitions.Subp* because the compiler can determine that there definitely is no package body to worry about in this case

* *pragma Pure*

  This pragma places sufficient restrictions on a unit to guarantee that no call to any subprogram in the unit can result in an elaboration problem. This means that the compiler does not need to worry about the point of elaboration of such units, and in particular, does not need to check any calls to any subprograms in this unit.

* *pragma Preelaborate*

  This pragma places slightly less stringent restrictions on a unit than does pragma Pure, but these restrictions are still sufficient to ensure that there are no elaboration problems with any calls to the unit.

* *pragma Elaborate_Body*

  This pragma requires that the body of a unit be elaborated immediately after its spec. Suppose a unit *A* has such a pragma, and unit *B* does a *with* of unit *A*. Recall that the standard rules require the spec of unit *A* to be elaborated before the *with*ing unit; given the pragma in *A*, we also know that the body of *A* will be elaborated before *B*, so that calls to *A* are safe and do not need a check.

  Note that, unlike pragma *Pure* and pragma *Preelaborate*, the use of *Elaborate_Body* does not guarantee that the program is free of elaboration problems, because it may not be possible to satisfy the requested elaboration order. Let's go back to the example with *Unit_1* and *Unit_2*. If a programmer marks *Unit_1* as *Elaborate_Body*, and not *Unit_2*, then the order of elaboration will be:

  ```
  Spec of Unit_2
  Spec of Unit_1
  ```

```
Body of Unit_1
Body of Unit_2
```

Now that means that the call to *Func_1* in *Unit_2* need not be checked, it must be safe. But the call to *Func_2* in *Unit_1* may still fail if *Expression_1* is equal to 1, and the programmer must still take responsibility for this not being the case.

If all units carry a pragma *Elaborate_Body*, then all problems are eliminated, except for calls entirely within a body, which are in any case fully under programmer control. However, using the pragma everywhere is not always possible. In particular, for our *Unit_1/Unit_2* example, if we marked both of them as having pragma *Elaborate_Body*, then clearly there would be no possible elaboration order.

The above pragmas allow a server to guarantee safe use by clients, and clearly this is the preferable approach. Consequently a good rule is to mark units as *Pure* or *Preelaborate* if possible, and if this is not possible, mark them as *Elaborate_Body* if possible. As we have seen, there are situations where neither of these three pragmas can be used. So we also provide methods for clients to control the order of elaboration of the servers on which they depend:

* *pragma Elaborate (unit)*

  This pragma is placed in the context clause, after a *with* clause, and it requires that the body of the named unit be elaborated before the unit in which the pragma occurs. The idea is to use this pragma if the current unit calls at elaboration time, directly or indirectly, some subprogram in the named unit.

* *pragma Elaborate_All (unit)*

  This is a stronger version of the Elaborate pragma. Consider the following example:

```
Unit A |withs| unit B and calls B.Func in elab code
Unit B |withs| unit C, and B.Func calls C.Func
```

  Now if we put a pragma *Elaborate (B)* in unit *A*, this ensures that the body of *B* is elaborated before the call, but not the body of *C*, so the call to *C.Func* could still cause *Program_Error* to be raised.

  The effect of a pragma *Elaborate_All* is stronger, it requires not only that the body of the named unit be elaborated before the unit doing the *with*, but also the bodies of all units that the named unit uses, following *with* links transitively. For example, if we put a pragma *Elaborate_All (B)* in unit *A*, then it requires not only that the body of *B* be elaborated before *A*, but also the body of *C*, because *B* *withs* *C*.

We are now in a position to give a usage rule in Ada for avoiding elaboration problems, at least if dynamic dispatching and access to subprogram values are not used. We will handle these cases separately later.

The rule is simple:

If a unit has elaboration code that can directly or indirectly make a call to a subprogram in a |withed| unit, or instantiate a generic package in a |withed| unit, then if the |withed| unit does not have pragma 'Pure' or 'Preelaborate', then the client should have a pragma 'Elaborate_All'for the |withed| unit. *

By following this rule a client is assured that calls can be made without risk of an exception.

For generic subprogram instantiations, the rule can be relaxed to require only a pragma *Elaborate* since elaborating the body of a subprogram cannot cause any transitive elaboration (we are not calling the subprogram in this case, just elaborating its declaration).

If this rule is not followed, then a program may be in one of four states:

* *No order exists*

  No order of elaboration exists which follows the rules, taking into account any *Elaborate*, *Elaborate_All*, or *Elaborate_Body* pragmas. In this case, an Ada compiler must diagnose the situation at bind time, and refuse to build an executable program.

* *One or more orders exist, all incorrect*

  One or more acceptable elaboration orders exist, and all of them generate an elaboration order problem. In this case, the binder can build an executable program, but *Program_Error* will be raised when the program is run.

* *Several orders exist, some right, some incorrect*

  One or more acceptable elaboration orders exists, and some of them work, and some do not. The programmer has not controlled the order of elaboration, so the binder may or may not pick one of the correct orders, and the program may or may not raise an exception when it is run. This is the worst case, because it means that the program may fail when moved to another compiler, or even another version of the same compiler.

* *One or more orders exists, all correct*

  One ore more acceptable elaboration orders exist, and all of them work. In this case the program runs successfully. This state of affairs can be guaranteed by following the rule we gave above, but may be true even if the rule is not followed.

Note that one additional advantage of following our rules on the use of *Elaborate* and *Elaborate_All* is that the program continues to stay in the ideal (all orders OK) state even if maintenance changes some bodies of some units. Conversely, if a program that does not follow this rule happens to be safe at some point, this state of affairs may deteriorate silently as a result of maintenance changes.

You may have noticed that the above discussion did not mention the use of *Elaborate_Body*. This was a deliberate omission. If you *with* an *Elaborate_Body* unit, it still may be the case that code in the body makes calls to some other unit, so it is still necessary to use *Elaborate_All* on such units.

9.4 Controlling Elaboration in GNAT - Internal Calls

In the case of internal calls, i.e., calls within a single package, the programmer has full control over the order of elaboration, and it is up to the programmer to elaborate declarations in an appropriate order. For example writing:

```
function One return Float;

Q : Float := One;

function One return Float is
begin
    return 1.0;
```

```
              end One;
```

will obviously raise *Program_Error* at run time, because function One will be called before
its body is elaborated. In this case GNAT will generate a warning that the call will raise
Program_Error:

```
     1. procedure y is
     2.    function One return Float;
     3.
     4.    Q : Float := One;
                        |
        >>> warning: cannot call "One" before body is elaborated
        >>> warning: Program_Error will be raised at run time

     5.
     6.    function One return Float is
     7.    begin
     8.        return 1.0;
     9.    end One;
    10.
    11. begin
    12.    null;
    13. end;
```

Note that in this particular case, it is likely that the call is safe, because the function *One*
does not access any global variables. Nevertheless in Ada, we do not want the validity of
the check to depend on the contents of the body (think about the separate compilation
case), so this is still wrong, as we discussed in the previous sections.

The error is easily corrected by rearranging the declarations so that the body of *One* appears
before the declaration containing the call (note that in Ada 95 as well as later versions of
the Ada standard, declarations can appear in any order, so there is no restriction that would
prevent this reordering, and if we write:

```
function One return Float;

function One return Float is
begin
      return 1.0;
end One;

Q : Float := One;
```

then all is well, no warning is generated, and no *Program_Error* exception will be raised.
Things are more complicated when a chain of subprograms is executed:

```
function A return Integer;
function B return Integer;
function C return Integer;

function B return Integer is begin return A; end;
function C return Integer is begin return B; end;
```

```
        X : Integer := C;

        function A return Integer is begin return 1; end;
```

Now the call to C at elaboration time in the declaration of X is correct, because the body of C is already elaborated, and the call to B within the body of C is correct, but the call to A within the body of B is incorrect, because the body of A has not been elaborated, so *Program_Error* will be raised on the call to A. In this case GNAT will generate a warning that *Program_Error* may be raised at the point of the call. Let's look at the warning:

```
 1. procedure x is
 2.    function A return Integer;
 3.    function B return Integer;
 4.    function C return Integer;
 5.
 6.    function B return Integer is begin return A; end;
                                                |
    >>> warning: call to "A" before body is elaborated may
                  raise Program_Error
    >>> warning: "B" called at line 7
    >>> warning: "C" called at line 9

 7.    function C return Integer is begin return B; end;
 8.
 9.    X : Integer := C;
10.
11.    function A return Integer is begin return 1; end;
12.
13. begin
14.    null;
15. end;
```

Note that the message here says 'may raise', instead of the direct case, where the message says 'will be raised'. That's because whether A is actually called depends in general on run-time flow of control. For example, if the body of B said

```
        function B return Integer is
        begin
          if some-condition-depending-on-input-data then
             return A;
          else
             return 1;
          end if;
        end B;
```

then we could not know until run time whether the incorrect call to A would actually occur, so *Program_Error* might or might not be raised. It is possible for a compiler to do a better job of analyzing bodies, to determine whether or not *Program_Error* might be raised, but it certainly couldn't do a perfect job (that would require solving the halting problem and is provably impossible), and because this is a warning anyway, it does not seem worth the effort to do the analysis. Cases in which it would be relevant are rare.

In practice, warnings of either of the forms given above will usually correspond to real errors, and should be examined carefully and eliminated. In the rare case where a warning is bogus, it can be suppressed by any of the following methods:

* Compile with the *-gnatws* switch set

* Suppress *Elaboration_Check* for the called subprogram

* Use pragma *Warnings_Off* to turn warnings off for the call

For the internal elaboration check case, GNAT by default generates the necessary run-time checks to ensure that *Program_Error* is raised if any call fails an elaboration check. Of course this can only happen if a warning has been issued as described above. The use of pragma *Suppress (Elaboration_Check)* may (but is not guaranteed to) suppress some of these checks, meaning that it may be possible (but is not guaranteed) for a program to be able to call a subprogram whose body is not yet elaborated, without raising a *Program_Error* exception.

9.5 Controlling Elaboration in GNAT - External Calls

The previous section discussed the case in which the execution of a particular thread of elaboration code occurred entirely within a single unit. This is the easy case to handle, because a programmer has direct and total control over the order of elaboration, and furthermore, checks need only be generated in cases which are rare and which the compiler can easily detect. The situation is more complex when separate compilation is taken into account. Consider the following:

```
package Math is
    function Sqrt (Arg : Float) return Float;
end Math;

package body Math is
    function Sqrt (Arg : Float) return Float is
    begin

        ...
    end Sqrt;
end Math;

with Math;
package Stuff is
    X : Float := Math.Sqrt (0.5);
end Stuff;

with Stuff;
procedure Main is
begin

    ...
end Main;
```

where *Main* is the main program. When this program is executed, the elaboration code must first be executed, and one of the jobs of the binder is to determine the order in which the units of a program are to be elaborated. In this case we have four units: the spec and body of *Math*, the spec of *Stuff* and the body of *Main*). In what order should the four separate sections of elaboration code be executed?

There are some restrictions in the order of elaboration that the binder can choose. In particular, if unit U has a *with* for a package *X*, then you are assured that the spec of *X* is elaborated before U , but you are not assured that the body of *X* is elaborated before U. This means that in the above case, the binder is allowed to choose the order:

```
spec of Math
spec of Stuff
body of Math
body of Main
```

but that's not good, because now the call to *Math.Sqrt* that happens during the elaboration of the *Stuff* spec happens before the body of *Math.Sqrt* is elaborated, and hence causes *Program_Error* exception to be raised. At first glance, one might say that the binder is misbehaving, because obviously you want to elaborate the body of something you *with* first, but that is not a general rule that can be followed in all cases. Consider

```
package X is ...

package Y is ...

with X;
package body Y is ...

with Y;
package body X is ...
```

This is a common arrangement, and, apart from the order of elaboration problems that might arise in connection with elaboration code, this works fine. A rule that says that you must first elaborate the body of anything you *with* cannot work in this case: the body of *X* *with*s *Y*, which means you would have to elaborate the body of *Y* first, but that *with*s *X*, which means you have to elaborate the body of *X* first, but ... and we have a loop that cannot be broken.

It is true that the binder can in many cases guess an order of elaboration that is unlikely to cause a *Program_Error* exception to be raised, and it tries to do so (in the above example of *Math/Stuff/Spec*, the GNAT binder will by default elaborate the body of *Math* right after its spec, so all will be well).

However, a program that blindly relies on the binder to be helpful can get into trouble, as we discussed in the previous sections, so GNAT provides a number of facilities for assisting the programmer in developing programs that are robust with respect to elaboration order.

9.6 Default Behavior in GNAT - Ensuring Safety

The default behavior in GNAT ensures elaboration safety. In its default mode GNAT implements the rule we previously described as the right approach. Let's restate it:

If a unit has elaboration code that can directly or indirectly make a call to a subprogram in a |withed| unit, or instantiate a generic package in a |withed| unit, then if the |withed| unit does not have pragma 'Pure' or 'Preelaborate', then the client should have an 'Elaborate_All' pragma for the |withed| unit.

In the case of instantiating a generic subprogram, it is always sufficient to have only an 'Elaborate' pragma for the |withed| unit.

By following this rule a client is assured that calls and instantiations can be made without risk of an exception.

In this mode GNAT traces all calls that are potentially made from elaboration code, and puts in any missing implicit *Elaborate* and *Elaborate_All* pragmas. The advantage of this approach is that no elaboration problems are possible if the binder can find an elaboration order that is consistent with these implicit *Elaborate* and *Elaborate_All* pragmas. The disadvantage of this approach is that no such order may exist.

If the binder does not generate any diagnostics, then it means that it has found an elaboration order that is guaranteed to be safe. However, the binder may still be relying on implicitly generated *Elaborate* and *Elaborate_All* pragmas so portability to other compilers than GNAT is not guaranteed.

If it is important to guarantee portability, then the compilations should use the *-gnatel* (info messages for elaboration pragmas) switch. This will cause info messages to be generated indicating the missing *Elaborate* and *Elaborate_All* pragmas. Consider the following source program:

```
with k;
package j is
  m : integer := k.r;
end;
```

where it is clear that there should be a pragma *Elaborate_All* for unit *k*. An implicit pragma will be generated, and it is likely that the binder will be able to honor it. However, if you want to port this program to some other Ada compiler than GNAT. it is safer to include the pragma explicitly in the source. If this unit is compiled with the *-gnatel* switch, then the compiler outputs an information message:

```
1. with k;
2. package j is
3.   m : integer := k.r;
                     |
     >>> info: call to "r" may raise Program_Error
     >>> info: missing pragma Elaborate_All for "k"

4. end;
```

and these messages can be used as a guide for supplying manually the missing pragmas. It is usually a bad idea to use this option during development. That's because it will tell you when you need to put in a pragma, but cannot tell you when it is time to take it out. So the use of pragma *Elaborate_All* may lead to unnecessary dependencies and even false circularities.

This default mode is more restrictive than the Ada Reference Manual, and it is possible to construct programs which will compile using the dynamic model described there, but will run into a circularity using the safer static model we have described.

Of course any Ada compiler must be able to operate in a mode consistent with the requirements of the Ada Reference Manual, and in particular must have the capability of implementing the standard dynamic model of elaboration with run-time checks.

In GNAT, this standard mode can be achieved either by the use of the *-gnatE* switch on the compiler (*gcc* or *gnatmake*) command, or by the use of the configuration pragma:

```
pragma Elaboration_Checks (DYNAMIC);
```

Either approach will cause the unit affected to be compiled using the standard dynamic run-time elaboration checks described in the Ada Reference Manual. The static model is generally preferable, since it is clearly safer to rely on compile and link time checks rather than run-time checks. However, in the case of legacy code, it may be difficult to meet the requirements of the static model. This issue is further discussed in [What to Do If the Default Elaboration Behavior Fails], page 298.

Note that the static model provides a strict subset of the allowed behavior and programs of the Ada Reference Manual, so if you do adhere to the static model and no circularities exist, then you are assured that your program will work using the dynamic model, providing that you remove any pragma Elaborate statements from the source.

9.7 Treatment of Pragma Elaborate

The use of *pragma Elaborate* should generally be avoided in Ada 95 and Ada 2005 programs, since there is no guarantee that transitive calls will be properly handled. Indeed at one point, this pragma was placed in Annex J (Obsolescent Features), on the grounds that it is *never useful*.

Now that's a bit restrictive. In practice, the case in which *pragma Elaborate* is useful is when the caller knows that there are no transitive calls, or that the called unit contains all necessary transitive *pragma Elaborate* statements, and legacy code often contains such uses.

Strictly speaking the static mode in GNAT should ignore such pragmas, since there is no assurance at compile time that the necessary safety conditions are met. In practice, this would cause GNAT to be incompatible with correctly written Ada 83 code that had all necessary *pragma Elaborate* statements in place. Consequently, we made the decision that GNAT in its default mode will believe that if it encounters a *pragma Elaborate* then the programmer knows what they are doing, and it will trust that no elaboration errors can occur.

The result of this decision is two-fold. First to be safe using the static mode, you should remove all *pragma Elaborate* statements. Second, when fixing circularities in existing code, you can selectively use *pragma Elaborate* statements to convince the static mode of GNAT that it need not generate an implicit *pragma Elaborate_All* statement.

When using the static mode with *-gnatwl*, any use of *pragma Elaborate* will generate a warning about possible problems.

9.8 Elaboration Issues for Library Tasks

In this section we examine special elaboration issues that arise for programs that declare library level tasks.

Generally the model of execution of an Ada program is that all units are elaborated, and then execution of the program starts. However, the declaration of library tasks definitely does not fit this model. The reason for this is that library tasks start as soon as they are declared (more precisely, as soon as the statement part of the enclosing package body is reached), that is to say before elaboration of the program is complete. This means that if such a task calls a subprogram, or an entry in another task, the callee may or may not be elaborated yet, and in the standard Reference Manual model of dynamic elaboration checks, you can even get timing dependent Program_Error exceptions, since there can be a race between the elaboration code and the task code.

The static model of elaboration in GNAT seeks to avoid all such dynamic behavior, by being conservative, and the conservative approach in this particular case is to assume that all the code in a task body is potentially executed at elaboration time if a task is declared at the library level.

This can definitely result in unexpected circularities. Consider the following example

```
package Decls is
  task Lib_Task is
     entry Start;
  end Lib_Task;

  type My_Int is new Integer;

  function Ident (M : My_Int) return My_Int;
end Decls;

with Utils;
package body Decls is
  task body Lib_Task is
  begin
     accept Start;
     Utils.Put_Val (2);
  end Lib_Task;

  function Ident (M : My_Int) return My_Int is
  begin
     return M;
  end Ident;
end Decls;

with Decls;
package Utils is
  procedure Put_Val (Arg : Decls.My_Int);
end Utils;
```

```
with Text_IO;
package body Utils is
  procedure Put_Val (Arg : Decls.My_Int) is
  begin
     Text_IO.Put_Line (Decls.My_Int'Image (Decls.Ident (Arg)));
   end Put_Val;
end Utils;

with Decls;
procedure Main is
begin
   Decls.Lib_Task.Start;
end;
```

If the above example is compiled in the default static elaboration mode, then a circularity occurs. The circularity comes from the call *Utils.Put_Val* in the task body of *Decls.Lib_Task*. Since this call occurs in elaboration code, we need an implicit pragma *Elaborate_All* for *Utils*. This means that not only must the spec and body of *Utils* be elaborated before the body of *Decls*, but also the spec and body of any unit that is *with*ed by the body of *Utils* must also be elaborated before the body of *Decls*. This is the transitive implication of pragma *Elaborate_All* and it makes sense, because in general the body of *Put_Val* might have a call to something in a *with*ed unit.

In this case, the body of Utils (actually its spec) *with*s *Decls*. Unfortunately this means that the body of *Decls* must be elaborated before itself, in case there is a call from the body of *Utils*.

Here is the exact chain of events we are worrying about:

*   In the body of *Decls* a call is made from within the body of a library task to a subprogram in the package *Utils*. Since this call may occur at elaboration time (given that the task is activated at elaboration time), we have to assume the worst, i.e., that the call does happen at elaboration time.

*   This means that the body and spec of *Util* must be elaborated before the body of *Decls* so that this call does not cause an access before elaboration.

*   Within the body of *Util*, specifically within the body of *Util.Put_Val* there may be calls to any unit *with*ed by this package.

*   One such *with*ed package is package *Decls*, so there might be a call to a subprogram in *Decls* in *Put_Val*. In fact there is such a call in this example, but we would have to assume that there was such a call even if it were not there, since we are not supposed to write the body of *Decls* knowing what is in the body of *Utils*; certainly in the case of the static elaboration model, the compiler does not know what is in other bodies and must assume the worst.

*   This means that the spec and body of *Decls* must also be elaborated before we elaborate the unit containing the call, but that unit is *Decls*! This means that the body of *Decls* must be elaborated before itself, and that's a circularity.

Indeed, if you add an explicit pragma *Elaborate_All* for *Utils* in the body of *Decls* you will get a true Ada Reference Manual circularity that makes the program illegal.

In practice, we have found that problems with the static model of elaboration in existing code often arise from library tasks, so we must address this particular situation.

Note that if we compile and run the program above, using the dynamic model of elaboration (that is to say use the *-gnatE* switch), then it compiles, binds, links, and runs, printing the expected result of 2. Therefore in some sense the circularity here is only apparent, and we need to capture the properties of this program that distinguish it from other library-level tasks that have real elaboration problems.

We have four possible answers to this question:

* Use the dynamic model of elaboration.

  If we use the *-gnatE* switch, then as noted above, the program works. Why is this? If we examine the task body, it is apparent that the task cannot proceed past the *accept* statement until after elaboration has been completed, because the corresponding entry call comes from the main program, not earlier. This is why the dynamic model works here. But that's really giving up on a precise analysis, and we prefer to take this approach only if we cannot solve the problem in any other manner. So let us examine two ways to reorganize the program to avoid the potential elaboration problem.

* Split library tasks into separate packages.

  Write separate packages, so that library tasks are isolated from other declarations as much as possible. Let us look at a variation on the above program.

```
package Decls1 is
  task Lib_Task is
     entry Start;
  end Lib_Task;
end Decls1;

with Utils;
package body Decls1 is
  task body Lib_Task is
  begin
     accept Start;
     Utils.Put_Val (2);
  end Lib_Task;
end Decls1;

package Decls2 is
  type My_Int is new Integer;
  function Ident (M : My_Int) return My_Int;
end Decls2;

with Utils;
package body Decls2 is
  function Ident (M : My_Int) return My_Int is
  begin
     return M;
  end Ident;
```

```
end Decls2;

with Decls2;
package Utils is
   procedure Put_Val (Arg : Decls2.My_Int);
end Utils;

with Text_IO;
package body Utils is
   procedure Put_Val (Arg : Decls2.My_Int) is
   begin
      Text_IO.Put_Line (Decls2.My_Int'Image (Decls2.Ident (Arg)));
   end Put_Val;
end Utils;

with Decls1;
procedure Main is
begin
   Decls1.Lib_Task.Start;
end;
```

All we have done is to split *Decls* into two packages, one containing the library task, and one containing everything else. Now there is no cycle, and the program compiles, binds, links and executes using the default static model of elaboration.

* Declare separate task types.

A significant part of the problem arises because of the use of the single task declaration form. This means that the elaboration of the task type, and the elaboration of the task itself (i.e., the creation of the task) happen at the same time. A good rule of style in Ada is to always create explicit task types. By following the additional step of placing task objects in separate packages from the task type declaration, many elaboration problems are avoided. Here is another modified example of the example program:

```
package Decls is
   task type Lib_Task_Type is
      entry Start;
   end Lib_Task_Type;

   type My_Int is new Integer;

   function Ident (M : My_Int) return My_Int;
end Decls;

with Utils;
package body Decls is
   task body Lib_Task_Type is
   begin
      accept Start;
      Utils.Put_Val (2);
```

```
      end Lib_Task_Type;

      function Ident (M : My_Int) return My_Int is
      begin
         return M;
      end Ident;
   end Decls;

   with Decls;
   package Utils is
      procedure Put_Val (Arg : Decls.My_Int);
   end Utils;

   with Text_IO;
   package body Utils is
      procedure Put_Val (Arg : Decls.My_Int) is
      begin
         Text_IO.Put_Line (Decls.My_Int'Image (Decls.Ident (Arg)));
      end Put_Val;
   end Utils;

   with Decls;
   package Declst is
       Lib_Task : Decls.Lib_Task_Type;
   end Declst;

   with Declst;
   procedure Main is
   begin
      Declst.Lib_Task.Start;
   end;
```

What we have done here is to replace the *task* declaration in package *Decls* with a *task type* declaration. Then we introduce a separate package *Declst* to contain the actual task object. This separates the elaboration issues for the *task type* declaration, which causes no trouble, from the elaboration issues of the task object, which is also unproblematic, since it is now independent of the elaboration of *Utils*. This separation of concerns also corresponds to a generally sound engineering principle of separating declarations from instances. This version of the program also compiles, binds, links, and executes, generating the expected output.

* Use No_Entry_Calls_In_Elaboration_Code restriction.

The previous two approaches described how a program can be restructured to avoid the special problems caused by library task bodies. in practice, however, such restructuring may be difficult to apply to existing legacy code, so we must consider solutions that do not require massive rewriting.

Let us consider more carefully why our original sample program works under the dynamic model of elaboration. The reason is that the code in the task body blocks immediately on the *accept* statement. Now of course there is nothing to prohibit elaboration code from making entry calls (for example from another library level task), so we cannot tell in isolation that the task will not execute the accept statement during elaboration.

However, in practice it is very unusual to see elaboration code make any entry calls, and the pattern of tasks starting at elaboration time and then immediately blocking on *accept* or *select* statements is very common. What this means is that the compiler is being too pessimistic when it analyzes the whole package body as though it might be executed at elaboration time.

If we know that the elaboration code contains no entry calls, (a very safe assumption most of the time, that could almost be made the default behavior), then we can compile all units of the program under control of the following configuration pragma:

```
pragma Restrictions (No_Entry_Calls_In_Elaboration_Code);
```

This pragma can be placed in the **gnat.adc** file in the usual manner. If we take our original unmodified program and compile it in the presence of a **gnat.adc** containing the above pragma, then once again, we can compile, bind, link, and execute, obtaining the expected result. In the presence of this pragma, the compiler does not trace calls in a task body, that appear after the first *accept* or *select* statement, and therefore does not report a potential circularity in the original program.

The compiler will check to the extent it can that the above restriction is not violated, but it is not always possible to do a complete check at compile time, so it is important to use this pragma only if the stated restriction is in fact met, that is to say no task receives an entry call before elaboration of all units is completed.

9.9 Mixing Elaboration Models

So far, we have assumed that the entire program is either compiled using the dynamic model or static model, ensuring consistency. It is possible to mix the two models, but rules have to be followed if this mixing is done to ensure that elaboration checks are not omitted.

The basic rule is that **a unit compiled with the static model cannot be |withed| by a unit compiled with the dynamic model**. The reason for this is that in the static model, a unit assumes that its clients guarantee to use (the equivalent of) pragma *Elaborate_All* so that no elaboration checks are required in inner subprograms, and this assumption is violated if the client is compiled with dynamic checks.

The precise rule is as follows. A unit that is compiled with dynamic checks can only *with* a unit that meets at least one of the following criteria:

* The *with*ed unit is itself compiled with dynamic elaboration checks (that is with the *-gnatE* switch.

* The *with*ed unit is an internal GNAT implementation unit from the System, Interfaces, Ada, or GNAT hierarchies.

* The *with*ed unit has pragma Preelaborate or pragma Pure.

* The *with*ing unit (that is the client) has an explicit pragma *Elaborate_All* for the *with*ed unit.

If this rule is violated, that is if a unit with dynamic elaboration checks *with*s a unit that does not meet one of the above four criteria, then the binder (*gnatbind*) will issue a warning similar to that in the following example:

```
warning: "x.ads" has dynamic elaboration checks and with's
warning:  "y.ads" which has static elaboration checks
```

These warnings indicate that the rule has been violated, and that as a result elaboration checks may be missed in the resulting executable file. This warning may be suppressed using the *-ws* binder switch in the usual manner.

One useful application of this mixing rule is in the case of a subsystem which does not itself *with* units from the remainder of the application. In this case, the entire subsystem can be compiled with dynamic checks to resolve a circularity in the subsystem, while allowing the main application that uses this subsystem to be compiled using the more reliable default static model.

9.10 What to Do If the Default Elaboration Behavior Fails

If the binder cannot find an acceptable order, it outputs detailed diagnostics. For example:

```
error: elaboration circularity detected
info:   "proc (body)" must be elaborated before "pack (body)"
info:     reason: Elaborate_All probably needed in unit "pack (body)"
info:     recompile "pack (body)" with -gnatel
info:                             for full details
info:       "proc (body)"
info:          is needed by its spec:
info:       "proc (spec)"
info:          which is withed by:
info:       "pack (body)"
info:   "pack (body)" must be elaborated before "proc (body)"
info:     reason: pragma Elaborate in unit "proc (body)"
```

In this case we have a cycle that the binder cannot break. On the one hand, there is an explicit pragma Elaborate in *proc* for *pack*. This means that the body of *pack* must be elaborated before the body of *proc*. On the other hand, there is elaboration code in *pack* that calls a subprogram in *proc*. This means that for maximum safety, there should really be a pragma Elaborate_All in *pack* for *proc* which would require that the body of *proc* be elaborated before the body of *pack*. Clearly both requirements cannot be satisfied. Faced with a circularity of this kind, you have three different options.

* *Fix the program*

  The most desirable option from the point of view of long-term maintenance is to rearrange the program so that the elaboration problems are avoided. One useful technique is to place the elaboration code into separate child packages. Another is to move some of the initialization code to explicitly called subprograms, where the program controls the order of initialization explicitly. Although this is the most desirable option, it may be impractical and involve too much modification, especially in the case of complex legacy code.

* *Perform dynamic checks*

If the compilations are done using the *-gnatE* (dynamic elaboration check) switch, then GNAT behaves in a quite different manner. Dynamic checks are generated for all calls that could possibly result in raising an exception. With this switch, the compiler does not generate implicit *Elaborate* or *Elaborate_All* pragmas. The behavior then is exactly as specified in the *Ada Reference Manual*. The binder will generate an executable program that may or may not raise *Program_Error*, and then it is the programmer's job to ensure that it does not raise an exception. Note that it is important to compile all units with the switch, it cannot be used selectively.

* *Suppress checks*

The drawback of dynamic checks is that they generate a significant overhead at run time, both in space and time. If you are absolutely sure that your program cannot raise any elaboration exceptions, and you still want to use the dynamic elaboration model, then you can use the configuration pragma *Suppress (Elaboration_Check)* to suppress all such checks. For example this pragma could be placed in the `gnat.adc` file.

* *Suppress checks selectively*

When you know that certain calls or instantiations in elaboration code cannot possibly lead to an elaboration error, and the binder nevertheless complains about implicit *Elaborate* and *Elaborate_All* pragmas that lead to elaboration circularities, it is possible to remove those warnings locally and obtain a program that will bind. Clearly this can be unsafe, and it is the responsibility of the programmer to make sure that the resulting program has no elaboration anomalies. The pragma *Suppress (Elaboration_Check)* can be used with different granularity to suppress warnings and break elaboration circularities:

  * Place the pragma that names the called subprogram in the declarative part that contains the call.

  * Place the pragma in the declarative part, without naming an entity. This disables warnings on all calls in the corresponding declarative region.

  * Place the pragma in the package spec that declares the called subprogram, and name the subprogram. This disables warnings on all elaboration calls to that subprogram.

  * Place the pragma in the package spec that declares the called subprogram, without naming any entity. This disables warnings on all elaboration calls to all subprograms declared in this spec.

  * Use Pragma Elaborate.

    As previously described in section [Treatment of Pragma Elaborate], page 291, GNAT in static mode assumes that a *pragma* Elaborate indicates correctly that no elaboration checks are required on calls to the designated unit. There may be cases in which the caller knows that no transitive calls can occur, so that a *pragma* Elaborate will be sufficient in a case where *pragma* Elaborate_All would cause a circularity.

These five cases are listed in order of decreasing safety, and therefore require increasing programmer care in their application. Consider the following program:

```
package Pack1 is
```

```
      function F1 return Integer;
        X1 : Integer;
      end Pack1;

      package Pack2 is
        function F2 return Integer;
        function Pure (x : integer) return integer;
        --  pragma Suppress (Elaboration_Check, On => Pure);   -- (3)
        --  pragma Suppress (Elaboration_Check);               -- (4)
      end Pack2;

      with Pack2;
      package body Pack1 is
        function F1 return Integer is
        begin
          return 100;
        end F1;
        Val : integer := Pack2.Pure (11);       -- Elab. call (1)
      begin
        declare
          --  pragma Suppress(Elaboration_Check, Pack2.F2);   -- (1)
          --  pragma Suppress(Elaboration_Check);             -- (2)
        begin
          X1 := Pack2.F2 + 1;                    -- Elab. call (2)
        end;
      end Pack1;

      with Pack1;
      package body Pack2 is
        function F2 return Integer is
        begin
          return Pack1.F1;
        end F2;
        function Pure (x : integer) return integer is
        begin
          return x ** 3 - 3 * x;
        end;
      end Pack2;

      with Pack1, Ada.Text_IO;
      procedure Proc3 is
      begin
        Ada.Text_IO.Put_Line(Pack1.X1'Img); -- 101
      end Proc3;
```

In the absence of any pragmas, an attempt to bind this program produces the following diagnostics:

```
error: elaboration circularity detected
info:     "pack1 (body)" must be elaborated before "pack1 (body)"
info:        reason: Elaborate_All probably needed in unit "pack1 (body)"
info:        recompile "pack1 (body)" with -gnatel for full details
info:          "pack1 (body)"
info:             must be elaborated along with its spec:
info:          "pack1 (spec)"
info:             which is withed by:
info:          "pack2 (body)"
info:             which must be elaborated along with its spec:
info:          "pack2 (spec)"
info:             which is withed by:
info:          "pack1 (body)"
```

The sources of the circularity are the two calls to *Pack2.Pure* and *Pack2.F2* in the body of *Pack1*. We can see that the call to F2 is safe, even though F2 calls F1, because the call appears after the elaboration of the body of F1. Therefore the pragma (1) is safe, and will remove the warning on the call. It is also possible to use pragma (2) because there are no other potentially unsafe calls in the block.

The call to *Pure* is safe because this function does not depend on the state of *Pack2*. Therefore any call to this function is safe, and it is correct to place pragma (3) in the corresponding package spec.

Finally, we could place pragma (4) in the spec of *Pack2* to disable warnings on all calls to functions declared therein. Note that this is not necessarily safe, and requires more detailed examination of the subprogram bodies involved. In particular, a call to *F2* requires that *F1* be already elaborated.

It is hard to generalize on which of these four approaches should be taken. Obviously if it is possible to fix the program so that the default treatment works, this is preferable, but this may not always be practical. It is certainly simple enough to use *-gnatE* but the danger in this case is that, even if the GNAT binder finds a correct elaboration order, it may not always do so, and certainly a binder from another Ada compiler might not. A combination of testing and analysis (for which the information messages generated with the *-gnatel* switch can be useful) must be used to ensure that the program is free of errors. One switch that is useful in this testing is the *-p (pessimistic elaboration order)* switch for *gnatbind*. Normally the binder tries to find an order that has the best chance of avoiding elaboration problems. However, if this switch is used, the binder plays a devil's advocate role, and tries to choose the order that has the best chance of failing. If your program works even with this switch, then it has a better chance of being error free, but this is still not a guarantee.

For an example of this approach in action, consider the C-tests (executable tests) from the ACATS suite. If these are compiled and run with the default treatment, then all but one of them succeed without generating any error diagnostics from the binder. However, there is one test that fails, and this is not surprising, because the whole point of this test is to ensure that the compiler can handle cases where it is impossible to determine a correct order statically, and it checks that an exception is indeed raised at run time.

This one test must be compiled and run using the *-gnatE* switch, and then it passes. Alternatively, the entire suite can be run using this switch. It is never wrong to run with the dynamic elaboration switch if your code is correct, and we assume that the C-tests are indeed correct (it is less efficient, but efficiency is not a factor in running the ACATS tests.)

9.11 Elaboration for Indirect Calls

In rare cases, the static elaboration model fails to prevent dispatching calls to not-yet-elaborated subprograms. In such cases, we fall back to run-time checks; premature calls to any primitive operation of a tagged type before the body of the operation has been elaborated will raise *Program_Error*.

Access-to-subprogram types, however, are handled conservatively in many cases. This was not true in earlier versions of the compiler; you can use the *-gnatd.U* debug switch to revert to the old behavior if the new conservative behavior causes elaboration cycles. Here, 'conservative' means that if you do *P'Access* during elaboration, the compiler will normally assume that you might call *P* indirectly during elaboration, so it adds an implicit *pragma Elaborate_All* on the library unit containing *P*. The *-gnatd.U* switch is safe if you know there are no such calls. If the program worked before, it will continue to work with *-gnatd.U*. But beware that code modifications such as adding an indirect call can cause erroneous behavior in the presence of *-gnatd.U*.

These implicit Elaborate_All pragmas are not added in all cases, because they cause elaboration cycles in certain common code patterns. If you want even more conservative handling of P'Access, you can use the *-gnatd.o* switch.

See *debug.adb* for documentation on the *-gnatd...* debug switches.

9.12 Summary of Procedures for Elaboration Control

First, compile your program with the default options, using none of the special elaboration-control switches. If the binder successfully binds your program, then you can be confident that, apart from issues raised by the use of access-to-subprogram types and dynamic dispatching, the program is free of elaboration errors. If it is important that the program be portable to other compilers than GNAT, then use the *-gnatel* switch to generate messages about missing *Elaborate* or *Elaborate_All* pragmas, and supply the missing pragmas.

If the program fails to bind using the default static elaboration handling, then you can fix the program to eliminate the binder message, or recompile the entire program with the *-gnatE* switch to generate dynamic elaboration checks, and, if you are sure there really are no elaboration problems, use a global pragma *Suppress (Elaboration_Check)*.

9.13 Other Elaboration Order Considerations

This section has been entirely concerned with the issue of finding a valid elaboration order, as defined by the Ada Reference Manual. In a case where several elaboration orders are valid, the task is to find one of the possible valid elaboration orders (and the static model in GNAT will ensure that this is achieved).

The purpose of the elaboration rules in the Ada Reference Manual is to make sure that no entity is accessed before it has been elaborated. For a subprogram, this means that the spec and body must have been elaborated before the subprogram is called. For an object, this means that the object must have been elaborated before its value is read or written. A violation of either of these two requirements is an access before elaboration order, and this section has been all about avoiding such errors.

In the case where more than one order of elaboration is possible, in the sense that access before elaboration errors are avoided, then any one of the orders is 'correct' in the sense that it meets the requirements of the Ada Reference Manual, and no such error occurs.

However, it may be the case for a given program, that there are constraints on the order of elaboration that come not from consideration of avoiding elaboration errors, but rather from extra-lingual logic requirements. Consider this example:

```
with Init_Constants;
package Constants is
   X : Integer := 0;
   Y : Integer := 0;
end Constants;

package Init_Constants is
   procedure P; --* require a body*
end Init_Constants;

with Constants;
package body Init_Constants is
   procedure P is begin null; end;
begin
   Constants.X := 3;
   Constants.Y := 4;
end Init_Constants;

with Constants;
package Calc is
   Z : Integer := Constants.X + Constants.Y;
end Calc;

with Calc;
with Text_IO; use Text_IO;
procedure Main is
begin
   Put_Line (Calc.Z'Img);
end Main;
```

In this example, there is more than one valid order of elaboration. For example both the following are correct orders:

```
Init_Constants spec
Constants spec
Calc spec
Init_Constants body
Main body
```

and

```
Init_Constants spec
Init_Constants body
Constants spec
Calc spec
Main body
```

There is no language rule to prefer one or the other, both are correct from an order of elaboration point of view. But the programmatic effects of the two orders are very different. In the first, the elaboration routine of *Calc* initializes Z to zero, and then the main program runs with this value of zero. But in the second order, the elaboration routine of *Calc* runs after the body of Init_Constants has set X and Y and thus Z is set to 7 before *Main* runs.

One could perhaps by applying pretty clever non-artificial intelligence to the situation guess that it is more likely that the second order of elaboration is the one desired, but there is no formal linguistic reason to prefer one over the other. In fact in this particular case, GNAT will prefer the second order, because of the rule that bodies are elaborated as soon as possible, but it's just luck that this is what was wanted (if indeed the second order was preferred).

If the program cares about the order of elaboration routines in a case like this, it is important to specify the order required. In this particular case, that could have been achieved by adding to the spec of Calc:

```
pragma Elaborate_All (Constants);
```

which requires that the body (if any) and spec of *Constants*, as well as the body and spec of any unit *with*ed by *Constants* be elaborated before *Calc* is elaborated.

Clearly no automatic method can always guess which alternative you require, and if you are working with legacy code that had constraints of this kind which were not properly specified by adding *Elaborate* or *Elaborate_All* pragmas, then indeed it is possible that two different compilers can choose different orders.

However, GNAT does attempt to diagnose the common situation where there are uninitialized variables in the visible part of a package spec, and the corresponding package body has an elaboration block that directly or indirectly initialized one or more of these variables. This is the situation in which a pragma Elaborate_Body is usually desirable, and GNAT will generate a warning that suggests this addition if it detects this situation.

The *gnatbind -p* switch may be useful in smoking out problems. This switch causes bodies to be elaborated as late as possible instead of as early as possible. In the example above, it would have forced the choice of the first elaboration order. If you get different results when using this switch, and particularly if one set of results is right, and one is wrong as far as you are concerned, it shows that you have some missing *Elaborate* pragmas. For the example above, we have the following output:

```
$ gnatmake -f -q main
$ main
 7
$ gnatmake -f -q main -bargs -p
$ main
 0
```

It is of course quite unlikely that both these results are correct, so it is up to you in a case like this to investigate the source of the difference, by looking at the two elaboration orders that are chosen, and figuring out which is correct, and then adding the necessary *Elaborate* or *Elaborate_All* pragmas to ensure the desired order.

9.14 Determining the Chosen Elaboration Order

To see the elaboration order that the binder chooses, you can look at the last part of the file:*b~xxx.adb* binder output file. Here is an example:

```
System.Soft_Links'Elab_Body;
E14 := True;
System.Secondary_Stack'Elab_Body;
E18 := True;
System.Exception_Table'Elab_Body;
E24 := True;
Ada.Io_Exceptions'Elab_Spec;
E67 := True;
Ada.Tags'Elab_Spec;
Ada.Streams'Elab_Spec;
E43 := True;
Interfaces.C'Elab_Spec;
E69 := True;
System.Finalization_Root'Elab_Spec;
E60 := True;
System.Os_Lib'Elab_Body;
E71 := True;
System.Finalization_Implementation'Elab_Spec;
System.Finalization_Implementation'Elab_Body;
E62 := True;
Ada.Finalization'Elab_Spec;
E58 := True;
Ada.Finalization.List_Controller'Elab_Spec;
E76 := True;
System.File_Control_Block'Elab_Spec;
E74 := True;
System.File_Io'Elab_Body;
E56 := True;
Ada.Tags'Elab_Body;
E45 := True;
Ada.Text_Io'Elab_Spec;
Ada.Text_Io'Elab_Body;
E07 := True;
```

Here Elab_Spec elaborates the spec and Elab_Body elaborates the body. The assignments to the **Exx** flags flag that the corresponding body is now elaborated.

You can also ask the binder to generate a more readable list of the elaboration order using the -*l* switch when invoking the binder. Here is an example of the output generated by this switch:

```
ada (spec)
```

```
interfaces (spec)
system (spec)
system.case_util (spec)
system.case_util (body)
system.concat_2 (spec)
system.concat_2 (body)
system.concat_3 (spec)
system.concat_3 (body)
system.htable (spec)
system.parameters (spec)
system.parameters (body)
system.crtl (spec)
interfaces.c_streams (spec)
interfaces.c_streams (body)
system.restrictions (spec)
system.restrictions (body)
system.standard_library (spec)
system.exceptions (spec)
system.exceptions (body)
system.storage_elements (spec)
system.storage_elements (body)
system.secondary_stack (spec)
system.stack_checking (spec)
system.stack_checking (body)
system.string_hash (spec)
system.string_hash (body)
system.htable (body)
system.strings (spec)
system.strings (body)
system.traceback (spec)
system.traceback (body)
system.traceback_entries (spec)
system.traceback_entries (body)
ada.exceptions (spec)
ada.exceptions.last_chance_handler (spec)
system.soft_links (spec)
system.soft_links (body)
ada.exceptions.last_chance_handler (body)
system.secondary_stack (body)
system.exception_table (spec)
system.exception_table (body)
ada.io_exceptions (spec)
ada.tags (spec)
ada.streams (spec)
interfaces.c (spec)
interfaces.c (body)
system.finalization_root (spec)
```

```
system.finalization_root (body)
system.memory (spec)
system.memory (body)
system.standard_library (body)
system.os_lib (spec)
system.os_lib (body)
system.unsigned_types (spec)
system.stream_attributes (spec)
system.stream_attributes (body)
system.finalization_implementation (spec)
system.finalization_implementation (body)
ada.finalization (spec)
ada.finalization (body)
ada.finalization.list_controller (spec)
ada.finalization.list_controller (body)
system.file_control_block (spec)
system.file_io (spec)
system.file_io (body)
system.val_uns (spec)
system.val_util (spec)
system.val_util (body)
system.val_uns (body)
system.wch_con (spec)
system.wch_con (body)
system.wch_cnv (spec)
system.wch_jis (spec)
system.wch_jis (body)
system.wch_cnv (body)
system.wch_stw (spec)
system.wch_stw (body)
ada.tags (body)
ada.exceptions (body)
ada.text_io (spec)
ada.text_io (body)
text_io (spec)
gdbstr (body)
```

10 Inline Assembler

If you need to write low-level software that interacts directly with the hardware, Ada provides two ways to incorporate assembly language code into your program. First, you can import and invoke external routines written in assembly language, an Ada feature fully supported by GNAT. However, for small sections of code it may be simpler or more efficient to include assembly language statements directly in your Ada source program, using the facilities of the implementation-defined package *System.Machine_Code*, which incorporates the gcc Inline Assembler. The Inline Assembler approach offers a number of advantages, including the following:

* No need to use non-Ada tools

* Consistent interface over different targets

* Automatic usage of the proper calling conventions

* Access to Ada constants and variables

* Definition of intrinsic routines

* Possibility of inlining a subprogram comprising assembler code

* Code optimizer can take Inline Assembler code into account

This appendix presents a series of examples to show you how to use the Inline Assembler. Although it focuses on the Intel x86, the general approach applies also to other processors. It is assumed that you are familiar with Ada and with assembly language programming.

10.1 Basic Assembler Syntax

The assembler used by GNAT and gcc is based not on the Intel assembly language, but rather on a language that descends from the AT&T Unix assembler *as* (and which is often referred to as 'AT&T syntax'). The following table summarizes the main features of *as* syntax and points out the differences from the Intel conventions. See the gcc *as* and *gas* (an *as* macro pre-processor) documentation for further information.

Register names
> gcc / *as*: Prefix with '%'; for example %eax
> Intel: No extra punctuation; for example eax

Immediate operand
> gcc / *as*: Prefix with '$'; for example $4
> Intel: No extra punctuation; for example 4

Address
> gcc / *as*: Prefix with '$'; for example $loc
> Intel: No extra punctuation; for example loc

Memory contents
> gcc / *as*: No extra punctuation; for example loc
> Intel: Square brackets; for example [loc]

Register contents
> gcc / *as*: Parentheses; for example (%eax)
> Intel: Square brackets; for example [eax]

Hexadecimal numbers
> gcc / *as*: Leading '0x' (C language syntax); for example *0xA0*
>
> Intel: Trailing 'h'; for example *A0h*

Operand size
> gcc / *as*: Explicit in op code; for example *movw* to move a 16-bit word
>
> Intel: Implicit, deduced by assembler; for example *mov*

Instruction repetition
> gcc / *as*: Split into two lines; for example
>> *rep*
>>
>> *stosl*
>
> Intel: Keep on one line; for example *rep stosl*

Order of operands
> gcc / *as*: Source first; for example *movw $4, %eax*
>
> Intel: Destination first; for example *mov eax, 4*

10.2 A Simple Example of Inline Assembler

The following example will generate a single assembly language statement, *nop*, which does nothing. Despite its lack of run-time effect, the example will be useful in illustrating the basics of the Inline Assembler facility.

```
with System.Machine_Code; use System.Machine_Code;
procedure Nothing is
begin
   Asm ("nop");
end Nothing;
```

Asm is a procedure declared in package *System.Machine_Code*; here it takes one parameter, a *template string* that must be a static expression and that will form the generated instruction. *Asm* may be regarded as a compile-time procedure that parses the template string and additional parameters (none here), from which it generates a sequence of assembly language instructions.

The examples in this chapter will illustrate several of the forms for invoking *Asm*; a complete specification of the syntax is found in the *Machine_Code_Insertions* section of the *GNAT Reference Manual*.

Under the standard GNAT conventions, the *Nothing* procedure should be in a file named `nothing.adb`. You can build the executable in the usual way:

```
$ gnatmake nothing
```

However, the interesting aspect of this example is not its run-time behavior but rather the generated assembly code. To see this output, invoke the compiler as follows:

```
$ gcc -c -S -fomit-frame-pointer -gnatp nothing.adb
```

where the options are:

*

  `-c`

    compile only (no bind or link)

*

```
      -S
                  generate assembler listing
*

      -fomit-frame-pointer
                  do not set up separate stack frames
*

      -gnatp
                  do not add runtime checks
```

This gives a human-readable assembler version of the code. The resulting file will have the same name as the Ada source file, but with a *.s* extension. In our example, the file `nothing.s` has the following contents:

```
            .file "nothing.adb"
            gcc2_compiled.:
            ___gnu_compiled_ada:
            .text
               .align 4
            .globl __ada_nothing
            __ada_nothing:
            #APP
                nop
            #NO_APP
                jmp L1
                .align 2,0x90
            L1:
                ret
```

The assembly code you included is clearly indicated by the compiler, between the *#APP* and *#NO_APP* delimiters. The character before the 'APP' and 'NOAPP' can differ on different targets. For example, GNU/Linux uses '#APP' while on NT you will see '/APP'.

If you make a mistake in your assembler code (such as using the wrong size modifier, or using a wrong operand for the instruction) GNAT will report this error in a temporary file, which will be deleted when the compilation is finished. Generating an assembler file will help in such cases, since you can assemble this file separately using the *as* assembler that comes with gcc.

Assembling the file using the command

```
            $ as nothing.s
```

will give you error messages whose lines correspond to the assembler input file, so you can easily find and correct any mistakes you made. If there are no errors, *as* will generate an object file `nothing.out`.

10.3 Output Variables in Inline Assembler

The examples in this section, showing how to access the processor flags, illustrate how to specify the destination operands for assembly language statements.

```
with Interfaces; use Interfaces;
with Ada.Text_IO; use Ada.Text_IO;
with System.Machine_Code; use System.Machine_Code;
procedure Get_Flags is
   Flags : Unsigned_32;
   use ASCII;
begin
   Asm ("pushfl"           & LF & HT & -- push flags on stack
        "popl %%eax"        & LF & HT & -- load eax with flags
        "movl %%eax, %0",               -- store flags in variable
        Outputs => Unsigned_32'Asm_Output ("=g", Flags));
   Put_Line ("Flags register:" & Flags'Img);
end Get_Flags;
```

In order to have a nicely aligned assembly listing, we have separated multiple assembler statements in the Asm template string with linefeed (ASCII.LF) and horizontal tab (ASCII.HT) characters. The resulting section of the assembly output file is:

```
#APP
   pushfl
   popl %eax
   movl %eax, -40(%ebp)
#NO_APP
```

It would have been legal to write the Asm invocation as:

```
Asm ("pushfl popl %%eax movl %%eax, %0")
```

but in the generated assembler file, this would come out as:

```
#APP
   pushfl popl %eax movl %eax, -40(%ebp)
#NO_APP
```

which is not so convenient for the human reader.

We use Ada comments at the end of each line to explain what the assembler instructions actually do. This is a useful convention.

When writing Inline Assembler instructions, you need to precede each register and variable name with a percent sign. Since the assembler already requires a percent sign at the beginning of a register name, you need two consecutive percent signs for such names in the Asm template string, thus *%%eax*. In the generated assembly code, one of the percent signs will be stripped off.

Names such as *%0, %1, %2,* etc., denote input or output variables: operands you later define using *Input* or *Output* parameters to *Asm*. An output variable is illustrated in the third statement in the Asm template string:

```
movl %%eax, %0
```

The intent is to store the contents of the eax register in a variable that can be accessed in Ada. Simply writing *movl %%eax, Flags* would not necessarily work, since the compiler might optimize by using a register to hold Flags, and the expansion of the *movl* instruction would not be aware of this optimization. The solution is not to store the result directly but rather to advise the compiler to choose the correct operand form; that is the purpose of the *%0* output variable.

Information about the output variable is supplied in the *Outputs* parameter to *Asm*:

```
Outputs => Unsigned_32'Asm_Output ("=g", Flags));
```

The output is defined by the *Asm_Output* attribute of the target type; the general format is

```
Type'Asm_Output (constraint_string, variable_name)
```

The constraint string directs the compiler how to store/access the associated variable. In the example

```
Unsigned_32'Asm_Output ("=m", Flags);
```

the "*m*" (memory) constraint tells the compiler that the variable *Flags* should be stored in a memory variable, thus preventing the optimizer from keeping it in a register. In contrast,

```
Unsigned_32'Asm_Output ("=r", Flags);
```

uses the "*r*" (register) constraint, telling the compiler to store the variable in a register.

If the constraint is preceded by the equal character '=', it tells the compiler that the variable will be used to store data into it.

In the *Get_Flags* example, we used the "*g*" (global) constraint, allowing the optimizer to choose whatever it deems best.

There are a fairly large number of constraints, but the ones that are most useful (for the Intel x86 processor) are the following:

=	output constraint
g	global (i.e., can be stored anywhere)
m	in memory
I	a constant
a	use eax
b	use ebx
c	use ecx
d	use edx
S	use esi
D	use edi
r	use one of eax, ebx, ecx or edx
q	use one of eax, ebx, ecx, edx, esi or edi

The full set of constraints is described in the gcc and *as* documentation; note that it is possible to combine certain constraints in one constraint string.

You specify the association of an output variable with an assembler operand through the *%n* notation, where *n* is a non-negative integer. Thus in

```
Asm ("pushfl"          & LF & HT & -- push flags on stack
     "popl %%eax"      & LF & HT & -- load eax with flags
     "movl %%eax, %0",            -- store flags in variable
     Outputs => Unsigned_32'Asm_Output ("=g", Flags));
```

%0 will be replaced in the expanded code by the appropriate operand, whatever the compiler decided for the *Flags* variable.

In general, you may have any number of output variables:

* Count the operands starting at 0; thus *%0*, *%1*, etc.

* Specify the *Outputs* parameter as a parenthesized comma-separated list of *Asm_Output* attributes

For example:

```
Asm ("movl %%eax, %0" & LF & HT &
     "movl %%ebx, %1" & LF & HT &
     "movl %%ecx, %2",
     Outputs => (Unsigned_32'Asm_Output ("=g", Var_A),    -- %0 = Var_A
                 Unsigned_32'Asm_Output ("=g", Var_B),    -- %1 = Var_B
                 Unsigned_32'Asm_Output ("=g", Var_C)));  -- %2 = Var_C
```

where *Var_A*, *Var_B*, and *Var_C* are variables in the Ada program.

As a variation on the *Get_Flags* example, we can use the constraints string to direct the compiler to store the eax register into the *Flags* variable, instead of including the store instruction explicitly in the *Asm* template string:

```
with Interfaces; use Interfaces;
with Ada.Text_IO; use Ada.Text_IO;
with System.Machine_Code; use System.Machine_Code;
procedure Get_Flags_2 is
   Flags : Unsigned_32;
   use ASCII;
begin
   Asm ("pushfl"        & LF & HT & -- push flags on stack
        "popl %%eax",               -- save flags in eax
        Outputs => Unsigned_32'Asm_Output ("=a", Flags));
   Put_Line ("Flags register:" & Flags'Img);
end Get_Flags_2;
```

The "a" constraint tells the compiler that the *Flags* variable will come from the eax register. Here is the resulting code:

```
#APP
    pushfl
    popl %eax
#NO_APP
    movl %eax,-40(%ebp)
```

The compiler generated the store of eax into Flags after expanding the assembler code.

Actually, there was no need to pop the flags into the eax register; more simply, we could just pop the flags directly into the program variable:

```
with Interfaces; use Interfaces;
with Ada.Text_IO; use Ada.Text_IO;
with System.Machine_Code; use System.Machine_Code;
procedure Get_Flags_3 is
   Flags : Unsigned_32;
   use ASCII;
begin
   Asm ("pushfl"  & LF & HT & -- push flags on stack
          "pop %0",            -- save flags in Flags
          Outputs => Unsigned_32'Asm_Output ("=g", Flags));
   Put_Line ("Flags register:" & Flags'Img);
end Get_Flags_3;
```

10.4 Input Variables in Inline Assembler

The example in this section illustrates how to specify the source operands for assembly language statements. The program simply increments its input value by 1:

```
with Interfaces; use Interfaces;
with Ada.Text_IO; use Ada.Text_IO;
with System.Machine_Code; use System.Machine_Code;
procedure Increment is

   function Incr (Value : Unsigned_32) return Unsigned_32 is
      Result : Unsigned_32;
   begin
      Asm ("incl %0",
             Outputs => Unsigned_32'Asm_Output ("=a", Result),
             Inputs  => Unsigned_32'Asm_Input ("a", Value));
      return Result;
   end Incr;

   Value : Unsigned_32;

begin
   Value := 5;
   Put_Line ("Value before is" & Value'Img);
   Value := Incr (Value);
  Put_Line ("Value after is" & Value'Img);
end Increment;
```

The *Outputs* parameter to *Asm* specifies that the result will be in the eax register and that it is to be stored in the *Result* variable.

The *Inputs* parameter looks much like the *Outputs* parameter, but with an *Asm_Input* attribute. The "=" constraint, indicating an output value, is not present.

You can have multiple input variables, in the same way that you can have more than one output variable.

The parameter count (%0, %1) etc, still starts at the first output statement, and continues with the input statements.

Just as the *Outputs* parameter causes the register to be stored into the target variable after execution of the assembler statements, so does the *Inputs* parameter cause its variable to be loaded into the register before execution of the assembler statements.

Thus the effect of the *Asm* invocation is:

* load the 32-bit value of *Value* into eax

* execute the *incl %eax* instruction

* store the contents of eax into the *Result* variable

The resulting assembler file (with *-O2* optimization) contains:

```
_increment__incr.1:
    subl $4,%esp
    movl 8(%esp),%eax
#APP
    incl %eax
#NO_APP
    movl %eax,%edx
    movl %ecx,(%esp)
    addl $4,%esp
    ret
```

10.5 Inlining Inline Assembler Code

For a short subprogram such as the *Incr* function in the previous section, the overhead of the call and return (creating / deleting the stack frame) can be significant, compared to the amount of code in the subprogram body. A solution is to apply Ada's *Inline* pragma to the subprogram, which directs the compiler to expand invocations of the subprogram at the point(s) of call, instead of setting up a stack frame for out-of-line calls. Here is the resulting program:

```
with Interfaces; use Interfaces;
with Ada.Text_IO; use Ada.Text_IO;
with System.Machine_Code; use System.Machine_Code;
procedure Increment_2 is

   function Incr (Value : Unsigned_32) return Unsigned_32 is
      Result : Unsigned_32;
   begin
      Asm ("incl %0",
           Outputs => Unsigned_32'Asm_Output ("=a", Result),
           Inputs  => Unsigned_32'Asm_Input ("a", Value));
      return Result;
   end Incr;
   pragma Inline (Increment);
```

```
                    Value : Unsigned_32;

                begin
                    Value := 5;
                    Put_Line ("Value before is" & Value'Img);
                    Value := Increment (Value);
                    Put_Line ("Value after is" & Value'Img);
                end Increment_2;
```

Compile the program with both optimization (-*O2*) and inlining (-*gnatn*) enabled.

The *Incr* function is still compiled as usual, but at the point in *Increment* where our function used to be called:

```
            pushl %edi
            call _increment__incr.1
```

the code for the function body directly appears:

```
            movl %esi,%eax
            #APP
                incl %eax
            #NO_APP
                movl %eax,%edx
```

thus saving the overhead of stack frame setup and an out-of-line call.

10.6 Other *Asm* Functionality

This section describes two important parameters to the *Asm* procedure: *Clobber*, which identifies register usage; and *Volatile*, which inhibits unwanted optimizations.

10.6.1 The *Clobber* Parameter

One of the dangers of intermixing assembly language and a compiled language such as Ada is that the compiler needs to be aware of which registers are being used by the assembly code. In some cases, such as the earlier examples, the constraint string is sufficient to indicate register usage (e.g., "a" for the eax register). But more generally, the compiler needs an explicit identification of the registers that are used by the Inline Assembly statements.

Using a register that the compiler doesn't know about could be a side effect of an instruction (like *mull* storing its result in both eax and edx). It can also arise from explicit register usage in your assembly code; for example:

```
        Asm ("movl %0, %%ebx" & LF & HT &
             "movl %%ebx, %1",
             Outputs => Unsigned_32'Asm_Output ("=g", Var_Out),
             Inputs  => Unsigned_32'Asm_Input  ("g", Var_In));
```

where the compiler (since it does not analyze the *Asm* template string) does not know you are using the ebx register.

In such cases you need to supply the *Clobber* parameter to *Asm*, to identify the registers that will be used by your assembly code:

```
Asm ("movl %0, %%ebx" & LF & HT &
     "movl %%ebx, %1",
     Outputs => Unsigned_32'Asm_Output ("=g", Var_Out),
     Inputs  => Unsigned_32'Asm_Input  ("g", Var_In),
     Clobber => "ebx");
```

The Clobber parameter is a static string expression specifying the register(s) you are using. Note that register names are *not* prefixed by a percent sign. Also, if more than one register is used then their names are separated by commas; e.g., "*eax, ebx*"

The *Clobber* parameter has several additional uses:

* Use 'register' name *cc* to indicate that flags might have changed

* Use 'register' name *memory* if you changed a memory location

10.6.2 The *Volatile* Parameter

Compiler optimizations in the presence of Inline Assembler may sometimes have unwanted effects. For example, when an *Asm* invocation with an input variable is inside a loop, the compiler might move the loading of the input variable outside the loop, regarding it as a one-time initialization.

If this effect is not desired, you can disable such optimizations by setting the *Volatile* parameter to *True*; for example:

```
Asm ("movl %0, %%ebx" & LF & HT &
     "movl %%ebx, %1",
     Outputs  => Unsigned_32'Asm_Output ("=g", Var_Out),
     Inputs   => Unsigned_32'Asm_Input  ("g", Var_In),
     Clobber  => "ebx",
     Volatile => True);
```

By default, *Volatile* is set to *False* unless there is no *Outputs* parameter.

Although setting *Volatile* to *True* prevents unwanted optimizations, it will also disable other optimizations that might be important for efficiency. In general, you should set *Volatile* to *True* only if the compiler's optimizations have created problems.

11 GNU Free Documentation License

Version 1.3, 3 November 2008

Copyright 2000, 2001, 2002, 2007, 2008 Free Software Foundation, Inc http://fsf.org/

Everyone is permitted to copy and distribute verbatim copies of this license document, but changing it is not allowed.

Preamble

The purpose of this License is to make a manual, textbook, or other functional and useful document "free" in the sense of freedom: to assure everyone the effective freedom to copy and redistribute it, with or without modifying it, either commercially or noncommercially. Secondarily, this License preserves for the author and publisher a way to get credit for their work, while not being considered responsible for modifications made by others.

This License is a kind of "copyleft", which means that derivative works of the document must themselves be free in the same sense. It complements the GNU General Public License, which is a copyleft license designed for free software.

We have designed this License in order to use it for manuals for free software, because free software needs free documentation: a free program should come with manuals providing the same freedoms that the software does. But this License is not limited to software manuals; it can be used for any textual work, regardless of subject matter or whether it is published as a printed book. We recommend this License principally for works whose purpose is instruction or reference.

1. APPLICABILITY AND DEFINITIONS

This License applies to any manual or other work, in any medium, that contains a notice placed by the copyright holder saying it can be distributed under the terms of this License. Such a notice grants a world-wide, royalty-free license, unlimited in duration, to use that work under the conditions stated herein. The **Document**, below, refers to any such manual or work. Any member of the public is a licensee, and is addressed as **"you"**. You accept the license if you copy, modify or distribute the work in a way requiring permission under copyright law.

A **"Modified Version"** of the Document means any work containing the Document or a portion of it, either copied verbatim, or with modifications and/or translated into another language.

A **"Secondary Section"** is a named appendix or a front-matter section of the Document that deals exclusively with the relationship of the publishers or authors of the Document to the Document's overall subject (or to related matters) and contains nothing that could fall directly within that overall subject. (Thus, if the Document is in part a textbook of mathematics, a Secondary Section may not explain any mathematics.) The relationship could be a matter of historical connection with the subject or with related matters, or of legal, commercial, philosophical, ethical or political position regarding them.

The **"Invariant Sections"** are certain Secondary Sections whose titles are designated, as being those of Invariant Sections, in the notice that says that the Document is released under this License. If a section does not fit the above definition of Secondary then it is not allowed to be designated as Invariant. The Document may contain zero Invariant Sections. If the Document does not identify any Invariant Sections then there are none.

The **"Cover Texts"** are certain short passages of text that are listed, as Front-Cover Texts or Back-Cover Texts, in the notice that says that the Document is released under this License. A Front-Cover Text may be at most 5 words, and a Back-Cover Text may be at most 25 words.

A **"Transparent"** copy of the Document means a machine-readable copy, represented in a format whose specification is available to the general public, that is suitable for revising the document straightforwardly with generic text editors or (for images composed of pixels) generic paint programs or (for drawings) some widely available drawing editor, and that is suitable for input to text formatters or for automatic translation to a variety of formats suitable for input to text formatters. A copy made in an otherwise Transparent file format whose markup, or absence of markup, has been arranged to thwart or discourage subsequent modification by readers is not Transparent. An image format is not Transparent if used for any substantial amount of text. A copy that is not "Transparent" is called **Opaque**.

Examples of suitable formats for Transparent copies include plain ASCII without markup, Texinfo input format, LaTeX input format, SGML or XML using a publicly available DTD, and standard-conforming simple HTML, PostScript or PDF designed for human modification. Examples of transparent image formats include PNG, XCF and JPG. Opaque formats include proprietary formats that can be read and edited only by proprietary word processors, SGML or XML for which the DTD and/or processing tools are not generally available, and the machine-generated HTML, PostScript or PDF produced by some word processors for output purposes only.

The **"Title Page"** means, for a printed book, the title page itself, plus such following pages as are needed to hold, legibly, the material this License requires to appear in the title page. For works in formats which do not have any title page as such, "Title Page" means the text near the most prominent appearance of the work's title, preceding the beginning of the body of the text.

The **"publisher"** means any person or entity that distributes copies of the Document to the public.

A section **"Entitled XYZ"** means a named subunit of the Document whose title either is precisely XYZ or contains XYZ in parentheses following text that translates XYZ in another language. (Here XYZ stands for a specific section name mentioned below, such as **"Acknowledgements"**, **"Dedications"**, **"Endorsements"**, or **"History"**.) To **"Preserve the Title"** of such a section when you modify the Document means that it remains a section "Entitled XYZ" according to this definition.

The Document may include Warranty Disclaimers next to the notice which states that this License applies to the Document. These Warranty Disclaimers are considered to be included by reference in this License, but only as regards disclaiming warranties: any other implication that these Warranty Disclaimers may have is void and has no effect on the meaning of this License.

2. VERBATIM COPYING

You may copy and distribute the Document in any medium, either commercially or noncommercially, provided that this License, the copyright notices, and the license notice saying this License applies to the Document are reproduced in all copies, and that you add no other conditions whatsoever to those of this License. You may not use technical measures to obstruct or control the reading or further copying of the copies you make or distribute.

However, you may accept compensation in exchange for copies. If you distribute a large enough number of copies you must also follow the conditions in section 3.

You may also lend copies, under the same conditions stated above, and you may publicly display copies.

3. COPYING IN QUANTITY

If you publish printed copies (or copies in media that commonly have printed covers) of the Document, numbering more than 100, and the Document's license notice requires Cover Texts, you must enclose the copies in covers that carry, clearly and legibly, all these Cover Texts: Front-Cover Texts on the front cover, and Back-Cover Texts on the back cover. Both covers must also clearly and legibly identify you as the publisher of these copies. The front cover must present the full title with all words of the title equally prominent and visible. You may add other material on the covers in addition. Copying with changes limited to the covers, as long as they preserve the title of the Document and satisfy these conditions, can be treated as verbatim copying in other respects.

If the required texts for either cover are too voluminous to fit legibly, you should put the first ones listed (as many as fit reasonably) on the actual cover, and continue the rest onto adjacent pages.

If you publish or distribute Opaque copies of the Document numbering more than 100, you must either include a machine-readable Transparent copy along with each Opaque copy, or state in or with each Opaque copy a computer-network location from which the general network-using public has access to download using public-standard network protocols a complete Transparent copy of the Document, free of added material. If you use the latter option, you must take reasonably prudent steps, when you begin distribution of Opaque copies in quantity, to ensure that this Transparent copy will remain thus accessible at the stated location until at least one year after the last time you distribute an Opaque copy (directly or through your agents or retailers) of that edition to the public.

It is requested, but not required, that you contact the authors of the Document well before redistributing any large number of copies, to give them a chance to provide you with an updated version of the Document.

4. MODIFICATIONS

You may copy and distribute a Modified Version of the Document under the conditions of sections 2 and 3 above, provided that you release the Modified Version under precisely this License, with the Modified Version filling the role of the Document, thus licensing distribution and modification of the Modified Version to whoever possesses a copy of it. In addition, you must do these things in the Modified Version:

A. Use in the Title Page (and on the covers, if any) a title distinct from that of the Document, and from those of previous versions (which should, if there were any, be listed in the History section of the Document). You may use the same title as a previous version if the original publisher of that version gives permission.

B. List on the Title Page, as authors, one or more persons or entities responsible for authorship of the modifications in the Modified Version, together with at least five of the principal authors of the Document (all of its principal authors, if it has fewer than five), unless they release you from this requirement.

C. State on the Title page the name of the publisher of the Modified Version, as the publisher.

D. Preserve all the copyright notices of the Document.

E. Add an appropriate copyright notice for your modifications adjacent to the other copyright notices.

F. Include, immediately after the copyright notices, a license notice giving the public permission to use the Modified Version under the terms of this License, in the form shown in the Addendum below.

G. Preserve in that license notice the full lists of Invariant Sections and required Cover Texts given in the Document's license notice.

H. Include an unaltered copy of this License.

I. Preserve the section Entitled "History", Preserve its Title, and add to it an item stating at least the title, year, new authors, and publisher of the Modified Version as given on the Title Page. If there is no section Entitled "History" in the Document, create one stating the title, year, authors, and publisher of the Document as given on its Title Page, then add an item describing the Modified Version as stated in the previous sentence.

J. Preserve the network location, if any, given in the Document for public access to a Transparent copy of the Document, and likewise the network locations given in the Document for previous versions it was based on. These may be placed in the "History" section. You may omit a network location for a work that was published at least four years before the Document itself, or if the original publisher of the version it refers to gives permission.

K. For any section Entitled "Acknowledgements" or "Dedications", Preserve the Title of the section, and preserve in the section all the substance and tone of each of the contributor acknowledgements and/or dedications given therein.

L. Preserve all the Invariant Sections of the Document, unaltered in their text and in their titles. Section numbers or the equivalent are not considered part of the section titles.

M. Delete any section Entitled "Endorsements". Such a section may not be included in the Modified Version.

N. Do not retitle any existing section to be Entitled "Endorsements" or to conflict in title with any Invariant Section.

O. Preserve any Warranty Disclaimers.

If the Modified Version includes new front-matter sections or appendices that qualify as Secondary Sections and contain no material copied from the Document, you may at your option designate some or all of these sections as invariant. To do this, add their titles to the list of Invariant Sections in the Modified Version's license notice. These titles must be distinct from any other section titles.

You may add a section Entitled "Endorsements", provided it contains nothing but endorsements of your Modified Version by various parties—for example, statements of peer review or that the text has been approved by an organization as the authoritative definition of a standard.

You may add a passage of up to five words as a Front-Cover Text, and a passage of up to 25 words as a Back-Cover Text, to the end of the list of Cover Texts in the Modified Version. Only one passage of Front-Cover Text and one of Back-Cover Text may be added by (or through arrangements made by) any one entity. If the Document already includes a cover text for the same cover, previously added by you or by arrangement made by the same entity you are acting on behalf of, you may not add another; but you may replace the old one, on explicit permission from the previous publisher that added the old one.

The author(s) and publisher(s) of the Document do not by this License give permission to use their names for publicity for or to assert or imply endorsement of any Modified Version.

5. COMBINING DOCUMENTS

You may combine the Document with other documents released under this License, under the terms defined in section 4 above for modified versions, provided that you include in the combination all of the Invariant Sections of all of the original documents, unmodified, and list them all as Invariant Sections of your combined work in its license notice, and that you preserve all their Warranty Disclaimers.

The combined work need only contain one copy of this License, and multiple identical Invariant Sections may be replaced with a single copy. If there are multiple Invariant Sections with the same name but different contents, make the title of each such section unique by adding at the end of it, in parentheses, the name of the original author or publisher of that section if known, or else a unique number. Make the same adjustment to the section titles in the list of Invariant Sections in the license notice of the combined work.

In the combination, you must combine any sections Entitled "History" in the various original documents, forming one section Entitled "History"; likewise combine any sections Entitled "Acknowledgements", and any sections Entitled "Dedications". You must delete all sections Entitled "Endorsements".

6. COLLECTIONS OF DOCUMENTS

You may make a collection consisting of the Document and other documents released under this License, and replace the individual copies of this License in the various documents with a single copy that is included in the collection, provided that you follow the rules of this License for verbatim copying of each of the documents in all other respects.

You may extract a single document from such a collection, and distribute it individually under this License, provided you insert a copy of this License into the extracted document, and follow this License in all other respects regarding verbatim copying of that document.

7. AGGREGATION WITH INDEPENDENT WORKS

A compilation of the Document or its derivatives with other separate and independent documents or works, in or on a volume of a storage or distribution medium, is called an "aggregate" if the copyright resulting from the compilation is not used to limit the legal rights of the compilation's users beyond what the individual works permit. When the Document is included in an aggregate, this License does not apply to the other works in the aggregate which are not themselves derivative works of the Document.

If the Cover Text requirement of section 3 is applicable to these copies of the Document, then if the Document is less than one half of the entire aggregate, the Document's Cover Texts may be placed on covers that bracket the Document within the aggregate, or the electronic equivalent of covers if the Document is in electronic form. Otherwise they must appear on printed covers that bracket the whole aggregate.

8. TRANSLATION

Translation is considered a kind of modification, so you may distribute translations of the Document under the terms of section 4. Replacing Invariant Sections with translations requires special permission from their copyright holders, but you may include translations of some or all Invariant Sections in addition to the original versions of these Invariant Sections. You may include a translation of this License, and all the license notices in the Document, and any Warranty Disclaimers, provided that you also include the original English version of this License and the original versions of those notices and disclaimers. In case of a disagreement between the translation and the original version of this License or a notice or disclaimer, the original version will prevail.

If a section in the Document is Entitled "Acknowledgements", "Dedications", or "History", the requirement (section 4) to Preserve its Title (section 1) will typically require changing the actual title.

9. TERMINATION

You may not copy, modify, sublicense, or distribute the Document except as expressly provided under this License. Any attempt otherwise to copy, modify, sublicense, or distribute it is void, and will automatically terminate your rights under this License.

However, if you cease all violation of this License, then your license from a particular copyright holder is reinstated (a) provisionally, unless and until the copyright holder explicitly and finally terminates your license, and (b) permanently, if the copyright holder fails to notify you of the violation by some reasonable means prior to 60 days after the cessation.

Moreover, your license from a particular copyright holder is reinstated permanently if the copyright holder notifies you of the violation by some reasonable means, this is the first time you have received notice of violation of this License (for any work) from that copyright holder, and you cure the violation prior to 30 days after your receipt of the notice.

Termination of your rights under this section does not terminate the licenses of parties who have received copies or rights from you under this License. If your rights have been terminated and not permanently reinstated, receipt of a copy of some or all of the same material does not give you any rights to use it.

10. FUTURE REVISIONS OF THIS LICENSE

The Free Software Foundation may publish new, revised versions of the GNU Free Documentation License from time to time. Such new versions will be similar in spirit to the present version, but may differ in detail to address new problems or concerns. See http://www.gnu.org/copyleft/.

Each version of the License is given a distinguishing version number. If the Document specifies that a particular numbered version of this License "or any later version" applies to it, you have the option of following the terms and conditions either of that specified version or of any later version that has been published (not as a draft) by the Free Software Foundation. If the Document does not specify a version number of this License, you may choose any version ever published (not as a draft) by the Free Software Foundation. If the Document specifies that a proxy can decide which future versions of this License can be used, that proxy's public statement of acceptance of a version permanently authorizes you to choose that version for the Document.

11. RELICENSING

"Massive Multiauthor Collaboration Site" (or "MMC Site") means any World Wide Web server that publishes copyrightable works and also provides prominent facilities for anybody to edit those works. A public wiki that anybody can edit is an example of such a server. A

"Massive Multiauthor Collaboration" (or "MMC") contained in the site means any set of copyrightable works thus published on the MMC site.

"CC-BY-SA" means the Creative Commons Attribution-Share Alike 3.0 license published by Creative Commons Corporation, a not-for-profit corporation with a principal place of business in San Francisco, California, as well as future copyleft versions of that license published by that same organization.

"Incorporate" means to publish or republish a Document, in whole or in part, as part of another Document.

An MMC is "eligible for relicensing" if it is licensed under this License, and if all works that were first published under this License somewhere other than this MMC, and subsequently incorporated in whole or in part into the MMC, (1) had no cover texts or invariant sections, and (2) were thus incorporated prior to November 1, 2008.

The operator of an MMC Site may republish an MMC contained in the site under CC-BY-SA on the same site at any time before August 1, 2009, provided the MMC is eligible for relicensing.

ADDENDUM: How to use this License for your documents

To use this License in a document you have written, include a copy of the License in the document and put the following copyright and license notices just after the title page:

> Copyright © YEAR YOUR NAME. Permission is granted to copy, distribute and/or modify this document under the terms of the GNU Free Documentation License, Version 1.3 or any later version published by the Free Software Foundation; with no Invariant Sections, no Front-Cover Texts, and no Back-Cover Texts. A copy of the license is included in the section entitled "GNU Free Documentation License".

If you have Invariant Sections, Front-Cover Texts and Back-Cover Texts, replace the "with ... Texts." line with this:

> with the Invariant Sections being LIST THEIR TITLES, with the Front-Cover Texts being LIST, and with the Back-Cover Texts being LIST.

If you have Invariant Sections without Cover Texts, or some other combination of the three, merge those two alternatives to suit the situation.

If your document contains nontrivial examples of program code, we recommend releasing these examples in parallel under your choice of free software license, such as the GNU General Public License, to permit their use in free software.

Index

www.ingramcontent.com/pod-product-compliance
Lightning Source LLC
Chambersburg PA
CBHW062348220526
45472CB00008B/1734